Praise for

DAUGHTERS OF THE SAMURAI

"*Daughters of the Samurai* reads like a novel that happens to be true: three girls uprooted by fate, bridging the gulf between the elegant rhythms of Old Japan and the exhilarating opportunities of America. Janice P. Nimura paints history in cinematic strokes and brings a forgotten story to vivid, unforgettable life."   —Arthur Golden, author of *Memoirs of a Geisha*

"Nimura captures both the broad sweep of social movements as well as the intimate details of these girls' lives, filling in gaps and holes in history that we didn't even know were there. Touching on cultural hybridity, multiculturalism, women's education, *Daughters of the Samurai* is history writing at its finest and required reading for anyone interested in Japan."
     —Ruth Ozeki, author of *A Tale for the Time Being*

"Surprising and richly satisfying. . . . In Nimura's skillful telling, Sutematsu, Shige, and Ume become ambassadors once again, bringing to life an era from which we can learn important lessons about intercultural understanding, conflict, and compromise, still vital to our survival in the global twenty-first century."   —Megan Marshall, author of *The Peabody Sisters* and *Margaret Fuller: A New American Life*, winner of the 2014 Pulitzer Prize in Biography

"Nimura achieves the elusive dream of the historian, producing a work that will engage and satisfy academic and non-specialist audiences alike. She offers both sets of readers a magnificently and meticulously detailed account of three women whose lives epitomize key features of the changing landscape of late 19th and early 20th century Japan. . . . *Daughters of the Samurai* is, perhaps, less a story of Japanese out of place in their country, than of women ahead of their time."   —Miriam Kingsberg, *Los Angeles Review of Books*

"At a reform-minded moment, Japan in 1871 dispatched five young girls to be educated in America. . . . Patiently, vividly, Janice Nimura reconstructs their Alice-in-Wonderland adventure: the girls are so exotic as to qualify as

'princesses' on their American arrival. One feels 'enormous' on her return to Japan. A beautifully crafted narrative, subtle, polished, and poised."

　　　　　　—Stacy Schiff, Pulitzer Prize–winning author of *Cleopatra*

"Briskly paced and engaging. . . . What's most interesting is Nimura's skillful documentation of Japan's ambivalent and ever-shifting relationship with the outside world—echoes of which you can still see today."

　　　　　　—Hanya Yanagihara, *Condé Nast Traveler*

"[Nimura's] descriptions of landscapes are poetic, and you'd be hard-pressed to find a novelist who is as deft at portraying relationships and inner thoughts."　　　　　　—Becky Krystal, *Washington Post*

"Set aside ample time: You won't welcome intrusions while reading this unprecedented, *true* story . . . *Daughters* proves memorably illuminating, a unique story full of firsts."　　　　—Terry Hong, *Christian Science Monitor*

"A superb history. . . . This remarkable and beautifully written story—often as riveting as a page-turning novel—is both scholarly and accessible to non-specialists."　　　　　　—Wingate Packard, *Seattle Times*

"Nimura has done an impressive amount of research to tell her story. . . . *Daughters of the Samurai* reads like a novel about the meeting of East and West and how it transformed the lives of three extraordinary young women."　　　　　　—Elizabeth Bennett, *Dallas Morning News*

"An extraordinary, elegantly told story of the beginning of Japan's education and emancipation of its women."　　—*Kirkus Reviews*, starred review

"A captivating read for biography lovers, readers interested in America's Gilded Age or late Meiji Japan, and fans of Arthur Golden's *Memoirs of a Geisha*."　　　　　　—*Library Journal*, starred review

"Nimura brings the girls and their late nineteenth-century exploits to life in a narrative that feels like an international variation on Louisa May Alcott's *Little Women*, so very appealing and delightful are their historic stories."

　　　　　　—*Booklist*, starred review

DAUGHTERS OF THE SAMURAI

N

W E

S

China

Russia

HOKKAIDO
(EZO)

Korea

• Hakodate

MUTSU
(now AOMORI)

Sea
of
Japan

HONSHU

Wakamatsu

AIZU

Tokyo (Edo)

Yokohama •

CHOSHU

SHIKOKU

5,136 mi. to
San Francisco

SATSUMA   KYUSHU

East China
Sea

Japan
at the Dawn of the Meiji Era

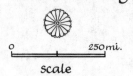

0   250 mi.

scale

DAUGHTERS
OF THE
SAMURAI

A JOURNEY FROM EAST
TO WEST AND BACK

JANICE P. NIMURA

W. W. NORTON & COMPANY
Independent Publishers Since 1923
NEW YORK LONDON

For information about permission to reproduce selections from this book,
write to Permissions, W. W. Norton & Company, Inc.,
500 Fifth Avenue, New York, NY 10110

For information about special discounts for bulk purchases, please contact
W. W. Norton Special Sales at specialsales@wwnorton.com or 800-233-4830

Manufacturing by LSC Harrisonburg
Book design by Marysarah Quinn
Production managers: Ruth Toda and Devon Zahn

Library of Congress Cataloging-in-Publication Data

Nimura, Janice P.
Daughters of the samurai : a journey from East to West and back / Janice P. Nimura.
— First edition.
pages cm
Includes bibliographical references and index.
ISBN 978-0-393-07799-5 (hardcover)
1. Japanese—United States—Biography. 2. Young women—United States—
Biography. 3. Schoolgirls—United States—Biography. 4. Acculturation—United
States—History. 5. Young women—Japan—Biography. 6. Samurai—Family
relationships—History. 7. Women—Education—Japan—History. 8. Japan—
Relations—United States. 9. United States—Relations—Japan. 10. East and
West—History. I. Title.
E184.J3N484 2015
920.72—dc23
[B]

2014046933

ISBN 978-0-393-35278-8 pbk.

W. W. Norton & Company, Inc.
500 Fifth Avenue, New York, N.Y. 10110
www.wwnorton.com

W. W. Norton & Company Ltd.
15 Carlisle Street, London W1D 3BS

5 6 7 8 9

FOR YOJI

Little Granddaughter, unless the red barbarians
and the children of the gods learn each other's
hearts, the ships may sail and sail, but the two
lands will never be nearer.

—ETSU INAGAKI SUGIMOTO, *A Daughter of the Samurai*, 1926

CONTENTS

AUTHOR'S NOTE · 11

PART I

PROLOGUE · 15

1. SAMURAI DAUGHTER · 19

2. THE WAR OF THE YEAR OF THE DRAGON · 32

3. "A LITTLE LEAVEN" · 42

4. "AN EXPEDITION OF PRACTICAL OBSERVERS" · 55

PART II

5. "INTERESTING STRANGERS" · 69

6. FINDING FAMILIES · 97

7. GROWING UP AMERICAN · 108

8. AT VASSAR · 127

9. THE JOURNEY "HOME" · 144

PART III

10. TWO WEDDINGS · 161

11. GETTING ALONG ALONE · 183

12. ALICE IN TOKYO · 208

13. ADVANCES AND RETREATS · 225

14. THE WOMEN'S HOME SCHOOL OF ENGLISH · 246

15. ENDINGS · 269

ACKNOWLEDGMENTS · 279

NOTES · 281

BIBLIOGRAPHY · 313

CREDITS · 321

INDEX · 323

AUTHOR'S NOTE

THIS IS THE STORY of three girls who were born in one world and sent, by forces beyond their comprehension, to grow up in an entirely different one. There, like all children, they absorbed the lessons of their surroundings. Though they were, each of them, purebred daughters of the samurai, they became hybrid by nurture. Ten years later, they returned to a homeland grown alien in their absence.

I live in the city where I was born, like my parents and grandparents before me. But my story converges with the one I'm telling. On the first day of college, I met a boy who was born in Japan. His family had left Tokyo for Seattle when he was very small, and announced their decision to return "home" when he was sixteen. For him, home was America. They left, and he stayed.

Two years after our graduation and two months after our wedding, we moved to Tokyo ourselves. In many ways, my sojourn there was easier than my husband's. As my Japanese improved, I was praised for my accent, my manners, my taste for sea urchin and pickled plums. My face excused me from my failures—I was a foreigner, after all. My husband enjoyed no such immunity. He looked Japanese, he sounded Japanese— why didn't he act Japanese?

Upon our return to New York three years later, I went to graduate school in East Asian studies and fell into a fascination with Meiji-era Japan, the moment when the Land of the Gods wrenched its gaze from the past and turned toward the shiny idols of Western industrial progress. One day, in the basement stacks of a venerable library, I found a slim green volume titled *A Japanese Interior*, by Alice Mabel Bacon, a Connecticut schoolteacher. It was a memoir of a year she had spent in Tokyo in the late 1880s, living with "Japanese friends, known long and intimately in America." This was strange. Nineteenth-century American women didn't generally have Japanese friends, certainly not ones they had met in America.

Alice came from New Haven, where I had spent my college years; she moved to Tokyo and lived not among foreigners, but in a Japanese household, as I had; she taught at one of Japan's first schools for girls, founded within a year of the one I attended in New York a century later. She wrote with a candid wit that reminded me of my own teachers, unfussy bluestockings with no patience for pretension. Following where Alice led, I discovered the entwined lives of Sutematsu Yamakawa Oyama, Alice's foster sister and the first Japanese woman to earn a bachelor's degree; Ume Tsuda, whose pioneering women's English school Sutematsu and Alice helped to launch; and Shige Nagai Uriu, who juggled seven children and a teaching career generations before the phrase "working mother" was coined.

I recognized these women. I knew what it felt like to arrive in Japan with little or no language, to want desperately to fit into a Japanese home, and at the same time to chafe against Japanese attitudes toward women. I had a husband who did not see the world through a Japanese lens, though his parents had never meant to raise an American child. A hundred years before "globalization" and "multiculturalism" became the goals of every corporation and curriculum, three Japanese girls spanned the globe and became fluent in two worlds at once—other to everyone except each other. Their story would not let me go.

PART

I

Samurai training will prepare one
for any future.

—ETSU INAGAKI SUGIMOTO,
A Daughter of the Samurai, 1926

The girls on the occasion of their audience with the empress. From left to right:
Tei Ueda, Shige Nagai, Sutematsu Yamakawa, Ume Tsuda, Ryo Yoshimasu.
(Courtesy Tsuda College Archives.)

PROLOGUE
NOVEMBER 9, 1871

IN THE NARROW STREETS surrounding the Imperial Palace, newfangled rickshaws clattered around corners, past the indigo hangings in the doorways of the merchants, past the glowing vermilion of a shrine's *torii* archway, past the whitewashed walls of samurai compounds. The runners between the shafts gleamed with sweat and whooped at those in the way; the passengers, mostly men, sat impassively despite the jolting of the iron-rimmed wheels. Shops selling rice or straw sandals stood alongside others offering pocket watches and horn-rimmed spectacles. Soldiers loitered on corners, in motley uniforms of peaked caps and wooden clogs, short zouave jackets and broad silk *hakama* trousers. They stared at the occasional palanquin passing by on the shoulders of several bearers, wondering at the invisible occupant: an official, in a stiff-shouldered tunic? a retainer's wife, on a rare outing to the local temple? Servant girls in blue cotton darted in and out of traffic, their sleeves tied back.

Tiny alongside the forbidding bulk of the palace's massive stone embankments, five girls filed past. Two of them were teenagers; the others younger, the smallest no more than six. They were swathed in rich silk, the three older ones in paler shades embroidered all over with leaves and trailing grasses, cherry blossoms and peonies; the other two in darker robes emblazoned with crests. Each girl's hair was piled high in heavy coils and loops secured with combs and pins. They held themselves carefully, as if their elaborate coiffures might overbalance them. Their painted lips were crimson bows against the powder that whitened their cheeks. Only their eyes suggested anything other than perfect composure.

Imposing timbered gates rumbled open to admit them, and then rolled closed again. Inside, all was quiet. Within this maze of fortresses and pleasure gardens, time flowed more slowly: everything seemed choreographed, from the movements of the guards to the gentle fluttering of each flaming red maple leaf. The girls padded along corridor after twisting corridor, taking small pigeon-toed steps in their gorgeous new kimonos, the finest they had ever owned, each tightly tied with a broad stiff *obi* in a contrasting hue. Grand court ladies escorted them, hissing instructions: to keep their eyes on the polished floor just in front of their white split-toed socks, their hands glued flat to their thighs, thumbs tucked behind fingers. Floorboards creaked, silk rustled. The subtle perfume of incense wafted from behind sliding doors. Stolen glances revealed screens painted with cranes and turtles, pine and chrysanthemum; lintels carved with tigers and dragons, wisteria and waterfalls; flashes of vivid fabric, purple and gold.

At last they arrived in a cavernous inner chamber. A heavy bamboo screen hung there, though the girls dared not look up. Seated behind it, they knew, sat the Empress of Japan. The five girls knelt, placed their hands on the *tatami*-matted floor, and bowed until their foreheads touched their fingertips.

Had the screen been moved aside, and had the girls been brazen enough to lift their eyes, they would have beheld a diminutive woman of twenty-two. Her head was the only part of her that emerged from a cone of ceremonial robes: snow-white inner kimono, wide divided trousers of heavy scarlet silk, an outer coat of lavish brocade, edged in gold. Though she held a painted fan bound with long silken cords, her hands were invisible within her sleeves. Oiled hair framed her oval face in a stiff black halo, gathered behind into a tail trailing nearly to the floor, and tied at intervals with narrow strips of white paper. She had a strong chin, and prominent ears that lent her an almost elfin look. Her face was powdered white, her eyebrows shaved and replaced with smudges of charcoal high on her forehead. Her teeth were blackened, in the style appropriate for a married woman, with iron filings dissolved in tea and sake, and mixed with powdered gallnuts. Though her husband had just been fitted for his first Western-style clothing, personal grooming for the women of the imperial court remained, for the moment, much as it had been for centuries.

Lacquered trays on low stands appeared before the girls, bearing bolts of red and white crêpe—auspicious colors—as well as tea and ceremonial cakes, also red and white. The girls bowed, and bowed again, and again, staring down at the woven tatami between their hands. They did not touch the refreshments. A lady-in-waiting emerged, holding a scroll before her. Her hands were graceful and astonishingly white as she unfurled it. In a high clear voice, using language so formal the girls could barely understand her, she read the words the empress had brushed with her own hand, words no empress had hitherto dreamed of composing.

"Considering that you are girls, your intention of studying abroad is to be commended," she chanted. Girls, studying abroad—the very words were bizarre. No Japanese girl had ever studied abroad. Few Japanese girls had studied much at all.

The reedy voice continued. "When, in time, schools for girls are established, you shall be examples to your countrywomen, having finished your education." The words were impossible. There was no such thing as a school for girls. And when they returned—if they returned—what kind of examples would they be?

The lady-in-waiting had nearly reached the end of the scroll. "Bear all this in mind," she concluded, "and apply yourself to your studies day and night." This, at least, the girls could do: discipline and obedience were things they understood. In any case, they had no choice. The emperor was the direct descendant of the gods, and these were the commands of his wife. As far as the girls knew, a goddess on earth—seeing but unseen, speaking with another's voice—had given them their orders.

The audience was over. The girls withdrew from the scented stillness of the empress's chamber and retraced their steps through the labyrinth of corridors to the clamor of the world outside the walls, no doubt light-headed with relief. They returned to their lodgings laden with imperial gifts: a piece of the rich red silk for each, and beautifully wrapped parcels of the exquisite court cakes. So sacred were these sweets, it was said, that a single bite could cure any illness. The girls might be the newly anointed vanguard of enlightened womanhood, but their families were not about to trifle with divine favor. Portions of the cake were carefully conveyed to relatives and friends.

In a month, the girls would board a ship for America. By the time they returned, if all went as planned, they would be grown women.

1

SAMURAI DAUGHTER

OF THE FIVE GIRLS on their way to America, the middle one in age, Sutematsu Yamakawa, had traveled the farthest, whether the distance was reckoned in miles or memories. She was born a warrior in the waning days of an era without war, February 24, 1860. The youngest child of the late Shigekata Yamakawa, chief retainer of the lord of Aizu, she was called Sakiko then: "blossom child." In that northern domain of dramatic peaks and paddy-terraced valleys, she would be one of the last to live the rhythms and rituals of a samurai family.

Perched high on a hill, the gleaming white walls and swooping tiered roofs of Tsuruga Castle dominated the town of Wakamatsu, seat of Aizu's leaders. An inner moat ringed the castle keep, and an outer moat enclosed an area of more than five hundred acres, within which stood granaries, stables, and the homes of the highest-ranking samurai. Earthworks rose from the inner bank, pierced by sixteen gates.

The Yamakawa compound, itself comprising several acres, stood near a northern gate of the castle. It was a traditional *bukeya-shiki*, or samurai mansion, a sprawling walled maze of single-story buildings and courtyard gardens, home to the family for genera-tions. The newer part of the compound was pristine and spare, comprising graceful rooms floored with hay-scented tatami mats, perfectly empty of everything except what might be required in the moment: floor cushions and low, lacquered tables at mealtimes; thick sleeping quilts at night, along with the wooden headrests used instead of pillows to protect carefully dressed hair from disarray. The only ornaments were to be found in the alcoves known as *tokonoma*, where might hang an antique scroll appropriate to the season, accompanied perhaps by a single spray of blossoms from the garden arranged in a ceramic vase.

The garden itself provided the decorative element absent from the interiors. A hidden spring in its center fed a tiny waterfall, which in turn filled a miniature lake stocked with goldfish darting beneath pink and white lotus blossoms. A diminutive series of carefully sculpted hills surrounded the lake, creating the illusion of a more expansive landscape. A rustic bridge crossed a stream and led to a ceremonial teahouse. In warm weather the paper-paned *shoji* screens that formed the outer walls of the main building slid back, allowing the breezes and the meticulous beauty of the garden to enter every room.

Serene and elegant as the setting might be, this was yet the home of warriors. The main gate of the compound, never unattended, was itself an imposing edifice, its tiled roof sweeping outward in deep eaves over massive timbers. Anterooms in which guards might keep watch unseen were tucked behind walls. The lavatory was roofed with unsupported tile; an intruder intending to catch an adversary in a vulnerable position would tumble straight through.

For a child like Sutematsu, the compound's walls were the edges of the world. Everyone she knew lived within them: her mother, grandfather, brothers and sisters and sisters-in-law, as well as stewards, maids, pages, gardeners, gatekeepers, and the children's nurse, who had her own tiny cottage on the grounds. The servants were like family themselves, many having been raised in the compound from childhood.

As new structures were added to the complex, older ones fell into disuse. A casual visitor could become lost. A child's imagination could roam free. Sutematsu and the other children would gather in an abandoned room after dark to play the *hyaku monogatari*, or hundred tales. Gathered around a lamp in the middle of the tattered tatami-matted floor, each child would take a turn telling a *kaidan*, a ghost story of the past: *Kitsune Yashiki*, or "The Foxes' Mansion"; *Yuki-Onna*, "The Snow-Woman"; *Jikininki*, "The Flesh-Eating Goblin." After each telling the light was lowered, until the children sat trembling in the haunted darkness, determined not to betray their samurai training by showing fear.

THE SAMURAI WERE a hereditary warrior class, and though by Sutematsu's time battles were largely the stuff of legend, samurai culture was shaped by ideals of courage, obedience, austerity, and martial prowess that led directly back to a more warlike age. Totaling about seven percent of Japan's thirty million people, the samurai as a class contributed nothing to the Japanese economy. They administered public life and cultivated the arts of war and of peace—including poetry, calligraphy, and scholarship—supported by a stipend from the lord of their particular domain, to whom they owed ultimate allegiance. Holding themselves to a lofty code of loyalty and honor, they left the baser necessities of production and trade to commoners.

According to Japanese mythology, the first emperor had descended from the sun goddess Amaterasu two thousand years before. Over the centuries, however, true power had come to rest with the shogun, a military dictator nominally appointed by the emperor, who served as a kind of divine endorsement. Ieyasu, the first shogun of the Tokugawa clan, had established his headquarters at Edo (modern Tokyo) in the late sixteenth century. The Tokugawas consolidated administrative control over hundreds of territorial warlords, or *daimyo*, leaving the emperor enshrined in virtually powerless seclusion as a living symbol of Japan's divine heritage. Rarely seen, and insulated from the outside world by a small city of pureblood imperial courtiers, the emperor lived "above the clouds" in tranquil Kyoto, while nearly three hundred miles to the northeast in bustling Edo, the shogun ran the country.

Once in power, the Tokugawas' first priority was their own stability.

To that end they devised an ingenious administrative system to preserve the delicate balance between the shogun, in Edo, and the hundreds of daimyo spread across the islands of Japan—each with his own domain, his own castle stronghold, his own loyal samurai retainers. Each daimyo was free to collect his own taxes, make his own local laws, and arm his own troops, as long as he also agreed to contribute money and laborers for Tokugawa projects including highway maintenance, mining, and palace construction. The shogun, attending to international relations, left the daimyo largely alone.

Largely, but not entirely. In a masterstroke of administrative cunning called *sankin kotai*, or "alternate attendance," the shogun required each daimyo to maintain a second palatial residence in Edo, where in alternating years his presence in attendance on the shogun was mandatory. And though the daimyo returned to their own territories roughly every other year, their wives and children were required to remain in Edo, safely under the shogun's eye.

Alternate attendance was essentially a ritualized hostage system, with an extra twist: it was fabulously expensive. Not only did each daimyo need to build, staff, and maintain an Edo compound appropriate to his rank; he also had to pay for the lavish procession to or from his own domain each year—an important opportunity to advertise his own power and dignity. All of which served to discourage unrest: it was much harder for a power-hungry daimyo to cause trouble for the shogun when he had no revenue left to spend on making war.

The unintended benefits of the system were considerable. The continuous tide of daimyo and their retinues flowing to and from Edo required a well-maintained highway network and provided regular trade for inns and teahouses along the road. News, ideas, and fashions flowed constantly from the vibrant whirl of Edo to the most remote castle towns. And every daimyo's heir, no matter how provincial his ancestral home, grew up a city boy, sharing experiences in common with the elites of every region of Japan.

.   .   .

To the north, remote from both Kyoto's ancient refinements and Edo's brash urbanity, lay the domain of Aizu, Sutematsu's home, harsher in both climate and culture. Walled in by mountains, Aizu was unusually isolated even for Japan, whose extreme topography made travel and communication a continual challenge. Getting in or out of the domain entailed scrambling over high mountain passes where deer and monkeys were more numerous than people, and bear and wild boar more of a threat than brigands. Aizu was a land unto itself, its local dialect all but incomprehensible to rare sojourners from other regions.

Aizu was the fiefdom of the Matsudairas, a collateral branch of the Tokugawa family, which by 1860 had governed Japan in relative peace for two and a half centuries. In a country formed of rival domains, Aizu was known for its martial prowess, its substantial standing army, its code of conduct for soldiers and commanders alike, and its fierce loyalty to the Tokugawas. "Serve the shogun with single-minded devotion," the Aizu code began. "Do not measure your loyalty by the standard of other domains." Sharing the triple hollyhock crest of the Tokugawas, the Matsudairas established their seat in the castle town of Wakamatsu, a hundred miles north of Edo at the convergence of five roads spidering across northeastern Honshu, Japan's main island. It was a strategic spot, linking the Tokugawa stronghold with northern regions more distant both geographically and politically.

Just as the castle in Wakamatsu presided over the landscape, the injunctions of the Aizu code dominated the lives of the samurai families living within the castle precincts. Confucian morality—placing men over women, parents over children, benevolent rulers over dutiful subjects—blended easily with martial hierarchy. "Do not neglect military readiness," the Aizu code instructed. "Do not confuse the duties of the higher and lower ranks. Older brothers should be respected and younger brothers loved. Lawbreakers should not be treated with lenience." An Aizu retainer, whether escorting his lord on the road to Edo or overseeing domain affairs at home, was to comport himself with discipline at all times, setting aside personal pettiness in the service of his daimyo. And last, "the words of women should be totally disregarded."

At the turn of every year, the retainers gathered in the presence of their lord while the head of the domain school read the Aizu code aloud. Aizu's school, the Nisshinkan, or "Hall of Daily Progress," rose on the west side of the castle. Here, starting at the age of ten, the sons of Aizu's samurai families—including Sutematsu's brothers—studied the Chinese classics and the arts of war, but also mathematics, medicine, and astronomy. It was a forward-looking curriculum that tapped the steady trickle of Western ideas entering Japan through the solitary Dutch trading post at Nagasaki, far to the south. Domain schools had been established throughout Japan during the Tokugawa period. The Nisshinkan, with its two-story lecture halls and its own observatory, was among the finest.

The Nisshinkan's schoolboys were members of neighborhood "ten-men groups," officially sanctioned gangs who pledged loyalty to each other and hostility to other groups in a miniature imitation of domain politics. Each group's leader rounded up his mates in the morning, marched them to school, and presided over the ritual of surrendering their swords to the sword rack for the duration of classes. After school he marched them home again. Even outside of school, behavior followed strict rules, read out periodically by the head boy: a junior version of the code followed by their fathers.

1. We must not disobey our elders.
2. We must always bow to our elders.
3. We must not lie.
4. We must not act in a cowardly manner.
5. We must not pick on those who are weaker.
6. We must not eat in public.
7. We must not talk to girls.

The boys responded in unison: "Those things that are forbidden, we must not do." And then they were free: to explore each other's houses, swim in the river Yukawa, or slide down pine-needled hillsides on empty rice bags. Those who broke the rules suffered ostracism or a beating.

The conduct of girls, though less public, was no less carefully policed. A set of seventeen "Instructions for the Very Young" exhorted all children to wake early, wash and rinse their mouths, and refrain from eating until their parents had taken up their own chopsticks. Yawning in front of elders was strictly prohibited. The samurai of Aizu encouraged their daughters to develop strength of character by excelling in their studies, but girls learned to read and write at home. Unlike her brothers, Sutematsu rarely had occasion to venture beyond her own front gates.

After breakfast the adults would gather for tea in her mother's room. While they chatted, the children might savor a few pieces of *kompeito*, the knobbly sugar candy that was a traditional treat among the refined classes.* Then it was time for the girls and younger boys to gather in the schoolroom, where their tutor waited.

While boys learned passages by rote from the ancient *Classic of Filial Piety*, a girl's syllabus would include the eighteenth-century treatise *Onna daigaku* ("Greater Learning for Women"), which placed Confucian moral obligations in the context of a woman's life. "The only qualities that befit a woman are gentle obedience, chastity, mercy, and quietness," it instructed, placing obedience—to parents, and subsequently to husband and in-laws—above all. Obedience did not necessarily entail meekness, though. An Aizu girl received a dagger as part of her trousseau, and her mother made sure she knew how to use it—not only in self-defense, but to take her own life, should her honor be stained.

As part of their daily recitation, Sutematsu and her sisters chanted

---

* *Kompeito*, from the Portuguese *confeito*, was introduced to Japan by Portuguese missionaries in the sixteenth century. Like many other imports, from Zen Buddhism to tempura, it was adopted so completely that its foreign origins are often forgotten.

in unison passages like: "The five worst maladies that afflict the female mind are: indocility, discontent, slander, jealousy, and silliness." Silliness included vanity: "It suffices for her to be neat and cleanly in her person and in her wearing apparel. It is wrong in her, by an excess of care, to obtrude herself on other people's notice." For writing practice, the girls copied out the same passages once more, engraving them in their minds as truth even while still too young to grasp their full implications.

During the lengthy lessons, the children knelt formally on the tatami, permitted to move only their hands and lips. On frigid days, when the temperature within the paper-walled schoolroom matched that in the garden outside, no charcoal *hibachi* burned, but no one dared tuck her hands into the front of her kimono. When the summer sun turned the room into an oven, no one fluttered a fan. To discipline the body was to discipline the mind.

Not all traditions were so harsh. Handed down from mother to daughter in every samurai family was a precious set of elaborately costumed dolls representing the imperial court. The Yamakawa collection numbered more than a hundred, and a whole room was reserved for them. For most of the year this was a playroom for the girls, who could rock their favorite babies and play house, unmolested by their brothers. The third day of the third month, however, brought the excitement of *hinamatsuri*, the Doll Festival, when the dolls took pride of place in the main reception room of the house, arrayed on a tiered stand draped in red. At the top stood the emperor and empress, their courtiers, musicians, and soldiers arrayed beneath them, along with doll-sized furniture, carriages, and tiny dishes filled with real delicacies. And since the dolls themselves were never seen to taste these offerings, could a little girl help it if she tasted on their behalf?

Life was rhythm and ritual, discipline and etiquette; it was impossible to imagine any other way. But after two and a half centuries of relative calm, a political shift as violent as any earthquake was about to shake Japan.

JAPAN UNDER THE Tokugawas was a place preoccupied with preserving the status quo. In 1606, as part of his consolidation of power, the first

Tokugawa shogun, Ieyasu, had declared Christianity illegal. The notion that every man owed his first allegiance to God was an unacceptable threat to the Confucian hierarchy, not to mention Ieyasu's still fragile supremacy. In addition, Christian missionaries might become the vanguard of European colonization, as had happened in the Philippines.

The Tokugawas expelled the Portuguese and Spanish missionaries who had proselytized in Japan since the 1550s. They drastically curtailed trade with Europe, eventually limiting it to a single Dutch vessel permitted to dock each year at the man-made and closely guarded islet of Dejima in Nagasaki harbor. And within four decades, they killed tens of thousands of Japanese Christian converts.

The antiforeign stance of the Tokugawas only hardened over time. In 1630, the shogunate passed laws prohibiting its subjects from ever leaving its shores or returning from abroad. A hapless fisherman, driven out to sea by a sudden storm and shipwrecked on a foreign shore, would be arrested immediately upon his return, were he lucky enough to find his way home. Though limited trade continued with China and Korea, and the Dutch provided a yearly infusion of information from Europe, Japan had essentially placed its own security above the attractions of commercial profit and global engagement. After centuries of territorial warfare, the Tokugawas presided over an extended peace.

By the first decades of the nineteenth century, however, it was increasingly hard to ignore the wider world. Russia was eager for access to the rich fisheries and timber of Japan's northernmost island of Ezo, modern-day Hokkaido. British and American whaling ships, having extended their reach to the Pacific, appeared in Japanese ports seeking provisions and did not appreciate being turned away. When news of China's defeat in the Opium Wars of the 1840s filtered in, the threat of military aggression from the West was no longer theoretical.

Sutematsu's home in landlocked Aizu may have been remote from these encounters, but its warriors were hardly unaware. As early as 1806, the shogunate deployed hundreds of Aizu samurai to patrol coastlines for years at a time as far north as Ezo, as well as southward to the areas around Edo. Back in Aizu, their leaders bore the cost of their deployment, borrowing heavily from local merchants and slashing samurai stipends.

The dynamic domestic growth of the Pax Tokugawa was beginning to slow, and its relative calm to fray. The old social hierarchy tilted and tottered. Commoners groaned under the pressure of taxes levied to pay the stipends of the warrior class, while merchant entrepreneurs amassed new fortunes and bought themselves the right to wear the two swords of the samurai. Ancient samurai families, their stipends reduced, found themselves unable to afford the trappings required by their station; men raised never to touch money now had to borrow it or find a way to earn some. Leaders of the outer domains, those without deep-rooted loyalties to the Tokugawas, began to rely more on their own opinions and less on the directives of the shogun. Uncomfortably aware of the foreign vessels visible on the horizon, many began to pay closer attention to "Dutch learning," especially Western military technology.

An interest in Dutch ideas, or *rangaku* (from the Japanese transliteration of "Holland": *Oranda*), had begun to take hold among intellectual innovators in Japan in the middle of the eighteenth century. Though the shogunate continued to treat foreigners with extreme suspicion, foreign books—on astronomy, geography, medicine, and technology, if not Christianity—were welcome, collected and carefully preserved. Some of the most distinguished scholars in Japan shifted their reverence from things Chinese to things Dutch, taking Dutch sobriquets, studying the language, and even drawing detailed landscapes complete with windmills. Though Japan remained nominally closed to Western trade, many Japanese elites were quite familiar with Western ideas. Most of the population, however, continued to think of foreigners as distant cousins of the long-nosed, goblin-faced *tengu* spirits that haunted forests and mountains.

THIS STATE OF affairs persisted until July 8, 1853, when Commodore Matthew Perry piloted his squadron of four "black ships" into Edo Bay and demanded the right to trade on behalf of the United States. Two of the ships were steam frigates belching ominous clouds of coal smoke, and all four bristled with cannon, including the latest in naval armament, the Paixhans gun, capable of firing explosive shells rather than the inert cannonballs upon which naval warfare had previously relied. It was a demonstration not just of military strength, but of technological supremacy.

The island nation of Japan possessed not a single naval vessel, and what coastal batteries existed were outdated and poorly maintained. The sword was still the signature weapon of the samurai, the physical embodiment of his prowess and his honor. This had been a conscious choice on the part of the shogunate more than a century earlier. Japan's metalworkers had rapidly adopted gunsmithing when the Portuguese first introduced firearms in 1543, and they were soon producing matchlock guns and cannon of the highest quality. But guns were impersonal, inelegant, and inappropriate in heroic hand-to-hand combat. A weapon as indiscriminately lethal as a gun made no distinction between daimyo and peasant. An unskilled, anonymous foot soldier, armed with a matchlock, could fell an elite swordsman from a safe distance. Was this the way of the warrior? Taking over production of guns and gunpowder, the shogunate gradually reduced its orders over the course of the seventeenth century—a trend aided by the fact that under Tokugawa rule, there were no battles to fight. Japan's gunsmiths faded into oblivion, and the warrior class reverted to the sword.

Most of the cannon mounted in Edo's defense were more than two hundred years old, designed to fire balls of six to eight pounds. Perry's guns were sixty-four-pounders. One of his officers bragged that the Americans could have loaded their guns with the diminutive Japanese cannon and fired them back at their owners.

The night of Perry's arrival, an unusually bright meteor appeared in the sky over Edo, bathing the bay in an eerie blue light and adding a shiver of divine portent to the feeling of dread that gripped the city. (Perry's men, naturally, took it as an encouraging sign.) Nine days later, having presented a letter from President Millard Fillmore and fired off a few rounds for dramatic effect, Perry sailed away, promising to return for an answer the following spring.

The shogunate was in turmoil, compounded by the inconvenient fact that the shogun himself, Ieyoshi, had dropped dead during the month of Perry's visit, and his twenty-nine-year-old successor, Iesada, had the emotional and intellectual faculties of a child. Clearly, the isolationist policies of the preceding centuries were doomed, but how could Japan engage with the West from a position of such weakness? Was there a way to adopt Western technologies without bowing to the barbarians? Officials in Edo took the unprecedented step of asking the daimyo for advice—in itself an admission of weakness. The daimyo, for the most part, rejected the prospect of trade with the Americans, but only a few advocated for war. It wasn't much of a mandate.

When Perry returned in February 1854 with twice as many ships, the shogunate compromised, reluctantly granting the Americans two treaty ports and the right to establish a consulate. The door having now opened a crack, the mercantile nations of the West proceeded to wrench it wide: within five years, the shogunate had signed agreements with the French, the British, the Russians, and the Dutch, opening yet more ports, fixing low import duties, and granting foreign nationals extraterritorial immunity.

The lopsided treaties were humiliating and seriously undermined the authority of the shogun. The ways of the past were increasingly irrelevant, while the way forward remained frighteningly unclear. "Our historians bid us to obey the maxims, to follow in the footsteps of our ancestors, to change nothing in them," a senior official in Edo told Henry Heusken, secretary to the new American consulate. "If you do this, you will prosper; if you change anything, you will fall into decay. This is so strong that if your ancestors bid you to go by a roundabout way to go to a certain spot, even though you discover a route which goes directly there, you may not follow it. You must always follow the path of your ancestors." Now foreigners with modern guns had forced the shogun from his ancestors' path.

Edo's woodblock artists were quick to capitalize on Perry's visit and the arrival of subsequent embassies, printing hundreds of thousands of broadsides depicting the monstrous black ships, the long-nosed and strangely hairy sailors, the bizarre uniforms that encased men's arms and legs in tight-fitting tubes, their feet in thump-heeled boots. Were the barbarians' feet made without heels, to require such footwear?

As these images, along with news of the treaties, spread throughout the islands of Japan, waves of opposition to Edo's concessions rippled in their wake. In addition to the grumbling daimyo of the outer domains, disaffected low-ranking samurai emerged as a threat to the shogun's control. Calling themselves *shishi*, or "men of high purpose," many renounced their domain loyalties and took the emperor, secluded in Kyoto, as a symbol of Japan's divine heritage. "*Sonno joi*," rang their rallying cry: revere the emperor, expel the barbarians. Preferring heroic action to diplomacy, they espoused a virulently xenophobic strain of terrorism, attacking the shogun's officials as well as traders who had dealings with foreigners, and sometimes targeting the foreigners themselves.

Sutematsu had never seen a foreigner. Despite the astronomical observatory at the domain school, despite the Western-style homes popping up to house European traders and diplomats in the treaty ports, despite the rising interest in military technology and European languages, and the sporadic eruptions of violence perpetrated by disgruntled samurai, in towns and villages across Japan the traditional rhythms of everyday life persisted—nowhere more so than in isolated Aizu.

By the 1860s there was still no one in a position of power anywhere in Japan with a truly intimate understanding of the West. A tiny handful of men had ventured to America, England, and continental Europe, sent officially by the shogun or smuggled out and back by reform-minded daimyo, but their brief sojourns served only to prove the urgency of learning more. The most extreme enthusiasts of "Dutch learning" had only the foggiest notion of what life in America or Europe was really like.

2

THE WAR OF THE YEAR
OF THE DRAGON

NEWS FROM THE SOUTH reached Aizu slowly, and most of it was unsettling. Her brothers' sober discussions were not for Sutematsu to join, but in houses with paper walls, no conversation was ever completely private. She could hear the intensity in their voices, and she wondered at the unfamiliar words: *kobu gattai*, the vague goal of reconciliation between the imperial court and the shogunate. Yet weren't the emperor and the shogun on the same side? Didn't the samurai of Aizu swear to uphold the shogun, whose power was granted by the emperor? Why did her brothers look so serious, and so fierce?

Yoshinobu, last of the Tokugawa shoguns, was a thwarted visionary, a man whose fondness for pork, Western-style horsemanship, and portrait photography did not sit well with those conservatives who wished only for all foreigners to go away. Pushed reluctantly into a doomed office in 1867, he imagined sweeping changes: Western-style cabinet ministries in place of the shogunate's council of elders; a professional standing army equipped with modern weapons and financed by a new tax system; the promotion of industry. But it was too late to convince the southern domains to support him.

Those who muttered against the shogunate were not limited to any one region, but they were concentrated in the prosperous southern domains of Satsuma (on the island of Kyushu) and Choshu (on the southwestern tip of Japan's main island, Honshu). Bitter rivals historically, the two domains had by 1866 sealed a secret alliance, vowing to replace the shogunate with a new government led by a restored emperor. These southern domains were better armed and better organized than the shogun's allies, and they had shrewdly wrapped their cause in the "brocade banner" of imperial legitimacy, neatly casting their adversaries in the role of traitors.

Ironically, the positions of the two fiercely opposed sides were roughly aligned by this time. After more violent encounters with Western warships over the years, the reactionary xenophobia of the *shishi*—the disaffected "men of high purpose"—had come to seem quixotic. No one actually harbored delusions about expelling foreigners any longer, and both sides had moved toward the conviction that a unified Japan—grounded in Confucian ethics and strengthened by imported Western weapons and industrial technology—was critical to dealing with threats both internal and external. But the brash young reformers of Satsuma and Choshu were determined to slash away the impenetrable thicket of bureaucracy that had grown up around the shogun over the centuries.

As these imperial loyalists consolidated power in the south, the Tokugawa leadership teetered. Rather than provoke full-scale civil war, Yoshinobu resigned—a move that disgusted his most loyal allies but revealed his clearer grasp of the political reality, and helped avoid a certain amount of bloodshed. In January 1868 imperial forces occupied Edo Castle, abolished the shogunate, and proclaimed the "restoration" of the fifteen-year-old Emperor Mutsuhito, known by his reign name as Meiji. A new era had begun.

IN THE NORTHERN domains, however, the old era endured a little longer. Though the Tokugawas were finished, their staunchest vassals were not ready to concede to the upstart southerners. Sutematsu's homeland of Aizu was at the center of this northern alliance of five domains, which fought a series of losing battles against the emperor's well-equipped forces in what would become known as the Boshin War, the War of the Year of the Dragon, 1868.

Bound by the Aizu code, these men fought on, even though their cause was now obsolete, determined to clear the unjust stain of treason from their honor. Or so they told themselves. It was easier to reconcile their grim last stand with the "Way of the Warrior" rather than the messier political reality. In fact, Aizu's daimyo, the able and determined Katamori Matsudaira, was risking the survival of his domain for the chance to lead Japan forward—and perhaps even claim the shogunate itself. Unfortunately, his arsenal fell short of his ambition, and his enemies in the south exacted a terrible revenge.

Recognizing that power lay with Western military technology, and having more funds at their disposal than were available to the cash-strapped shogunate, the southern domains had bought Minié rifles and shell-firing cannon directly from foreign traders years earlier. Aizu, on the other hand, had little in the way of modern weaponry; hastily constructed wooden cannon, reinforced with hoops of bamboo, could fire rocks but had an unfortunate tendency to burst after a few rounds. The daimyo of Aizu had at last begun to purchase weapons from foreign dealers, but his supplies were low and his forces untrained in comparison to the well-armed warriors from the south. The technological superiority of the emperor's forces had little effect on Aizu defiance, however: to an Aizu warrior, a Satsuma man was nothing but a "potato samurai." (Sweet potatoes were known as *satsuma-imo*.)

That spring, as Sutematsu and her sisters arranged the tiers of dolls for *hinamatsuri*, their mother stared grimly at the figurine representing the emperor, now the symbolic leader of their enemies. With summer came a sound like distant thunder: cannon fire, echoing in the mountains. Girls of the samurai class tied back their sleeves and bound their hair with white headbands to practice with the *naginata*, a wickedly curved blade at the end of a long pole, preparing to defend their homes. The length of the weapon enabled a woman to keep a larger attacker at a distance, mitigating her disadvantage in height or weight. The weapons were a familiar sight to Sutematsu, hanging on their rack in the guardroom of the Yamakawa compound, their slender shafts marching up the wall like the rungs of a ladder. She had only ever seen them used for practice. The boys stayed home now, their classes suspended—the Nisshinkan had become a field hospital. Aizu was bracing for the worst: a desperate last stand in defense of a world that had already ended.

The graceful, winglike roof lines of Tsuruga Castle—*tsuru* means "crane"—belied its massive fortifications. Sheer walls twenty feet thick rose vertically from the moats, each massive block of stone bearing the chisel marks of the laborers who had wrestled it into place centuries earlier. In places, the drop from the top of the wall to the algae-green surface of the moat was fifty feet. On the inside, the walls were a maze of stone steps, some flights broad enough for fifteen men to run straight up toward the outer edge; others, barely wide enough for one, tracing diagonal paths up and down at intervals. The castle itself rested on a stone foundation two stories high.

Atop one corner of the wall surrounding the castle stood a bell tower, a squat, square lookout of studded timbers rising from a base of stone, tapering slightly to a tiled roof. On August 23, 1868, the bell clanged urgently, summoning all who could hear it to take shelter within the castle walls. Imperial forces, as many as thirty thousand of them, had entered the town. Sutematsu's mother, Toi, gathered her four youngest children and her daughter-in-law—two older sons were off fighting—and headed toward the sound of the bell.

The scene was chaos: those who sought shelter struggled through driving rain and enemy fire. The rain-soaked wooden houses burned slowly, sending up choking clouds of dense smoke. Crowds jammed the streets. After a couple of hours, the castle gates were shut—there was no more room within. Desperate refugees milled outside the walls, enemy bullets whizzing overhead. The Yamakawa women were, for the moment, safe inside.

Hundreds of others had not left their homes when the bell began its clamor. Determined not to hinder their side, they opted for a ceremonial exit. Donning the white robes of the dead, the wives of absent warriors helped their elderly parents to commit ritual suicide before killing their children and finally themselves. In the home of one senior councillor alone, his mother, wife, two sisters, and five daughters died. Two of the teenage daughters composed their farewell poem together:

> *Hand in hand, we will not lose our way,*
> *So let us set forth on the mountain path to death.*

Now the sounds of enemy cannon boomed within the ring of mountains that cradled Wakamatsu; the very air seemed to shake. The rhythmic pop of rifle fire sounded to the children like beans roasting in a pan.

Sutematsu's brother Kenjiro, a few weeks shy of fourteen, had joined the Byakkotai, or "White Tiger Brigade," a reserve unit of teenagers. Not quite strong enough to manage a rifle, he was soon sent back with other younger boys to help guard the castle. He was lucky. On August 22, a unit of twenty White Tigers had lost their commander and become separated from the main force. At dawn the next day, gazing down from a hilltop at their castle wreathed in smoke, they assumed the worst: that their stronghold had been taken, their lord slain, their domain defeated. Kneeling together in despair, they killed themselves. Only one of the twenty survived. The tale is retold to this day in textbooks, tourist brochures, and manga as a paradigm of warrior honor.

AT TWENTY-THREE, Sutematsu's eldest brother, Hiroshi, was a respected commander in the Aizu hierarchy. When word of the siege at Wakamatsu reached him, it was clear that the enemy lines would be impenetrable by the time he could return with his unit to defend the castle. And so Hiroshi resorted to guile: dressing his men as peasants, he commandeered flutes and drums and the feathered costumes of the region's annual lion dance. Posing as a troupe of performers, his men paraded into the castle in broad daylight. The daimyo, impressed, promptly put Hiroshi in charge of defense for the duration of the siege.

Besieged inside the castle walls along with three thousand of their men, fifteen hundred women and children broke into work brigades—some to wash and cook rice, some to clean the crowded and increasingly filthy interior spaces, some to nurse the wounded, and some to make gun cartridges. Sutematsu, a sturdy child of eight with wide-set eyes that missed little, trotted back and forth, bringing lead shot from one storehouse and stacking finished cartridges in another.

Her sister was among the cartridge makers. Yearning for a more active role, the teenager scavenged pieces of discarded armor, chopped off her hair, pulled down the corners of her mouth in a classic samurai grimace, and announced that she was off to join the fighting. Obedience, however, was as deeply ingrained in her as the warrior spirit, and when her mother forbade her to leave the castle, she grudgingly stayed put.

During the last days of the month-long siege, as the sixty cannon of the imperial forces continued to pound the castle, Toi sent Sutematsu with the other girls to fly kites high above the walls, as if it were a holiday. *We are still here*, the kites declared. *We do not fear you.* As shells rained down, it fell to the women to smother them with wet quilts before they exploded. Hiroshi's wife, Tose, was running toward one when it burst. The shrapnel just grazed Sutematsu's neck, but it caught her sister-in-law in the chest. Tose's wounds festered, and she begged Toi to fulfill her duty as a warrior: to give Tose a good death.

"Mother, mother, kill me!" she cried. "Where is your courage? Remember you are the wife of a samurai!"

But though Toi wore on her belt the razor-sharp dagger carried by all women of her rank, she could not bring herself to kill her daughter-in-law. She had, after all, elected to seek shelter in the castle when the shelling began, rather than committing ritual suicide. Tose died in agony.

On September 22, the daimyo of Aizu reluctantly surrendered. Over the castle flew a white flag sewn by the women besieged within. The sudden silence, after a month of constant shelling, was eerie. Every house within the outer moat of the castle had burned to the ground. The elegant rooms and exquisite gardens of Sutematsu's childhood lay in ruins. The white walls of the castle itself were scarred and blistered, its tiled roofs pocked with holes.

Casualties on both sides in the Boshin War numbered nearly six thousand, with Aizu alone accounting for almost half of that total. Despite their decisive victory, the imperial forces took no chances, for the determination of Katamori Matsudaira, Aizu's daimyo, was undisputed. The night of his surrender they placed him under guard in a temple, with six cannon carefully aimed at his door.

Along with her mother and sisters, Sutematsu left the wreckage of Wakamatsu for a prison camp a few miles away. She was filthy, hungry, and crawling with lice. The world she had known was gone.

A YEAR WENT by before the new Meiji government decided the fate of the defeated Aizu: exile to the newly created province of Tonami, a barren and nearly uninhabited region at the northern tip of Honshu. The Meiji government chartered American ships to ferry them, and in the spring of 1870 the Yamakawa women boarded the paddle wheel steamer *Yancy* at Niigata—their first glimpse of the sea. The American sailors gave them biscuits, and they nibbled the strange new food while standing at the rail and watching the coast unfurl. But the novelty faded quickly; as the ship slowly threaded its way north, there was ample time for doubt and depression to take hold, compounded, miserably, by seasickness.

Hiroshi, the oldest Yamakawa brother, was now one of Aizu's leaders, chief of the domain office in Tonami, and responsible for the lives of seventeen thousand refugees. Weary warriors were reunited with their wives and children, and for a time their lot seemed to improve. It was summer, conditions were far cleaner and less crowded than at the camps they had left behind, and there were mushrooms to gather and fish to catch. But the exiled samurai of Aizu were not farmers, and as the weather turned colder the gravity of the situation became clear: not enough rice, no proper shelter or warm clothes. Supplies of firewood ran out. Porridge froze solid in the pot. The settlers dug for the roots of bracken under the snow, collected the seaweed that washed up on the shore, and tried to make meager stores of soybeans and potatoes last. The lucky ones ate dog meat.

Hiroshi's position did not help the Yamakawas' plight; on the contrary, he led by example, putting the needs of his people before those of his family. Desperate to feed his mother and sisters, Hiroshi quietly negotiated with the local tofu dealer to buy *okara*, the pulpy by-product of tofu production often used as animal feed. When other samurai got wind of this humiliating arrangement, they forced Hiroshi to abandon his plan. An Aizu warrior did not eat fodder. Hiroshi expressed his despair only obliquely, in poetry:

> *To those who ask of Tonami in the north,*
> *tell them this;*
> *It is a land before human time.*

Samurai training had not included any of the practical skills these harsh surroundings demanded, save one: endurance, stiffened by the strict code that had put the Aizu on the losing side in the first place. "If those scoundrels from Satsuma and Choshu ever hear that the Aizu samurai have died of starvation, they'll ridicule us," one father told his son. "Our domain will go down in infamy. This is a battlefield, do you hear? It's a battlefield until the day Aizu wipes the stain from its honor."

In spite of cold and hunger, the exiles soon established a school for their sons, though the curriculum took a striking new direction. The boys now read the works of Yukichi Fukuzawa, an educational innovator and leading proponent of Western learning, chanting rhythmic couplets on world geography and history instead of Confucian philosophy. Taking his cue from the Western writers he was translating, Fukuzawa sorted the countries of the globe into categories: Savage, Barbarous, Half-Civilized, and Enlightened. "Although Europe is now without doubt the most civilized and enlightened continent in the world," he wrote, "it was in a chaotic and ignorant state in the old days." Japan might not be as enlightened as Europe, but at least it wasn't savage, like Africa, and given time, there was hope for improvement.

Western technology had helped the imperial forces win the war. It was clear to Aizu's leaders what their sons needed to learn, but books did not fill hungry bellies. The refugees suffered from malnutrition, intestinal parasites, and anemia. Sutematsu, turning eleven, spent her days spreading nightsoil on the fields and looking for shellfish to contribute to her family's meager meals.

WITH THE CESSATION of hostilities, the young Emperor Meiji and his court settled into new rhythms and rituals in their "eastern capital." Townspeople reminded themselves to call their city Tokyo now, rather than Edo. Sutematsu's second brother, Kenjiro, now sixteen, had managed to make his way there. Posing as a temple acolyte, he had escaped an Aizu prison camp under the protection of a monk. His exceptional academic ability soon attracted the patronage of sympathetic Choshu leaders, and for the next year, living under an alias, he was able to study, moving frequently when the rumor of his fugitive status resurfaced. Eventually he was able to settle in Tokyo, but his origins still counted against him, blocking his access to the most prestigious schools. Though there was less snow in Tokyo than in the wilds of Tonami, Kenjiro found himself nearly as hungry as his exiled family.

It wasn't just the defeated people of Aizu who found life a struggle in the early years of Meiji. The name of the new era signified the intent of the new leadership: Meiji means "enlightened rule." A circle of energetic, reform-minded, and startlingly young men emerged to lead a new and improved Japan, packaging their agenda as the divine word of the "restored" emperor. With his endorsement, they rapidly began to dismantle the status quo.

The wave of change that had swept the shogun from power left behind an uneasy coalition of men whose loyalties were ancient and fundamentally provincial. "Japan" was an abstract concept; each domain was a country unto itself. With the common enemy defeated, old rivalries threatened to reemerge. The "potato samurai" from Satsuma and Choshu had ousted the Tokugawas and confiscated their base, but they and all the other domains remained intact, each with its own army.

In August of 1871, the emperor summoned the lord of every domain to Tokyo for an announcement that, while predictable, was no less stunning: the domains were henceforth abolished, their age-old boundaries erased, replaced by a system of prefectures administered by Tokyo-appointed governors. The former daimyo, generously compensated with money and titles, their debts now assumed by the new central government, put up little resistance. Lower-ranking samurai, on the other hand—even those who had backed the winning side in the recent conflict—lost their stipends, their rank, their accustomed place in the social hierarchy. The forward-thinking ones found their way into business or government service. The rest opened their ancestral storehouses and sold what they could, sinking into genteel poverty. Foreign visitors to Japan were delighted with the buyer's market in souvenirs. "The curio-shops displayed heaps of swords which, a few months before, the owners would less willingly have parted with than with life itself," declared one popular guidebook.

The Yamakawa men—capable Hiroshi and his clever younger brother Kenjiro—would be among the forward-thinking ones. Their family might have lost the security and prestige that their affiliation with the shogun had once provided, but with their Aizu pride intact, they were determined to reclaim it. Neither could have imagined the part their little sister would play in the fulfillment of that vow.

3 | "A LITTLE LEAVEN"

THE FATES OF TWO of the Yamakawas would be determined in part by a broad-faced, bull-necked man named Kiyotaka Kuroda, whose Satsuma origins would once have marked him decisively as their enemy. A man of intense enthusiasms—for liquor as well as for national development—Kuroda embodied the quantum leap of Meiji leadership. Less than a decade earlier, traveling in the retinue of the lord of Satsuma on the road to Edo, Kuroda had been appalled to see a party of British day-trippers on horseback—including a *woman*—gawking at his lord's elaborate palanquin as it passed, flanked by retainers and servants all wearing the cross-within-a-circle crest of xenophobic Satsuma. Oblivious to the townspeople prostrating themselves in the dust, the barbarians had lingered, chatting, by the side of the road—until the horsemen closest to them charged with drawn swords, killing one man, wounding two others, and separating the lady's hat from her head, along with some of her hair. The Richardson Incident of 1862, named for the dead man, provoked Britain to bombard the Satsuma seat of Kagoshima within a year. It was this demonstration of Britain's military might that hastened the realization in Satsuma that "expelling the barbarians" might not be a particularly practical course.

Several years later, the two-sworded, silk-robed samurai Kuroda, attacker of foreigners, had become a mustachioed Meiji bureaucrat in a well-tailored Western-style military uniform.

Turning to the West for guidance, he traveled to the United States, touring coal mines, lumber mills, and breweries; observing American farming and mining techniques; and inviting American experts to advise the newly created Hokkaido Colonization Board, formed to strengthen the Japanese presence in the northern territories, which were eyed covetously by neighboring Russia. Richly endowed with forests and fishing grounds, Hokkaido was inhabited only by indigenous hunter-gatherer tribes of bear-worshiping Ainu. What better place, Kuroda argued, to send the displaced and disaffected remnants of the cash-strapped warrior class?

Upon his return to Japan, Kuroda recruited promising young men to study abroad and help him in his cause—among them Sutematsu's brother Kenjiro, still a struggling student in Tokyo. Kenjiro was selected despite, but also because of, his lineage: though the stain of defeat still tarnished the name of Aizu, no one doubted the strength and resolve of its warriors, and its cold winters were thought to be good preparation for life in Hokkaido. In January 1871 sixteen-year-old Kenjiro sailed for America, with a Tokyo-made "Western-style" suit that looked more like a kimono, and secondhand shoes, conspicuously white and several sizes too big.

IT WASN'T JUST the men of business Kuroda had observed in America. Throughout the trip, he had been astonished by American women. At home, females of his rank stayed largely out of sight; the teahouses and reception rooms where men transacted business were strictly off limits. Samurai wives sewed, served, bore children, and managed the household for their husbands, who spent their leisure hours in the pleasure quarters, enjoying the attentions of a different sort of woman, trained in music, dance, and sparkling conversation rather than the domestic arts. Women were obedient or entertaining; beyond that, they were unimportant.

But these American women! They had opinions, which they didn't hesitate to offer—and the men listened. They joined their husbands at social gatherings and official ceremonies. They presided at table. Men gave up their seats for women, doffed their hats to them, made way for them on the sidewalk, fetched and carried for them. In public. Clearly, American women had a happier lot than their Japanese sisters. Why?

The answer, Kuroda concluded, was education. American women of the higher classes were well-informed and well-read, and though naturally they did not aspire to lead businesses or armies, they were the intellectual companions of their husbands and sons, who turned to them not just for practical needs, but for emotional and spiritual strength. Surely this rich home life helped explain the staggering successes of American men in industry and commerce. Upon reaching Washington and the company of his friend Arinori Mori, the young and rather dashing Japanese chargé d'affaires there, Kuroda shared his conclusions, even going so far as to exhort Mori to find himself an American wife. Reassuring Kuroda of his patriotism, Mori politely declined.

Undaunted, Kuroda went back to Japan and drafted a memorandum to the Meiji government. The goal of colonizing wild Hokkaido would never be accomplished by sending mostly untrained men north and hoping for the best. The first thing to do, he wrote, was to educate Japanese women, who bore the responsibility for the first decade of their children's lives. Educated mothers would raise enlightened sons, who would then grow up to lead Japan, "as a little leaven leavens the whole lump." Unwritten, but perhaps implied, was a warning: as long as the Japanese kept their women in the shadows, Westerners would have trouble recognizing Japan as a civilized nation.

Young men like Kenjiro Yamakawa were already studying abroad and returning with invaluable tools. It was time to send young women to join them. Upon their return, they would be qualified to teach in the girls' schools that Kuroda envisioned; they would also make excellent wives for the new statesmen of Japan as they emerged onto the global stage.

Kuroda's thoughts were well received, aligned as they were with the fundamental goals of the reform-minded Meiji leaders. One of their first acts upon seizing power had been to draft a statement of purpose: the Charter Oath, proclaimed by the emperor at his enthronement in 1868. The oath announced the radical intentions of the new government: to overhaul Japan's political, economic, and social institutions and guide the country toward equal footing with the West. "Evil customs of the past shall be broken off and everything based upon the just laws of Nature," it read. "Knowledge shall be sought throughout the world so as to strengthen the foundation of imperial rule." The restrictions on engagement with the wider world, enforced over the preceding two and a half centuries, were thus reversed at a stroke.

Kuroda's timing was excellent. In the fall of 1871, Tomomi Iwakura, a former courtier and newly minted Meiji minister, announced a plan to lead an embassy to the nations with whom Japan had signed treaties, starting with the United States. It was time to heed the call of the Charter Oath and seek knowledge throughout the world. The delegates would observe Western institutions and technology firsthand, introduce Japan's new leadership to foreign governments, and broach the issue of renegotiating the unequal trade agreements forced on the doomed shogunate more than a decade earlier. Dozens of students would travel with the embassy. Why not add a few girls?

IN THE YEARS following the arrival of Commodore Perry's black ships, Japan had sent other official embassies abroad, with mixed success. The first, to the United States in 1860, was largely ceremonial: a chance for the shogunate to assert its dignity in the wake of the first humiliating unequal treaty signings, as much for the Japanese audience as for the Americans. A middle-ranking and rather motley group, the members of this first delegation had only the sketchiest concept of life outside Japan; many were selected merely for their willingness to consider going abroad. Inexperienced, nervous, and deeply wary of the West, they shuffled through their diplomatic obligations hurriedly, refusing many invitations and determined to get home as soon as possible.

The Americans, flattered that Japan had chosen to visit their nation first, greeted the Japanese "princes" with ecstatic enthusiasm. In New York, hundreds of thousands of spectators watched the procession of ambassadors down Broadway on June 16, 1860, escorted by seven thousand welcoming troops, a spectacle immortalized by Walt Whitman in "The Errand-Bearers":

> *Over sea, hither from Niphon,*
> *Courteous, the Princes of Asia, swart-cheek'd princes,*
> *First-comers, guests, two-sworded princes,*
> *Lesson-giving princes, leaning back in their open barouches,*
>   *bare-headed, impassive,*
> *This day they ride through Manhattan.*

But those impassive faces belied bewilderment and discomfort. Yukichi Fukuzawa, the prolific author and educator whose works would one day enlighten Aizu's exiled sons, was a twenty-five-year-old member of that first delegation. Despite years of study in Dutch and English, he found himself baffled by such novelties as horse-drawn carriages, ice cubes, and ballroom dancing. Even a smoke was a challenge: seeing nothing he recognized as an ashtray, Fukuzawa emptied the bowl of his pipe into a wad of paper that he stashed in his sleeve. Wisps of smoke began to emerge from his robe. "The light that I thought I had crushed out was quietly setting me afire!"

Though the press coverage of the 1860 embassy was almost universally respectful, the behavior of the average American citizen did not always rise to that standard. When the envoys arrived in Washington, mobs surrounded their carriages and gaped. "One burly fellow swore that all [the Japanese men] wanted was to have a little more crinoline and be right out decent looking nigger wenches," noted a reporter.

The group led by Tomomi Iwakura in 1871 would be far more impressive. Eleven years after the journey of Whitman's inscrutable princes, Japan had not just a new government but a new attitude on the part of its young statesmen: active, curious, determined, embracing the future rather than protecting the past. Many of Iwakura's men had already studied abroad, and several spoke competent English. The average age of the forty-six ambassadors was thirty-two.

Among them were most of the rising stars of Japan's new leadership, including the very men who had written the Charter Oath. Many of them would become household names in the decades to come: Takayoshi Kido, a senior councillor; Hirobumi Ito, minister of public works; and Toshimichi Okubo, minister of finance. Kunitake Kume, a Confucian scholar, was the embassy's official scribe; his monumental *True Account of the Ambassador Extraordinary & Plenipotentiary's Journey of Observation through the United States of America and Europe* would fill five volumes and sell thousands of copies.

The addition of a few girls to the sizable contingent of young male students joining the delegation would not be a problem. The American ambassador, Charles DeLong, would be traveling with the group, and his wife, Elida Vineyard DeLong, would make a convenient chaperone. In his position as deputy chair of the Hokkaido Colonization Board, Kuroda began recruiting for his pet project. The offer was generous: ten years in America, all expenses paid, with a stipend of eight hundred dollars per year—a stunning sum to spend on anyone, let alone untested girls.

Yet there were no applicants. Who would send a small daughter away while she was still useful at home, only to get her back too late to marry, assuming anyone would want to marry a girl untutored in the duties of a Japanese wife? And to America, of all places, where the loud, smelly, yellow-haired, blue-eyed barbarians wore their filthy shoes right into the house and gorged on animal flesh at every meal? For most families high placed enough to see the recruiting notices, it was unthinkable. As the Iwakura Mission's departure date approached, Kuroda was forced to launch a second round of recruiting. This time he received responses from a handful of applicants, all of whom were accepted at once.

SUTEMATSU KNEW NOTHING of this. In the spring of 1871, after the Aizu exiles' first hungry winter in snowbound Tonami, her brother Hiroshi had sent her to Hakodate, just across the Tsugaru Straits in Hokkaido. Already far from her homeland, she would now be isolated from her family as well—but at least she would be fed. Compared to barren Tonami, Hakodate was a bustling oasis; one of the first ports opened to foreign trade as a result of Commodore Perry's negotiations in 1854, it was now a regular destination for diplomats and missionaries, as well as traders. Sent to lodge with Takuma Sawabe, one of Japan's first Russian Orthodox converts, Sutematsu later moved to the home of a French missionary family and spent six months in a town whose harbor buzzed with international shipping. Western-style buildings had sprung up to house the consular staffs of nine different countries—with sash windows that slid up instead of sideways, white clapboard siding instead of unpainted wood, shingled roofs instead of tile or thatch, wrought-iron fences instead of plastered walls. Sutematsu had never seen homes built without tatami floors and shoji screens. Hakodate was a first taste of the West.

By the time Kuroda issued his recruitment notices, Sutematsu's brother Kenjiro had already left for America. Hiroshi, leader of the exiled Aizu domain, had no trouble imagining his youngest sister there as well. She had acquitted herself admirably, during both the siege of Wakamatsu and the longer trials of prison camp and exile. She showed promise as a student, and Hiroshi had confidence she could rise to the challenges of a foreign classroom at least as honorably as she had faced the struggles of the previous three years. At the very least, her departure would mean one less sister to support. And who knew? If she managed to return someday, accustomed to American ways and speaking fluent English, perhaps she could contribute somehow to Japan's modernization—and to the rehabilitation of her family's good name.

In October of 1871 Hiroshi traveled to Hakodate to inform his sister that she would be leaving immediately for Tokyo. There she would board a ship for America, where she would study at government expense for a decade. Sutematsu had no way to comprehend his words. He might as well have told her she was moving to the moon. But her Aizu training left no room for disobedience. She packed to leave without question.

On her way south to Tokyo, she stopped in Tonami to bid her mother farewell. Toi was horrified by the decision to send her daughter away, but

Hiroshi was the head of their household, and his decision was final. When they parted, Toi bestowed a new name on her youngest child—a common practice among the literate classes to mark a new life phase. From now on, the erstwhile Sakiko would be called Sutematsu, an odd name to the Japanese ear, written with the characters for "discard" and "pine tree": 捨松. The second character contained an echo of the Matsudaira family, lords of Aizu, and of Wakamatsu, seat of the domain, to signify her origins; the first could be read as bitter acknowledgment that such a proud lineage had come to an end. It was time to let go of the past. But *matsu* ("pine") is also a homonym for the verb "to wait." A girl cast to the winds, then—sacrificed to circumstance, yet noble and enduring like the pine. Her mother would await her return.

A GIRL OF eleven, under normal circumstances, is betwixt and between: too big for dolls and playing house, eager to be entrusted with "real" responsibilities, yet not quite wise enough to make out the road ahead. But Sutematsu had already seen more horror than most adults: the heaps of bodies left unburied during the siege of Tsuruga Castle, the dying agony of her sister-in-law, the slower deaths from hunger and cold in Tonami, the separation from her family in Hakodate. The festival dolls arranged on their red-draped tiers each spring in Aizu were but a hazy memory of a life that now seemed to have belonged to someone else. Her home no longer existed, her mother had bid her a final farewell, and now she would leave Japan itself behind, along with the only language she could speak. Hiroshi hurried her to Tokyo, where officials from the Hokkaido Colonization Board and the Ministry of Education were waiting—along with four other girls, looking every bit as bewildered as Sutematsu felt.

Two of them were already young women: Ryo Yoshimasu and Tei Ueda, both fourteen years old. The other two, Sutematsu was relieved to note, were younger, even smaller than she was. Shige Nagai, stocky and round-faced with laughing eyes, was ten. Ume Tsuda, exquisitely pretty, was only six. Ryo and Tei instinctively took Sutematsu under their wing—she had come from so far away, and had no one to help her in Tokyo—while Sutematsu, always the littlest sister, suddenly acquired two littler ones in Shige and Ume.

After so much loss, here was a new family of sorts. All five were samurai daughters, all five from families on the losing side of the recent upheaval. These were the chosen girls, if chosen they were, as there exists no record of any others having applied. Life accelerated quickly. The girls' recruitment having been a hasty afterthought, their departure with the Iwakura Mission was already upon them.

WHETHER IN REMOTE Aizu or bustling Tokyo, a samurai girl's life had always been lived largely within her family compound's walls. Now every day seemed to consist of dashing from place to place. Hitherto, people moved about on foot, or else rode in a *kago*, a basketlike palanquin swinging queasily from bamboo poles borne on the shoulders of trotting bearers. The passenger might be cushioned by a folded futon, but the dusty and jolting journey was never comfortable. In Tokyo, however, the kago had been replaced by the smoother and more maneuverable *jinrikisha*. The two-wheeled, canopied buggies raced up and down Tokyo's narrow streets, pulled by wiry runners wearing leggings and broad bowl-shaped hats to keep off the sun. By 1871, not two years after their invention, there were twenty-five thousand jinrikishas plying Tokyo's narrow streets, their rattling wheels and shouting runners adding considerably to the urban din.

Bowling along on wheels was novelty enough, but the girls also received an invitation to ride the new seventeen-mile railway from Tokyo to Yokohama, financed by the British and so recently completed it was not yet open to the public. The Japanese contractors who built the line (under close foreign supervision) had never seen a train. It had an English chief engineer and a foreign crew, and, to the girls' astonishment, it pulled itself.

There were formal functions to attend, hosted by high-ranking officials. There was no time to have Western-style clothes made, but unlike Western dresses, kimonos were sewn with straight seams from cloth of standard width and needed no fitting. The new finery, paid for by the government, was urgently required. These were the first girls ever selected to receive a foreign education, and in honor of that extraordinary circumstance, they would be the first girls of samurai rank ever granted an audience with the empress herself.

THE EMPRESS HARUKO had only recently undergone her own transformation into the first lady of the court. A pedigreed daughter of the Kyoto nobility—an ancient and inbred class distinct from the samurai—she was something of a prodigy: reading at the age of three, composing poetry at five, studying calligraphy at seven, and plucking the *koto* (a stringed instrument) at twelve. She was equally adept in the traditional arts of tea ceremony and flower arrangement. Her family was one of the five from which the imperial consort was traditionally chosen. Her suitability was unquestioned except for a single detail: she was older than her intended. This in itself was not insurmountable; there was precedent for imperial unions with older women. The problem was that the difference in their ages was three years—an inauspicious number. But no matter. The girl's official birth date was quickly shifted later by one year, and in January 1869 the marriage went forward—the groom sixteen, his bride, officially, eighteen.

Until her marriage, Haruko—along with all her foremothers—had lived a life confined strictly within the limits of etiquette, protocol, and the precincts of the imperial palace. Within the year, she and the Emperor Mutsuhito had relocated to Tokyo. Two more years had passed, and the cascade of changes had been dizzying. Most recently, the Meiji leaders had decided that the "delicate and effeminate old aristocrats" who had heretofore managed every aspect of daily life in the imperial household in Kyoto should be replaced by "manly and incorruptible samurai" as the emperor's most intimate advisers. These advisers had a new responsibility: tutoring the young emperor in history and current affairs, both foreign and domestic. Japan's emperors had always lived in seclusion, kept in ignorance of the wider world by the shoguns who held true power. All Mutsuhito's

father had seen of Commodore Perry's visit in 1853 were the demonic cari-
catures of Edo's woodblock artists. Breaking the precedent of centuries,
the young emperor would henceforth become a student of the times.

More shocking yet, the empress and her ladies were expected to
attend these lectures as well, and listen closely. Not only would the young
empress be the highest-ranking woman in Japan; she would be the most
well-informed too. The wife of an emperor had hitherto functioned solely
as the bearer of his heirs, her life lived behind screens, unseen by any but
her ladies-in-waiting. Haruko would be a modern consort, appearing
beside her husband to encourage the efforts of Japan's modernizers, and to
represent a unified nation to the world.

On the morning of November 9, 1871, the Empress Haruko had yet to
emerge onto the global stage. Nor could the girls who bowed before her in
awe that day have imagined that one day they would join her there.

WITH THEIR VISIT to the empress, the girls had become part of the
official chronicle of Japanese history. Their next stop was a photographer's
studio, for a formal portrait commemorating the imperial audience.

Though the first photographs had reached Japan via Dutch traders in
Nagasaki as early as the 1840s, professional photographers did not arrive
until the 1860s—just in time to capture Old Japan as it confronted the
onslaught of the new. Superstitions regarding the preternaturally accurate
images were rife at first. "Once photographed, your shadow will fade," one
warned; "twice photographed, your life will shorten." Another insisted that
if three people sat for a portrait together, the one in the middle would die
early. Within a few years, however, photography had become one of seven
"tools of civilization and enlightenment," along with newspapers, the postal
system, gaslights, steam engines, international exhibitions, and dirigible
balloons. By 1871, sitting for a formal photograph was a proud event, the
privilege of a select few that rarely included women, let alone young girls.

Still strangers to each other, the girls must have felt as uncomfortable as they appear in the photo. Tei and Ryo sit as stiff as bookends on

either side, toes together and heels apart. The photographer has angled their seats precisely toward each other; swathed in similar kimonos of pale silk, elaborately embroidered with fruits and flowers, they stare blankly past each other's ears. Tei folds her fingers demurely inside her sleeves. Between them, the three younger girls are less carefully composed. Seated in the center, Sutematsu clasps her hands in her flowered lap, lips pursed slightly to one side, hair sculpted into high loops like butterfly wings. Shige stands to her right, her dark kimono in somber contrast, and both girls gaze frankly at the unfamiliar contraption pointing their way. Perched on Sutematsu's other side, Ume is distracted by something beyond the camera, her diminutive features dwarfed by her own complicated coiffure. Ryo holds one of Ume's hands in hers, perhaps steadying her. Though the new wet-plate collodion process had taken firm hold among the growing ranks of Japan's studio photographers—reducing exposure time from minutes to seconds—it was nevertheless hard for a six-year-old to sit perfectly still.

Stylized and expressionless, the girls look like dolls. Their portrait leaves out as much as it preserves: no suggestion of the violent upheaval just past, no trace of the bewilderment and gut-gripping fear with which the girls must have contemplated their immediate future. Five daughters of the losing side had been repackaged for the coming victories of the new Japan, and their own feelings on the subject were irrelevant.

That same evening the girls were invited to a dinner at the home of Toshimichi Okubo, a Satsuma samurai who, having risen to the post of finance minister, was now, at forty-one, one of the highest-ranking members of the embassy about to depart. With his chiseled features, expressive eyes, and wavy hair cropped in the new style and parted on the side—no samurai topknot—Okubo cut a dashing figure. Many years later the girls would still remember the long tatami-matted room full of men drinking sake while geisha played music, danced, and kept the cups always full. Unmarried girls were not usually the dinner guests of statesmen.

Girls weren't usually the subject of newspaper articles either. Japanese journalism was still in its infancy, but Takayoshi Kido, another leader of the imminent embassy and an author of the Charter Oath, saw it as a key component of modernization. His newspaper, the *Shimbun Zasshi*, founded just months earlier to educate the people on the aims of the new government and "urge them on toward civilization," covered the story. "Five Young Girls Leave for Study in America," ran the astonishing headline. Fewer than twenty years had passed since Commodore Perry's black ships first sailed into Edo Bay.

4 "AN EXPEDITION OF PRACTICAL OBSERVERS"

ON THE OCCASION OF a state dinner just before the embassy sailed, the emperor addressed his court and the men who would lead the Iwakura Mission with a speech of startling frankness. "If we would profit by the useful arts and sciences and conditions of society prevailing among more enlightened nations," the emperor said, "we must either study these at home as best we can, or send abroad an expedition of practical observers, to foreign lands, competent to acquire for us those things our people lack, which are best calculated to benefit this nation." The Emperor of Enlightened Rule was effectively declaring his own land unenlightened.

"Travel in foreign countries, properly indulged in, will increase your store of useful knowledge," the emperor continued. Two hundred and fifty years of staying home made venturing abroad seem fundamentally unnatural—tempting, perhaps, but perilous, to be sampled sparingly, like strong drink. "Great national defects require immediate remedies," he declared. The Land of the Gods, defective! But there was more. "We lack superior institutions for high female culture. Our women should not be ignorant of those great principles on which the happiness of daily life frequently depends. How important the education of mothers, on whom future generations almost wholly rely for the early cultivation of those intellectual

tastes which an enlightened system of training is designed to develop!"
The happiness of women was suddenly a goal of national policy; Japan
could not progress to enlightenment without them.

"Liberty is therefore granted wives and sisters to accompany their relatives on foreign tours, that they may acquaint themselves with better forms
of female education, and, on their return, introduce beneficial improvements in the training of our children," the emperor went on. Though the
assembled notables remained impassive as they listened to these words—
written for the emperor, no doubt, by some of their own number—they
were not yet ready to heed them. None of the Iwakura Mission's ambassadors brought their women along. If it was important for women to learn
foreign ways, let the vanguard be the expendable younger daughters of
other men.

FRIENDS AND RELATIVES of the Iwakura delegates, many a bit worse
for wear after the previous evening's farewell parties, thronged the Yokohama waterfront as the girls stepped into a launch bobbing beside the pier,
careful not to tread on the long kimono sleeves—the style for unmarried
women—that draped nearly to their feet. Though a heavy frost covered
the ground, the late-December sun was strong. Gawkers pressed in, hoping for a glimpse of the most famous men of the age, and wondering at
the little girls included incongruously among them. Sitting stiffly under a
white canopy alongside their chaperone, Mrs. DeLong, the girls searched
the crowd on the dock for familiar faces as the rest of the embassy boarded
other small boats.

"What heartless people their parents must be," Ume's aunt overheard
another bystander mutter. "Sending them to a barbarous land like America!" No one contradicted her. Some of those present may have been aware
that the girls were not actually the first Japanese females to venture to
America. In the wake of Aizu's defeat, one John Henry Schnell, a Prussian
arms dealer and military adviser to the daimyo, had led a small contingent
of Aizu samurai and peasants (including his own Japanese wife) to Cali-

fornia, bringing tea seeds and silkworms. The Wakamatsu Tea and Silk Colony, established in June 1869 in Placerville, east of Sacramento, had quickly shriveled in the unforgiving climate, its settlers dead or dispersed in poverty. "What wonder," Ume wrote later, "that even five girls were found in the length of the kingdom whose parents would permit them to start on this perilous and daring undertaking!"

Little thought had been spared for the practical aspects of preparing young girls for ten years in an alien land. The men of the mission had managed to acquire Western-style suits, perhaps not at the leading edge of fashion, but nevertheless serviceable. Many of the delegates also possessed sizable English vocabularies. The girls had neither. Little Ume was the only one whose trunk contained any items useful for a girl traveling to America: an English primer with the Roman alphabet, a small book entitled *A Pocket Edition of Japanese Equivalents for the Most Common English Words*, and a bright red woolen shawl, which looked rather odd with her kimono.

They were gifts, she told the older girls, from her father, Sen Tsuda, who had been telling her stories of America for as long as she could remember. He knew how to speak English, she reported proudly; he had worked as an interpreter for the shogun, and had even once traveled to San Francisco, the very port for which they were bound. He returned with trunkfuls of reference books and manuals, but without his samurai top-knot, which, in a fit of enlightened enthusiasm, he had cut off and shipped home en route. Ume had never forgotten her mother's speechless shock when she opened the package.

Tsuda's time abroad had broadened his views on girl children. Upon his return, he insisted that Ume learn to read and write; not quite four years old, she was soon taking lessons morning and evening. A bright child, she learned the *kana* syllabary rapidly, progressing to the Chinese ideographs, or *kanji*, used in Japanese writing.

Ume's family, like Sutematsu's, had found itself on the wrong side of the recent conflict, and having lost his position in the service of the shogun, her samurai father now struggled to regain his footing. Under the circumstances, he, too, was open to the possibility of reducing the number of mouths he had to feed. With Ume's two little brothers to carry on his line, a daughter was, frankly, expendable. The plan to send girls to America intrigued him twice over, then: not only would he be relieved of the burden of the girl's expenses, but an American-educated daughter might eventually return to him a little welcome prestige. Having a daughter who spoke English fluently and to whom Western customs were second nature could only raise his standing with the new government.

At first, Tsuda planned to send his eldest daughter, Koto, but the girl balked. Ume, two years younger, was substituted at the last moment. When Ume was born on the last day of 1864, her father had stormed from the house at the news that his second child was a second daughter. He was still absent on the seventh day, when tradition dictated a baby should be named. Next to her mother's bed stood a bonsai plum tree, *ume* in Japanese, so Ume it was—a name evoking the beauty and fortitude of the plum, which blooms before the snow has melted. Now, that strength would be tested. Still a month shy of her seventh birthday, Ume was less aware than Koto of the gravity of the decision. A strange and distant land called America? It sounded like a fairy story, and she was curious. Her English skills, at that point, were limited to "yes," "no," and "thank you."

IWAKURA, IN HIS courtier's robes, stood regally on the deck of the steam-powered lead boat, while sailors plying long oars steered the small fleet of launches in his wake. Tiny Ume, in a flaming-red silk kimono embroidered with soaring cranes, chrysanthemums, and her namesake plum blossoms, made a bright spot that remained visible long after her boat had pulled away from the pier. Anchored farther out was the Pacific Mail steamship *America*, one of the largest paddle wheel steamers in the world: 363 feet from stem to stern, with more than an acre of deck. Today it flew the Japanese *hinomaru*, the red-on-white "Circle of the Sun," alongside the American Stars and Stripes. The ship dwarfed the launches bearing the ambassadors as they drew alongside. A nineteen-gun salute rang out, then another fifteen salvos in honor of the departing American ambassador. Cannon smoke drifted over the water, and the echoes bounced back and forth across the harbor.

At last more than a hundred delegates and their mountain of luggage were safely aboard. At noon one final cannon exploded, and as the ship's anchors rose out of the water, the towering paddle wheels began to turn. The *America* was under way. "Sailors on the decks of the many foreign warships in Yokohama Bay all manned the rigging and doffed their caps in salute as we passed," wrote Kunitake Kume, the official scribe. "We were followed for several miles by a crowd of well-wishers in a flotilla of boats."

It would be hard to overstate the high-minded sense of purpose with which these men set off, charged with opening a new era in the chronicle of Japan's relations with the wider world. In the larger context of their mission, the five girls traveling with them were insignificant. In his account of their departure, Kume mistakenly noted only four.

Beyond the waves, Mount Fuji rose in snow-robed majesty, the view from the ship's deck unobstructed and stunning. "It was a very beautiful day when the vessel started," Ume would write in one of her first English compositions, barely two years later. "How my heart beat as I saw the land fading away! I tried not to think about it." The sun sank behind the mountains, but the travelers remained on deck, gazing west until the sea gleamed in the moonlight, serene and exquisite. But during the night the wind rose, and the exaltation of the view faded as the ship began to roll.

THE THREE-WEEK VOYAGE was difficult. The Pacific in midwinter was full of storms, and the five girls were crammed into a single cabin, Ryo sharing a berth with Ume ("as she was such a tiny little tot"), while Shige made do with a luggage rack for her bed. Shige's sister had given her an old *zori*, a rice-straw sandal, instructing her to keep it under her pillow as a charm against seasickness. Sandal or no sandal, all five girls were soon bedridden and miserable.

Just as Shige fell between Sutematsu and Ume in age, her life experience to this point fell somewhere between theirs as well. Like Ume, she had spent most of her childhood in Tokyo among elders intrigued by Western ideas and loyal to the shogunate. Her father, Takanosuke Masuda, had been governor of Hakodate, the northern treaty port from which Sutematsu had just come; her much older brother, Takashi, had begun to study English at the age of eleven. The family had moved back to Edo in 1861, the year Shige was born. She could just remember her father and teenage brother embarking on an embassy to Europe two years later. They had traveled via Shanghai and India and up the Red Sea to the Mediterranean. Shige had seen a photograph of the group posing in blinding sunlight before a vast stone head: the Great Sphinx.

As with Sutematsu, the Boshin War had put an end to life as Shige knew it and separated her from her family. As the domains of the Northern Alliance had struggled to resist the emperor's forces in July of 1868, gunfire had also shattered the leafy peacefulness of Koishikawa, Shige's neighborhood just north of Edo Castle. Though the southern forces had already taken the castle and replaced the shogun with the young Emperor Meiji, pockets of resistance remained. More than a thousand of the deposed shogun's men had formed a base at a temple in Ueno, barely a mile away. On the morning of Takashi's wedding day, the emperor's forces, wearing blue Western-style uniforms and the shaggy "red bear" wigs of the southern samurai, attacked.

All day long Shige and her family listened to the whoosh and thump of shells. Smoke from acres of burning houses darkened the air. The groom hurried off with the other men of the house, their wedding finery discarded in favor of whatever weapons were at hand. "The bride was left alone with mother and the little ones," Shige recalled, "but the house was in great commotion[,] for friends came hurrying in to take shelter from the shells." By evening, the battle of Ueno was over, the last holdouts of the shogun's forces routed. The heads of the losers were mounted on poles, and Shige was taken to gaze at them. "It was a terrible sight."

The city was in chaos, and especially dangerous for anyone who harbored loyalties to the losing side. Because Shige's father and brother had made their careers in the service of the shogun, their family was directly threatened. Triumphant imperial soldiers roamed the streets, harassing Tokugawa loyalists for sport. Takashi had already lost two sisters to disease in early childhood, and he was determined not to lose another. To keep Shige safe, he decided the best course was to give her away.

Takashi's friend Gen'ei Nagai, a doctor he had met while serving in the shogun's cavalry, was moving his family out of Tokyo with the exiled shogun's retinue. Nagai would adopt Shige and take her far from the turbulent capital. With bewildering speed, Shige had a new surname, a new family, and a new home. Riding in a kago, she swayed and bumped along dusty roads for five days to the village of Mishima, southwest of Tokyo, which for the next three years would be her home.

Thanks to the influence of well-placed friends on the winning side, Takashi soon secured a position in the Ministry of Finance. When the call for female students went out, he was intrigued. Not bothering to inform his little sister or her foster family, he submitted an application to the Hokkaido Colonization Board on Shige's behalf. The Nagai family was startled when one day a horseman clattered up to their house, bearing word from Tokyo of Shige's imminent departure for America.

Ten-year-old Shige was stunned. After three years at the temple school in the village, she could read and write in Japanese, but she had never uttered a word of English. How could she possibly fulfill the government's expectations for her future? Takashi had played a hunch, however, when he submitted his sister's application. Shige's situation was hardly idyllic: her adoptive mother, who took a harsh approach to child rearing, had never warmed to her. Frightening as the prospect of America seemed, the unknown future might offer an improvement over the difficult present. Shige was not sorry to say goodbye to the Nagais.

TWO DAYS AND nights of nausea passed in the cramped cabin. Well-wishers had sent the girls off with boxes of sweets that were now stacked to the ceiling, making the small space even smaller. Chinese waiters brought unrecognizable meals they could not bring themselves to touch. Mrs. DeLong, their chaperone, spoke no Japanese, and the men of the delegation, while occasionally helpful as interpreters, knew nothing about the needs of young girls. Their stewardess had been taught the Japanese for "what do you want?" but the girls had no words to respond with in English. When hunger did penetrate their queasiness, they picked at the pile of sweets, which only made things worse.

On the third day they had a visit from the delegate in the cabin next door. A dapper, outspoken Finance Ministry official who would go on to become a pioneer of Japanese journalism, Gen'ichiro Fukuchi was a veteran of two previous overseas missions. The challenges of an ocean voyage were not new to him. He swept into the girls' cabin, quickly taking in the five pale and clammy faces and the half-empty boxes of confectionary, and sprang into action. Opening the porthole, he seized the remaining cakes and flung them overboard. "All our entreaties and wails were in vain," Shige recalled.

It was a week before any of the girls left their cabin. Ume recovered first, venturing up the metal steps that led to the deck and gazing, awestruck, at the tall American sailors and their smartly uniformed officers. Once all the girls were up, they had a proper tour: the luxurious saloons and dining rooms, the thunderous engines and the churning paddle wheels, whose sound was the only proof that the ship was moving on the featureless expanse of ocean. "Passengers are forbidden to approach the cages over the paddlewheels or wander outside the deck railings," read the rules posted aboard ship. "Do not talk to officers on watch." Each day the captain announced their degree of longitude, which the ambassadors dutifully recorded. Those who had acquired pocket watches carefully adjusted them to the new time.

Rain fell, and kept falling for nearly half the voyage. Once the ship itself had become familiar, there was nothing to look at. "We did not see so much as the silhouette of a single island," the embassy's scribe Kume noted. "Although it was the time of the full moon, the fact that we could hardly ever see it intensified our feelings of loneliness." Hirobumi Ito, one of the senior ambassadors and a close friend of the cake-flinging Fuku-chi, came to check on the girls, who were still mourning the loss of their sweets. A small man with a large personality, lowborn but aiming high, Ito was something of a peacock, handsome and gallant and fond of life's pleasures, his boyish smile verging on a smirk. At twenty-two he had smuggled himself out of Japan to study in London; now, at thirty, he was the minister of public works. "He told us to come to his room and he would give us something nice, if we behaved properly," Shige later remembered. To each girl he gave a precious piece of *misozuke* pickle, a taste of home that settled both their stomachs and their nerves. It would not be the last time Ito changed the girls' circumstances for the better.

The enforced idleness of shipboard life lay heavily on the delegates. The men of the Iwakura Mission were ambitious, determined, proud, and insecure. Samurai from the southern domains savored the triumph of their rise to power, but still felt more deeply loyal to their own domains than to each other. Those who had once served the toppled shogunate held deep-seated grudges. Enemies until just recently, they had not entirely finished becoming allies. Now they faced the daunting challenge of introducing their new leadership to the wider world.

Those with some experience abroad patronized those who had never left Japan. One delegate, an official with the judicial department, held tutorials on Western table manners: forks on the left, knives on the right, cut your meat into pieces first instead of picking up a whole chop and gnawing off a bite. Don't slurp. The younger and more arrogant junior delegates, resenting such schoolmarmish meddling, only slurped and stabbed with greater abandon.

The presence of young girls in this idle and simmering group was provocative. The two oldest, Ryo and Tei, both fourteen, were nearly of marriageable age. They were the only Japanese females the men would see until the mission returned home, and not every delegate was as appropriately solicitous as Ito and Fukuchi. One day, Ryo was alone in the girls' cabin when a man named Nagano, a secretary with the foreign department, stumbled in, drunk. Ryo was struggling to fend him off when her roommates returned. Sutematsu, shaking with outrage, ran for Ambassador Okubo.

Though there were two secretaries called Nagano with the embassy, it is easier to suspect the lecherous one as having been Keijiro Nagano, a man with a colorful history. Back in 1860, at the tender age of sixteen, he had joined the first mission to America as an apprentice interpreter. His youthful high spirits, in contrast to his stiffly straight-faced countrymen, had instantly attracted the attention of the American press; dubbing him "Tommy," reporters swarmed him, and everywhere he went the ladies swooned. The daily papers tracked his activities almost more assiduously than those of the ambassadors he served. He wrote love notes to American girls on pink stationery and inspired a polka composed in his honor, with a refrain that captured the odd ardor of his fans, at once admiring and condescending:

Wives and maids by scores are flocking
Round that charming, little man,
Known as Tommy, witty Tommy,
Yellow Tommy, from Japan.

Now twenty-eight, still slight of stature if no longer quite so pretty, Nagano may yet have considered himself a ladies' man. But flirting with anonymous foreign girls was not the same as groping the daughter of a samurai. Perplexed by this unprecedented situation, and painfully aware of the eyes of the American crew upon them, the mission's leaders decided to hold a trial; wasn't that what enlightened Westerners would do? It would be an edifying exercise in foreign legal protocol, it would hold the transgressor to account, and (to be honest) it would provide a little entertainment. The voyage was long, and the delegates were bored.

The strutting Ito, having observed courtrooms in London during his sojourn there, would play the judge. Other delegates would take the roles of prosecutor and defense attorney. Takayuki Sasaki, the embassy's senior official in charge of judicial affairs, was appalled. It was one thing, he argued, to hold a mock trial with a fictitious case, but the offense here was real. Whether it had been a serious crime or just a bit of minor mischief, making a show of bringing it to "court" risked yet more disgrace to the girl, her molester, and, by extension, the embassy itself. All this before their ship even reached shore. What would the foreigners think?

Predictably, the trial was a farce, with no judgment reached. "Little irregularities might not affect big countries of the West," wrote a fuming Sasaki in his journal, "but our country has just begun to take the path of progress and is, as it were, still a child without learning, having achieved nothing. It had better be cautious of doing anything amiss." Nagano, for his part, was nonchalant. "To divert our boredom," his journal entry reads, "a sham trial, inspired by a little happening, was held." None of the delegates recorded a word about Ryo's humiliation or the discomfort of the other girls.

THE *AMERICA* PLOWED steadily toward San Francisco, sighting nothing but an occasional albatross riding the wind like a kite. "Goonies," the sailors called them. Two days from port, seagulls appeared, swooping so low they nearly touched the heads of the passengers. "Apparently, when crossing the ocean," Kume wrote, "if you see goonies you are far from land, but if you see gulls you know you are nearing land." The first leg of the journey, then, was almost over.

Sent off by their families, largely ignored by the men of the mission, and unable to converse with their American chaperone, the five girls in their tiny cabin had nothing to do but wonder.

PART II

The customs of all countries are strange to untrained eyes.

—ETSU INAGAKI SUGIMOTO,
A Daughter of the Samurai, 1926

Ume, Sutematsu, and Shige in Philadelphia, 1876. (Courtesy Tsuda College Archives.)

THE SUN HAD RISEN hours since, but fog still lingered in San Francisco Bay as the steamer *America* made her slow and regal way through the Golden Gate. It was Monday, January 15, 1872. As Fort Alcatraz slid past, salvos of artillery rang out—a thirteen-gun salute, one shot fired for each of the original states. In the first-class cabins, a few of the Japanese delegates were counting. They were somewhat disappointed not to reach a higher number. "America is a democratic country and practices simplicity with respect to the level of politeness and etiquette displayed," the scribe Kunitake Kume confided philosophically to his journal.

Flags decorated every mast, the Stars and Stripes and the Circle of the Sun fluttering fore and aft of the smokestacks amidships. As the ship settled into her berth, an unusual group gathered on the promenade deck, led by two men. One, gazing eagerly at his home port after long absence, wore a dark beard, a winter coat, and an Astrakhan hat of Persian lamb: Charles DeLong, American ambassador, returning from two years of service in Japan. A native New Yorker, DeLong had chased adventure to the gold fields of California by the age of seventeen. Supplementing his speculative ventures with a law practice, he moved into politics, where he proved more of an opportunist than an idealist. He had accepted the post of minister to Japan in 1869 and had taken to the glamour of diplomatic life like a duck to water. His natural charm had always served him well.

But it was the other man who drew the stares of those watching from the pier. He stood, straight and slim and solemn, in midnight-blue robes of embroidered silk tied with cord. Two swords of different lengths swept down from his sash. The sides of his head were shaved and the remaining hair drawn up into a topknot, over which he wore a black lacquered headdress—more like a box than a hat—tied securely under his chin. Strong black brows slashed downward to an aquiline nose and a mouth turned down at the corners. Heavy-lidded eyes surveyed the crowds of people gathered below. Tomomi Iwakura, minister of the right, ambassador extraordinary and plenipotentiary, made an imposing first impression. Once a chamberlain in the court of the Emperor Meiji's father, and then a key player in the maneuverings that restored the son to power, he embodied both Japan's past and its future.

Behind him stood dozens of his entourage, inelegant by comparison, dressed, as one reporter noted, "in the most outlandish English readymade garments of all styles since the flood." When the ship was safely moored, a more sharply tailored party of local notables came on board to greet the exotic visitors, their genial smiles and outstretched hands met with stiff bows.

Twenty-three days after leaving Yokohama, the men of the Iwakura Mission were ready to set foot on foreign soil. As the sober group filed down the gangplank, a splash of vivid color brought up the rear. A wave of excitement rippled through the crowd. Emerging from behind the ample girth of their chaperone, Mrs. DeLong, five girls stepped carefully into view. They were swathed in bright silk, lavishly embroidered from collar to hem and tied with broad contrasting sashes. Two carried themselves with the reserve of young women, hatless, their hair upswept and crowned with tortoiseshell combs. The other three, clearly younger, wore gay floral ornaments in their lacquered coiffures, though their faces were carefully composed. So these were the princesses sent by the Mikado!

They may not have been princesses, but they were the first Japanese females ever to venture abroad in the service of their nation. The two eldest would retrace their steps within the year, but the three younger ones would not see their homeland again for a decade. Sutematsu was eleven. Shige was ten. And Ume, her eyes darting in wonder from the houses to the carriages to the well-dressed women in the crowd, had turned seven at sea.

THE DOCKSIDE CROWDS parted to allow the members of the embassy to reach a line of waiting carriages. Walking between walls of onlookers, the girls kept their eyes down, uncomfortably conscious of their clothes, their hair, the staring eyes on every side. Mrs. DeLong strutted alongside them like a proud hen with unusually colorful chicks, enjoying the sensation they made.

The carriage ride from the Embarcadero to the Grand Hotel lasted only a few blocks—hardly enough time to savor the novelty of horse-drawn transport. The streets were filled with the rattle of carriage wheels, churning up clouds of gritty dust between rows of buildings "as densely packed as the teeth of a comb," wrote Kume. The hotel, a gleaming white confection of pediments and cupolas and oriel windows, rose four splendid stories at the corner of Market and New Montgomery Streets.

The Grand Hotel was only a few years old, and its appointments dazzled the delegates. The lobby floor, paved with marble, was waxed to a treacherous sheen. The sparkle of crystal chandeliers vied with the glitter of gilt. Each suite had its own bathroom, with pure drinking water available at the twist of a faucet, and mirrors of limpid clarity. The scribe Kume, furiously scribbling notes on everything, waxed poetic with delight. "At night when one loosens a screw and sets the gas afire, the planets and stars circle above one as light glows inside white jade," he wrote of the lamps in his room. "There are lace curtains on the windows that make one think one is looking at flowers through mist." A button on the wall, when pressed, rang a bell hundreds of feet away to summon the hotel staff. But most extraordinary of all was what happened when a porter ushered Kume into a tiny chamber off the lobby, in which a few hotel guests were already standing, quite still and oddly expectant. A metal grille clanged shut. "I was shocked when it suddenly started to move and we were pulled upward," he wrote of his first elevator ride.

The procession of welcoming parties began first thing the next morning: the handful of Japanese students already in San Francisco; the city's mayor, William Alvord; the gentlemen of the press, with each of whom Iwakura and his colleagues shook hands. The reporter from the *San Francisco Chronicle* had prepared carefully for this moment. "*Annata, anaata ohio doko morrow morrow!*" he exclaimed, beaming with pride at being able to address the dignified visitor in his native tongue. Iwakura bowed gravely and, through his interpreter, thanked the man for his good wishes and his perfect command of Japanese. The reporter took his leave, quite satisfied with himself, though what he had actually uttered was gibberish.*

At noon it was time for the officers of the army and navy, though it was almost one o'clock by the time everyone had assembled in the hotel's ballroom. The floor had been covered with canvas, the walls draped in the flags of both nations. Iwakura and DeLong sat on an upholstered sofa—a posture that was more comfortable for the American. None of the Japanese visitors were accustomed to sitting on chairs, which made their dangling legs go numb.

By two o'clock the military men had left and it was time for the consular corps. The doors of the ballroom were by now crowded with well-dressed onlookers, and while the embassy waited for the consuls to appear, a gaggle of young ladies entered, holding hands for mutual support. They introduced themselves to Iwakura, who chuckled and shook their hands. The spectators were charmed, and the delegates kept their shock to themselves. Women—and not even of age!—at a diplomatic ceremony?

Representatives of England, Denmark, Sweden, Norway, Argentina, Austria, Belgium, Bolivia, Colombia, Chile, France, Germany, Greece, Guatemala, Italy, Mexico, the Netherlands, Peru, Switzerland, Sicily, and

---

* The *Chronicle* reporter possessed more enthusiasm than expertise. In standard transliteration, *anata* is a casual form of "you," *ohayo* means "good morning," *doko* means "where," and *morrow* remains indecipherable.

Portugal presented their credentials. "The city of San Francisco, standing at the threshold of this continent, holds out her hands and bids you welcome," proclaimed the president of the Chamber of Commerce, for whom good fellowship was clearly good business. San Francisco's merchants stood ready to extend the doctrine of Manifest Destiny across the Pacific, expanding the market for American products and American ideas. Iwakura was gracious but clear in reply. Japan was eager to trade, but his mission had a more specific mandate: to open the question of negotiating more equitable terms than the United States and the other treaty nations had hitherto allowed.

The parade of dignitaries had worn on for more than five hours. For the delegates, unaccustomed to any form of salute more intimate than a bow—even from their own mothers—the endless clasping of hands was overwhelming. They retired to their rooms, followed by the eyes of hotel guests who gathered in knots near the entrances to the reception areas, hoping for a glimpse. The luxurious accommodations provided little relief, though—at least not until the tables and chairs and desks had been pushed aside, and the exhausted men could repose at last on the carpeted floor.

Their rest was brief. The daily papers had announced that the Japanese embassy would be serenaded that evening, and by the appointed hour of ten o'clock, well-wishers and gawkers choked the streets surrounding the hotel. The Second Artillery Band was punctual. Making their first formal appearance, the five Japanese girls joined the delegates, necks craning all around them as they took their seats. "They were all attired in elegant costumes and appeared to know that they were attracting attention, and shrank from it as all well bred young ladies should do," a reporter noted approvingly. Well-bred or not, the girls were genuinely uncomfortable; unlike the men of the delegation, they were powerless to secure the camouflage of Western clothing without assistance, and that, Mrs. DeLong so far refused to give. Attention was not something she shrank from.

The stately chords of "Hail Columbia"—composed for George Washington's first inaugural in 1789, and used as the national anthem for most of the nineteenth century—were soon blaring triumphantly from the parlor windows and out to the streets below. Earlier Japanese travelers had returned with reports of the headache-inducing unpleasantness of barbarian music. Sitting appreciatively in a crowded parlor just a few feet from a full military band must have been a strain.

At the concert's conclusion, lusty cheers and applause from outside were redoubled when Iwakura and DeLong emerged onto a balcony. The noisy enthusiasm, while gratifying, was somewhat startling to the delegates. "Western people are ever eager to promote trade and like to extend a warm welcome to foreign visitors," Kume wrote. "Such gatherings, which are part and parcel of American customs, are unusual in Japan." Iwakura drew a scroll from his sash and unrolled it to a length of several yards, though the speech he read from it in Japanese was brief. Both men withdrew. The crowd, however, was not ready to go home, shouting for the popular DeLong to say a few words. He demurred: it went against protocol for him to speak publicly; this wasn't the setting for bending the rules; his heart was too full at this important moment for him to express his feelings . . . oh, very well, if you insist.

Ambassador DeLong's remarks instructed his audience to consider these visitors in a distinctly different light from the "Orientals" already among them. "Let the Chinese be not confounded with the Japanese," he told the people of San Francisco. "California need never fear an influx of coolie labor from the Japanese Empire." Depraved China had no choice but to export its impoverished masses; noble Japan, on the contrary, would shortly be forced to look abroad for labor to fuel its new and gleaming industries. "While the Chinese have been forced to wear the chain of slavery, the Japanese have never had a master; their intellects are as sharp as their weapons," DeLong declaimed.

His argument was not new. A dozen years earlier, when the first Japanese embassy had visited the United States, an up-and-coming new magazine devoted to the "American idea" had crystallized the attitude toward the exotic East. In a lengthy essay, the *Atlantic Monthly* had described a Japan poised to eclipse its larger Asian neighbor. The focus of the world would shift away from China, "for, in spite of all Celestial and Flowery preconceptions, it is impossible to view with any sincere interest a nation

so palsied, so corrupt, so wretchedly degraded, and so enfeebled by mis-
government, as to be already more than half sunk in decay; while, on
the other hand, the real vigor, thrift, and intelligence of Japan, its great
and still advancing power, and the rich promise of its future are such as
to reward the most attentive study." China, at that point on the brink of
defeat in the Second Opium War, hobbled by addiction and humiliated
by the mercantile nations, was no match in the American imagination for
virtuous, vigorous Japan. Here was a nation with grit and goals, eager to
emulate American progress, like-minded in every way.

This perspective had only intensified over the succeeding decade as
the economic boom fueled by the gold rush faded, nowhere more than
among white San Franciscans, unanimous in their scorn. The Chinese
"hordes" undercut white workers for jobs and then sent their earnings
home, they made no attempt to adopt local customs or costumes, and then
they returned to a country that was inexplicably uninterested in Ameri-
can-made telegraph lines and railroads. The progressive and enlightened
Japanese, on the other hand, having been awakened from their centuries-
long sleep by America's own Commodore Perry, seemed to embrace
everything they found on this side of the Pacific.

While immigrant Chinese men continued to wear their hair in braided
queues down their backs, most of these Japanese visitors had cut off their
samurai topknots, and within days of their arrival were sporting black silk
hats to complement their ill-fitting Western suits. The city's fashionable
hatters were quick to pounce on this high-profile market, and soon all the
delegates were vying for the prize of highest and shiniest topper. Iwakura
ordered samples brought to his room. When none proved a decent fit, the
hatter sent one of his staff with a conformator, an elaborate mechanical
contraption of wooden slats and metal pins used to take precise measure-
ments of clients' heads. The ambassador, it turned out, had a remarkably
small head. His aides had a hilarious time trying on the conformator. "And
that is what we want with Japan," commented the *Chronicle*, "—to sell
them 'plug' hats—and the wise man will soon see to what extent the prin-
ciple can be carried."

. . .

THE NEXT TWO weeks were a whirl of tours and entertainments for the men of the mission. They visited factories, hospitals, schools, courthouses, barracks, forts, and rail yards, asking endless questions and taking copious notes. One of the first stops was the San Francisco Assaying and Refining Works, just a few blocks down Montgomery Street from the Grand Hotel. The gold rush may have slowed to a trickle, but mining companies were still processing what remained. The delegates looked on as workers weighed, tested, and melted the precious stuff; each got the chance to heft a gold bar in his hands. Then it was on to the Kimball Carriage Manufactory, the Mission Woolen Mills, the Bank of California, the Union Foundry, and on, and on.

It wasn't all work. On the way back to the hotel one afternoon, a beaming middle-aged gentleman hailed the delegation at the corner of Fourteenth and Mission Streets, in front of a rococo stone entrance topped with statues, flagpoles, and a sign in letters three feet high: WOODWARD'S GARDENS. R. B. Woodward himself, "the Barnum of the West," beckoned them into his personal pleasure grounds. A wealthy hotelier, Woodward had converted a mansion on six acres into the most popular attraction in San Francisco. Visitors could explore picture galleries and greenhouses, ogle peacocks and buffalo, and visit the Museum of Natural Wonders, which featured fossils, taxidermy, and a gold nugget weighing ninety-seven pounds. A purveyor of exotica himself, Woodward could hardly resist the appeal of such exotic visitors, though he did not go so far as to waive the twenty-five-cent admission fee. Public amusements of this sort were as yet unknown in Japan. Finance Minister Okubo and future prime minister Ito were persuaded to try the box swings, and everyone took a ride on the rotary boat, a wind-powered floating merry-go-round circling a fountain.

A trip to the theater was that evening's featured entertainment—a drama entitled *Rouge et Noir*, about the evils of gambling, at the opulent California Theatre. The place was packed by the time the silk-robed Iwakura arrived with his more soberly suited entourage. Squeezing through at last, they

found that the attention of the audience turned more often toward their
flag-decked boxes than toward the action on stage. Adding to the excitement was the presence of Mrs. DeLong, escorting the two oldest girls,
still in kimonos. "Several milliners are at present engaged in making them
English outfits," the *Chronicle* reported with a note of disappointment. "If
we mistake not, the romance attached to these ladies will all wear off when
their Oriental habiliments are doffed for our more common attire . . . No
doubt they are the most beautiful Japanese ladies in the United States today—there are no others—but if they accept the garments of our fashionable belles, thousands can be found much more beautiful than they." The
report was, in fact, premature; it would be several more weeks before the
powerless girls managed to secure Western-style wardrobes.

The trip to the theater was a rare outing. Though the Japanese men
were making appearances all over the city, the girls kept to their rooms to
avoid the "*furore*" their presence caused, taking all their meals there. The
older ones could receive visitors in Mrs. DeLong's rooms in the afternoons,
but the three youngest were almost never seen. The days were long and
bewildering. Without a word of English, the girls were entirely dependent
on Mrs. DeLong. "We hardly dared to go out into the hotel corridors by
ourselves, for fear we would get lost, and not know our rooms again, as we
had no way of asking in any case," Ume later remembered. One day, when
Ume ventured into the hall with another of the girls, a group of women
and children happened by. Delighted by this encounter with the "Japanese
princesses," the women carried the girls off to their rooms, where they
fingered the silk of their costumes, traced the embroidery on their sashes,
and stroked their hair to their heart's content. They brought out toys and
pictures for their doll-like guests, chattering unintelligibly while the girls
waited in increasing discomfort, wondering when they might be released
and how on earth they would find their way back.

Language was only the most obvious of the barriers the girls faced.
None of them having ever encountered a black person, they were terri-
fied of the hotel's waiters. When Mrs. DeLong took all five of them to see
Emerson's Minstrels perform at the Alhambra Theatre one evening, the

spectacle only confused them further: the white performers in blackface, thought Ume, "could not be creatures of this world."

The girls were perplexed as well by the women they saw: the chambermaids and laundresses who worked in the hotel seemed to be made straight, like themselves, but the female hotel guests all sprouted odd humps from their backsides. Was there some sort of magic that deformed the bodies of the wealthy? Mrs. DeLong soon explained the strange mechanics of the bustle—and dined out on the anecdote for days. "The simplicity of these daughters of the Orient is really touching," the *Chronicle* chuckled fondly.

SAN FRANCISCO WAS now seized with enthusiasm for things Japanese. The firm of Haynes & Lawton, specializing in silver plate, was quick to publicize its stock of Japanese bronzes and porcelain "to impart a classic inspiration to the drawing-room and boudoir." "Japonisme," a term first used that very year, need not be limited to the salons of Paris, promised these advertisements. Those who had made their fortunes on the American frontier could now grace their parlors with antique *objets* by reaching across the Pacific instead of the Atlantic—and how fortuitous that Haynes & Lawton was so conveniently located on the ground floor of the Grand Hotel. "Lovers of the quaint and curious in art, and who are interested in this ingenious and progressive people," should hasten to Market Street, instructed the *Chronicle*.

Within a few weeks the leading photographic studio of Bradley & Rulofson, just a stone's throw from the hotel, was advertising an exhibition of portraits of the embassy, including "a splendidly executed group representing the 'high Japs.'" This photo, along with one of Mrs. DeLong and the girls, was later published as an etching in *Harper's Weekly*, providing the rest of the country with a glimpse of "our Japanese visitors."

Crowds dogged them everywhere. Four days after their arrival the city honored the embassy with a parade and military review. A grandstand for the dignitaries rose in front of the hotel, but ordinary bystanders had to risk the sidewalks; there were reports of women and children badly hurt in the crush. The crowd, estimated at fifty thousand, somewhat marred the martial spectacle, as onlookers spilling into the street prevented the Second Brigade of the National Guard from marching in straight lines. "The streets were so densely packed with hat-covered heads that there was no room to insert even a needle," Kume wrote. Iwakura, perhaps wisely, pleaded indisposition and kept to his room.

The whirl of excursions only intensified as the days passed. In every situation, however unforeseen, the Japanese proved themselves to be good sports. For dessert at one official luncheon, a huge cake in the shape of a woman—representing "America"—was set down in front of Iwakura. Baffled, he turned to his host, who advised him to cut it and distribute the pieces to the lunch guests. Inspired, Iwakura cut off the two hands of the figure and presented them to two ladies nearby, explaining as he did so that likewise "Japan extends the hand of friendship to her American friends."

A week after arrival Iwakura made his way to the offices of Western Union, where a private office had been equipped with telegraphic equipment linked directly to the East Coast. He exchanged greetings with Secretary of State Hamilton Fish in Washington, and then sent a message to Samuel Morse himself. "The Embassy from Japan desires to inform the inventor of the Electric Telegraph that his fame is well known in Japan, and that within a few months one thousand miles of telegraph wire will be opened for business in their country," the telegraph read. In reply, the eighty-year-old Morse welcomed the Japanese "to the sphere of telegraphic intercourse." The moment was one of mutual—though perhaps not mutually understood—satisfaction: Japan striding with determination toward a future on equal footing with the West, America proudly and paternally bestowing its technological advancements on a nation still entangled with its benighted feudal past. But Iwakura's mission was to gather ideas in the service of Japanese sovereignty. His men were studying the West in order to resist Western incursions in the future.

Before leaving the telegraph office, Iwakura sent a personal message to his three young sons, who, having preceded him across the Pacific, were now studying in New Jersey, at Rutgers Grammar School. Among the very first Japanese students to come to America under the auspices of the new Meiji leadership, they were planning to meet him in Chicago as the embassy traversed the continent. "Affectionate Father," they responded immediately, "we rejoice to hear from you."

The climax of the embassy's stay in San Francisco was a lavish banquet. Dinner for two hundred was served at eight o'clock in the flag-bedecked, flower-strewn dining room of the Grand Hotel. The menu, printed in gold, silver, crimson, blue, and mauve, was dizzying: oysters, soups, fish, cold appetizers (including the intriguing "Westphalia Ham, décoré à la Japonaise"), four boiled offerings, eight entrées, and seven kinds of roasted meat. There were a dozen vegetable dishes, and twice that number of desserts. The champagne was courtesy of Krug and Roederer, and the tables were crowned with edible ornaments including a Temple of Fame, an Arc de Triomphe, a Treble Horn of Plenty, and a "Gothic Pyramid."

When all appetites had been sated, the speeches began. Newton Booth, the newly installed governor of California, declared that Japan was "the Great Britain of the Pacific—the England of the Orient," thus banishing Japan's foreignness with a single rhetorical flourish. "It is something new in history for a nation to apply for matriculation as a student in the university of the world, where the modern professors are the telegraph, the steam-engine and the printing press, and where the course taught is what we call Christian civilization," he continued, deftly defining Japan as a sort of visiting scholar, gratifyingly clever, somewhat awestruck, and completely unthreatening.

Iwakura thanked him but quickly ceded the floor to his charismatic vice-envoy, Hirobumi Ito. Extended sojourns in England and America had taught the younger man an ease and comfort among foreigners that many of his colleagues lacked. Now in charge of modernizing Japan's infrastructure, Ito spoke—in English—of dazzling progress in the construction of railroads, lighthouses, and oceangoing vessels, skipping nimbly over the turmoil that had recently convulsed Japan. "Our Daimios magnanimously surrendered their principalities, and their voluntary action was accepted by a General Government," he declared. Japan's progress included social as well as technological advancement, Ito insisted. "By educating our women, we hope to ensure greater intelligence in future generations. With this end in view, our maidens have already commenced to come to you for their education." Though not, perhaps, for their entertainment. The girls were not among the invited guests that evening.

Speech after speech followed, but no one placed Ito's vision of Japan ascendant in clearer context than the Reverend Horatio Stebbins, of San Francisco's First Unitarian Church. The arrival of the embassy, he said, "seems a repetition of the old story where the magii [*sic*] of the East was led to where the Child lay. That star still lives and stands where it is most cherished. Welcome, most illustrious descendants of the old stock. Your presence is more welcome than the incense of frankincense and myrrh." Stebbins's hyperbole may have been champagne fueled, but it captured the Americans' mood: the guests from the East were welcome, their tribute graciously received, but the star they followed was American. The assembled guests roared their approval.

A FEW DAYS before the embassy was to leave San Francisco, Mrs. DeLong received a letter from the State Central Woman Suffrage Committee of California, to be translated for the girls. "Your visit to this country has an especial significance to those women of America who have been and are laboring for the rights and privileges belonging to a broader field of action than has before been open to them; and they rejoice that this movement is simultaneous in Japan and other enlightened nations, marking, as it does, a new era in the history of the world." The encounter may have been good publicity for the suffrage committee, but it is doubtful the girls had the faintest idea what they were talking about. Nothing resembling representative government yet existed in Japan. It would be nearly two decades before even the wealthiest Japanese men had the right to vote. (As for woman suffrage, Japanese women would not win the right to vote until 1945, when the American Occupation enforced it.)

But as baffling and overwhelming as these two weeks of hectic welcome in San Francisco had been, they were only a prelude. Early on the morning of January 31, the Iwakura embassy boarded a special train to begin a journey that was still a novelty even for most Americans: crossing the continent by rail. It was not yet three years since the pounding of the golden spike at Promontory Summit, at the edge of the Great Salt Lake in Utah Territory. By the time they reached Washington, DC, their final destination, the girls would see more of their new country than most of their American hosts ever had, or would.

They traveled in style. George M. Pullman had introduced his revolutionary sleeper cars just in time to capitalize on transcontinental travel, and five of them had been ordered to accommodate the embassy. During the day, long plush-upholstered seats faced each other across a central table in each compartment; at night, porters reclined the seats to form lower berths and released overhead latches to drop the upper berths down. There were curtains for privacy, ornate floral paintings on the ceiling, mirrored panels, carpets on the floor, and glass wall-sconces to make the gilt accents sparkle. "It is all quite opulent," wrote Kume in awe. At a breathtaking average speed of twenty miles per hour, the train seemed to soar above the ground. On straightaways it could go nearly thirty.

Their first stop was Sacramento, California's capital. The schedule included a tour of the insane asylum at Stockton, and then it was on to the chambers of the state legislature. (Wags insisted that the delegates wouldn't be able to tell the difference.) As usual, the girls stayed in their rooms at the Orleans Hotel, which afforded privacy but continued to hinder their education in American manners. They ate what was placed before them without much understanding of what it was or how it should taste, and because they usually dined alone, they remained unenlightened. When a pot of butter appeared on the table that evening, each girl took her spoon and scooped up a mouthful, there being no one to demonstrate its use as a condiment. At least their isolation allowed them to grimace and gag unobserved.

Though the legislature had spent the previous few days bickering about who should be responsible for the entertainment expenses of the embassy (breaking off their arguments only when the delegates themselves entered the chambers for a visit), Sacramento saw the Japanese off with yet another banquet on their final evening, complete with miniature statues of President Grant gracing each table. The festivities ended with rousing choruses of "America," "Auld Lang Syne," and "Home, Sweet Home," sung with more spirit than harmony. In the wee hours of the morning on February 2, the delegates began their transcontinental trip in earnest.

THE SUN WAS high and the passengers still groggy when the train reached Cape Horn, a particularly stunning stretch of track high above the American River. "Far below, at the foot of the valley, was a tiny village near the river, which meandered like a winding sash," marveled Kume. "We could see people the size of peas and inch-high horses moving along a thread-like road." Two more locomotives were added for the climb above the snow line and across the Sierra Nevada. Flurries whipped past the double-hung windows, which began to fog over, obscuring tier upon tier of jagged peaks. Snowsheds covered the tracks for miles at a time, with shafts of sunlight reflecting off the snow and slashing into the darkened cars through gaps in the boards. At Summit, seven thousand feet above sea level, the train was coupled to a snowplow for the long descent.

From there it was on to the Great Basin, with endless sagebrush desert replacing the dramatic Sierra. From the train the travelers could see Indians in the dome-shaped thatched dugouts of their winter camps—a long way from the cupolas of the Grand Hotel. "Having journeyed through a realm of civilization and enlightenment, we were now crossing a very ancient, uncivilized wilderness," Kume wrote. He found no romance in the scene: "Their features display the bone structure often seen among our own base people and outcasts."

The next stop was Ogden, Utah Territory, which they reached on February 4—and were then unable to leave. Snow had blockaded the Union Pacific Railroad. They could consider themselves lucky: passengers trapped for days aboard snowbound trains farther east were surviving on salt fish and crackers, and piling out to help railroad workers shovel snow that had drifted as high as the smokestacks of the engines. Resigned, the delegates transferred to a branch line to wait out the delay in Salt Lake City, thirty-five miles to the south.

In 1872, Salt Lake City was a handful of muddy streets with board sidewalks, frequented by ranchers, miners, soldiers, and new Mormon converts attracted from as far east as England. The Japanese travelers put up at the Townsend House, Salt Lake City's leading hotel: a wood-frame building with a long veranda and a corral out back for cattle. Though there was a spacious "ball-room" upstairs, the bedrooms were tiny and the partitions between them thin.

Within hours of arrival, Iwakura received an invitation from Brigham Young, patriarch of the Mormon Church, requesting the pleasure of his company. As diplomatic etiquette dictated that Young should be the caller and not the called-upon, the ambassador politely declined. The messenger insisted that Young was eager to meet the Japanese visitors but found it impossible to present himself at the Townsend House. Why?, the ambassador inquired. Well, said the messenger, the prophet Brigham unfortunately found himself detained at home in the custody of a federal officer. The first target of President Grant's antipolygamy campaign, Young had been arrested for "lascivious cohabitation" several months earlier and was awaiting trial. He had sixteen wives and forty-eight children.

Iwakura frowned. "We came to the United States to see the President of this great nation," he said, choosing his words with care. "We do not know how he would like for us to call on a man who had broken the laws of his country and was under arrest." A few days later, however, a party of touring delegates did make an official stop at Brigham Young's house, in the company of Charles DeLong. "His power is equivalent to a feudal lord's," Kume wrote of Young, describing his house as "dignified and looking like a castle." DeLong later claimed he hadn't realized where their guides were taking them, but non-Mormon leaders were not amused. Iwakura, perhaps cannier than DeLong, had somehow arranged not to be part of the group that evening.

For the duration of his stay, Iwakura maintained a discreet distance from Salt Lake City's Mormons. Crowning the visit was a banquet hosted by the city's leading gentiles—dinner for 120, followed by dancing. For once, the girls were in attendance. "Mrs. DeLong, with the bearing and mien of a queen, and the Japanese girls, in their rich, quaint costumes, absorbed the constant attention of the guests," the *Chronicle*'s reporter relayed to San Francisco by telegraph. After dinner, the dignified speeches gave way to dancing—something the Japanese delegates found uncomfortable to watch. "The social customs in this remote mountain area were, we thought, somewhat less than refined," Kume wrote delicately.

Days of anticlimax followed, as departure was postponed again, and yet again. "We had seen everything which might possibly be interesting and the bright moon was now full," Kume wrote. Many of the delegates frequented the Warm Springs Bath House, a mile away, where for a quarter they could soak chest-deep in heated pools—a pleasure denied to them since leaving Japan.

Still kimono clad, the girls stayed out of sight; their clothes, in addition to making them conspicuous, did little to keep them warm. In addition, Ryo, having endured the embarrassment of the shipboard mock trial, was now suffering the effects of snow blindness, her eyes painful and watering from gazing at the dazzling landscape without protection. From the windows of the Townsend House, the girls saw snowball fights and sleigh riding for the first time. Hirobumi Ito, again more solicitous than the other ambassadors, visited their rooms to entertain them with ghost stories, switching to fairy tales when it was time for bed.

After nearly three weeks the rails were cleared at last, and on February 22 the embassy left Salt Lake City for Chicago. Now two dining cars—Pullman's latest innovation—were coupled to their train, which eliminated the need to stop for meals. After more than a month spent mostly confined to hotel rooms, the girls were overwhelmed by the vast landscapes through which they passed. Faces pressed to the windows, they watched the craggy peaks of the Wasatch Front glide by. After dark, the edges of the canyons were etched in moonlight against the sky.

. . .

HALFWAY THROUGH WYOMING Territory they crossed the Continental Divide and began the descent toward the Great Plains. Hours went by without a glimpse of anything that could be called a town. "Although one may tire of hearing about the vastness of the United States," Kume wrote, "when one experiences it, it is even more astonishing than one could believe." The Rockies had receded below the western horizon, and there was nothing in any direction but grass, cropped by herds of buffalo and bands of wild horses.

As they approached the Missouri River, the scenery changed again: plowed fields and pastureland now, with wooded areas visible in the distance. Crowds gathered in the towns they passed. At Omaha, memorably, a group of schoolgirls came to the station, clapping and waving and blowing kisses; for the Japanese girls, it was a reassuring glimpse of friendly peers, however bewilderingly strange their behavior or the setting might be. Not all the onlookers were so welcoming. "Show yourselves, you yaller duffers," men shouted, shoving up against the windows of the train. "Come out here, and let us see you."

A reception committee came out from Chicago to welcome the embassy at Aurora, a western suburb of the city. Thousands were on hand at the station, and the mood was festive. When the train pulled in, Aurora's nimbler citizens leaped onto the couplings between the cars, climbed onto their roofs, and perched on each other's backs. Faces crowded every window. The delegates were in the dining car, wielding their knives and forks with calm decorum at window-side tables draped with white linen, in stark contrast to the melee raging outside.

The welcoming committee boarded, the train gathered speed, and within a mile the young Aurorans who had climbed atop the train jumped to the ground. As the aldermen of Chicago shook hands with the ranking ambassadors, the girls withdrew to a corner of the car, though the stripes and flowers of their kimonos were, as usual, conspicuous among the dark suits of the men. "Their features are less intellectual than those of the males, the noses and chins being indistinct of outlines, and indicating a want of firmness," a *Chicago Tribune* reporter commented, and then he contradicted himself: "They seem to bear their isolation from the parental fireside, and the loss of fond mothers, with firmness." Having read reports of these "intelligent, bright, and vivacious"—not to mention attractive—young ladies in the previous weeks, he was somewhat surprised by the quiet group, unable to communicate with the Americans and largely ignored by their male compatriots. They looked lonely.

Carriages were waiting at the depot when the train reached Chicago on February 26. The vast station roared with freight and passenger cars trundling ceaselessly over an intricate web of track. "Most of the stations up to now had been rather insignificant places," Kume noted. Chicago was a metropolis.

The girls were wrapped against the cold in heavy red woolen shawls, as yet their only item of Western clothing. This was about to change, though; Mrs. DeLong's intransigence had at last driven the girls to appeal directly to Iwakura, who ordered the necessary purchases to be made during this stop.

Mayor Joseph Medill was on hand to receive the visitors when they reached their next hotel, Tremont House. His city was not at its best; just four months earlier, the Great Chicago Fire had left much of it a smoking ruin. Devastating fire was commonplace in the dense wood-and-paper streetscapes of Japanese towns. Iwakura expressed his sympathy and complimented "the wonderful recuperative powers of the American people after suffering severe injuries." Before he left Chicago, he surprised his hosts with a donation of five thousand dollars for fire relief: a princely sum, and "the first money contribution ever made by heathen or pagan donors for the relief of Christian recipients," noted the *Tribune*. One more gratifying sign that the Japanese were ready to lay aside their ancient ways and join the ranks of modern civilization.

Iwakura's three sons, who had left their studies in New Jersey and arrived in Chicago weeks earlier, now joined their father's embassy. The "little almond-eyed gentlemen" had already succeeded in charming their hosts in Chicago: no "American boys of the same age, taken at random from our schools, would have passed through the ordeal of an interview with a 'foreign' journalist with half so much credit," wrote the *Tribune* admiringly. That evening, Iwakura's sons joined the girls for a walk, strolling through the burned-out blocks of the South Side. The boys had already spent a couple of years in American classrooms: here at last were a few sympathetic souls—teenagers, rather than ambassadors—who could tell the girls something of what awaited them.

The train carrying the embassy pulled out of Chicago's East Station the following evening. As the delegates rolled through Indiana and Ohio, the novelty of travel by rail wore thin. The girls were tired of sitting, but taking a stroll to the end of the car and back carried its own risks: a bump in the track could hurl an unwary passenger against the exposed stove, or send her toppling into the drinking-water tank. Opening the window meant a faceful of cinders and dust, and there was no venturing into the cars ahead or behind; the vestibule car, allowing passengers to pass from one car to the next in a moving train, had not yet been invented. There was no separate car for females either, so the girls, having nowhere to undress discreetly for bed, remained mostly clothed. The thin curtains did nothing to block the sound of the delegates' snores. The tiny washroom contained a basin, a roller towel, a piece of soap, and very little privacy. On to Pittsburgh, Philadelphia, and Baltimore, where the tracks ran through the center of town, and the cars were uncoupled and pulled by horses, with drivers on each car blowing horns to warn pedestrians. And finally, Washington.

SNOW WAS FALLING in the District of Columbia on leap day, February 29, when the five Pullman cars at last rolled to a stop. Waiting on the platform was a lithe young Japanese man with a mane of black hair swept back from his brow, wise eyes and full lips framed by a strong brow and full beard. In contrast to his recently arrived compatriots, he seemed very much at home, his suit well cut, his linen freshly starched. Arinori Mori, Japanese chargé d'affaires in Washington, had, after all, spent most of his adult life abroad. Then again, he was only twenty-four.

Mori's early training as the son of a Satsuma samurai would have felt familiar to Sutematsu's brothers in Aizu: discipline, stoicism, high standards. The difference, in Mori's case, was his early attraction to English, in a domain whose leaders quickly realized the power of England and America. At the age of seventeen, Mori had joined a small group of students chosen by Satsuma leaders to be smuggled out of Japan. Three years of travel in England, Europe, and the American Northeast had accelerated his education. By 1871, the new Meiji government had appointed him the first official representative of Japan in Washington. Brilliant, precociously self-possessed, iconoclastic, and stubborn, he would be described by his friend Hirobumi Ito in later years as "a Westerner born of Japan."

Facilitating an encounter between the most powerful men in Japan and the most powerful men in America was part of Mori's job—a challenge he faced with confident assurance. Taking charge of the five young females the ambassadors had brought with them, however, was daunting. Neither his samurai training nor his more recently acquired diplomatic skills had prepared Mori for this. Aside from a vague mandate to get them educated, the girls came with no instructions.

As Iwakura and the rest took their time to disembark, the girls emerged onto the platform, wearing the ready-made clothes hastily purchased for them in Chicago beneath the red shawls that shielded them from the swirling snow. "The princesses, five in number, appeared to keep their conversation to themselves," noted a reporter for the *Evening Star*, "but their eyes were not inactive—every movement about the depot was watched by them." Mori's eyes swept from Ryo and Tei, now wearing rather unbecoming black hats perched on their foreheads, past Sutematsu and Shige, in similar ruffled dresses, and down to doll-like Ume, all but engulfed in her shawl. "What am I to do?" he blurted into the ear of his American secretary, Charles Lanman. "They have sent me a baby!"

Mori had been at his post for a year, with Lanman at his side for the last five months. An avuncular man in his midfifties, with a broad forehead and a shock of dark hair, Charles Lanman was a genial foil for Mori's intensity. His path to the Japanese legation was eclectic. Born in Michigan, educated in Connecticut, and trained as an accounting clerk in New York, Lanman had settled in the capital in his early thirties, working first as a journalist and then as librarian to several branches of the federal government. He was the author of a shelf of books, an accomplished painter, an avid angler, and an eager explorer of the American wilderness, especially by canoe. He told good stories and cultivated a wide circle of friends. As a navigator of Washington's social and diplomatic currents, he was enormously helpful.

He was also—though married for more than two decades to a Georgetown heiress—childless. To Mori's profound relief, Lanman and his wife, Adeline, had volunteered to look after the girls during their stay in Washington. As Mori began shepherding the delegates toward the twenty-nine carriages and two omnibuses standing ready to convey them to lavish accommodations at the Arlington Hotel, Lanman gathered the girls for the slightly longer ride to his house. After more than two months of steamship cabins, hotel rooms, and sleeping cars, they would bid the delegates and the DeLongs farewell and spend their first night in an American home. "It is said they parted from the Minister with great reluctance, as a very warm friendship had existed between them and Mrs. DeLong," reported the Washington papers. Any reluctance on the part of the girls probably had more to do with fear of the unknown than actual affinity for the self-satisfied Elida DeLong, however. At the Lanmans', they would find themselves in much better hands.

CHARLES AND ADELINE Lanman lived in a stately brick house behind a white picket fence at 120 West Street (later known as P Street) in Georgetown. Built by Mrs. Lanman's father sixty years earlier, it had been her wedding gift. Ivy climbed its walls, and towering trees shaded the spacious garden. Its interiors reflected the aesthetic and intellectual refinement of its inhabitants: stately Hepplewhite furniture with gleaming brass fittings, shelves of books and family silver, and walls hung with oil paintings and watercolors by English and American artists, including

Lanman's own work. His fishing paraphernalia had a room to itself. Since the beginning of his tenure with Mori, Lanman had also begun to collect Japanese bits and pieces: a vase, a sword, a kimono.

Mori arrived at his secretary's door the next day to check on his young charges. The girls were delighted with their gracious surroundings, but the Lanmans seemed overwhelmed: a houseful of children, even ones as well behaved as these, was clearly a strain. The plan was quickly modified. Sutematsu, Shige, and Tei would move to the nearby home of Mrs. Lanman's sister, Mrs. Hepburn, while Ryo and young Ume—whose precocious chatter had already won the Lanmans over—would remain at 120 West Street.

That was all the attention Mori could spare; the embassy was waiting. Washington's social calendar was in full swing, its hotels and rooming houses full of legislators and lobbyists, diplomats and military men. The scribe Kume, still faithfully noting every detail, was impressed by the breadth and impeccable smoothness of Pennsylvania Avenue, its wide brick sidewalks lined with poplars. Washington was a city of visitors, it seemed to him, with no local products except legislation and national pride. Everyone was from somewhere else.

Those who braved the snow for a glimpse of the Japanese men were mostly disappointed: even had the weather been pleasant, the delegates had preparations to make over the weekend. President Grant would receive them formally on Monday, and there would be a State Department reception at the Masonic Temple Tuesday night. Thwarted reporters seized on the appearance of Keijiro Nagano, "the veritable 'Japanese Tommy' who visited this country several years ago and was so much admired by the ladies."

After the terrible darkness of the Civil War—coinciding with Japan's own period of domestic turmoil—the first glimmerings of the Gilded Age were emerging. The economy, fueled by rail expansion, was growing again; speculation was rampant. The mood of opportunism penetrated government to such a degree that "Grantism" had become a synonym for political corruption. Meanwhile, black Americans, including more than a third of Washington's 130,000 residents, had yet to feel the benefits of emancipation. "The separation between white and black people," Kume noted, "is as distinct as that between clear and muddy water."

Where the Japanese fit in this racially polarized moment was hard to tell. They were the talk of the town, even inspiring a cameo in Mark Twain and Charles Dudley Warner's novel *The Gilded Age*:

> "Did you see those Japs, Miss Leavitt?"
>
> "Oh, yes, aren't they queer. But so high-bred, so picturesque. Do you think that color makes any difference, Mr. Hawkins? I used to be so prejudiced against color."
>
> "Did you? I never was. I used to think my old mammy was handsome."

High-bred or picturesque? Noble or weird? For the formal presentation of their credentials to the president, the leaders of the embassy arrived in full court dress: purple and blue silk robes, richly inlaid swords, strange head-gear. The papers covered every detail. The cornucopia-shaped hats of some of the ambassadors reminded one reporter "of the helmets worn by Roman warriors of old," while their flowing black silk jackets were "worn similarly to the same garment in use by American ladies." Iwakura, though possessed of "great natural dignity," had "a feminine cast of features." A strip of carpet was laid under the White House portico "upon which the Japanese were to walk in their dainty silken shoes." Were they warriors or women?

At the very least, they were entertainment. At the State Department dinner the following evening, one legislator's wife captured the titillated mood as the assembled guests waited for the ambassadors—now in Western suits—to appear. "A confused idea had prevailed, to some extent, that we were to have some kind of a tub-and-tight-rope exhibition, that they would spin tops and swallow pokers, and balance themselves on one another's noses," she reported. "To such expectant lookers-on it must have been a source of disappointment to see a line of small, yellow-skinned gentlemen wearing those badges of our social servitude, the regulation dress coat and white necktie."

The delegates felt a similar kind of ambivalence toward their hosts that night, though they were apparently better at hiding it. The Americans promenaded past the dais with their ladies on their arms and then formed up for dancing, "the members of the Embassy being spectators and seeming to greatly admire the 'giddy mazes of the waltz,'" the *Evening Star* reported. But what the delegates had learned at their audience with President Grant the day before made the dancing seem an especially frivolous distraction. "It will be a pleasure to us to enter upon that consultation upon international questions in which you say you are authorized to engage," Grant had told them. But the delegates were not, in fact, authorized to engage. The mission's intent had been merely to open the question of treaty renegotiation. The ambassadors bore no written mandate from their emperor to actually act. Meanwhile, Grant was ready to negotiate now. What to do?

Two weeks later, on March 20, Hirobumi Ito and Toshimichi Okubo, two of Iwakura's highest-ranking deputies, boarded a train once again. Retracing the seven-thousand-mile journey they had just concluded, they would return to Tokyo for the necessary credentials. The embassy would remain in Washington, and wait.

To these uncertainties the girls remained happily oblivious. After a few days of fascination with the "princesses"—"Their mission is to be educated here, and to return to Japan to assist in rearing female wall flowers to adorn the court of the Mikado," one skeptical reporter commented—the press had moved on. In the care of attentive hosts, enjoying the luxury of more settled surroundings for the first time in months, the girls did not miss their countrymen, preoccupied as they were with all things American.

They felt awkward and exposed at first in their new clothes: the stiff fabric buttoning snugly at throat and wrist, hugging the curves of waist and hip. Their high-buttoned leather boots creaked, and squeezed their toes. But now when they played tag, they could run with long strides instead of the old pigeon-toed, kimono-wrapped shuffle. They could leap over the flagstone paths, their skirts swirling. They could sit on a garden bench and spread their knees wide, catching the windblown petals of spring in their unfamiliar laps. They watched the neighbor children, astonished at their antics. At home, boys might walk on stilts, but never girls. The neighbor children stared back. Sometimes their parents stopped to stare too.

Charles and Adeline Lanman, however, had nothing but warm respect for their unusual charges. Within days of their arrival, Mrs. Lanman wrote to Ume's mother, enclosing photographs of herself, her husband, and their house. "Ume, in particular, is quick to learn. Everyone who meets her praises her manners, which we attribute to her upbringing," she told Hatsuko Tsuda. "Ume and we already feel so close to each other that we worry how we will lament when the time comes for us to part." In her reply, Hatsuko expressed gratitude, stiffened with sternness: "I wish you to understand that I shall be glad to have you treat her strictly, just exactly as you think will be best for her welfare without regard to our opinion, and that you and your husband will be, while she is in your country, the same as her father and mother."

In samurai families, discipline was the guiding spirit: even in sleep, girls were expected to fold their bodies into the curved letter *ku* く, though their brothers were free to sprawl across their futons like the five-pointed character *dai* 大, for "big." In America the girls slept in four-legged beds raised high off the floor, and no one scolded them to keep their legs together under the blankets. The feather pillows had smothered them at first—so unlike the wooden headrests they had once used to preserve their carefully combed and oiled hair at night. Now the young ones wore their hair loose down their backs. Without the oil, it hung in soft waves.

A week after the girls' arrival, a guest joined the Lanmans for dinner. Joseph Niijima, Amherst College's first Japanese graduate, had come to Washington to interpret for the embassy. A decade earlier, Niijima had stowed away on an American ship, determined to study in the West. Now he was preparing for the ministry at Andover Theological Seminary, but he still remembered his equally English-obsessed school friend in Edo, Sen Tsuda, Ume's father. How strange to meet his daughter here! Ume and Ryo soon looked forward to Niijima's visits. "They don't understand what the ladies in the families speak to them," he wrote, "so when I go there to see them they are delighted to see me, and ask me ever so many questions."

A gossip columnist for the *New York Times*, invited for an evening at the Hepburns', was equally charmed by the other three girls, though perhaps in spite of himself. "Their faces are quite pretty when not in repose," he commented, "and their motions are graceful in the extreme." He approved of their delicate manners, their croquet skills, their rapid mastery of the game of Parcheesi, and their sense of mischief. At dinner, Sutematsu turned to the young man next to her and addressed him in Japanese.

"Do you understand?" she asked with a twinkle.

The young wag, enjoying the attention of the assembled company, launched into his best impression of someone speaking an incomprehensible Asian language. "*Me gum gum forum chow chow sa ke no go.*"

"You talk Chinese," the girl retorted, "not Japanese."

THE DAYS AND weeks passed with no particular schedule. Despite the constraints of the language barrier, despite the pinching shoes and fitted bodices, the girls were oddly unbound. By the end of May, Mori had found a house on Connecticut Avenue and moved all five girls in together, along with a cook and a governess, Miss Annie Loring. They studied English for two hours each morning, took piano lessons, and were otherwise left mostly to themselves. This domestic arrangement did little to acclimate the girls, but it was awfully fun. Mrs. Lanman stopped in to see them frequently, and they visited the Japanese legation, where the junior officials spoiled them. Long after bedtime they would light the gas and romp some more, unheard and unchecked by Miss Loring, who was soon succeeded by Miss Lagler. Five clever girls who could conspire in an unintelligible language made a challenging assignment for any governess.

Six months after they had boarded the steamship in Yokohama, it was becoming harder for the girls to remember the rhythms of their earlier lives and the turmoil that had followed. Though Sutematsu could trace the faint scar on her neck where the shrapnel had struck her during the terrible siege of the castle, it felt like something that had happened to someone else. Shige seemed more like a sister than the ones she had left behind. To her mother, little Ume wrote in Japanese:

> First I am happy to know you are all well. I am fine. As I already told you, we live together in Washington. At first Miss Loring taught us, but she went back to her home, so another teacher came. We study from 10 to 12 in the morning. Where we live now is 13 blocks from the Lanmans, but do not worry, Mrs. Lanman comes often to look after us. Ryo would have written to you, but her eyes are bad and she cannot study. She says to tell you she is sorry. I am reading a book for beginners. I am also reading a book about the Earth, and practicing handwriting. Please do not worry about me too much. From Ume.

It was the last letter she would write in her mother tongue.

AFTER A FOUR-MONTH ROUND-TRIP home and back, Ito and Okubo reached Washington in July of 1872, diplomatic credentials at last in hand, with imperial instructions to open international negotiations and not simply hammer out a bilateral treaty with the United States. But Secretary of State Hamilton Fish flatly refused to widen the scope of the discussion. Ito and Okubo had completed their exhausting errand in vain. There was nothing now to hold the frustrated Iwakura delegates in America. After brief stops in Philadelphia, New York, and Boston, they would sail for London.

On a balmy evening in late July, the grounds of the Japanese legation glowed with dozens of paper lanterns. Arinori Mori had invited everyone—departing ambassadors, Japanese students remaining in America, the five girls, and the Lanmans—for a farewell dinner. The *Evening Star*'s reporter was vaguely disappointed that the much-discussed "princesses" attended in Western dress, but otherwise "everything passed off pleasantly."

Iwakura and his men left for Philadelphia on the noon train the next day. Over the next fourteen months they would see England, Scotland, France, Belgium, Holland, Prussia, Russia, Denmark, Sweden, Germany, Italy, Austria, and Switzerland, returning to Japan via the four-year-old Suez Canal, Ceylon, Singapore, and Hong Kong. They had a nation to build, and all the systems of the

Western world to learn. If anyone spared a thought for the girls left behind, it was presumably a fleeting one.

Without the delegates to look after, Mori could at last turn his attention to the students in his charge. He invited the five girls to dinner, accompanied by Charles Lanman and their teacher. "The ordinary dinner parties of Washington are noted for their sham dignity and stupidity," Lanman wrote years later. This one he remembered for its simple elegance and earnestness—startling, really, when one considered the paths followed by each of the guests to this point. But there they sat, Lanman mused, remarkably at home in their unremarkable new clothes, with Ume in the place of honor to Mori's right, her chin not much higher than her plate. "By implied consent, the conversation was monopolized by Mr. Mori, and the readiness with which he spoke the different languages at his command, was truly wonderful, and he was kept very busy, by the necessity of explaining questions that were put to him by his American and Japanese friends," Lanman remembered fondly. "At one time he expatiated at considerable length upon the deplorable condition of the Japanese woman, and his revealings were made intensely interesting by the presence of the Japanese girls; he would then address a remark to one of the older girls, with a view to drawing her out on the fashions of the American women, when he would obtain, in return, a sentiment teeming with common sense or wit."

When dusk ended an after-dinner game of croquet, the party moved inside to admire a collection of books and photographs newly arrived from Japan. Mori presented each girl with a fan, and Lanman gave them each a bouquet, "and thus ended one of the most unique dinner parties, in the spirit of its composition, which ever occurred in Washington." But where Lanman was swept away by the picturesque novelty of the cross-cultural scene, Mori noticed something else: after more than five months in Washington, the girls were still chattering away in Japanese.

Mori knew all too well the bewilderment of arriving in an alien land. But as a young man in London, he had been expected to look after himself, and learning English had been a matter of survival. Safe and well tended with their governess on Connecticut Avenue, the girls felt no such imperative. They were no closer to being able to study in an American classroom than they had been when they arrived. If they were to fulfill the empress's mandate, something had to change.

KIYOTAKA KURODA, THE girls' original recruiter, and Mori, their current guardian, may have believed wholeheartedly in the rightness of bringing girls to America, but even an imperial mandate wasn't enough to convince Sutematsu's brother Kenjiro. After a year of study in Norwich, Connecticut, Kenjiro's English was more than serviceable, his penmanship quite elegant. Though still not yet eighteen, he had no qualms about expressing his reservations to the men in Washington who controlled his sister's fate.

How could it possibly be a good idea to send Japanese girls to America before they had finished learning what it meant to be Japanese? "If these girls are not taught about our moral science, they will do every thing as the Americans do, or of their own choice," Kenjiro wrote to Charles Lanman in English, his indignation rising with every line. "If they do as the Americans do, that is, according to the bible, they will be punished by our Government. Although I do not know whether the Americans are sorry to find their sisters in punishment, or not; yet I, a Japanese, am very sorry for that."

Shaped by the "moral science" of the Aizu samurai, Kenjiro's priorities were fixed: Confucian obedience, hierarchy, honor. Loyalty to his defeated domain had been redirected as pride in his emerging nation and its new leadership. The word "government" warranted an initial capital; the Bible did not. As he crammed for the entrance exam to Yale's Sheffield Scientific School that summer, Kenjiro had no doubts about his mission: learn English, study physics and engineering, return home, and use his new skills to help lead Japan forward. But what was Sutematsu's mission? How could a half-grown girl, virtually alone in an alien land for ten years, not be irrevocably changed? How could such a woman ever reenter Japanese society, let alone become a role model?

Mori's concern was more immediate: the girls must begin to make better progress in English, and for that, they must be separated. That one of them had an opinionated older brother in New Haven suddenly looked like an opportunity. Having passed his exams and won a place at Yale (his trigonometry was shaky, but he had promised to do extra work over the summer), Kenjiro would make his home for the next three years in New Haven. If Sutematsu went to live with a New Haven family, her brother would at least be able to keep an eye on her—a situation that would satisfy both Kenjiro and Mori.

Other factors were turning Mori's attention toward Connecticut as well. That same summer of 1872, a group of thirty Chinese boys, ages ten to sixteen, had arrived in New England as the vanguard of the Chinese Educational Mission, the brainchild of Yung Wing, the first Chinese man to graduate from Yale, in 1854. The arrival of the Chinese boys on the heels of the Iwakura Mission was not a coincidence; though Yung had been advocating such a plan for years, his government was finally spurred to act by a dawning awareness of Japan's modernization efforts. Yung's Yale connections steered him toward Birdsey Grant Northrop, secretary of Connecticut's Board of Education. Together, Yung and Northrop solicited "cultured families" in which the Chinese boys could begin their American educations. The response was overwhelming: 122 families in Connecticut and southern Massachusetts volunteered—far more than were needed.

Mori and Northrop were already good friends. Part of Mori's job as Japanese chargé d'affaires in Washington was to keep track of the nearly two hundred Japanese students already in the United States, most of them sponsored by the Japanese government. Because of these young men, Mori had become a student of the American educational system, touring schools in Massachusetts and Connecticut, where the establishment of public education was already well under way. When the question of what to do with the girls arose, Northrop was the obvious man to ask, and his work with Yung made it clear that appropriate host families would not be hard to find. Especially since Mori was no longer trying to place five girls, but three.

Ryo's eyes had never recovered from the glare of the western snows.

Though she wore a green eyeshade to protect them, chronic inflammation made studying nearly impossible. Doctor after doctor examined her, and all agreed: if she continued to strain her eyes, she risked blindness. No longer physically able to carry out her role as foreign student, she would have to return home, Mori decided. Tei, closest to Ryo in age and temperament and showing signs of acute homesickness, would go with her.

Perhaps following Yung Wing's example of placing pairs of students together, Mori set out to find a home for Sutematsu and Shige, now twelve and eleven. Consultation with Kenjiro, Northrop, and Addison Van Name, a scholar of the Far East who was Yale's librarian, yielded a likely prospect: the family of Leonard Bacon, a prominent Congregational minister in New Haven. Letters discussing the terms of the arrangement were soon flying between New Haven and Washington.

"I went to see Mrs. Van Name today about the little Jap," wrote Bacon's eldest daughter, Rebecca, to her father that summer. "She was very glad to hear that perhaps we would like Miss Yamagawa [sic] and will write to her brother right away. In the mean time, some one may have snapped her up, but that is not likely. I told her that Mr. Van Name & B. G. Northrop might say what they thought would be a fair price for her, and you would see."*

Ume, having imprinted on the older girls like an orphaned chick, was horrified by the news that they would be leaving her behind. But her distress was soon mitigated by Mori's next decision: Ume was to return to the Lanmans, at least for now. Still only seven, Ume needed a mother as much as a teacher, and Adeline Lanman had fallen in love with the child, her "sunbeam from the land of the rising sun."

LEONARD BACON WAS a pillar of New Haven's intellectual elite: the pastor of First Church in the center of the town green for more than four

---

* Already acquainted with Kenjiro, the Bacons focused their correspondence in the summer of 1872 on Sutematsu alone, but the eventual plan called for both Sutematsu and Shige to join their household.

decades, a professor of theology at Yale, a prolific writer and editor. At seventy he had the craggy visage of a biblical patriarch: domed forehead, imposing eyebrows, white beard, and a mouth whose corners seemed pressed down by the weight of his thoughts. He had nine children from his first wife, and five more with his second; firstborn Rebecca was forty-six, and Alice, the youngest, fourteen.

New Haven was a stronghold of Congregationalism, which traced its ideology directly back to the Puritan settlers of New England, and Bacon's pulpit was one of the most influential. He was a magisterial moderate, always eloquently seeking the middle ground, confident in the power of Protestant orthodoxy to promote both moral and social progress. Throughout his career he had been vocal in his support of the antislavery movement, while remaining a harsh critic of the extremist approach of the abolitionists. Blacks were not inherently inferior, he agreed, but as they could surely never shake off the crushing degradation of white racism, the solution was not to give them equal rights as Americans but rather to send them back to Africa. There they could prosper, and, not coincidentally, share the gospel with the rest of their unenlightened race.

The Japanese girls, too, would be able to spread enlightenment in another remote land struggling in darkness: when they returned to Japan in ten years, they would carry Christianity with them. Meanwhile, the years they spent in New Haven would bring a different, if no less significant, benefit. Though rich in ideas, the sprawling Bacon household was perennially short of cash. Here, then, was a doubly attractive prospect: an opportunity to enhance the family finances and uplift the distant heathen without ever leaving New Haven.

The question of race was peripheral. In 1872 the few Japanese in America—nearly all of them from the samurai class—had come to learn and return home, not to demand equality or take American jobs. Freed slaves were a problem and Chinese coolies were a plague, but Japanese students were a worthy project. They would study hard, and then leave. The presence of Kenjiro in New Haven offered convenient insurance: if something went awry, he would be right there.

Unmarried, middle-aged Rebecca, a teacher who had helped raise her own siblings and now served as her father's right hand, sounded a note of caution, however. She had met one of the young Japanese men studying near New Haven and was not impressed, especially after a report that he was gravely ill. "They don't stand this climate too well and there is that responsibility to be counted in about this child," she wrote to Bacon, who had fled New Haven's heat for the relative cool of the Litchfield Hills. "They are puny folks & can hardly lift the end of a trunk—the men. But they selected healthy ones to send over."

As Kenjiro and Van Name batted the question of compensation back and forth, Rebecca rolled up her sleeves and did the due diligence, consulting other host families in the area on weekly stipends. "Mrs. Hotchkiss suggests $13.00," she told her father, "but evidently doesn't think $15.00 too much." Catherine, Bacon's second wife, was often bedridden; a boarding student might provide some welcome companionship, and the younger Bacon daughters could help with English and music instruction.

Following Rebecca's advice, Bacon approved the deal: for fifteen dollars a week per girl, he would provide room, board, and laundry, along with instruction in English, arithmetic, and geometry. Clothing, books, piano lessons, and medical attention were extra. (Rebecca had done very well for the Bacons. Northrop's original call for families to host the Chinese boys stipulated sixteen dollars per week for each *pair* of boys—though this disparity may also have had something to do with the prevailing American attitude toward Japan versus China, or the relatively greater Japanese enthusiasm, and hence budget, for sending students abroad.)

In contrast to his hardheaded daughter, Bacon framed the arrangement as more familial than financial. "What we propose," he wrote to Van Name, "is to receive her not simply as a boarder and lodger, but as if she were the child of some relative or near friend, who would expect us to have a parental care over her and to treat her with all parental kindness. She will be in the family as if she were one of our grandchildren."

Kenjiro approved, and even gave permission for his sister to attend church with Bacon and his family. "However I beseech him not to give her any religious instructions, which I will give her," Kenjiro wrote. The practice of Christianity was, after all, still illegal in Japan. His impressionable sister must be shielded from its influence.

As Washington's swampy humidity gave way to the drier breezes of fall, the odd little household on Connecticut Avenue prepared to disband. Ryo and Tei were the first to leave, retracing their journey across the continent and then the Pacific in the care of Mrs. Thomas Antisell, the wife of an Irish-American engineer employed by the same Hokkaido Colonization Board that had sponsored the girls. By the end of October they were back at the Grand Hotel in San Francisco. "During their stay in the East"—the East Coast this time, not the mysterious Orient—"the young ladies acquired a good knowledge of English, discarded their rich Oriental costumes, and assumed the garb of fashionable American girls, and now present a stylish appearance," chirped the *San Francisco Bulletin* approvingly. The two teenagers were anything but cheerful, though. They had failed in their mission, and upon returning to Tokyo, would soon disappear into anonymity. The bond that had formed between them and the three younger girls was broken forever.

Ume, for her part, was delighted at the prospect of moving back to Georgetown. The girls were practicing letter writing in their morning English classes, so Ume wrote to Adeline Lanman. "My Dear American mother," she began,

> You are a very nice woman. You are kind to me. You love me. Yesterday we will go to the woods and we have a very nice time. You are kind and I never forget. I am very glad this winter stay at your house.

The words loop across the page, the letters beautifully formed but not quite connected, as if written one at a time, with pauses for effort. "Your affectionate Japan daughter," Ume signed off. She might be losing the girls she had come to regard as older sisters, but she was gaining parents more solicitous and indulgent than any adults she had ever known.

On the evening of October 30, 1872, Sutematsu and Shige boarded the night train bound for New Haven, escorted by Mori. After eight months, Washington had begun to feel familiar; now here was yet another journey to a place they couldn't imagine, full of people they had never met, but on whom they would again be utterly dependent. In Sutematsu's case, however, apprehension was edged with excitement. She did know one person in New Haven. The last time she had seen her brother was in the smoking ruins of Wakamatsu, four long years earlier. She couldn't recall his face clearly, but at the moment he was the only Japanese man in New Haven. He wouldn't be hard to spot.

Ten hours later their train pulled into New Haven's Union Station—not the monumental red-brick edifice that stands today, but its smaller predecessor on Chapel Street, an eccentric building graced by a central tower that looked startlingly like the topmost tiers of Tsuruga Castle. But the girls had no time to wonder at this odd vision. Begrimed and bleary from their night of travel, they were whisked along Church Street. The vast town green, with its three stately churches, opened out to the left, with the buildings of Yale College just visible beyond. A few moments later they pulled up in front of a well-tended white clapboard house on the right.

"The two Japanese girls came today," Leonard Bacon wrote in his date book for October 31. "Mr. Mori, the Japanese embassador [sic] dined with us." The two men found much to discuss; Mori was drafting a recommendation to his government arguing against the ban on Christianity in Japan, and Bacon, naturally, had plenty to offer on the subject. Mori would incorporate many of Bacon's ideas, which eventually found their way into the Meiji government's revised laws on religious tolerance. Kenjiro needn't have worried. The man who would raise his sister was himself helping to ensure that Japan would not condemn her Christian upbringing.

Bacon and Mori wasted no time making the girls' situation official. That same day, Bacon presented Mori with a document outlining their terms. "Mrs. Bacon and my daughters will be watchful over the health, morals, and manners of these young ladies, and will take care that their training is like that of daughters in the best New England families," it read in part. The girls would study at home until they had acquired the skills they needed to go to school. "When they shall have learned to read English with sufficient facility," Bacon continued, "we shall take care to interest their minds in such books as will be useful to them." Useful to them in becoming educated ladies, that is—teachers, perhaps, but not scholars.

Bacon's opinion of female scholarship was mixed. His younger sister, Delia—considered an intellectual prodigy—had won fame as an author, speaker, and playwright, only to become fixated on the idea that authorship of Shakespeare's plays should actually be attributed to a group of wits including Francis Bacon, Edmund Spenser, and Sir Walter Raleigh. "I have all along regarded her darling theory as a mere hallucination," her brother wrote. Delia had died in an asylum at the age of forty-eight.

In Leonard Bacon's mind, a girl's highest goal was not to dazzle the intellectual world but to run a well-organized household. His memorandum to Mori on the girls reflected this view:

> We expect them to acquire that knowledge of domestic duties and employments which qualifies an American lady to become the mistress of a family. We expect that they will be taught and will be willing to learn whatever our own daughters learn of work proper to a lady who may have occasion not only to direct the servants in her house but often to teach them how to perform their work.

Mori was more than satisfied; here was the very attitude that had created the women the Meiji reformers had noticed and admired. "Good wife, wise mother," or *ryosai kenbo* in Japanese—that was the phrase that would soon enter the argot of the Meiji era, and that was the kind of woman Japan needed in order to move forward. Her contribution would be vital, but limited to the domestic sphere.

But these larger goals were far from the girls' minds as they learned their way around the house on Church Street. After just a few days at the Bacons', two things had become clear: Sutematsu and Shige were delightful children, and they weren't going to get very far with their English as long as they lived in the same house. By the end of the week, Shige had left for Fair Haven, a mile or two away, where another prominent minister, John S. C. Abbott, had agreed to take her in. "We were sorry to part with her eminently Mongolian features and her propensity to see the comical side of things," Bacon wrote. "She was almost the more interesting one." But having come to know Kenjiro, Bacon couldn't very well pack his sister off to another family—and anyway, Bacon continued, Sutematsu "had charmed us all with her simplicity, her intelligence, and her affectionately confiding ways."

It had been a year—almost to the day—since the Empress Haruko had gazed at five kneeling girls from behind her screen. Now there were three, and for the first time each of the three was on her own. Their American education could begin in earnest.

THOUGH SHIGE AND UME looked to her as the senior member of their unusual trio, Sutematsu settled into the Bacon family as the littlest sister. With the exception of the imposing Leonard Bacon, it was a household of women: Catherine, Leonard's second wife, whose arthritis often confined her to her bed; Rebecca, more Catherine's peer than her stepdaughter, briskly efficient manager of the family's daily details; and Nelly and Alice, the last of the fourteen Bacon children still living at home, ages sixteen and fourteen.

Within a few months, Sutematsu—or "Stemats," as her name was pronounced and written by her American friends—had become a treasured member of the family. Even the crusty hired Irishwomen who helped with the washing and cooking thought so, "and if they are aware that she is a 'haythen,'" wrote Bacon, "that makes no difference to them."

The formidable minister himself quickly developed something of a soft spot for his new ward. In the spring of Sutematsu's first year in New Haven, P. T. Barnum's "Grand Traveling Museum, Menagerie, Caravan & Hippodrome" stopped there, attracting every child in the area like a magnet. "Barnum's great menagerie was here two days, but, to my great disappointment, we were unable to give Stemats the opportunity of seeing it," Bacon wrote. "The little girl's disappointment we could not doubt, but she did not exhibit any sort of vexation." Only a year earlier, the girl herself had been the object of just the kind of stares drawn by Tom Thumb and the Feejee Mermaid. She may have missed the circus, but she had clearly crossed over to the side of the gawkers.

Each day, Sutematsu went to Mrs. Bacon's room after breakfast and spent several hours studying with her. Nelly was her music teacher, sitting next to her on the piano bench in the parlor. But it was with Alice that Sutematsu formed the strongest bond. Similar both in age and in scholarly intensity, the two girls were soon inseparable. And though Sutematsu worked diligently at her lessons, it was undoubtedly the time spent with this new sister that made the most immediate impact on her progress. Chattering away to Alice, instead of to Shige and Ume, she improved her English by the day.

In Alice Mabel Bacon, the youngest of fourteen, one might have expected a pampered pet, but Alice was a serious-minded soul with a sharp wit, a passion for books, and an unusually open mind. She was not the first studious female in the family. Her oldest half-sister Rebecca had only recently returned home to help her invalid stepmother; before that, Rebecca had held the position of assistant principal at the Hampton Normal and Agricultural Institute in Virginia, founded to educate free blacks after the Civil War. A couple of years earlier, when Alice was twelve, she had spent a year living with Rebecca at Hampton, attending classes and even teaching a bit. The other teachers had called Alice "the Little Professor." Like Sutematsu, she possessed a self-reliance that belied her years, and she understood what it meant to live among people unlike herself.

Before long, Sutematsu was ready to walk with Alice to Grove Hall Seminary, a small primary school for girls run by Miss Maria Monfort just a block away. A three-story frame building, it was topped with a cupola and set well back from the brick herringbone sidewalk. Sutematsu's world suddenly expanded from the Bacon women to a whole classroom full of girls. As she had studied at home as a child, and then not at all during the years of war and dislocation, it was her first experience in a large group of her peers.

Autograph books were all the rage at Grove Hall, and a classmate named Carrie had a beautiful one, bound in tooled green leather, with "Autographs" stamped in fancy gilt letters. When it was her turn to sign, Sutematsu turned the little oblong book so that her page was tall rather than wide, and wrote her name in Japanese, four kanji characters marching down the page. Alice, never one to suffer fools, was equally unafraid of making a statement. "Cease your chatter, and follow me," she wrote in Carrie's book—in elegant Greek. Then, switching back to English, "Yours truly, A. M. Bacon." One wonders whether autograph-seeking Carrie ever deciphered that page.

Meanwhile, Kenjiro made sure that Sutematsu's English did not replace her native tongue entirely, and that her growing comfort with American ways did not eclipse her identity as a dutiful subject of the Japanese empire. They met for weekly lessons in Japanese language and Confucian philosophy. Sutematsu complained these were far more onerous than all the rest of her schoolwork in English, but underneath the griping her samurai pride was intact—enough to show off her calligraphy in Carrie's autograph book, at least. When Kenjiro completed his degree and returned to Japan in 1875, he continued his tutelage remotely, sending his sister long letters on Japanese politics. She appreciated his attentiveness, though she did wish he'd tell her more about their family.

Sutematsu's education continued outside the classroom as well. Though the Bacons were far from wealthy, Leonard Bacon's stature won him membership in the Hillhouse Society, a group of New Haven's leading academics and businessmen who met regularly to discuss scholarship, art, and civic affairs. Hillhouse Avenue, lined with mansions and stately elms, was home to most of them; just a few years earlier, Charles Dickens had declared it the most beautiful street in America. The Hillhouse wives had their own group, Our Society, founded to provide aid to needy women and children. Sutematsu attended meetings with Alice, sewing clothes and making diapers for struggling black families or refugees from the Franco-Prussian War. It was her first exposure to charity; private philanthropy was unknown in Japan.

The days had room in them for play as well as work. Across the street from the Bacons lived the family of William Dwight Whitney, professor of Sanskrit at Yale and secretary of the American Oriental Society. Whitney's eldest daughter, Marian, fell just between Alice and Sutematsu in age, and she was their schoolmate as well as their neighbor. Another serious scholar growing up in a family that prized learning above most things, Marian was also tremendous fun. In the cold months the girls played checkers and went sleighing and skated in the frozen back yards of their friends; in warmer weather they climbed trees and swam. Sutematsu joined in with grace and enthusiasm. "I remember how, when we began to learn to dive, her lithe figure would spring into the air from the little raft and go down straight as an arrow into the water, while we splashed and floundered and fell flat upon the surface," Marian wrote.

New Haven's summers were sweltering, and the Bacons were in the habit of escaping northward to the deeper shade and cooler breezes of Colebrook, a village high in the Litchfield Hills. It was fifty miles by train to Winsted, and another dusty hour by cart from there. Not much more than an inn, a store, and a church, Colebrook was home to the Carrington sisters, Catherine Bacon's unmarried cousins, both in their late twenties. Miss Kate and Miss Sarah took in boarders to supplement the income from their parents' farm, and their city cousins were regular summer guests. There were lakes to bathe in, fish to catch, and evenings filled with poetry and charades.

In the summer of 1874 there was another lodger at the Carringtons' white frame house down the hill from the center of the village: Tan Yaoxun (or Yew Fun Tan, as he was known at the time), one of two boys from the Chinese Educational Mission whom Miss Kate and Miss Sarah had agreed to host. Tan was twelve. Like Sutematsu, two years his senior, the boy enjoyed Catherine Bacon's motherly attentions. At the end of that summer, when Catherine left with the girls for the start of school in New Haven, Tan's letters followed her. "Do you remember saying that you would like to hear from me frequently?" he wrote. "I have not forgotten what you have said, if you have." He told Mrs. Bacon of his triumphs and travails at fishing—"I was provoked because I could not catch that *big trout*, though I ought not to let my angry passions rise"—and sent his best "to the Miss Bacons and all." "All," presumably, included the Bacons' unusual ward. Tan's path and Sutematsu's would continue to intersect in the years to come.

By 1875 Sutematsu was ready to sit the entrance examination for Hillhouse High School, the jewel in the crown of New Haven's young public education system. Its graduates, if they were boys, tended to matriculate at Yale; if girls, to become teachers—at least until they married. The exam covered arithmetic, grammar, geography, and US history, along with penmanship, music, and drawing. "Analyze the following sentence," read one grammar question: "They who are set to rule over others, must be just." In geography, applicants were instructed to name a country corresponding to each of the following: "1. Savage, 2. Barbarous, 3. Half civilized, 4. Civilized, 5. Enlightened." If she had ever peeked into her brothers' schoolbooks—the progressive ones by Fukuzawa, that is, which they had studied in exile—this would have rung a bell.

Three years earlier Sutematsu had lacked enough English to beg for a Western-style dress. She passed the test easily. There is no record of how she answered the geography question.

AMONGST LESSONS, SKATING parties, trips to Colebrook, and tutorials with Kenjiro, Sutematsu looked forward to her visits with the one person whose company she particularly craved: Shige. No matter how rapid their progress in English or how kind their hosts, each found the other's company a relief. Shige lived barely a half hour's walk across town, but she and Sutematsu saw each other only occasionally, limited by their studies and the rhythms of their respective families.

Though Leonard Bacon had regretted Shige's departure, he had approved of her destination: the home of John Stevens Cabot Abbott, a Congregational minister as prominent as Bacon himself, though in a more secular sphere. A graduate of Bowdoin College, where his classmates had included Nathaniel Hawthorne and Henry Wadsworth Longfellow,

Abbott found more success and satisfaction as a best-selling author than as a pastor. His first book, *The Mother at Home, or The Principles of Maternal Duty*, published some forty years earlier, had catapulted him to fame; since then, he had penned voluminous illustrated histories on topics including the French Revolution, Napoleon, Frederick the Great, and Captain Kidd. Like Bacon, Abbott held views quite consistent with the Meiji reformers' "good wife, wise mother" ideal of women's education: "As the mother is the guardian and guide of the early years of life, from her, goes the most powerful influence, in the formation of the character of man."

The Abbotts were unusually well equipped to host a student: their home on East Grand Street—a squat, two-story house on a spacious corner lot—was also a school. The Civil War had taken a generation of young men and left a generation of single women, many of whom became teachers. Abbott's eldest daughter Ellen, in her midthirties, was one of these. Unable to bear her own children, she helped mold the minds of others'. Miss Abbott's School, operating out of two well-appointed parlors, served nearly a hundred children in three divisions: the Primary Department, introducing the basics to scholars as young as five; the Academic Department, for those ages ten to fifteen; and the Higher Course, offering philosophy, rhetoric, and languages. First among Miss Abbott's staff was her mother, who taught English and natural science; four other teachers and a music master completed the faculty.

Though boys made up half of the Primary Department, they tended to move on—to other schools, or private tutors—as they grew older. Nearly all of Miss Abbott's more advanced students were girls, and it was a constant struggle to keep them focused on their studies. "To Parents," she wrote in the school's explanatory pamphlet:

> A single day's absence, or an evening party, greatly interferes with educational advancement; for the next day, in nine cases out of ten, the pupil is unfitted or unprepared. Not having been present at the previous recitation, she has not known the new lesson, and entails upon herself difficulties which follow her often for weeks. *A lesson lost can never be made up.*

The stern tone belied the jolly mood that prevailed at the Abbotts', several degrees livelier and more relaxed than the Bacons' Puritan uprightness. To Shige, Miss Abbott was soon "Aunt Nelly": her teacher, to be sure, but also something between mother and friend. It was Nelly who introduced Shige to the Bible and taught her how to pray. In the summer, when the school was closed, Aunt Nelly took Shige on field trips: to the Berkshires in southwestern Massachusetts; to Boston, where Shige went strawberry picking and visited the Japanese art objects at the Athenaeum; to the beach at Nantucket, where Reverend Abbott had once led a congregation; to the White Mountains of New Hampshire, where Shige spotted tiny goats perched on the slopes of Mount Washington. When Abbott traveled to Bowdoin to preach at commencement, Shige tagged along and got Long-fellow's autograph.

As Sutematsu had Alice Bacon and Marian Whitney for her companions, Shige had the Pitman girls: her classmate Helen, and Helen's younger sisters Leila and Lizzie, whose parents were neighbors and close friends of the Abbotts. When Aunt Nelly was busy with home and school, the Pitmans were always nearby. In their company, gregarious Shige moved from the schoolroom out into the larger community, attending church and Sunday school, and the occasional social. One memorable evening she went with Helen and Leila to a spelling bee pitting the women of their church against those of another. There was a breathless moment when Mrs. Pitman misspelled "catastrophe," but then her opponent erred in turn, and the match was saved. The winner received a silk umbrella, and the runner-up, a collection of Dickens.

In the summer of 1875, fourteen-year-old Shige lost the dubious distinction of being the only Japanese student in the neighborhood. The Pitmans, following the Abbotts' example, invited an aspiring naval cadet named Sotokichi Uriu* to live with them while he prepared to enter the academy at Annapolis. Ironically, the curriculum at the United

---

* Though the modern transliteration of the name is "Uryu" rather than "Uriu," the family always used the older spelling in English, and continues to do so to this day.

States Naval Academy, established in 1845, was conceived in large part by Commodore Matthew Perry, who could never have imagined a Japanese midshipman at Annapolis when he sailed his black ships into Edo Bay in 1853.

Small and slim, with delicate features, Uriu was eighteen. Unlike the girls, blindsided by the announcement of their selection as foreign students, Uriu had been in training since the age of twelve, chosen by the elders of his domain—Kaga, on the Sea of Japan coast—to study English, physics, chemistry, navigation, and engineering with foreign teachers at the domain school. At fifteen, he traveled three hundred miles on foot to enter the Imperial Naval Academy in Tokyo, where he was a star English student and also became interested in Christianity. At the same time, he was something of a traditionalist: a fine calligrapher, a formidable opponent at the board game called *go*, and fond of chanting the haunting lyrics of classical *noh* drama.

Uriu's ambitions matched his talents, but he kept his ferocious drive largely to himself. Plucky and popular, he was a good citizen and a loyal friend, if a bit serious-minded. "The fear of the Lord is the beginning of wisdom," he wrote in Shige's autograph book, "and the Knowledge of the holy is understanding." The Pitmans were fond of him, and even after he enrolled at Annapolis he continued to return to them for vacations. He made his foster family proud—though he tipped the scales at barely 115 pounds, his fellow midshipmen quickly acknowledged his superior moral stature. "It used to be a joke in our class that we included one Christian, and that one was Uriu," one of his classmates remembered. When it came to soothing the "unruly spirits" in the class, Uriu was the one they turned to. What a lovely boy, Mrs. Pitman would tell Shige approvingly. He'd make a nice match for you.

THOUGH INCREASINGLY AT home in New Haven, and secure in each other's friendship, Sutematsu and Shige did not forget Ume back in Georgetown, and they made periodic trips to see her. Birdsey Northrop, keeping a paternal eye on the girls as Connecticut's secretary of education, escorted Sutematsu and Shige to Washington at Christmas in 1874.

"Ume is as talkative as ever," Sutematsu wrote to Mrs. Bacon from Georgetown. "She can read, and recite poetries very well, and it was true that she received four prizes, do you not remember, that we read about it in news paper in Colebrook?" In contrast to the frugal Bacons, the Lanmans were lavish hosts. "After dinner," Sutematsu wrote later the same day. "I can not write to you any more for I ate so much oysters, that I can not write."

In New Haven, Sutematsu and Shige spent hours thinking and talking about Japan, with Sutematsu's brother Kenjiro and then Shige's neighbor Sotokichi Uriu adding to the conversation. In sharp contrast, Ume could barely remember life before the Lanmans, who treated her as a pampered daughter rather than an emissary from a foreign government. She had been such a little girl when she arrived, and the move to their home such a relief after the nomadic year that preceded it. Undistracted by family matters or financial concerns, Adeline Lanman devoted all her attention to Ume, who returned her affection in equal measure.

"Dear Mrs. Lanman, I thought I would write you this note to tell you how I spent the evening and to tell you what time I went to bed so that if I was asleep when you came home you would know all," she wrote the first time her new mother left her to go out for the evening. "I am now undressing. I shall try to be a good girl tomorrow, better than today. I have a hard time to find my nightgown. I have said my prayers and going to jump right into bed." It is hard to imagine the youngest daughter of a samurai household scribbling such an intimate note to her absent mother, even assuming samurai mothers ever went visiting after dark.

Ume's orientation in the world was shifting. To her own mother, Hatsuko, she wrote—in English—of a dream she'd had: "I dreamt that I went home to get Koto [Ume's older sister] to come with me to America. Mrs. Lanman went with me, and after we inquired a good many times, we were shown to a house. That was Mr. Tsuda's. It was a American three story house and I rang the door bell and Koto came there she was so glad to see me." For her part, Hatsuko was both startled by and grateful for the degree of attention her daughter was receiving. "I am always thinking that Ume is a great deal happier in your home than in Japan[,] for she enjoys such comfort under your care, and is loved as if she were your own child," Hatsuko wrote (in Japanese) to Adeline Lanman. Ryo, the oldest of the original five girls, now back in Tokyo, had visited the Tsudas and described the Lanmans' home in glowing terms.

The Lanmans enrolled Ume at Miss Lucy Stephenson's grandly named Georgetown Collegiate Institute, a small school for girls that had just opened its doors a few blocks away. A neighbor child, Martha Miller, also attended the school, and Ume and Mattie were soon fast friends. It was Mattie's job to fend off the unwelcome attentions of children—both black and white—who tried to pull Ume's long thick braid on their morning walk to school. It wasn't long, however, before Ume established herself as something of a force. She excelled in croquet and lawn tennis, and always took the lead when friends came to play under the trees in the side garden. She was a fiercely competitive chess player, and a rather fussy eater, steering clear of unfamiliar dairy products—even ice cream—and preferring cured meats to fresh. The Lanmans delighted in her strong will. "She always decidedly objected to being interfered with by the offer of outside suggestions," Charles Lanman wrote.

By the end of her second year at Miss Stephenson's, Ume was at the top of her class, covered with glory at the school's second annual commencement ceremony, the news of which had reached Sutematsu and the Bacons in Colebrook. "A large number of premiums were distributed, and it will surprise the public to learn that not less than four of them were received by the young Japanese, Miss Ume Tsuda, for composition, writing, arithmetic and deportment," the *Daily National Republican* announced. "And it may be stated here that, at a previous examination of the class in elocution, while the remainder of the pupils read their pieces from a book, this child recited hers from memory, without making a single mistake, and her piece was the White-footed Deer, by Bryant."

At eighteen stanzas, William Cullen Bryant's ballad was indeed a feat of memorization for a nine-year-old. Proud of his charge, Charles Lanman wrote to the poet himself of Ume's triumph. "If there is any merit in my poem," Bryant replied, "it consists in the spirit of humanity towards the inferior animals which it inculcates. She may forget the poetry, such as it is; but the lesson, I hope, will not be forgotten." Ume's accomplishments, commented another newspaper, "would imply that there is a live Yankee element in the Oriental mind."

As Ume's life in English blossomed, her Japanese withered, though at first the Lanmans did their best to preserve it. A month or two after Ume settled in Georgetown, the Lanmans invited Kiyo Kawamura, a sixteen-year-old student, to live with them. Sent by his father to acquire an American education, but more interested in becoming an artist, Kawamura received instruction in English and painting from Charles Lanman in exchange for tutoring Ume in Japanese. The arrangement was brief: Kawamura left to pursue his art in Paris after six months.

Two years later Ume was still without a tutor—a circumstance that the Japanese minister in Washington, Kiyonari Yoshida, deemed unacceptable. "Mr. Yoshida said I must learn Japanese," Ume wrote to her mother. "He has a lady, or a maid, to keep company with his wife, and she will teach me Japanese." These lessons, if they ever took place, were ineffective, however, and if Charles Lanman saw the situation as something of a "calamity," Ume's father did not share his dismay. In his correspondence with Lanman—always in English—Sen Tsuda expressed no concern at his daughter's loss of fluency; she would pick it up again when she returned. His daughter was only too happy to agree. "Ume herself was wont to say that as she had come to America to study English, there was no sense in bothering herself with Japanese," wrote Lanman.

Spongelike, Ume soaked up the Lanmans' upper-middle-class priorities: self-improvement and intellectual curiosity balanced by a Protestant piety convinced of its own righteousness and eager to rescue those still laboring in the dark. Charles Lanman's work at the Japanese legation kept him ever mindful of his responsibility to foster a sense of civic duty in Ume. Eager to show off his precocious charge, he assigned her essay topics and shared the results with both his colleagues and Ume's family in Tokyo. Her responses combined the Lanmans' sense of civilizing mission with a hazy impulse to defend her heritage. "Dear Mr. Lanman," she wrote for one assignment:

> You asked me to write you a letter or rather a composition on what I thought about the improvement in Japan and how they ought to make improvement. I think it wrong to make everything different in Japan . . . I would like Japan to keep the language and dress as they did and write the same but have America schools and have Japanese schools too. They ought to keep on making china and bronzes and sword just as they did but in a few things the Japanese ought to change, such things as the scissors, and a few others, for in a few things the Americans make better. I wish they would (all the people in Japan) become Christians and all the temples become churches it would be too much trouble to build new churches, but take all the idols and everything and change a few thing and have that as a church it would make beautiful churches.

In fact, Ume's exposure to the appeal of all things Western had begun before she ever left Japan. As a teenager, her father had been one of the young samurai manning the outdated coastal artillery as Commodore Perry steered his astonishing black ships toward Edo. From that moment Sen Tsuda had resolved to cast his lot with the West: leaving his domain behind, he set out for Edo and by his midtwenties had learned enough English to win a position as interpreter to the shogun. The restoration of the emperor ended that career, but in 1869 Tsuda landed on his feet: he became the manager of Tokyo's first hotel catering to foreigners.

The Hoterukan was a perfect symbol of the early Meiji era. Taking its name from the Japanese pronunciation of the English word "hotel" with the suffix -*kan* ("building") added, it was a spectacularly awkward convergence of East and West, with Western-style sash windows set into walls of traditional diamond-patterned *namako* tiles. The gardens were Japanese, but the interiors were plastered and painted in the foreign style. There were two hundred rooms on three stories, and a staff of more than a hundred. To the Japanese, the massive building was impressive, immortalized in dozens of popular prints, but it was expensive and inconvenient, built on mosquito-ridden reclaimed swampland, and foreigners found the food inedible. The business foundered, and Tsuda quit after less than two years. The Hoteru-kan burned to the ground in 1872, just after the girls arrived in America. It was a spectacular failure, but there Tsuda learned enough about Western ways to propel him into his next incarnation, as a pioneer importer and cultivator of exotic produce: strawberries, asparagus, eggplants, figs. Tsuda was soon advising the Meiji government on Western agriculture.

Like many Japanese reformers, Tsuda regarded Western strength and Christianity as inseparably entwined. Though he and his family did not actually convert until after Ume's departure, Tsuda never shared Kenjiro Yamakawa's wary hostility toward the barbarians' religion. Ume, embraced by an American family for whom piety was paramount, had no reason to resist. A year after arriving at the Lanmans', she asked to be baptized. Eager to grant her gratifying request, but mindful of the Japanese ambivalence toward Christianity, the Lanmans brought her to their friend Octavius Perinchief, pastor of a nonsectarian church in Pennsylvania and an adviser to Arinori Mori on educational policy. "I think I have baptised grown persons whose convictions and views were not so well defined as hers," Perinchief wrote. Ume's vision of turning temples into churches proved prescient. "Ume will be glad to know that I have hired a fine temple and have removed all the Idols and every Sunday afternoon Mr. Soper[*] preaches in the temple, which we all attend and many of the neighbours," Tsuda wrote to Lanman in 1875. Ume's sister Koto joined in her parents' embrace of Christianity. "You went away from us and I think you will have trouble," she wrote to Ume in English, "but if we believe in Jesus Christ and get help from Him then we shall be happy."

Ume certainly seemed to believe. In a small cottage in the Georgetown garden lived Jeffrey and Margaret Savell, a black couple who worked for the

---

[*] Junius Soper was an American Methodist missionary responsible for the conversions of Sen and Hatsuko Tsuda.

Lanmans. Charles Lanman liked to recount how Ume would visit the cottage on Sunday mornings with her Bible and prayer book, and conduct a miniature Sunday school for the elderly pair. Years later, Jeffrey, now a widower, wondered what had become of the girl from Japan. "O sir, she was a good child sure," he told Lanman, "and she told Margaret how to get to heaven."

For the time being, though, heaven was a home in Georgetown, where the little girl was praised by her teachers and adored by her foster parents, who traveled with her through New England and as far as Canada in the summers and introduced her to the most prominent members of their circle. She shook Senator Charles Sumner's hand and sat on Longfellow's lap. "A kiss to your little Japanese ward," Longfellow closed one letter to Lanman.

IN THE SUMMER of 1876, the three girls posed together for a rare photo. Sutematsu stands in the middle, tall and straight in bold stripes, belted narrowly at the waist with a broad ribbon tied at the side. Her hair is pulled back, with curly bangs cut in front. The full cheeks of her childhood have lengthened into more mature planes; her expression is both severe and serene. To her left stands Shige, half a head shorter, arm linked through her friend's striped sleeve. Shige's face, still round, is softer and less austere, framed with ruffles at the collar and the same curly bangs. Sutematsu's right arm encircles Ume's shoulders as the smaller girl leans into her hip, reaching up to hold her hand. Sutematsu and Shige have the shapely grace of young women; Ume, the simpler dress and gamine features of a girl. All three regard the world with striking poise. "The trio," as they called themselves, was united for a much-anticipated visit. Sutematsu was sixteen; Shige, fifteen; Ume, eleven. And the United States of America was one hundred.

In honor of the centennial, a great exposition was taking place in Philadelphia, an "International Exhibition of Arts, Manufactures and Products of the Soil and Mine" so prodigious that it became synonymous with the national birthday itself. "Have you been at the Centennial?" people asked each other. "How do you like the Centennial?" The traumas of the recent past—the Civil War, Reconstruction, and the Panic of 1873, with its ensuing economic depression—receded for a season as America celebrated the prodigious resources and innovations that would "sooner or later lift the nation from its slough of despond, and place it at the head of the phalanx of progress."

Two hundred and fifty pavilions rose on 285 acres in Fairmount Park, with a custom-built narrow-gauge railway to move the spectators from one building to the next. The colossal Main Building—at a symbolic 1,876 feet long, the largest building in the world—enclosed an area the size of six football fields and housed exhibitors from thirty-seven countries. The centennial art exhibition in Memorial Hall featured everything from shocking French and Italian nudes to *The Dreaming Iolanthe*, a bas-relief sculpted in butter by a farmer's wife from Arkansas. The milk pan that held the sculpture was nested in a bowl of ice for the duration of that unusually hot summer.

The most popular attraction was Machinery Hall, where foreign and local visitors alike could behold the proof of America's imminent shift from an agricultural nation to an industrial one. The Otis elevator, the Remington typewriter, and Alexander Bell's telephonic telegraphic receiver were all on display, but the central attraction was the majestic Corliss steam engine, an "athlete of steel and iron" that powered all the exhibits in the hall. William Dean Howells, editor of the *Atlantic Monthly*, waxed rhapsodic: "Wherever else the national bird is mute in one's breast, here he cannot fail to utter his pride and content." As a nation, America was coming of age, pivoting from brash upstart to mentor, and the proof was in Machinery Hall. "Let the new cycle shame the old!" proclaimed the last line of the hymn that John Greenleaf Whittier composed for the opening of the exhibition. The song threatened to eclipse "Hail Columbia" and "The Star-Spangled Banner" in its instant popularity.

Between May and November, nine million people paid fifty cents apiece to exult in their nation's achievements and travel the world without leaving Philadelphia. Many countries had built freestanding structures, and Japan had two: a model "dwelling" and a bazaar, filled with "dragons, and mats, tea cups, and lanterns, cabinets, and carved ivory" that entranced passersby, especially the ladies. The garden surrounding the bazaar was a classically miniaturized Japanese landscape, "a plesaunce for a palace of puppets," remarked one observer, "while a single American oak over-canopied the whole park." Visitors were delighted, though somewhat in the manner of visitors to a zoo. "The quaint little people, with their shambling gait, their eyes set awry in their head, and their grave and gentle ways, how can it be in them . . . to make such wonderful things?" commented one. "It is a great pity not to see them in their own outlandish gear, for picturesqueness' sake," lamented Howells. Most of the Japanese exhibitors had quickly found themselves Western clothes after several "Asiatics," both Japanese and Chinese, were harassed on opening day.

In July, Sutematsu and Shige traveled down from New Haven to meet Ume and the Lanmans and join the throngs in Philadelphia. Four years had passed since their first bewildering kimono-clad days in San Francisco. Now they strolled from pavilion to pavilion, well tailored and at ease. Amid so much that was exotic, they were relatively inconspicuous, enthralled along with everyone else by the scale and scope of the displays, from the gigantic torch-bearing hand of the Statue of Liberty, rising out of a kiosk at which you could make a donation toward the future construction of her pedestal, to the unfamiliar snacks for sale, including bananas, sold individually wrapped in foil for the exorbitant price of ten cents. In contrast, when 113 young members of the Chinese Educational Mission visited the Centennial Exhibition a month later, they became one of the attractions, touring the grounds in loose Chinese jackets and cloth shoes, their long queues hanging down their backs from beneath jaunty Western-style boaters. Their schoolwork was on display in the Connecticut pavilion, and each boy had the chance to shake hands with President Grant.

The girls might have been overlooked entirely, had it not been for the presence of Kiyonari Yoshida, the Japanese minister, who joined the Lanman party staying at the home of Octavius Perinchief, a forty-minute drive from the exhibition. The Perinchief house became an informal Japanese headquarters that summer, with members of Japan's Centennial delegation coming to pay their respects to Yoshida and his wife. The bicultural group made repeated visits to the exhibition and spent afternoons discussing its marvels, with Yoshida and his colleagues joining the girls on the Perinchiefs' lawn for croquet. Makoto Fukui, the head of the Centennial delegation, was bemused by the gargantuan spectacle of the exhibition: "The first day crowds come like sheep, run here, run there, run everywhere. One man start, one thousand follow. Nobody can see anything, nobody can do anything. All rush, push, tear, shout, make plenty noise, say damn great many times, get very tired, and go home."

Ume was less critical. "The Main Building is one third of a mile long, and is the most interesting of all the parts," she wrote to a friend in Georgetown. "The main entrance has over the door an organ, the largest in the United States." The Japanese department in the Main Building had "bronzes, laquer-ware, and china of greatest variety and splendor," Ume noted with the same intrigued curiosity as any American spectator, and Machinery Hall was "quite wonderful." If the Centennial Exhibition inspired national pride in Ume, that sentiment was at least as American as it was Japanese. But after several visits, she began to see Fukui's point: "After all, it is very tiresome work to walk about so much, looking at the things." The heat and the crowds took their toll: in the wake of the Philadelphia trip, Ume came down with typhoid fever, her only serious bout with illness during her years with the Lanmans.

THE FOLLOWING SPRING, in April 1877, Sutematsu graduated from Hillhouse High School. As at Miss Abbott's School, the students who received diplomas from Hillhouse were mostly female; the boys in the class had departed to prepare for the exams that would admit them to college. The commencement exercises were elaborate, with students speaking on "Dickens' Pictures of English Home Life," "The Turkish Question," and "The Woman of the Past, the Present, and the Future," among other topics, and interludes of music by Mendelssohn, Haydn, and Handel. The class of '77 had composed its own graduation song, a sentimental farewell to friends and teachers expressing a hope that God might "crown every life with richest love." Sutematsu was the only girl in the class who would go on to earn a college degree.

Graduations can give graduates an inflated sense of their own maturity. "I went to see Miss Abbott last evening, and I am glad I did," wrote Rebecca Bacon to her stepmother in high dudgeon that summer. It had just come to her attention that Sutematsu and Shige intended to spend some of their summer vacation on Long Island, at the beach in Southampton. "This enterprise, I find, is planned by the two Japanese girls on their own unassisted resposibility [sic]," she scrawled, her indignation evident in misspellings, underlined words, and uncharacteristic exclamation points. "The way in which the children have arranged it shows at once their intention to direct things for themselves and their incapacity to do it," Rebecca continued. The plan, she reported, was for the girls to

go *by themselves* to Southampton, where they intended to put up at a Hotel!!! They protested—or Stemats did—that they were quite competent to do it—"oh yes, *with* Shige"! for company—or talk of that kind. Miss A very promptly shut down on *that*—she told Stemats that she had no idea that Mrs. Bacon would allow her to go to a Hotel in that way; and that if she would, she herself would not permit Shige to do it . . . Now it is plain that Stemats is getting "too big for her breeches" and ought to be made to see that because she is an inexperienced child she does wrong to herself not to consult those who have her in charge.

Burdened as she was with the care of elderly parents and dependent siblings, all to be managed on a budget that did not stretch to frivolous beach trips, Rebecca's pique was not hard to understand. "I do not think it best for her to go to Southampton," she closed. "Miss A told me that yesterday Shige heard that Mrs. Lanman & Ume were to spend the summer there." That was the last straw, apparently—though the Lanmans were obvious chaperones for Sutematsu and Shige, Rebecca must have balked at the irksome image of Sutematsu spoiled by the indulgent Mrs. Lanman.

In the end, Sutematsu went, with the Japanese embassy forwarding a check for fifty dollars to cover expenses. The days of her dependence on the Bacons were coming to an end.

"MOST OF US IN Japan are radicals," wrote a student who used the nom de plume of "Stranger" in the inaugural issue of the *Gleaner*, published by Hillhouse High School students. "In this century of science and civilization, we don't like to live the life of the Middle Ages. We like changes and modern improvements."

It is likely that "Stranger" was Sutematsu. Though four boys from the Chinese Educational Mission were her schoolmates, she was the only Japanese student at Hillhouse at the time. The subject matter, too, seems to resonate with her experience. Kenjiro had done his work well: his sister may have come of age in America, but she still identified herself as a daughter of Japan. And despite Japan's determined leap toward Western civilization and enlightenment, there remained certain ideas too radical for a daughter of Japan to take seriously. "One is women's rights," Stranger declared. "We don't believe that woman was made to preside over a political assembly, or to pronounce judgement on the bench, or to ascend the pulpit and discourse on theology." Not that Susan B. Anthony or Elizabeth Cady Stanton were advocating goals as lofty as these, but their brand of extremely public activism in the service of equality for women made Sutematsu decidedly uncomfortable.

The other arena in which Japanese tradition triumphed over Western ways, Stranger continued, was the training of children. "We don't believe in children's independence," wrote the girl whose own family had sent her halfway around the world at the age of eleven. "In Japan children are taught to obey their elders, and to believe that the way of their parents' is always better and wiser than their own." She had obeyed, and continued to believe. That she was now more fluent in English than Japanese and cramming hard for college entrance examinations was a paradox she seemed not to see. No daughter of Japan had ever held a college degree, or dreamed of earning one. In heeding her empress's mandate to be educated, Sutematsu was leaving the way of her elders forever.

EVEN IN AMERICA, higher education for women was an idea in its infancy. Only a tiny handful of women's institutions—Wellesley, Smith, Vassar—had actually received charters as colleges, and of these, only Vassar had been admitting students for more than a decade. Catherine Bacon happened to pay a visit to Vassar, in Poughkeepsie, New York, several years after its opening. "I have never seen such a wonderful place as this college is, so quiet and at night after ten o'clock, there is something very striking, almost awful in the silences, when you remember that four hundred human beings are under the same roof," she wrote to her husband.

Matthew Vassar had no formal education. Building his family's modest brewery into the nation's largest, he took his rightful place among the Poughkeepsie elite while still in his thirties. In 1861, approaching the age of seventy and eager to invest in his own immortality, he placed a tin box containing $408,000—half his fortune—before the handpicked board of Vassar Female College, an institution that did not yet exist.

His family thought he was mad, but Vassar was firm. "I considered that the mothers of a country mold the character of its citizens, determine its institutions, and shape its destiny," he told his new trustees. "Next to the influence of the mother, is that of the female teacher, who is employed to train young children at a period when impressions are most vivid and lasting."

Vassar Female College was unlike any existing institution of higher learning, most notably because all of its students lived together in a single grand edifice: the spectacular Main Building, five hundred feet wide and five stories high, "heated by steam, lighted with gas, ventilated in the most perfect manner, and supplied throughout with an abundance of pure soft water." The building had its own elevator, along with a chapel, a library, an art gallery, lecture halls, and faculty apartments. Approached by a stately avenue lined with still-diminutive evergreens, it dominated the landscape. Observers compared it to the Palais des Tuileries in Paris.

"I think of Alice constantly & wish she might be able to come here[,] for I have never seen any thing more delightful, than the arrangements for health and out of door pleasures, and any body with the will, has opportunities for culture not offered I think, in any other place," Catherine marveled when she visited. "I mean for girls," she added.

As it turned out, the Bacons could not afford to send Alice to college. But in September of 1878, the opening of Vassar's fourteenth academic year, Sutematsu Yamakawa and Shige Nagai moved into the Main Building, their tuition paid by the Japanese government. They were the first nonwhite students to enroll. Shige would be a special student in the music department, and Sutematsu had been accepted for the full four-year baccalaureate degree.

Sutematsu had grown up with Alice for a sister, and matched her in ambition and ability. She rose to any challenge that presented itself. Vassar, the first of the group of women's colleges that would later be known as the Seven Sisters, claimed to offer women the same education that Yale and Harvard offered young men. In this, at least, Sutematsu had no qualms about claiming her equal right.

Vassar's student accommodations were elegant, with carpets and rockers, upholstered sofas and wall-mounted bookshelves, and imposing bedsteads carved of black walnut, wide enough for two girls to share. Servants kept the rooms tidy, and a formidable "lady principal" kept the girls in line. There were indoor bathrooms on each floor, and students were required to bathe twice a week. Each day ended with chapel after dinner, and Bible class and a longer service were held on Sundays. Meals were taken in the dining hall, where each girl had a regular place and provided her own napkin. For recreation, girls could stroll the gravel paths of the two-hundred-acre campus, go boating or skating on the lake, and visit the college's own bowling alley. Twenty minutes of quiet privacy were enforced twice a day, and it was recommended that students use that time for prayer. Everyone got up at 6:30, and lights-out was at ten. Board and tuition was four hundred dollars per year.

Vassar was a little world unto itself, and its professors formed the pantheon of deities. Truman Backus, head of the English department, riveted and inspired the girls with his youth and passion, both for literature and for current affairs. "He waked us up and kept us awake and we never wanted to miss a class for fear we should miss something," remembered one student. "He made us do our own thinking and that is the mark of a true teacher." Others seemed more interested in looking at him than listening to him. "You should see his Cassius-like proportions," gushed one girl to her mother. "'Long, and lank and brown as is the ribbed sea-sand,' and above all his keen blue eyes."

If Professor Backus was dazzling, the Dutchman Henry Van Ingen, head of the art department, was dear. Gentlemanly and approachable, he put every girl at ease with his quiet humor while holding them to his own high standard. When one student, copying a Raphael cherub, balked at completing the nude figure, Van Ingen was firm: "What's the matter? Finish it up! Put in everything you see. What the Lord made you don't need to be ashamed of." The girls adored him. "I expect to talk about him in every letter," wrote one. "He is our oasis in a sea of troubles—to mix metaphors."

Most memorable of all was Miss Maria Mitchell, astronomer. (At Vassar, male professors were addressed as "Professor"; female faculty were considered merely teachers and referred to as "Miss.") The first building to be completed on the Vassar campus was the Observatory—a trim, two-story brick building crowned with a dome and equipped with a powerful telescope—and from the college's inception Miss Mitchell claimed it as her domain. Stout, squat, and square-jawed, her hair styled in incongruously dainty ringlets, she cut an unforgettable figure. She had discovered a comet, which was named for her, and she counted among her personal friends all the notable women of the day, including Julia Ward Howe and Elizabeth Cady Stanton. She had no patience for etiquette or the ninnies who fretted over it.

Miss Mitchell's blunt candor discomfited many, but she was as unfiltered with praise as with criticism. Many a new girl took heart from her cheerful "How are you getting on?" during the first weeks of term. "Learn as if you will live forever; live as if you will die tomorrow" was her motto, and she insisted that female faculty be recognized for their accomplishments alongside the men. She was famous for her "dome parties," at which those lucky enough to receive an invitation enjoyed charades, strawberries and cream, and Miss Mitchell's own poetry, composed for the occasion. She knew, though, that even her most gifted students were unlikely to choose the life of a celibate scientist. At one party she offered this verse to her guests:

> *Who lifting their hearts to the heavenly blue*
> *Will do woman's work for the good and true;*
> *And as sisters or daughters or mothers or wives*
> *Will take the starlight into their lives.*

Reaching for the stars was lonely work. Vassar's students may have been pioneers in higher education for women, but after graduation most of them would dedicate their lives to marriage and motherhood, not scholarship.

ALL FRESHMEN TOOK Latin, math, and natural history; to this, Sutematsu's first-year schedule added English composition, German, and elementary drawing. Shige, enrolled as a special student in the School of Music, studied music history and theory, voice, piano, and organ. She also took English composition and French, and a little math in her first year (arithmetic had been a weak spot on her entrance exam). For the first time since those initial months in Washington, the two girls lived together and, at Sutematsu's insistence, added one more subject to their course of study:

Japanese. Every day they would retire to their room for an hour to chat in their mother tongue.

Though she submitted loyally to her friend's enforced language practice sessions, Shige would much rather have been out enjoying herself. Where Sutematsu was studious and elegant, Shige was excitable and full of fun. As a student she was not particularly distinguished, but she was beloved: indispensable at candy pulls and sleigh rides, or when someone gave a "spread" and ordered ice cream and cake from town. She loved to dance; her rendition of the Highland fling rendered her classmates helpless with laughter. And when they were laid up in the infirmary, it was Shige who came with get-well wishes. "I have no memory of an hour's indisposition at Vassar that I did not hear the click, click of Singhi's [*sic*] funny little walk as she came down the corridor bringing me a pitcher of lemonade and unlimited sympathy," wrote one friend.

Shige was a regular performer at college concerts, and her interpretations of Schubert, Mendelssohn, and Mozart were always greeted with warm applause; notices in the *Vassar Miscellany* praised her spirited expressiveness. The well-regarded musician and scholar Frederick Ritter, native of Strasburg, headed the School of Music, and Shige became his student. Though she studied the canon of European classical music, she did not forget the melodies of her childhood. "Japanese arias given me by Miss Shige Nagai," reads a note scribbled in Ritter's hand at the top of a sheaf of hand-notated staff paper.

Sutematsu cultivated a different image: graceful but reserved, intellectual, ambitious. She excelled at English and contributed highly polished essays to the *Miscellany*. She projected an air of cosmopolitanism. To her classmates she looked "like a beautiful Jewess of a poetic type"—less alien, though still exotic. Shige, on the other hand, "was broadly and indubitably Japanese." While Shige frolicked at blindman's buff, Sutematsu honed her chess game and beat all her teachers at whist. Another English instructor, Helen Hiscock, described "a sense of reserve power" in the tall, slender girl. "When the class-room was depressed by

that 'sleepiness' which experienced teachers dread, Stematz* could con-
found her languid American classmates with a brilliant recitation in literature or logic."

The only time anyone ever saw a flush of excitement on Sutematsu's
calm face was at the college post office, where from time to time she
received a letter that had traveled farther than any girl in Poughkeepsie—
except Shige—had ever dreamed of going. It might be from Kenjiro in
Tokyo, full of politics and international affairs. Or it might even be from
Russia. Sutematsu was not the only girl in her family who had been sent
abroad—one of her older sisters, Misao, was in St. Petersburg. Separated
for most of their lives, the two sisters shared little common experience and
no written language: Misao's life was lived in French. When a letter from
this distant sister arrived, Sutematsu convened an informal council of her
friends—some to help compose an appropriate letter in reply, others to put
it into decent French. Helping Sutematsu was so much more entertaining
and exotic than writing their own letters home.

Just as Shige and Ume had always deferred to Sutematsu as their leader,
her classmates soon looked to her as well. By the end of her first year she
had been elected president of her class for the year to come. "I believe it
was on account of her studiousness that she was appointed, or it may have
been because she was a favorite, I do not know which," fourteen-year-old
Ume wrote to her mother in Tokyo, betraying perhaps a touch of envy.
The accolades had to this point been mostly hers.

When she returned as a sophomore, Sutematsu's new office required
her to address the incoming freshmen at the Sophomore Party, a duty she
discharged with notable grace. She was invited to join the Shakespeare
Society, reserved for those of literary attainment. Her marks were among
the highest in the class, and her company was coveted. Each year the college observed Founder's Day, a holiday in honor of Matthew Vassar's

---

* Though her New Haven circle always wrote "Stemats," the newly fledged college girl
signed herself "Stematz" and continued to do so for the rest of her life.

birthday; in her junior year Sutematsu was named marshal for the event and led the festivities in Japanese dress. There was something of the fairy tale about this tall, dark girl who insisted she wasn't a princess: who among the other girls had ever needed to dispel a rumor like that?

The largest student organization on campus was the Philalethean Society, "Lovers of Truth," founded originally as a literary club. By the time Sutematsu and Shige arrived, the group was responsible for most of the entertainment on campus: recitations, lectures, music, and especially comic dramas. (Love of truth did not extend to trousers; girls playing male roles wore false mustaches but men's clothing only as far as the waist, over their usual long skirts.) Though Sutematsu refrained from taking the stage in a dramatic role, her name did appear on evening programs in other ways. "Miss Yamakawa's essay was perhaps the most enjoyable of the exercises," the *Vassar Miscellany* reported in the fall of 1880. "She told us of life in a Japanese household, and by her vivid description of some of the scenes of her childhood easily held the attention of all." Who could match the romance of Sutematsu's lost childhood world, where "the sacred lotus spread its broad, shield-like leaves" across the surface of an ornamental lake, "no profane shoes were allowed to make their defacing marks" on the soft paleness of the tatami-matted floors, and a small army of pages, maids, gardeners, and gatekeepers kept the expansive compound running smoothly?

DEPARTURE FOR VASSAR had not severed Sutematsu and Shige's earlier friendships. During their three-month summer vacations they returned to New Haven or traveled to cooler destinations, often in the company of Ume and the Lanmans. Charles Lanman had made it a decades-long habit to spend part of the summer on Block Island, a pristine spot off the coast of Rhode Island. The Lanmans stayed at the Ocean View Hotel, among the most lavish resorts in New England, where the girls shared veranda strolls and evening card parties with generals and judges, politicians and writers—the cream of Gilded Age society.

Ume delighted in the company of the older girls on these trips. Ocean bathing was a favorite activity, especially for Sutematsu, "who is a fine swimmer," Ume wrote admiringly, "and is perfectly at home in the water." Lanman took the girls driving to the cliffs at the island's southern end, where they could gaze at the waves foaming over the rocks. On one memorable evening they were invited for a moonlight sail. Ume recounted the scene for her mother: "The night was very still, and there was no breeze, so we went on very slowly. The reflection of the moon on the water was very beautiful, and as we went on, several persons began to sing songs of all kinds, which sounded very sweetly."

In June of 1881, Ume traveled to Poughkeepsie for commencement. The ten years granted the girls by the Japanese government were drawing to a close, and though Sutematsu and Ume had successfully petitioned for one-year extensions to complete their respective college and high school degrees, for Shige three years of college was enough. Her health was uncertain; her eyes were giving her trouble. She had earned a certificate in music from Vassar. And Sotokichi Uriu was graduating from the Naval Academy at Annapolis and returning to Japan.

Shige had never lost touch with the boy who had lived across the street in Fair Haven. Uriu had even come to Vassar once, part of a contingent of cadets invited to supply dance partners at a Vassar fête. He made his way to Poughkeepsie again that June. His life and Shige's had followed similar paths, ones that diverged profoundly from those of nearly every other Japanese on earth. It was becoming clear to both of them that the road forward was one they might walk together.

The close of the school year at Vassar comprised several acts: the president's baccalaureate address; a musical soiree, at which Shige and the other five music school graduates were the featured performers; Class Day, at which the seniors passed the torch to the juniors; and finally commencement. As Shige took her place with the graduates that year, and Sutematsu had her own responsibilities with the junior class, Ume, feeling quite grown-up, assumed the role of hostess at the festivities, finding seats for Shige's guests, including Uriu. "The girls say I was very convenient,"

Ume wrote to Mrs. Lanman. "I was on my feet all day going here & there, playing the agreeable & going to bed late, getting up early and seeing everything, that I felt utterly worn out."

At commencement, the graduates took the front rows of the chapel and the younger classes filled the galleries as Shige's teacher, Professor Ritter, played an organ voluntary. The centerpiece of the program was a debate between two seniors "as to whether the negro is doomed or not." The speaker for the affirmative declared that "wherever an inferior and superior race were brought together the inferior succumbed and went into servitude." Her opponent, though holding out more hope for the future of the black man, opened her remarks with "flat head, flat nose, and thick lip" and allowed as how "it could not be expected he would emerge from slavery with high ideas of literature and art."

If anyone suffered a moment of discomfort at the airing of this topic in the presence of Shige, Sutematsu, and their guests, it went unrecorded. In most minds, these polished college girls were in a separate racial category altogether: colored, to be sure, but also talented, dutiful, and deserving— a credit to their progressive (if still heathen) nation, as well as to Vassar. "It is evident from their actions that the president and faculty desire much to get me," Ume wrote, "but I guess they won't." One more year was all the Japanese government had granted.

BY OCTOBER, SHIGE was in San Francisco, ready to embark on the steamer *Oceanic*, bound for Japan. The city that had gawked at her nearly a decade earlier was now admiring, if still faintly patronizing. "Through her connection with the Abbott family she came into close association with other famous literary families of New-England, and imbibed the spirit as well as the habits and customs of those with whom she lived," reported the *San Francisco Chronicle*. "She is now a graceful girl, with petite figure, bright and intelligent face, and polished but unaffected manners, dressing prettily in American costume." A "thorough New-England girl in all her instincts," she offered a ringing valedictory comment:

My country will never become advanced until her women and mothers
are educated, and our women will never, as a class, be educated so long
as they marry so early, for the years from 15 to 20 they should spend
in school.

She made no mention of what she planned to do with her American education. She was twenty, and she had studied hard; by her own logic, she
was free to marry. Daunting though it might be to return to the land she
had last seen as a ten-year-old, her intended was waiting for her. Though
it had always been the tradition in samurai families to arrange appropriate
marriages between young people who had barely met, Shige would marry
a man of her own choosing. She sailed with more excitement than dread,
eager to join Sotokichi Uriu and embark on a new phase of her life, perma-
nently partnered by a husband uniquely able to understand her.

She was not the only Japanese female on board. Her companion for the
journey was a young girl named Shiori Louisa Wakayama, about the same
age as Shige had been when she first sailed for America—and her story
was a strange echo of Shige's own.

The girl was the daughter of Norikazu Wakayama, a member of the
Iwakura Mission with whom Shige had traveled to America in 1872.
While visiting New York with the embassy, Wakayama had stayed in a
boardinghouse run by a Jamaican-born woman named Julia Shanahan,
a divorcée "of Spanish descent, black eyed, stylish and well educated."
Mrs. Shanahan had followed Wakayama to Japan shortly after his departure. Three years later she returned to Brooklyn with his daughter in tow.
She had agreed, she said, to educate the girl in America, with Wakayama
paying her the lavish sum of a thousand dollars per annum. Years had
passed, the money had ceased to arrive, and then Wakayama brought suit
to reclaim his daughter. Despite a tearful appearance by the distraught
girl on the witness stand, the judge had ruled in her father's favor, and
now Shiori Louisa was on her way back to Japan, entrusted to Shige's care
for the journey.

The daily papers had covered the dispute avidly that summer. "When it came time for Louisa to part from Mrs. Shanahan, whom she calls 'Mamma,' she was greatly affected," reported the *New-York Tribune*. Though the papers were discreet, it seems clear that Mrs. Shanahan was Shiori Louisa's mother. "But for her queer little almond-shaped eyes she would readily have passed for an American girl," noted the *New York Times*, with "creamy skin, jet-black hair, and sweet, shy face, presenting physically a marked contrast to the usual type of Japanese girl, being large and nobly developed." Her father's country was notoriously wary of half bloods, and she spoke no Japanese. Shige, struck by the weird symmetry of their lives, must have been a comfort to her—and sighed in private relief at the relative security of her own situation.

As Shige sailed for Japan, Sutematsu returned to Vassar for her senior year. She missed her roommate's warm presence. "I think of Shige very often and wonder what she is doing so far away," she wrote to Ume. "I would give anything to know how she felt as she landed and met her friends." Ume had nearly completed her high school degree at the Archer Institute, a small secondary school for the daughters of Washington's elite; Mrs. Rutherford B. Hayes, wife of the president and a personal friend of Mrs. Archer, attended the closing exercises each June to present the medals and diplomas. Ume had continued to win the praise of all who taught her. Archer's Bavarian music master deemed her "an ambitious persevering & truly polite pupil—Her progress compares favorably with that of our European & American girls of her age."

Alone at Vassar and four years closer to adulthood, Sutematsu envied Ume. "If I could see you I should so like to have a regular old talk with you," she wrote from her dormitory. "I must manage to come down. Dear me how nice it will be to sit by that open fire in Mrs. Lanman's parlor. It makes me blue to think of the contrast between what is there and what is here. It is an awful wet day and there is nothing cheerful about anything here. I wish I was with you now. It makes me home-sick to think of Mrs. Lanman's house with all the comforts and luxuries."

Shige was thinking of Georgetown too, despite the joy and excitement of her return to Japan. She was officially engaged to Sotokichi Uriu, and reunited with her family: her older brother Takashi Masuda, who had steered her toward America so many years ago, was now president of the Mitsui Trading Company, which would soon come to dominate Japanese trade. But when Shige wrote to Adeline Lanman from Tokyo, her longing for "the past happy days" saturated every page. "I cannot, I must not, I will not go back to those days in reality, for God has given me to teach others the bright example which you and other American friends have shown me. I am a child to learn no longer, I am a teacher, every one comes to me to know what to do . . . and I am old in their eyes, if I cannot feel old myself," she wrote. "I came in the right time. I feel sure that with God's help I can do some good." But beneath her brave words was a homesickness more acute than Sutematsu's rainy-day blues. "I long now to be with you in your bright cheerful parlor to kiss Mr. Lanman's bearded cheek, to listen to Ume's nonsense, to hear the crackle of the burning timber from your bright hearth, to see your quick movement, always busy for some one's comfort, O! Mrs. Lanman."

Shige was careful to keep her letters to Vassar lighthearted, but they made Sutematsu uneasy nonetheless. Her friend was about to marry a man whose glittering career as a naval officer was all but assured. Though Shige wrote of the bewilderment of returning to a world now every bit as alien as America had once been, her happiness bubbled through; though there was dismay at forsaking the freedoms of a college girl for the constraints of a Japanese bride, there was also delight. "Bring lots of buttons," she wrote cheerfully, skipping nimbly past the larger questions she knew her friend faced. Whether or not Shige managed to find meaningful work in the service of women's education in Japan, her position in Japanese society, at least, was secure. But how did one go about reentering Japanese society as a single woman, one determined to work and not to marry? Sutematsu's classmates couldn't help noticing her uncharacteristic moodiness that year.

There was little time for gloom, though. Sutematsu was now president of the Philalethean Society, organizing meetings and dramatic productions on top of her classes in chemistry, composition, geology, history, philosophy, literature, and Greek. She also found time to instruct the Vassar community on her nation's recent political history. "In spite of modern sources of information," she wrote in the *Vassar Miscellany* that year, "most Americans seem to have the vaguest idea about the political or the social condition of the Island Empire." She followed this assertion with an essay that neatly summarized events from the heyday of the shoguns through the rise of the Meiji leadership. Kenjiro would have been proud.

AT CHRISTMASTIME SUTEMATSU returned to New Haven, where all thoughts of her studies and her future were suddenly banished by grief: on Christmas Eve of 1881, at the age of seventy-nine, Leonard Bacon died. His wife and his three youngest children were at his bedside, along with Sutematsu and Tan Yaoxun, the Chinese boy known from Colebrook summers, now a junior at Yale. It was Tan who ran for the doctor that night, but he was too late.

Two days later, Tan and Sutematsu stood with the family at Bacon's graveside. Noah Porter, Yale's president, was struck by this visible testament to Bacon's unusually large heart. "Could he have foreseen that among the multitude of devout men who followed him to his burial these representatives would be present from China and Japan, as members of his own household and of the household of faith, he would have said, in anticipation: 'I shall not have lived in vain,'" Porter wrote in his obituary.

Leonard Bacon had never faltered in his support of these two young people, whose foreignness had not prevented them from feeling like members of his family. Though the Chinese government had recalled its students, fearing the influence of Christianity, Bacon saw to it that Tan remained at Yale, raising funds from his own friends for Tan's support. "I have never expressed to you nor to Dr. Bacon nor to Nellie & Alice my gratitude for every comfort I have received at your hands because all these kindnesses were so much like home love and care that I could not do it," Tan wrote in a condolence letter to Catherine.

Back at Vassar after the funeral, Sutematsu was pleased to receive a photograph of Bacon as a keepsake from Catherine. "It is such a perfect likeness that every time I look at it I feel as if Dr. Bacon was speaking to me. It stands on my desk just above my head as I sit to read or write, and as I look up, I am reminded of that noble and beautiful life, which had done so much for me," she wrote to Catherine. "I am sure it will be a great help to me to have the picture[,] for when I look at it I can not but wish to be good and true as he would wish to have me to be."

Her foster father was gone, her years in America nearly done. But the mail that winter brought heartening reminders of what lay in store: a letter from her sister in St. Petersburg, enclosing a pearl ring and the news that she would be returning to Tokyo in April; and another from Shige. "I was nearly wild when I saw the well known handwriting and the envelope was torn up with lightening [*sic*] rapidity and its contents devoured with the greatest speed," Sutematsu wrote to Catherine Bacon. With Shige's letter was a present: a warm quilted hood, blue with a red lining. "I find it very useful in these cold piercing days when I go coasting or skating," she wrote.

ALL TOO SOON it was commencement time again. Class Day, June 13, was glorious, the trees in front of the Main Building dressed up with ribbons in the college colors of rose and silver, representing the dawn of women's education breaking through the gray of the past. In the chapel, the thirty-nine members of the class of 1882 listened with rapt attention to their chosen class representatives: an Orator, a Historian, and a Sibyl, whose job it was to deliver affectionate prophecies for each graduate.

Sutematsu received her full share of both giggles and respect. The Sibyl predicted that their Japanese classmate would be mightily relieved to return to a land where friends didn't express their friendship quite so physically (Sutematsu was notorious for her discomfort when greeted with an enthusiastic embrace). "However[,] she does not have much rest," the prophecy continued, "as the following slip from a Tokio newspaper will testify: 'The leader of reform among women in Japan is Stematz Yamakawa. She is of the élite of Japanese society, and is both stylish and popular.'" Her classmates nodded in recognition as the Sibyl concluded: "Her 'little brown hands' have almost more than they can do now, managing her boarding school. But she is doing good work, and is making better use than most of us of her Vassar education."

Emerging blinking into the sunshine, the seniors completed the ritual burial of their class records under their chosen tree and passed the ceremonial spade to the juniors with due solemnity. That evening, before joining their families and teachers in the dining hall for music and dancing, they gathered for their class supper, a last chance to share the intimacy of four years together. Seated at a single long table, they howled with laughter at the final toasts—"Ironic and Otherwise"—devised for each girl. Sutematsu, smirking good-naturedly, was named "Most Careless."

The weather held for commencement the next morning. At 10:30 the graduates took their seats in the front rows of the chapel, surrounded by alumnae and guests; the Japanese consul in New York, Saburo Takaki, was present with half a dozen of his staff. His government had provided Sutematsu with lavishly embroidered silk for her graduation dress, and the audience murmured as she stood before them, one of ten senior speakers.

Consul Takaki was not disappointed. Where her fellow orators had chosen as their themes "The Conscience of Science," "The Decline of Speculative Philosophy," or the relative merits of Alexander II, Sutematsu addressed "British Policy toward Japan," condemning the unequal trade agreement that persisted between the two nations. The speech was "the most interesting of the whole series," declared the *Poughkeepsie Eagle*, "an eloquent plea for the independent nationality of Japan." The *Chicago Tribune* called it "the most notable, as it was the most enthusiastically applauded oration of the day." Sutematsu had proved herself as canny as she was eloquent: without directly criticizing her adopted country, whose policies toward Japan were similarly patronizing, she had made her point nonetheless. The original goal of the Iwakura Mission—treaty revision—remained incomplete.

News of Sutematsu's achievement reached all the way to Japan. "Never before had a foreigner's speech moved an American audience so much," trumpeted the *Asahi Shimbun*. "Miss Yamakawa brought great honor not only to herself, but to her country." Tomomi Iwakura and his ambassadors, many now among the most prominent figures in Japan, never imagined they would read such news of the little girl who had traveled with them.

AND THEN THERE was nothing left to do but pack and fill out the form headed "To Students Leaving College": "By what train do you wish to leave Poughkeepsie? Do you wish the College to take your baggage to depot? If so, how many and what Pieces?" For thirty-eight members of the graduating class, the train would take them home—to teach, perhaps, but most likely to marry. For Sutematsu, it would be the first leg of a much longer journey.

In her graduation portrait, Sutematsu stands with regal calm, dazzling in embroidered white silk. She is twenty-two—the same age as the empress behind the screen had been more than a decade before.

CATHERINE BACON HAD NOT made the trip to Poughkeepsie to see her foster daughter graduate; her health had not permitted it. At the end of July she was buried beside her husband in New Haven's Grove Street Cemetery. For the second time in her life, Sutematsu found herself without parents.

"I cannot realize the great change that has taken place," she wrote to Alice a few days after Catherine's death. "It has been like a terrible dream to me and though I keep thinking about it, I cannot possibly realize it. To you of course it must seem more real and I cannot but keep thinking of your changed life." But her beloved foster sister's new status as an independent adult created an opportunity. "Whichever way you decide to spend your winter," Sutematsu continued, "the time will not be very long for I hope very earnestly that you will be able to come out to Japan next spring. I don't know whether your relatives will approve of your taking such a step, but I hope your wish to work with me for the good of Japan may be realized. You can do much here I know, but your opportunity to sacrifice yourself for the sake of others is indeed endless in Japan."

Though the Bacons had not been able to send Alice to college, she had continued her studies independently. Radcliffe College would not be chartered until 1894, but Harvard had begun to offer special examinations for women in 1874. Administered in several cities, the tests were the same as those given to male applicants to Harvard College. A woman who earned a passing mark would receive a certificate from Harvard's president confirming her achievement. In 1881, Alice received certificates in three subjects. Her results won her the right to study with Harvard professors at the Society for the Collegiate Instruction of Women in Cambridge, familiarly known as the Harvard Annex. But there was no money for her tuition, and besides, she was needed at home: her oldest half sister, the capable Rebecca, had died just as Sutematsu left for Vassar, and Catherine was failing. Now, with Catherine gone, Alice was on her own. Once she had tidied her family's affairs, she was free to pursue a career. Indeed, she had no choice.

A new chapter, daunting and exhilarating, was beginning for both women, aligned in their assumption that their lives would be devoted to work, not family. Yes, a woman's highest calling was that of good wife and wise mother, but an educated woman could also fulfill her moral mission in the classroom, where she might have an even greater impact on the next generation. To both of these ambitious young women, marriage seemed unlikely, even undesirable, whereas together they might do great work in a land that seemed in desperate need of their skills.

There would be no summer vacation in the Litchfield Hills for Sutematsu that year. As departure loomed, she was determined to soak up any information that might be useful to an advocate for women's education. For the months of July and August, she enrolled at the Connecticut Training School for Nurses. Alice's oldest half brother, Francis Bacon, was a professor of surgery at Yale's medical school; his wife, Georgeanna, had nursed soldiers during the Civil War and written the definitive work on the subject: *A Handbook of Nursing for Family and General Use*. A decade earlier they had helped to found the nursing school, and they made it possible now for Sutematsu to spend her summer studying there.

"I am now in the diet kitchen and I find the work pretty hard," she wrote to Alice in Colebrook. "Still I suppose it is good for me to have to wash pots and shovel coal and scrub the floor . . . I make from two to three gallons of beef tea every day and about a gallon and a half of chicken soup.

Besides these I have to make custards, gruels, porridges, etc. It is of course very interesting but I don't like it so well as regular nursing."

As New Haven sweltered in the summer heat, Sutematsu indulged in daydreams of a life in Japan that looked suspiciously like the one she had enjoyed in New England, full of meaningful work, genteel recreation, and stimulating company. She and Alice would keep house together, chaperoned by Sutematsu's mother in Tokyo, and hosting whatever Bacon relatives or Vassar alumnae happened by. Alice would teach English; and Sutematsu, physiology and gymnastics. "You see we would live in American style if you like while we can [procure] Japanese things for my mother, or we could live half and half," Sutematsu imagined. "When the summer vacations come we might go north and visit the home of my childhood and further up to Yesso [Ezo, or Hokkaido] and see the Ainus since you are so much interested in ethnology."

Suspended for the summer between the American college girl she had been and the Japanese educational reformer she was determined to be, Sutematsu strove mightily to keep her eyes on a rosy future instead of peering down into the gulf that lay between. It wasn't easy. "Perhaps I am counting the chickens before they are hatched and building castles in the air," she mused more soberly. "Still it is pleasant to think about it when there is no harm done by it."

As the fall approached, postcards and letters flew between Sutematsu and her Vassar friends. "I hope I shall see you before I start for the far-off Orient," she wrote to her classmate Jessie Wheeler, sounding more like a missionary contemplating a sojourn among the heathen than a Japanese woman about to return to her native land. A week later her airy tone had sharpened, betraying a building anxiety: "Do you mean to say that you won't go through New Haven before the tenth of Oct.?" she scribbled to Miss Wheeler. "It is disgusting of you to put it off so late, when you know I want to see you so much . . . So hurry up."

Alice was packing up her life as well. She and her siblings had inherited the white clapboard house on Church Street, but money was tight, and renting the house would provide a little income. By the end of September

Sutematsu was chagrined to realize she would not be able to invite her Vassar friends to stay after all: "Every thing is already upside down and the whole house is in a state of confusion." With little left in New Haven to hold her, and with the promise of a future with Alice in Japan to sustain her, Sutematsu left New Haven for New York in October to meet Ume and begin their journey back.

UME, NOW SEVENTEEN, had received her high school diploma from the Archer Institute just as Sutematsu graduated from Vassar. Like many only children an avid reader, Ume had continued to excel in high school, adding Shakespeare and Wordsworth to the novels by Dickens and Scott that she loved to devour. "Miss Tsuda's progress in Latin, Mathematics, Physics, Astronomy, and French has been much in advance of her class, she having a clear insight into all the branches to which she has devoted herself," read her certificate from Archer.

After a decade as the adored foster daughter of the Lanmans, Ume had grown into a sprightly, accomplished, affectionate, and opinionated girl—a familiar face in Georgetown social circles. Her farewell party was covered by the press. "The regret for her departure is as general as it is genuine," reported the *Evening Critic*. But although Ume's memories of Japan had faded almost completely, her adopted country could not quite see her as an American. "Miss Tsuda is a very intelligent young girl, and while her face is of a decidedly national type, it is attractive, and even pretty. Her hair is a marvel of length and thickness, and is a real burden to the small head that carries its weight. She has completed her education at one of our best schools, and goes back home a really good English scholar."

The Lanmans and Alice accompanied Sutematsu and Ume for much of the journey west. In Chicago, Ume's foster parents made their reluctant farewells and entrusted the travelers to the care of J. D. Davis and his wife, missionaries returning to Japan. The little party continued west, marveling all over again at the sight of antelope herds and prairie dog towns from the windows of the train, and stopping in Cheyenne, Wyoming, where Alice at last said goodbye to the young woman she regarded as a sister.

The girls were unprepared for their effect on the residents of Cheyenne, a railroad town that only fifteen years earlier had been a blank space on the western edge of the Great Plains. Stares and whispers had always been part of their lives in America, but their intimate circles in Georgetown and New Haven and Poughkeepsie had long since ceased to find them exotic. In Cheyenne, they were curiosities all over again. Davis was in town to speak about his work in Japan; he had helped to build the first church in Cheyenne a dozen years earlier. Naturally, the minister hosting them assumed the Japanese girls in his care were part of the package. Before a large gathering of the town's various congregations at the Cheyenne Opera House, the minister, a Mr. Sanders, announced that Mrs. Davis would address the Ladies' Missionary Meeting the next day—as would one of the Japanese young ladies.

"I was thunderstruck," Sutematsu wrote indignantly to Alice from the train afterward. "I never heard of such a thing. I thought it was impertinent of Mr. Sanders to speak in that way when he had not said anything to us at all." It wasn't the public speaking that daunted her—she had dazzled the commencement audience at Vassar only a few months earlier; it was the idea that she was a spectacle, and that the public expected her to perform for them.

The people of Cheyenne wanted to hear from a real Japanese girl, but Sutematsu was entirely uninterested in sharing her intimate memories with strangers. "I did not know what to say," she wrote, "but Mrs. Davis suggested that I should speak of the summer of our coming to this country and also of what I expect to do on my return." If the ladies of the Missionary Meeting were looking for a personal account of the far-off Orient, they must have been disappointed.

The girls were the talk of the town. "Indeed we have been lionized since we came to Cheyenne," Sutematsu wrote with incredulity. "Actually a reporter came to interview us! Fortunately we were out so we escaped the ordeal." It was with some relief that they boarded the westbound train.

"The people were very hospitable and warm hearted, but rather trying as they were rather inquisitive."

Ume, less self-conscious, managed to find some humor in the naked stares. At one point in their journey, two "real Indians" boarded the train, settling in the dining car. The children seated near Ume and Sutematsu begged for permission to go look. "Their mother remarked it might not be polite or agreeable," Ume wrote, "whereupon I said that if Stematz and I would go, it would only be a fair exchange of free shows, as probably the Japanese are as great curiosities to the Indians as they are to us."

Onward to San Francisco, where they were hosted in Berkeley by Charles Lanman's friend John H. C. Bonté, the secretary of the Board of Regents of the University of California. Their stay was a whirl of entertainment, as Sutematsu reported breathlessly to Jessie Wheeler: "We have since we've been here been invited to two parties and there is to be one at this house tomorrow and we go to a what is called Junior Day on Saturday which consists of speaking by the students followed by dancing." This was more like it: California may have seemed like another world, with gardens full of blooming fuchsia and green peas and strawberries on the table in October, but the elite social life of a university town felt perfectly familiar. For the moment, Sutematsu and Ume put aside their thoughts of what lay ahead. The Bonté girls were good company. "We all climbed a tree yesterday," Ume wrote to Mrs. Lanman. "Stematz and I had a hard time to get down, and were laughing so much that we could hardly hold on."

From the moment they had parted in Chicago, Ume had begun writing reams of chatty letters home to Adeline Lanman at a prolific pace that she would maintain almost without pause for the next three decades. Younger than Sutematsu in more than just years, Ume reacted to her changing surroundings like the sheltered American young lady she was: with breezy strokes of startling insensitivity. "It is so strange to see so many Chinese here," she wrote from Berkeley.

In San Francisco we saw the street that leads to Chinatown and dirty enough it is. Miss Fannie [the Bontés' daughter] said it would be unsafe for any ladies to walk there without gentlemen. It is a horrid part of the city. All the servants that are employed here are Chinese, and such contrary things they are sometimes, leaving without any warning or any reason. They are generally honest, do not steal and are thrifty, but one has to be careful and watch them to see they are neat. Many of them do not mind telling lies. You may be thankful you have colored servants. If 'niggers are overrunning Washington,' it is nothing to the Chinese here.

Now it was Ume's turn to sound like a missionary. "They smoke opium and go regularly to those awful dens, and there seems to be no way to reach them and make them better."

The girls had arrived in San Francisco at a moment of acute racial tension. Anti-Chinese rioting had become commonplace: the Chinese workers who had built the transcontinental railroad were blamed for the depressed wages and sagging economy that followed the end of the Civil War and the slowing of the gold rush. Just five months earlier Congress had passed the Chinese Exclusion Act, suspending all Chinese immigration. Blithely unaware of any irony, Ume wrinkled her nose and wrote, "I hardly wonder at the people out here not wanting any more of these Chinamen." Were it not for her elegant clothes and her prominent chaperones, she might have been mistaken for one herself.

Before they sailed, one of the Japanese diplomats paid a call. "You know he talked very bad English, and we could not exactly make out [what he was trying to say]," Ume wrote. Gradually the girls understood that the man was worried about protocol: how would Sutematsu and Ume be compensating the Bontés for their hospitality? Shocked, the girls protested that their hosts had welcomed them as friends; it would be appalling to offer them money in return. "Whereupon he said he would instruct the government to send them a present. For this I am glad, but it seemed such a queer proceeding as it was our own private affair what we did or [where we] stayed. Well there are funny people in the world," Ume concluded. It was their first reminder of something Ume had allowed to drift to the back of her consciousness: she was an official representative of Japan in

America, and as far as the Japanese government was concerned, her affairs were also theirs.

San Francisco was a brief idyll, shadowed by the approach of their departure. On her last day in Berkeley, Ume took a break from her packing to write one more time. "I think I realize that I am really leaving America," she confided to Mrs. Lanman. "Before, I felt as if I were on a summer trip, but a long sea voyage is entirely different." Surrounded by trunks and piles of clothing, she gazed out the window and wondered whether she would ever return. "I am hoping against hope that tomorrow will be bright and sunshiny, for I want America to look its brightest," she wrote. "We have not had one gloomy day yet, and if tomorrow is, I shall be so sorry." But mindful of her reader, bereft and anxious back in Washington, Ume forced a smile. "Let everything rest in God's hands, and feel that whatever happens all is best," she instructed her foster mother.

The steamer *Arabic* left San Francisco on October 31. "Ume Tsuda and Stematz Yamakawa are now at sea," John Bonté wrote to the Lanmans the next day. "We have the profoundest respect and the warmest love for both of them, and I cannot tell which sentiment is the strongest. Few American young ladies could, in the same period, win so much love and esteem. We part with them with great reluctance."

"I EXPECT AFTER the first days of seasickness to enjoy the trip very much," Ume had written to Mrs. Lanman before they sailed. "It will be like a seashore sojourn."

It wasn't. Despite the lateness of the season, the *Arabic*'s captain chose the northern route, shorter but rougher. The elegant cane-and-walnut steamer chair Sutematsu and Ume had bought for sunbathing on deck went unused. Though the *Arabic*'s inbound journey from Yokohama to San Francisco had set a new record of thirteen days and twenty-one hours, the outbound trip dragged on for three weeks.

"The purser who has crossed this ocean fifty seven times says that he never had so rough a passage before," Sutematsu wrote to Alice. "Actually it has been so stormy that most of the time we could not sit, walk, sleep or eat with any comfort at all. Sometimes I had to hold on to my seat and all I could do was to try not to be thrown down and at night I have been kept awake because I dare not go to sleep for fear I should be flung out of my berth." Dishes crashed to the floor at every meal; trunks burst open and scattered their contents over the staterooms. And with their course charted just south of the Aleutian Islands, it was bitterly cold.

The company on board did not add much to their comfort. Of nineteen first-class passengers, thirteen were missionaries. "Although it is very pleasant to be with such good, staid people, I wish we had some young people who are not quite so quiet and good," Ume wrote when she was feeling well enough to hold a pen. The captain apparently agreed: "He says that the storms are due to the fact that there are so many missionaries on board this vessel," Sutematsu told Alice. "I presume he thinks they are so many Jonahs, but it is to be hoped that he will not propose to throw any of them overboard." Sutematsu had brought along a pack of cards, but she and Ume hesitated to play—the missionaries would not approve.

Aside from these discomforts, shipboard life was plush—and this time the girls could enjoy it. There were electric bells by the berths for calling the stewardess, tea and toast in bed, multiple courses at lunch and dinner, a well-stocked library, a ladies' lounge, a smoking room for the gentlemen, and "plenty of waiters & China boys" to bring whatever was needed. Most of the passengers, including the Davises, sat at the captain's table. The Japanese girls, along with a couple of younger unmarried travelers and a Chinese gentleman and his wife, were at the purser's table. Both Sutematsu and Ume took note of the mealtime pecking order, with the nonwhites excluded from the captain's company, but Ume shrugged it off: "It is much nicer at our table, for we laugh and talk, and it is very pleasant indeed."

Ume found the Chinese couple "the object of some curiosity." A Chinese passenger in first class was indeed a rarity. Built specifically to capitalize on the flood of Chinese emigrants over the previous three decades, the *Arabic* carried far more human cargo in steerage than in its limited first-class accommodations. Beneath the spacious staterooms where Sutematsu and Ume picked queasily at their tea and toast, hundreds of Chinese coolies, likewise returning to their native land, were enduring the journey under very different conditions.

As the *Arabic* pitched and yawed across the unusually turbulent Pacific with its unusually placid first-class passengers, Sutematsu and Ume had nothing but time in which to contemplate their uncertain futures. What did they know of Japan? Ume had the photographs her mother had sent with her eleven years earlier: her parents' house, a family portrait with her grandmother, a picture of herself and her mother hand in hand. She had been petted by Japanese dignitaries and had heard her foster father discussing the affairs of the Japanese legation at home.

But at seven she had been too young to retain many memories of her Japanese childhood, and by the time she had matured enough to take an interest in her native country, she had already begun to feel like an American girl. She had absorbed from the Lanmans a worldview steeped in Christian morality. Her attitude toward "the Japanese" was not far different from that of any of the young missionary women aboard the *Arabic*: curiosity, a determination to bring enlightenment to the unenlightened, and a healthy dose of trepidation. "We must not make enemies, or offend their taste, but conform as much as possible yet improve their customs & method of dressing, of society, etc. in our own little circles," Ume wrote. Mrs. Davis warned that conversion to Christianity in Japan was as yet far more common among the poor. "Hard to be thought ignorant or of inferior mind because we follow Him," Ume mused. "I think we know something at least of the difficulties, but do not imagine that either of us feels any differently from what we did—we still want to go, and were it ten times darker and gloomier we would not[,] if we could[,] turn back." Japan is a "new beautiful country," Ume stoutly declared to Mrs. Lanman. "Come and see me sometime soon and you will see me in my home so happy indeed," she wrote, whistling a cheerful tune to banish her fear. She no longer spoke a word of her mother tongue.

Sutematsu's understanding of Japan was far more sophisticated. Nearly twice Ume's age when she had left Japan, she carried with her indelible memories of her ancestral home, her extended family, and the traumatic defeat of her domain at the hands of the emperor's forces. Her brother Kenjiro had kept her understanding of the rapidly shifting political situation in Japan current. While Ume had become, at her core, an American girl, Sutematsu still identified herself as Japanese—an identity she occasionally found uncomfortable.

"Japan is no longer a land of mysteries," she had proclaimed to the members of the Philalethean Society during her junior year:

> But in spite of many travelers and numberless books and lecturers, only a few Americans know truly what Japan is. Not long ago an intelligent and well educated young lady asked me seriously if we had lakes and rivers. Another innocently inquired, "Do you have grave-yards in Japan?" . . . Perhaps the most intelligent query I have ever received was from a little girl of seven years, who, after asking whether we considered a dish of mice a rare delicacy, looked at me earnestly for a moment, and then asked gravely, "What makes you look so different from us? Is it because you are Japaned?"*

Sutematsu may have been irritated by the tactless ignorance of certain Americans, but after eleven years, and despite her bravado, Japan had in some ways become a land of mysteries to her as well. Yet it was still, paradoxically, hers:

> It is not to be wondered at, that Americans have such peculiar ideas about our country, considering how very different it is from other parts of the world. You say we do every thing upside down. We turn the leaves of a book from left to right; we write up and down instead of horizontally; we place the surname before the Christian name; and so on. There is no limit to the list of our oddities.

---

* "Japanning" referred to the exceptionally hard black lacquer prized on decorative objects imported from Japan.

Her tone is sardonic, but it masks a note of uncertainty. Sutematsu could no longer read or write in Japanese; the books whose pages she turned (from right to left) were all in English. She signed herself "Stematz Yamakawa," and not the other way round. She may have claimed Japanese "oddities" as her own, but they were not much more comfortable to her than to the thoughtless young ladies who exclaimed over them.

The rest of the essay, which Sutematsu titled "Recollections of Japanese Family Life," dwelled on childhood memories of her family's sprawling compound: the lotus blossoms, the spare and elegant rooms, the loyal servants. She was describing a world that had begun to disappear even before she sailed for America. Her family had lost everything in the Boshin War, and the old domains had been reorganized into prefectures just before she left Japan. In 1876 the Meiji government had abolished the samurai class entirely. The world of Sutematsu's childhood had been erased.

"Consequently, you must constantly make the distinction between the Old Japan where the feudal system, and the darkness of the Middle Ages still held sway," she instructed her readers confidently, "and the New Japan with telegraphs and railroads, banks and universities, and a government rapidly transforming itself into a limited monarchy." This was the Japan in which she would be making her future. Soon she would see it for the first time; as yet, it existed for her only in her imagination.

For a New Haven–raised Vassar graduate, however, Sutematsu's sense of Japan was startlingly accurate. In the essay on Japanese politics she had written for the *Vassar Miscellany* in her senior year, she followed her summary of Japan's transformation with a conclusion that acknowledged the uncertainty of Japan's future:

> What will be the end of these agitations no one ventures to predict. In fact, the people of Japan could be divided into three most diverse parties: first, those who are conservative, who believe in the ancient regime and who strenuously oppose the introduction of any new principle or foreign civilization; the second class are those who advocate reform but believe in slow and sure progress; the third class are thoroughly discontented

with the past and present and desire a change at any cost. Which of these is strong enough to overcome the other two, can not yet be decided.

As a woman whose life was being uprooted and transplanted in the service of her country for the second time, whose mind had been shaped by a culture most of her countrymen had never encountered, Sutematsu could only hope the first party would not prevail.

AND THEN THE skies cleared, the water turned deep blue instead of grim gray, and the port of Yokohama was only a day ahead of them. Sutematsu, never one to pour out her feelings, wrote in her last shipboard words to Alice only of the glorious weather, and that she felt "splendid except for a nasty cold." Ume, as usual, confided her innermost thoughts to Mrs. Lanman. "I am wild with joy and can hardly contain myself—next moment I am filled with strange misgivings," she wrote. "You can imagine my face as red as a beet from now onward, from excitement." She rushed about the ship, fixing in memory the wheelhouse, the kitchen, the steerage decks, and the officer's quarters. Scanning the waves, she spotted a school of porpoises. "They swam all around us and so close that we could see them under the water and as they leapt up we could see their whole lengths. All around us the water foamed with their spoutings and we watched them with interest and curiosity[,] glad indeed to see something alive, in the water enjoying themselves."

It was a good omen. "Tomorrow turns a new page in my life," Ume closed her letter. "May it be a good one." Whatever happened after the *Arabic* docked, Ume was determined to fulfill the expectations of her family and her country. In the years to come, only a very few would ever be privy to the doubts that plagued her. Below her signature she added a postscript: "This letter intended only for your & Mr. L's own reading."

Sutematsu and Ume lay awake most of their last night on board, talking until the wee hours in their shared stateroom. As dawn broke on Monday, November 20, 1882, they dozed at last, only to be woken by a voice shouting outside their door: "Land!" They dove into their clothes and raced each other up on deck, where the outline of mountains was emerging from the mist.

"How do you feel now, since you have seen your country?" someone asked.

"I cannot tell you how I feel," Sutematsu replied, "but I should like to give one good scream."

It was several more hours before the *Arabic* dropped anchor. She was soon surrounded by small craft churning out to meet her. Sutematsu gave them only an idle glance; the *Arabic* was several days late, and the uncertainty of their arrival would surely have kept any welcoming party away. But Ume's eyes were sharper: suddenly she gasped and pointed. On the deck of an approaching tugboat stood a knot of people frantically waving handkerchiefs. As it drew closer, the girls recognized the excited faces: Ume's father and sister, Sutematsu's sisters, and their dear Shige.

Eleven years earlier they had watched from the deck of a different steamer as the edge of an alien land approached. Now, that once-foreign place was the only home they knew. It was the coastline ahead of them that was alien.

PART

III

The standards of my own and
my adopted country differed so
widely in some ways, and my love
for both lands was so sincere, that
sometimes I had an odd feeling of
standing upon a cloud in space, and
gazing with measuring eyes upon
two separate worlds.

—ETSU INAGAKI SUGIMOTO,
A Daughter of the Samurai, 1926

*From left to right: Ume, Alice, Shige, and
Sutematsu, circa 1901.* (Courtesy Vassar College
Library Special Collections.)

THE TUG FULL OF eager faces soon pulled alongside the *Arabic*. The rough crossing was over at last; Sutematsu and Ume had only to step onto the smaller boat for the short ride to the Yokohama docks, and solid ground. Yet as they thanked the American officers and said goodbye to the ship to which they had been confined for three weeks, their relief was tempered with regret. The crew had been kind to them, and the *Arabic*, despite its discomforts, was at least a familiar space. Once they disembarked, they would truly leave America behind.

On the dock, their party was engulfed by eager jinrikisha men, "who though very polite were very persistent," Sutematsu wrote. She and Shige, unwilling to delay their reunion a moment longer, got into a double one, while the others rode singly. The last time Sutematsu had ridden in a jinrikisha, eleven years earlier, she had felt very small; now, sitting in what felt like an "overgrown baby-carriage and whirled away through the narrow streets, lined on either side with tiny houses, I felt as if I were visiting Lilliput." Ume, for her part, was determined to be delighted with everything Japanese. The strange conveyances were "so nice and comfortable," she wrote to Mrs. Lanman. "You can't imagine how nice."

Their first stop was the nearby home of Saburo Takaki, familiar to the trio from his years of service as Japanese consul in New York. He and his wife had joined the welcoming party and invited the travelers to lunch in Yokohama before they pushed on to their final destinations in Tokyo. Takaki's wife inquired as to whether Sutematsu and Ume would prefer Japanese or Western-style cuisine. Japanese, of course, they eagerly assured her. But as the food was served, there was a nervous pause. Would the new arrivals remember how to use chopsticks?

To everyone's surprise—not least their own—the two young women took up the unfamiliar utensils without faltering. "I ate the lunch as naturally as one who has never left the soil of the Mikado's empire," Sutematsu wrote with bemused relief. "It is a strange fact that skill in using the chopsticks seems to be inherited and the last thing to be forgotten by Japanese otherwise denationalized." Ume was especially heartened—here at least was one thing she still knew how to do—and basked in the approbation of her hosts. "I get along as well as anybody ever does with them," she told Mrs. Lanman. "They all say so."

After lunch they walked to the train depot. The rail line between Tokyo and Yokohama, not quite complete when they had left, was by now an unremarkable part of the landscape. An hour brought them to Tokyo's Shimbashi Station, not far from the Imperial Palace, where eleven more members of Ume's family were on hand to meet their train, bowing and smiling. Another crowd of jinrikisha men gathered. But here the group divided—Sutematsu heading northwest to her mother's house in the neighborhood called Ushigome; Ume, southwest to her father's farm in the suburb of Azabu. They were on their own again, and their reeducation in being Japanese was under way.

AFTER ONE MORE jolting hour in a jinrikisha, Sutematsu stepped down at the gate of the Yamakawa home. There was her mother, Toi, whose resolve to wait for the daughter she'd lost was at last rewarded. There was Kenjiro, looking taller and more dignified since Sutematsu had last seen him in New Haven six years earlier, standing beside a wife she had never met. Kenjiro was now a professor of physics at Tokyo Imperial University, a position hitherto held only by visiting Western advisers.

And there were her sisters: the eldest, Futaba, who lived half the week at the Women's Higher Normal School—Japan's only teacher-training school for women—where she supervised a dormitory; Misao, back from Russia and working as a French interpreter; and Tokiwa, with her husband and small son, who promptly burst into tears at the sight of this strange new aunt, with her bizarre clothing and shoes and hair. He was the only one who betrayed his feelings so noisily, however. Sutematsu was safe now from flamboyant American embraces. After eleven years of separation, the Yamakawas expressed the joy of reunion with Japanese restraint.

The house was crowded and busy—in addition to three generations of Yamakawas, there were three boarding students, a manservant, and three maids—but somewhat to Sutematsu's embarrassment, she found herself the object of everyone's concern. "They are so afraid I should get sick on account of the change of climate and clothing that they all devote themselves to me and I am in a fair way to become spoilt," she wrote to Alice. Specially ordered foreign food arrived three times a day from a nearby restaurant—a degree of special treatment that Sutematsu had never received in her life and that, to her relief, was short-lived. "After the first week I have been allowed to eat Japanese food with meat twice a day."

Another nephew, oldest brother Hiroshi's ten-year-old son, was also glad to see the celebrity status of his "American Aunt" begin to subside. Apple of his grandmother's eye, he had feared that Sutematsu's return might displace him in Toi's favor. "Oh, she is too big for Grandma's baby," he exclaimed with relief when they met. (Sutematsu, appalled at the way her mother indulged the boy, found him a nuisance.)

Sutematsu was grateful now for the enforced study sessions with Kenjiro in New Haven, and the hours of Japanese conversation with Shige at Vassar. Her Japanese, though rusty, was surprisingly serviceable. "As soon as I touched my native soil, my tongue seemed to be loosened," she wrote. Spoken fluency, at least, was rapidly returning; reading and writing would be another project entirely. With calm resolve, Sutematsu settled down to relearn her past. "My knees at this moment are aching as if they are coming to pieces," she wrote to Alice from the tatami-matted floor. "I am busy making Japanese clothes for myself."

SUTEMATSU AND UME spent their second night in Japan with Shige, at her brother's elegant home in Shinagawa. Ryo Yoshimasu, whose eye trouble had cut short her own American education, arrived for a brief and bittersweet reunion. "She does not show the ten years' difference in her looks," Ume wrote to Mrs. Lanman. "She seemed glad to see me and asked after you and Mr. Lanman." No one seemed to know what had become of Tei Ueda, the fifth girl. Beyond the curiosity of seeing the woman whose life had so briefly and intensely converged with theirs, however, the returnees had little to say to Ryo—and no truly comfortable language in which to say it.

Once Ryo departed, the conversation could flow more freely. There was so much to discuss. Having extended her engagement until her friends' return, Shige could wait no longer: she and Sotokichi Uriu would be married in ten days' time. "The day the steamer sails with this letter she will be Mrs. Uriu," Ume wrote to Mrs. Lanman. "So often as Sutematsu and I have talked about it, we never dreamed of anything like this."

As bewildered now by their surroundings as they had been so long ago in San Francisco, Sutematsu and Ume had trouble imagining their friend setting up housekeeping in Japanese style. At dinner, Shige plied them with "every kind of mess imaginable," Ume reported, amazed at how the strange flavors seemed somehow familiar. Sutematsu and Shige dressed Ume in a kimono, "and you don't know how funny I looked," Ume reported. "Then I took a Japanese hot bath, which would be very odd to you all, but which is very neat and pleasant." It was certainly odd to Ume as well, whether or not she cared to admit it.

Tucked up at last in Shige's comfortable bedroom—the only one in the house with Western-style furniture—the three young women talked late into the night. "Shige is a great help, for she tells us what to do and what not," wrote Ume. "Japanese etiquette is so strict and I am in fear all the time of making a bad blunder, and of being unintentionally rude."

. . .

FOR UME, REENTRY into the Tsuda family was dismayingly difficult. The initial welcome had been glorious: relatives visiting, letters of congratulation arriving for her father, gifts of candy and fish and glowing red persimmons, celebratory *sekihan* (rice tinted pink with tiny red adzuki beans) for dinner. "So you see my return is a great thing," Ume wrote with pride on her third day at home. In addition, the Tsudas' house was reassuringly equipped with familiar objects. Ume's father had provided a Western-style bedstead on which Ume spread a Japanese quilt—"so much lighter and warmer than American things." She had a table in her room for her belongings, and a makeshift washstand. The house had a foreign-style parlor with chairs and carpet and a mantelpiece with a clock. Ume's parents and sister Koto had converted to Christianity in her absence too, so every meal—served at a table, with chairs—was preceded by grace.

But the house, isolated in the suburbs and surrounded by cultivated fields, was cramped and overflowing with siblings, most of whom had been born after Ume's departure. She was often physically uncomfortable, especially in the rooms that were not furnished in Western style. "The hardest thing is . . . taking off the shoes," she wrote. Koto had thoughtfully knitted house socks for her to wear, but it was strange to go shoeless in company. Instead of thonged sandals, Ume had only high-buttoned boots, and "it is the greatest nuisance to have to button and unbutton every time you go anywhere."

She couldn't bring herself to trade her dresses for kimonos, or to give up her accustomed underpinnings of corset, camisole, petticoat, and stockings. This reluctance led to other difficulties. "I can't yet sit down polite fashion"—kneeling with a straight back, heels tucked under bottom—"but they don't make me at all." "They," in fact, treated Ume like an exotic doll. All the family and everyone who came to call exclaimed over every detail of her appearance. "My dresses have been shown over and over again—all my various things, hats, ribbons and everything," she wrote to Mrs. Lanman. "You would have been astonished to see the regular show here one afternoon." Long ago, the San Francisco ladies who had waylaid her in the corridors of the Grand Hotel had clucked over her embroidered kimono and hair ornaments in just the same way.

And just as in that faraway hotel room, once again Ume had no idea what the people around her were saying. "If I could only speak my own language," she wrote. But the little girl whose unself-conscious chatter had delighted the Lanmans now found herself, on the cusp of adulthood, painfully mute. Her father, the erstwhile interpreter, and her sister Koto, who had learned serviceable English at a mission school in Tokyo, translated for her when they could, but letters to America became the only real outlet for Ume's distress. She poured her thoughts out in writing. "I am bound hand and foot, I am both deaf and dumb," she lamented. "My father promises to get me some instruction books, but has not yet, and I have learned but little, sad to say, though Koto tries to teach me. But when there are six or seven ways to say anything and they tell me all, I get in a muddle truly." Just as troubling, she had noticed that Shige, after only a year back in Japan, now occasionally stumbled when speaking English. "Oh, I don't want to lose my English as Shige has," she wrote in horror. "I must read and write and talk and keep it up."

For the first time in her life, Ume felt awkward. She had always been the little one, elfin, nimble, shinnying up a tree to reach her bedroom window in Georgetown. "But now in Japan I feel so big," she wrote. "Sutematsu is uncomfortably tall for Japan. What a land of little people it is anyway!" Surrounded by unfamiliar faces, Ume no longer recognized herself. Writing to her best friends in Georgetown—the alliterative threesome of Mattie, Maggie, and Mamie—she flickered between insecurity and disdain. "Much to my alarm and horror do you know, I am actually growing *more fat*!!!" she moaned. "It is Japanese food I assure you, and then Japanese dresses so loose, and padded make me immense. Why I am almost tempted to take anti-fat,* were it not for my too great indifference to personal looks." She was a scholar, chosen by her country—not a

---

* Allan's Anti-Fat, an elixir derived from seaweed, was a popular Victorian weight loss supplement.

girl trying to win a husband. Feeling defensive, she aimed a jab: "In this respect, I don't resemble my country women, because they think all the world of their looks and their beauty, for that is indeed their sole means of attraction."

For the first time in her memory, Ume physically resembled the women around her, yet she had never felt more conspicuous. Her face no longer drew stares, it was true; instead it was her actions that marked her. She was perpetually in the wrong place, doing the wrong thing, her bows clumsy, her smiles too broad. "I long to jump around, rush wildly about and yet not have it thought strange," she wrote. Ume was no longer a child, though; she was a young woman, with a heavy sense of responsibility to the government that had sent her abroad. "My father was talking the other day about the money spent on me," she wrote in a low moment, "and said that it would have been enough in Japan to support a family more than comfortably." Her American freedom and the freedom of her girlhood were suddenly and simultaneously at an end.

NOTHING SIGNALED THE momentous shift in the lives of these three more clearly than Shige's imminent wedding. "Sutematsu and I hate to have Shige married and no longer a girl like one of us, but of course we don't say anything," Ume wrote to Mrs. Lanman. The week following their arrival, she and Sutematsu went shopping for Shige's wedding gift. "If we had only known we could have bought her a lovely present in America, but here it was hard to find anything for her foreign home," complained Ume, somewhat disingenuously. They had known full well that Shige would soon be married, but from the comfortable distance of half a world away, it had been easier not to think about it. The daunting question of whether a woman could live happily in Japan without a husband remained unanswered.

Ume settled on a pair of pretty vases as a gift for Shige ("for twelve yen, and that was very reasonable"), while Sutematsu chose "a sort of tea concern which I cannot express in English with a tea set and a candy plate," as she described it to Alice. In this, at least, they did not worry about what was proper. Shige would appreciate their gifts whether or not they conformed to Japanese expectations.

At seven o'clock on the evening of Friday, December 1, 1882, a small group of relatives and intimate friends gathered for the ceremony. "Such a curious mixture," Ume wrote, "such a wedding never was before and never again will be known." Radiant, the Japanese bride and Japanese groom were perfectly comfortable in foreign style from head to toe: Uriu in his naval uniform; Shige in maroon silk trimmed with swan's down, specially ordered from Paris. Both devout Christians, the couple had arranged for a Christian service, though the officiant was a Japanese minister who read the vows in Japanese. The assembled guests included Uriu's Annapolis roommate, Tasuku Serata, also in his naval uniform; Takashi Masuda, brother of the bride, in the *haori* jacket and skirt-like *hakama* trousers worn by men of rank on formal occasions; Takashi's American colleague Robert Irwin, in a swallowtail coat; Sutematsu and Ume in their best black silk; and the rest of the female guests in kimonos. Western attire notwithstanding, all the guests sat on the tatami-matted floor.

When the ceremony was over, the guests enjoyed supper in foreign style, served by waiters in suits. There was even a wedding cake, "which Mr. Uriu had presented him by the Pitman girls ages ago, for his wedding, little thinking then who would cut it," Ume reported. (It must have been an especially durable confection; Uriu had taken his leave of his foster sisters in New Haven more than a year earlier.) "Shige looked so pretty and happy and truly it is a good match—love on both sides," Ume continued. A love match: of all the strange details of this most unusual wedding, here was—at least in Japanese eyes—the strangest.

THE EXCITEMENT OF the wedding was a welcome distraction from the looming question of what would come next for Sutematsu and Ume. The prospect was fairly bleak. Shige had had a much easier time upon her return, her path eased not only by her engagement but by her field of expertise: one did not need to be literate in Japanese in order to teach the piano. She had settled quickly into a position with the Ministry of Education's Music Investigation Committee, founded to introduce Western music into the Japanese national curriculum and soon to become the government-sponsored Tokyo Music School. Her position as a piano instructor paid her the highest salary of any woman in Japan.

With neither fiancés nor serious musical training, Sutematsu and Ume could not follow where Shige had led, though truth be told, their sights were set higher. Where Shige was content to teach and eager to start a family, Sutematsu and Ume dreamed of founding a school. So they decided to begin where they had left off: with Kiyotaka Kuroda, the man who had recruited them in the first place. This tactic was complicated by the fact that Kuroda's bureau, the Hokkaido Colonization Board, had ceased to exist earlier that very year, its demise tainted with scandal: Kuroda had attempted to sell off the board's assets to his Satsuma cronies. His wife's death around this time had added a tabloid edge to Kuroda's sudden notoriety: rumors flew that he had killed her in a drunken rage, though he was eventually cleared of this charge. (The negative publicity did little permanent harm to Kuroda's reputation. Before the decade was out, he would serve as Japan's second prime minister.)

Despite all this, Kuroda remained a logical first step. Within a week of their arrival, Sutematsu and Ume presented themselves at his house, escorted by Ume's father as translator. Kuroda received his young guests—perhaps the first women ever to pay him a personal call—in a Western-style room. "A fine distinguished soldier-like man he was," Ume wrote, "and he conversed with us kindly, passing many compliments as to our education according to Japanese custom and rather embarrassing us, but we managed to thank him." Kuroda pressed his unusual visitors to stay. He had gathered some colleagues and invited a troupe of blind musicians to entertain on traditional instruments: the three-stringed *samisen* and zither-like *koto*. "So we stayed, and he entertained us and we had refreshments and heard some queer music, but very fine according to their ideas." This was followed, to the young visitors' increasing discomfort, by geisha singing. After nearly three hours, Kuroda turned to his guests in their Western dresses. To their horror, he asked them to sing as well.

There was but one way out of this predicament. "As we could not refuse, and no one who knew music was present, Sutematsu and I dragged through 'In the Gloaming' and 'Jesus, Lover of My Soul'—a thing I never did before, and want to laugh at the idea of it even now," Ume reported later, utterly bemused. They had come to discuss the solemn question of their role in the future of Japan, and found themselves sharing a bill with professional entertainers—something no wellborn Japanese woman would ever contemplate. And while their renditions of the sentimental love song and the stately hymn were doubtless charming, with the exception of Ume's father no one in the room understood a word.

That night, at Ume's house, the two young women discussed the future. It had been a disheartening afternoon. "All these great men in Japan are not Christians and are, besides, very immoral," Ume wrote. "We feel as if we were a drop in an ocean." How could they win the support of influential men like Kuroda if they were seen as mere curiosities? And were those men, with their fondness for sake-pouring geisha (on Sundays, no less!), really likely to support the goal of raising the status of women through education?

Their impatience to get to work was driven by an increasing sense of unease in their own homes. The Yamakawas were an accomplished group, grateful to have left the hunger and hopelessness of exile far behind, but their lives were by no means luxurious. Kenjiro and his older brother Hiroshi, now a general in the Imperial Army, still retained a strong sense of obligation to the scattered remnants of Aizu's samurai. Twenty different relatives and friends received their financial support, and there were always several students boarding with the Yamakawas at any given moment. "I am not willing to be an added expense to my family," Sutematsu told Alice.

Ume, having grown up in a household far less preoccupied with budgeting than the Bacons' had been, was more concerned with the Tsuda family's expectations than with their finances. "My Father," she told Mrs. Lanman, "is very kind and indulgent, but seems to expect far too much from his foreign daughter. He introduces me to people, I think with a proud way, and already wants and asks me to do many things which I don't know. I hope his anticipations in me will not be too suddenly overthrown." Ume did not burden her foster mother with a list of those anticipations, but prominent among them was certainly the one Ume feared most: a good marriage.

AS FAR AS Ume could tell, there was no word in Japanese for "spinster." "Sutematsu and I inwardly lament over the fact that we shall do such an unprecedented thing as to live and die old maids," Ume wrote. "But we won't marry and don't care to, and if we did, we would find it hard, for Japanese husbands require so much attention and obedience and do not treat their wives with a bit of respect and love, if they have any." Well, there was Shige. "Of course, this is not always the case, but it is so in general," Ume insisted. To Ume's chagrin, Shige challenged her unequivocal stance— and as the weeks passed, Sutematsu, unnervingly, also seemed less and less firmly of Ume's mind. Ume felt abandoned by her two older friends. "They seem to think, both of them (which is *very* hard)," she wrote, "that we must decide now whether we are willing to live single all our lives or not." In other words, the question was still open—at least in Sutematsu's mind, if not in Ume's—and an answer was urgently required: "Everyone marries early, and if we put off, then we won't have any offers."

Eager for her dearest friends to share her happy state, Shige made her new home in Negishi, in the northeastern part of Tokyo, into a sort of clubhouse—a gathering place for the trio, as well as for friends of her husband: "young men who have been abroad and who are consequently more congenial than those who never have seen other countries," Sutematsu told Alice. "We have a society of our own very different from purely Japanese one or foreign." Here were men she could talk to, graduates of Amherst and Cornell and Yale who were fluent in English, certainly, but who also understood the language of Western scholarship and were not alarmed by a woman who spoke it. With the married Urius as chaperones, the young people discussed issues and played games from both sides of the Pacific. The unrestrained laughter of men and women enjoying themselves together, however, was purely American.

Ume, barely eighteen and with no college experience, was the little sister at these gatherings, but Sutematsu was in her element. At Shige's, she felt "perfectly at home," able to relax while still forging valuable connections with young men who had taken up promising positions at the university or in government as soon as they returned with their degrees. (She tried not to mind that no such offer had yet come her way.) The only irritation she felt was at Shige's tendency to play matchmaker. "[She] has presented me with no less than six lovers out of whom I may make my choice," she complained to her Vassar classmate Jessie Wheeler. "There is no probability, however, of my forsaking the noble army of spinsters."

In the face of Shige's happiness and the demoralizing lack of interest from the Ministry of Education, though, it was difficult to remain resolved. "Oh, Alice, I don't know what to do," Sutematsu wrote in January 1883, not two months after her return.

> It is perplexing this life. It is nothing but a perpetual struggle after some thing . . . What would you say if I were engaged? But never fear. I have so far refused to marry three distinct persons and perhaps I may not have another chance even if I were willing. One I might have married for position and money but I resisted the temptation . . . The others—well I suppose I might have married for love, for yet neither of them had money or rank—but I didn't. So when you come to Japan you will still find me an old maid. Do you know Alice that girls who are above twenty are old maids? I am one and mother says that I may not have another offer . . . I am sure I don't know what is going to become of Japan. I feel perfectly discouraged about my work.

Her ambition was at war with her pride. The truth was increasingly clear: an old maid in Japan, no matter how accomplished she might be, was an object of pity, if not outright scorn.

At the end of January, Shige's brother Takashi provided a welcome distraction from the grim challenges of life and work. He planned to throw a party to introduce the newlywed Urius to his wider circle; would the trio and friends like to entertain with a "private theatrical"? They quickly settled on the final two acts of Shakespeare's *The Merchant of Venice*—an English lesson and a cultural display in one. "The party will be a large affair and all sorts of swell people will come to it," Sutematsu wrote with excitement. "But since half of them won't understand English we have no fear of stage fright at all."

For ten days it was almost like being back at Vassar with the Philalethean Society: casting, rehearsals, costumes. "Can you imagine me as Portia?" Sutematsu asked Alice. Actually, it wasn't much of a stretch. Lovely, intelligent, regal, and completely convincing when disguised as a doctor of the law, Portia arrives at court to save noble Antonio from the bloodthirsty Shylock. In terms of beauty, bearing, and brilliance, surely there was no woman in Japan more qualified for the part. "At the trial scene I am to wear my fur cloak, a velvet cap and a black dress," Sutematsu reported. "In the next act I shall wear my commencement dress." Ume, appropriately, would play Portia's clever young lady-in-waiting, Nerissa, with a rubber raincoat for her law clerk's costume. They were indeed perfectly cast: two highly accomplished young women, playing characters who pose as young men in order to achieve otherwise impossible goals.

Uriu played the noble and generous Antonio, and Naibu Kanda, an Amherst graduate known as the finest English speaker in Japan, was Portia's ardent suitor, Bassanio. Shige took the part of the duke, arbiter of justice, in an "ermine" cloak that Sutematsu fashioned of black cotton. Shylock stole the show, as played by Shige's younger brother Eisaku, who had also studied abroad—"the best amateur performer I ever saw," Sutematsu declared.

The party, by all accounts, was a great success. Ume especially enjoyed herself: the polished woodwork of the Masuda reception rooms glowed in the candlelight, the guests were elegantly dressed, and best of all, she wrote to Mrs. Lanman, the players "were relieved from the formalities of sitting and talking all the time, and so we stayed in the other room and got our rather funny costumes fixed." A narrator hidden behind a curtain read a synopsis of the story in Japanese, "and then we had the scene which went off beautifully and seemed to be enjoyed and appreciated." At least they had demonstrated that "nice people" could enjoy entertainment at a social gathering without hiring professionals, Ume concluded, satisfied. But women in Japan had been banned from the stage for the last two hundred and fifty years. Aside from the trio in costume, the other female guests at the Masudas' that night would never have dared a "private theatrical"—or even a game of charades—in mixed company.

Though the evening was meant to honor Shige and her new husband, it was Sutematsu's turn as Portia that proved most memorable. Two men watched her that night with unusual interest. One was Naibu Kanda, who delivered his lines as Bassanio, Portia's lover, with an ardor entirely unfeigned. Kanda had enjoyed Sutematsu's company at Shige's gatherings ever since her return, and he had already made his feelings clear; he was one of the suitors she had mentioned in her letters to Alice. An instructor of English at the university, and a devout Christian, Kanda was, in every respect, a catch. On the advice of her mother and Shige, Sutematsu hadn't rejected him out of hand, informing him instead that she couldn't possibly make a decision so soon after her return. If he needed an answer now, however, it would have to be no. Kanda decided to wait. "So we met very often and were very good friends," Sutematsu told Alice later. "Of course it was very pleasant to have a young handsome man very attentive to you and to have him think your slightest wish is as a law."

The heightened excitement of the play must have brought the situation to a head. Three days after the party, Sutematsu wrote to Alice in a state. "What a trouble it is to live!" she scrawled. "I have got into most horrible trouble and I don't know what to do. You are my only comfort[,] for I can write to you and let off my feelings. I can't talk to even Shige[,] for with her began the trouble and I am afraid we will have no end of row." Flustered and apparently embarrassed, she would not explain herself, even to Alice. "I need not tell you the nature of the trouble," she wrote, "for it is sufficient to say I am in it."

It was another three weeks before Sutematsu told Alice the rest of the story. Playing Portia to Kanda's Bassanio had ended her indecision. "I did have serious thoughts of saying yes," she wrote, "for I liked him very much and he was in dead earnest." But did her future really depend on a Bassanio? Shakespeare's young hero is charming, impulsive, romantic, but somewhat hapless; in the end, it is Portia's quick-wittedness that saves the day. Sutematsu certainly identified with Portia's calm competence. "When I thought of it more, I did not think it would be best," she wrote, "for one thing he is very young and boyish. So finally I wrote to him and told him that we better forget all that passed between us."

Kanda did not give up easily. The very next day the "crazy boy . . . presented himself at our house demanding to see me," Sutematsu recounted. When she said she was sick, he asked for her sister Futaba, the teacher. But Futaba was at work, so off he went to the Women's Higher Normal School to plead his case. Futaba listened to him for more than an hour and brought his entreaties home that evening, but her little sister's mind was made up. "And now he has written me a long letter and I feel dreadfully," Sutematsu wailed to Alice, "for it seems more like a curse than any thing else."

Doors seemed to be closing rather than opening. Sutematsu was briefly galvanized by the news that a position teaching physiology and zoology might be available at the Normal School. "It is just the place for me and I should like to teach Physiology above all others," she gushed; it had been one of her strongest subjects at Vassar. The salary promised to be even higher than Shige's—a welcome boost to Sutematsu's tottering self-esteem. But the textbooks were all in Japanese, which Sutematsu still could neither read nor write. "I have to study it just like a new language and teach in that language within two weeks," she wrote. "My mother says it is impossible but I mean to try if I am asked." In the end, she was forced to concede that the obstacles were insurmountable. Meaningful, profitable employment seemed entirely out of reach, and marriage—if, indeed, she wasn't already too old for it—like an admission of defeat. Her twenty-third birthday that month did not feel like cause for celebration.

The models Sutematsu had looked to in New Haven—unmarried,

independent women like Shige's "Aunt" Nelly Abbott, director of her own school, and Alice Bacon's oldest sister Rebecca, assistant principal at Hampton Normal and Agricultural Institute—simply had no counterparts in Japan. "Oh Alice, my views on various subjects change so rapidly," she sighed. "I see now the necessity for Japanese women to be married . . . You can not tell till you have been in Japan and be a Japanese, but really it is necessary." She owed a debt to her country, but no one seemed to have any idea how she was meant to repay it. "I wonder if you think as I do that the happiest period of one's life is one's childhood," she wrote.

> I feel more than ever the heavy responsibility of my future . . . and wish those careless days at Vassar could come back again. Oh Alice what a tangle this life is! I never used to think much of the dark side of life and used to feel so confident of the future and of my own strength but now I am not certain of either. People talk of dying for one's country as a glorious thing, but to me, to live for one's country seems infinitely more self-sacrificing. If it is possible that by the death of someone Japan could be benefitted in some way I would willingly, rather gladly be that one, but that is impossible.

There seemed to be no way forward.

JUST WEEKS LATER, Ume wrote with intense urgency to Mrs. Lanman: "I have so much to write and tell you, you can't imagine, and I want this letter to hurry up and reach you." Several tantalizing pages on, she got to the point: "I have reached the climax of my letter, and the secret burning on the end of my pen is about to be put down. The secret is no longer a profound secret and Sutematsu says I may tell. This is it. Do you know our dear Sutematsu in a little while is going to be a great lady, one of the first in the land in position as she is now in mind?"

The second admirer whose eyes had followed Sutematsu as she delivered Shakespeare's lines two months earlier had been a member of the audience. A portly man of middle age, jowly and grave, one of the highest-ranking present that night, he had taken careful note of the young woman's cosmopolitan grace. Shortly following Sutematsu's triumph as Portia, her brothers received a formal and utterly unexpected inquiry: Iwao Oyama, minister of war, requested the hand of their youngest sister in marriage.

The proposal was shocking. Oyama was one of the most powerful men in the Meiji government. He was forty years old, a recent widower with three small daughters, a battlefield veteran whose barrel chest afforded barely enough room for his decorations. And he was a Satsuma man: sworn enemy of the Aizu.

This, more than anything, stunned Sutematsu's family. During the siege of Tsuruga Castle, in the last desperate days of the Boshin War, Oyama had been one of the "potato samurai" closing in on the beleaguered Aizu from the surrounding hills. He had himself fired the very cannonballs that Sutematsu and her sisters had dodged within the castle walls. He bore scars from that battle—perhaps from the very ammunition the girls had helped to make. Fifteen years had passed, the war was long over, and Oyama was now Hiroshi Yamakawa's superior officer in the army. But at a deeper level, he remained the enemy. The Yamakawas turned him down flat.

Oyama had more in common with Sutematsu, however, than was at first apparent. One month after she had sailed for San Francisco with the Iwakura Mission in 1871, he had boarded a French mail boat and headed in the other direction, via the Indian Ocean, to study European military technology. Determined to master French, he had settled in Geneva (there were too many Japanese expatriates in Paris for his taste). He had lived abroad for nearly three years and returned with a taste for all things European. He understood better than most that a modern Japanese statesman needed a consort who was comfortable with public life and conversant in current affairs, and he knew his daughters would benefit from a stepmother who could teach them Western ways.

Still mourning his first wife, a woman no older than Sutematsu who had succumbed to complications of childbirth just the summer before,

Oyama hadn't intended to remarry so soon. But Sutematsu was the only woman in Japan with a bachelor's degree. She spoke English like a native, and some French too. She was tall and slim and elegant and poised. She dressed well, and she knew how to dance. She was perfect.

Oyama's dapper cousin Tsugumichi Saigo, minister of agriculture and the ranking Satsuma leader in Tokyo, took it upon himself to act as go-between and bring the Yamakawas around. Honoring them with several personal visits, he shrewdly appealed to the family's outsized sense of duty. Yes, Satsuma and Aizu had a troubled history. But the new Japan depended on its most talented citizens to stand together and lead the nation forward. The union of such an accomplished daughter of Aizu with the heroic minister of war— the very man who had chosen the ancient poem that provided the lyrics for Japan's new national anthem—would set an example for all Japanese citizens to transcend the past. Couched in those terms, the offer was harder to reject. But while the Yamakawas retained many of the attitudes of their samurai heritage, they had absorbed enough of Western ways to agree that the decision was not theirs to make. Sutematsu would choose her own path.

A year earlier she would have found the idea of such a marriage absurd. Oyama was a stranger, a statesman, old enough to be her father—it would be as if Portia married the duke at the end of the play instead of Bassanio. All her life Sutematsu had planned to pursue the goal of promoting women's education in Japan. How could she possibly join her life to Oyama's? Or to anyone's?

But the months since her return had been chastening ones, in terms of both the work available to her and the larger issue of the place of women in her native country. She could toil away, tutoring English privately until her literacy in Japanese improved, and then perhaps join the faculty at the Normal School, like her sister. But would standing before a classroom of girls every day for the rest of her life really make much of a difference?

Uprooted at the age of eleven, she had spent half her life as the one who was not like the others, the only Japanese girl that most around her had ever met. Must she now spend the rest of her life as the only unmarried woman—still the odd one out, even in her native land? Before, at least, she'd had Shige to share her strange circumstances; with Shige married, there was only Ume, who had never been the same kind of soulmate. The future that Sutematsu had imagined now looked terrifyingly lonely. She did not love Iwao Oyama—she had only just met him—but he was intelligent and well respected, and he seemed to understand the strangeness of her position. With him, it might be possible to serve her country as well as herself: to be both useful and happy.

"What must be done is a change in the existing state of society," she wrote, "and this can only be accomplished by married women." Nine months earlier, she had stood before the assembled guests at Vassar's commencement as a star student, an orator, a leader. Newspapers had reported her remarks on international policy. Classmates and professors had spoken of her glittering future. As Oyama's wife, with access to the most rarefied levels of power, she might yet fulfill some of their expectations.

"By the way do you remember I told you that I had an offer from a gentleman in a rather high position," Sutematsu wrote to Alice with studied nonchalance. "Well, he has asked me again and I am thinking of it." It was the first week in April, and Sutematsu had in fact already made the difficult decision to accept Oyama's proposal. Telling Alice of her decision, however, was even harder. "If I thought that if I did not teach, I would be perfectly useless to Japan, I would not hesitate to devote my whole life to teaching, but I feel sure that I can do some service to the country by giving up my pet plan," she continued. "It is all so strange and confusing and I cannot tell what is right or what is wrong." Was it selfish or selfless to change her mind?

HOURS OF INTIMATE conversation with Shige and Ume had been spent debating Sutematsu's decision; "she grew thin with worrying and pondering and wavering," Ume told Mrs. Lanman. Ume's own response flickered between envy and relief. With this one dramatic step Sutematsu would vault past them all—even those they had once held in awe. Kiyonari Yoshida, the former Washington chargé d'affaires who had attended the Philadelphia Centennial with them, was now back in Tokyo as well. "I wonder what he thought and said when he heard of it first," Ume wrote, "because he always considered us children or girls, and now Sutematsu is as good and better in the Japanese sense than Mrs. Y,* and Sutematsu's husband older than he."

Sutematsu would never need to worry about money again. "Mr. Oyama is rich, has a lovely house entirely foreign, rather Frenchy, and Sutematsu will always wear foreign dress, and have everything she wants," Ume wrote. She could "have lovely entertainments, dances, dinner parties, bring ladies and gentlemen together, show the great men what a woman can be and can do, and be *Madam Oyama*," Ume imagined. At the same time Sutematsu would be "no more our Steam, our Vassar graduate, or hospital nurse, or school teacher." Oyama's powerful colleagues would never seek Sutematsu's counsel, and their wives could never match her intellect. There would be no more cozy late-night discussions at Shige's; Sutematsu's new rank would not permit such informality. And though Oyama's reputation was irreproachable—"He never drinks, or does any of those dreadful things others do, and he is very pleasant, and I am sure very, very kind"—to Ume he was a cipher: there was, for one thing, no language in which they could converse. No, she could not imagine making the choice on which Sutematsu had settled.

For Sutematsu, the marriage was not simply about wealth or influence. It was a chance to take root. By July, she could explain herself more clearly to Alice (who had already received the startling news, via Ume's indiscretion, from Mrs. Lanman). "Although they all love me at home, I am not absolutely needed," she wrote,

> and the feeling that if I were dead, people would miss me but not mourn for me for very long used to make me very blue indeed. Mother has a

---

* Mrs. Yoshida was a former geisha, a woman of rank by marriage only, not by birth. Several of the highest-ranking Meiji leaders took their favorite geisha as wives, perhaps because exposure to the West had taught them to look more favorably upon love matches, but also because a woman trained in the arts of music and conversation was useful as a consort for a Western-style statesman.

grandson to whom she is wholly devoted, besides having lots of other children beside myself. All my brothers and sisters are either married or have children. Shige has her husband, and so none of these people can be said to be dependent on me for their comfort, but now it is different. I have someone whose happiness is in my keeping and whose children's welfare is in my hands.

She had traveled a very long way from the day, eleven months earlier, when she had exhorted Alice to hurry up and move to Tokyo, where they would keep house together and found their own school. "I would never take such a step without due consideration and I think I have done right," she insisted to Alice. "He is so thoroughly good that I am sure I may trust my future to him. I suppose you will not like it and I have thought over that too, but I felt that in questions of this nature one can not hope to please everybody." Her words betrayed a lingering unease. "I felt somehow that I was ungrateful to you, but I know that you are too generous to think so," she wrote. "Besides, you would not wish that this feeling should prevent me from doing what I think would be for my future happiness and welfare." She tried not to dwell on how her decision would affect Alice's future happiness and welfare. "I hope you are not angry with me. It is for the best."

Alice's reaction has not survived, and Sutematsu did not write again for the better part of a year. She was busy, to be sure, with French lessons now on top of her Japanese studies, and social calls on Oyama's acquaintances, and dressmaker's fittings for her trousseau. But her letters to Alice from this point are few and far between. The Vassar girl's frank confidences cease. The wife of the minister of war would need to keep her feelings more to herself.

THE WEDDING WAS small and private, as befitted a widower embarking on matrimony for the second time. Neither Shige nor Ume was present. Ume had stolen a peek at the wedding dress at Sutematsu's house a few days earlier: exquisitely embroidered silk, with a long court train and custom-made lace at the throat, she reported to Mrs. Lanman. Oyama had given Sutematsu a diamond ring with three brilliant-cut stones, ordered from Switzerland. (It looked "all together too magnificent on my scraggy fingers," Sutematsu wrote to Alice.) But otherwise, as far as Ume was concerned, the great event was disappointingly anticlimactic: "so matter-of-fact, so simple and quiet, that it seems strange," Ume wrote. "She just left one house and went to the other, dressed in the gorgeous dress that no one saw except the people of the house, and there is no fuss, no wedding trip, no jollification, or sending off." What was the good of marrying an important man if you couldn't have an important wedding? "As it is," Ume complained, "I don't feel that she is married one single bit."

The ceremony took place at Oyama's house. Afterward, friends and relatives received wedding announcements engraved in spidery script on large squares of ivory card: *Le Ministre de la Guerre General Oyama Iwao à l'honneur de faire part de son mariage avec Mlle Yamagawa qui a eu lieu à Tokio le 8 Novembre 1883.* A handful of the couple's most intimate acquaintance were invited to dinner the following evening. Already, Sutematsu seemed different to Ume, "acting hostess to all the ladies so well that I could not see but a little of her." Ume longed to get her alone, hear about the ceremony, ask her what lavish presents she had received. But "Steam," the big sister, the confidante, was not available. "I must teach my tongue not to call her Stematz in the presence of others, but 'Okusan' (Madam) or else Mrs. Oyama," Ume resolved. "Shige is always Shige, company or not, but I can't be so familiar with Stematz except when we are alone, and we won't be alone often." Ume found the dinner uncomfortable: the conversation was all in Japanese, and Sutematsu—Madame Oyama—could be of no help to her.

Nor was Shige there to toast her dearest friend that night. A jolting jinrikisha ride to a formal dinner was not a good idea for her just then: four days later she gave birth to her first child, a girl named Chiyo.

Sutematsu was now married; and Shige, a mother. "I must get used to the idea," wrote Ume, "and not mind being all alone."

GETTING ALONG ALONE

"PLEASE DON'T WRITE MARRIAGE to me again—not once," Ume protested to Mrs. Lanman at the beginning of that first summer back in Tokyo. "I am so sick of the subject, sick of hearing about it and discussing it. *I am not going to marry unless I want to.*" She and Sutematsu and Shige had been a country of three—tiny, perhaps, but secure. Now everything had changed. Their friendships remained, but the country of three had become, at least in Ume's eyes, a country of one.

Having made her aversion to matrimony clear, Ume had no choice but to embrace the question of work. On the plus side, she was better qualified than almost anyone in Japan to teach English and Western ways. The trouble was that, all of a sudden, those skills weren't necessarily what everyone wanted to learn. After a decade of headlong enthusiasm for Western ideas, the blistering pace of change was making some reformers queasy. "A few years ago everything foreign was liked, and the cry was progress. Now, Japanese things are being put ahead, and everything foreign is not approved of, simply because it is foreign," Ume wrote. "If we wish the government to endow for us an English school for girls, we have come home at a bad time."

During the 1870s, while the girls were abroad, Japan had hired thousands of American and European engineers, technicians, and consultants, paying them handsomely. In the years immediately following the departure of the Iwakura Mission, the Meiji government had replaced the traditional lunar calendar with the Gregorian, created a conscript army, instituted a national land tax, and mandated four years of compulsory education for both boys and girls—huge strides toward national stability and international relevance. In 1877, just a year after participating in the Centennial Exhibition in Philadelphia, Japan held its first National Exhibition in Tokyo's Ueno Park, not far from the temple where the shogun's forces had made their last stand less than a decade earlier. There were displays of art, produce, manufactured goods, and livestock. Japan's own Machinery Hall featured a mechanical loom invented by a Japanese man.

Even as crowds of spectators in Tokyo celebrated Japan's progress, however, at the other end of the country a desperate last stand for the traditions of the past was under way. Takamori Saigo was a burly and charismatic statesman who had broken with the Meiji leadership over its rapid reforms: in his mind, the samurai class should remain in control and assert Japan's growing strength more aggressively.* Retreating to his Satsuma stronghold near the southern city of Kagoshima, Saigo dug in. Tens of thousands of disaffected samurai rallied to his cause, but the new imperial conscript army, equipped with state-of-the-art artillery, vastly outnumbered them. By the end of that summer the Satsuma Rebellion was over: the rebels in the south had been decimated, and the iconic Saigo had committed suicide. The forces of modernization seemed to have triumphed unequivocally.

Two years later, in 1879, former US president Ulysses S. Grant traveled to Japan. The Meiji leaders—especially those who remembered visiting the White House with the Iwakura Mission in 1872—were beside themselves. The hero of the American Civil War was a natural idol for a group of former samurai who had triumphed in Japan's upheaval and

---

* His younger brother Tsugumichi Saigo, mustachioed and trim in contrast to Takamori's imposing bulk, was the agriculture minister who would later persuade Sutematsu to accept Iwao Oyama's proposal.

had just finished using Western military technology to silence their own challenge from rebels in the south. No matter that Grant himself advised the Meiji leadership against liberalizing Japanese society too quickly. "It is said that Grant is receiving more honor from the Japanese than any crowned head has ever received," wrote eighteen-year-old Clara Whitney, an American missionary's daughter. "One Japanese lady remarked that General Grant is treated so much like a god here that a temple to his honor should be erected immediately." Geisha danced for him in red-and-white-striped kimonos with underrobes of star-spangled blue and circlets of silver stars in their hair—graceful personifications of the American flag. The emperor himself stood to shake Grant's hand—the first Western hand the sovereign had touched.

Mutsuhito had undergone his own transformation since the departure of the Iwakura Mission. His parting words to them in 1871 had been delivered in full court dress, the only clothing in which he had ever appeared. Within two years, he had set aside his robes in favor of Western-style military uniforms, and cropped his hair short. He appeared in public with some regularity now. Once an almost mythical figure, the emperor had emerged from behind the screens, his new wardrobe a powerful symbol of Japan's reinvention.

Books on foreign ways and places sold briskly, few more popular than a translation of the Scotsman Samuel Smiles's *Self-help*, which the Japanese read as a manual of Western success. "The spirit of self-help is the root of all genuine growth in the individual," Smiles declared, "and, exhibited in the lives of many, it constitutes the true source of national vigor and strength." America, in particular, was glorious proof of this wisdom, only a century after its independence. Surely Japan could do likewise, perhaps even more rapidly.

In 1872, as the Iwakura girls were studying their first English primers in Washington, the Meiji leaders had promulgated a new Fundamental Code of Education, with an emphasis on self-improvement and individual opportunity. The old domain schools had indoctrinated samurai boys in the ways of loyalty and filial piety; from now on, children from every level of society would attend school with the aim of "building up their characters, developing their minds, and cultivating their talents" in order to "make their ways in the world, employ their wealth wisely, make their businesses prosper, and thus attain the goals of life." Samuel Smiles would have approved.

But some who read Smiles closely noticed, as well, this corollary to his message: "Help from without is often enfeebling in its effects." What were all these foreign experts if not help from without? Had Japan gone too far in its emulation of the West? Was it in danger of compromising its newfound strength? In 1878, on a tour of the provinces accompanied (and strongly influenced) by Nagazane Motoda, his personal adviser on Confucian ethics, the emperor pronounced himself dismayed by the Western influences he observed in provincial classrooms. Upon their return, Motoda summarized the emperor's reactions in an imperial rescript, "Great Principles of Education." Published the same year as Grant's visit, it signaled the beginning of a retrenchment in educational policy. "In recent days, people have been going to extremes," it read.

> They take unto themselves a foreign civilization whose only values are fact-gathering and technique, thus violating the rules of good manners and bringing harm to our customary ways . . . The danger of indiscriminate emulation of Western ways is that in the end our people will forget the great principles governing the relations between ruler and subject, and father and son.

Morality, not technical knowledge, should be the primary purpose of universal education, the document continued, and to that end, "the study of Confucius is the best guide." Enlightenment must not undermine the moral authority of the emperor. Education should promote obedience, not self-reliance. Japan must resist the false gods of Western progress.

Japan's determined leap toward foreign ways had launched the trio on their adventures in America, but in their absence that momentum had begun to falter. The girls had become a paradox, sent by their emperor to learn what was increasingly condemned in his name. They had returned just as the general rage for novelties like beef and ballroom dancing was beginning to cool, replaced by a revival of interest in traditional arts like the tea ceremony. "There must be a certain kind of charcoal and teapot," Ume griped, "the cup must be wiped and dusted so many times and a half and placed just so and so, and the tea fixed just this way, and I could fill pages with description and rules, though I think them very tiresome and useless."

But the reaction was more than just a matter of fashions and pastimes. Confucian teachings—like the eighteenth-century treatise "Greater Learning for Women" that Sutematsu had learned by heart as a child in Aizu—held that women should be subordinate to men in all things. Women's education had no place in a society ruled by these principles. Many families preferred to keep their daughters at home, despite the new requirement to send them to school. If they were educated at all, young women should study to be good wives, wise mothers, and loyal subjects— not teachers. Anything beyond elementary education for women was virtually nonexistent, and what progress had been made now began to seem precarious. "In the normal school, Sutematsu told me, they are giving up the foreign rooms, floors, chairs, and cot beds, and going back to Japanese style," wrote Ume. "Well, they are fools because in a year or so they will buy them all back again, and keep on piling up the expenses in their changeable fickle ways, and why, when they take a step forward, need they take a half one back?"

As the months passed, however, it became clear even to Ume: these early signs of conservative backlash were real. The government that had sent the girls to America was no longer so committed to the ideas they had learned there.

BY THE END of that first spring, Ume despaired of ever repaying the debt she owed Japan. On bad days, she expressed her unhappiness in the same bleak terms Sutematsu had used before her decision to marry. "If

I thought that by my dying I could elevate these daughters of Japan, I should be glad to do so," she wrote to Mrs. Lanman. "Is it not easier to give up life, and see a work *done* than to blindly grope and try, and see the end unattained, and fret and worry over impossibilities?"

For Ume, the months following Sutematsu's engagement proved the grimmest. Stranded in the Azabu farmhouse, "devoured with fleas" and tormented by mosquitoes, Ume tried to make herself useful: serving tea to visitors, tidying her room, studying Japanese, and scolding her seven younger siblings into submission. She took solace in her precious piano, purchased for her by the Lanmans with the last of her stipend. Having survived its journey from Washington mostly unscathed, it now dwarfed the Tsuda family's small parlor.

In Georgetown, Ume had been a daughter of the elite; in Tokyo, her family's social standing was more ambiguous. Sen Tsuda, Ume's father, had pursued an eclectic assortment of progressive ideas during Ume's years in America. He had traveled to the Vienna Exposition in 1873, and in the years following his return he helped found a missionary school for girls, a school for the deaf and blind, and a school of agriculture. He was a member of the intellectual club known as the Meirokusha, where he fraternized with some of the brightest minds of the Meiji leadership. He enjoyed a brief commercial success with the "Tsuda rope," a pollination technique imported from Holland, involving a woolen rope painted with honey to brush against ears of grain. He arranged for a commemorative tree to be planted in honor of President Grant's visit.

But to his samurai peers, Tsuda's enthusiasm for farming seemed déclassé, and his embrace of American-style equality extreme: he had even gone so far as to change his official status from samurai to *heimin*, or commoner. His fervent embrace of Christianity likewise marked him as an eccentric. By the time of Ume's return, with the national appetite for foreign ways fading, her father's influence was in decline. And though she was comforted by his religious choice, Ume was appalled to discover that shortly before his conversion, Tsuda had fathered a child with a servant— perfectly acceptable by samurai standards but profoundly shocking to an upper-middle-class daughter of Georgetown. As a mentor and patron, then, Ume found her father less than ideal, especially in comparison with Shige's wealthy businessman brother or Sutematsu's powerful fiancé— both men paragons of cosmopolitan elegance.

Shige, always the most maternal of the trio, worried about Ume's isolation. She sent a colleague from the music school to tune Ume's piano, and shared her concerns in letters to America. "Mrs. Lanman she misses you, and your love, your home, your country, more than any of us," she wrote to Georgetown. "Our director at the School of Music is anxious to have Ume teach for us, but I think the distance is so great and she is needed at home." (The distance was a convenient excuse as far as Ume was concerned; to Mrs. Lanman she confided, "I think music would not do much to gain me influence.")

Ume was irked by Shige's report to Mrs. Lanman—"I think it very unwise and wild of Shige to write you such a letter"—and disgusted by everyone's harping on her least favorite subject: marriage. Sutematsu was trying to steer her toward her own disappointed suitor, Naibu Kanda, while Mrs. Lanman dropped hints about Sotokichi Uriu's Annapolis roommate. "Please don't write anything about Mr. Serata," Ume shot back. "I always laughed at such an idea, and at him, for I don't even like him particularly, and poor and everything." The youngest and smallest member of the trio, it seems, had the highest standards.

Perhaps betraying her own insecurities, Ume reserved her harshest disapproval for the American missionaries in Tokyo. "They are entirely too stuck up, and can not reach any but the lowest kind of people because they will not conform to Japanese ways," she wrote. "Talk of hardships and privations—they have their families, and their homes, the best of comforts, dress well, go off on holidays, have a good time, know nothing of Japanese, and still they are doing all this, for the work for God's sake. Doing what?" Here were people no different from those she had lived among in Washington: secure—even smug—in the knowledge that they were doing God's work, surrounded by the comforts of home, subsidized by their churches, and free from any imperative to adapt to their alien surroundings. And here was Ume, without a clear purpose or means of support, deeply discomfited by the awkwardness she felt in her native land, unwilling to admit even to herself that part of what she felt for the missionaries was envy. Her girlhood had been full of prizes and prominent acquaintance. Now, as one Japanese among many, she burned with the frustration of the underestimated.

To put it less charitably, Ume was something of a snob. When assessing her prospects for employment as a teacher, she quickly ruled out the missionary schools, "which only poorer classes attend, and to which no one of any rank would send a daughter," she wrote. But by May of 1883 her ennui had become unbearable. Back in 1874 her father had helped found Kaigan Jogakko ("Seaside Girls' School") under the auspices of the Methodist Mission in the foreign settlement at Tsukiji; it was there that Ume's older sister Koto had learned her English. The Methodists were happy to have Ume teach English, world history, and geography, and though the pay wasn't much and the commute was an hour each way by jinrikisha, it was only for the summer term—just six weeks.

Ume looked upon her appointment with a mixture of pride and disdain. "Now are you not surprised that I am going to be a school ma'am right away, and teach the little Japanese?" she wrote gaily to Mrs. Lanman. "Hurrah! for the first beginning, though so little. It will seem very funny to hear lessons and order the children and keep quiet, and really and truly earn money. Why, I feel like a child and a schoolgirl myself, and really I am only eighteen."

The weeks of teaching slid by swiftly. "I am so busy, you can't imagine," Ume exclaimed, though in fact she taught for only three hours each afternoon, and never more than eight girls at a time. Teaching felt a bit like playacting: "Indeed you would be surprised to see how I can be severe and dignified." She was careful, however, to qualify the pleasure she took in her pupils. "Do not suppose, Mrs. Lanman, that these girls have anything of the refinement, sense of true honor, or moral standards like girls I have known," she wrote. When the term was over Ume was pleased to be asked back for the fall, but she declined. Teaching was hard work, she had discovered. "I think I am young yet, and I hate sometimes to think of the drudgery and monotony of it always."

Her privileged Georgetown girlhood had left her unprepared for her own future. Marriage was abhorrent; anonymous teaching, a thankless grind. The recognition she craved now seemed a hopeless dream, but she clung to it anyway. "I want to have my school, and never marry, though I do not say I shall never do so, because it is so *hard*, so very *hard*, to get along alone." Especially when Sutematsu, having decided against getting along alone, had suddenly ascended to the glittering ranks Ume regarded with such fascination.

When Sutematsu shared a rumor that Ume was under consideration as interpreter to the empress, Ume's imagination exploded: "But what a position that might be—almost a sinecure! At New Year's and formal occasions only would the interpreter be needed, and when a wife of some minister or great lady is presented. Would it not be great? I could then see the best society." Prestige, elegant surroundings, minimal responsibilities—what could be better? But even as Ume gushed to Mrs. Lanman, she knew her Japanese skills barely allowed her to communicate with the Azabu housemaids, let alone translate the ornate language spoken at court. It was gratifying, still, to think of her name on the lips of the powerful.

An invitation to a grand fête hosted by Kaoru Inoue, the foreign minister, was another consolation. "I don't hide it that I do want to go to the government ball," she wrote, "for I shall meet a lot of the great people & I want to look nicely & may be it will help my school plans."

On November 3, the emperor's birthday, a thousand invited guests gathered at the foreign minister's official residence. Gaslight illuminated the imperial chrysanthemum crest on the front gate, and colorful lanterns glowed from the eaves of the house and across the grounds. The reception rooms were filled with flowers, outmatched in splendor only by the costumes of the revelers: military uniforms trimmed in gold, gowns from Paris, and several examples of traditional court dress, "very curious and very beautiful," Ume reported. There was dancing, for those who knew how, though the dancers were mostly foreigners. Fireworks burst overhead, momentarily blotting out the stars.

Shige, just days from the birth of her daughter, was forced to miss the fun, as she would miss Sutematsu's wedding later the same week. Uriu escorted Ume, in white (she decided against her train), and Sutematsu was "lovely in blue crepe." The American consul general was there, and the Lord Mayor of London. But the most intriguing person Ume met that evening was not a foreigner. Midway through the festivities, a slim and elegant older man, resplendent in military decorations and gold braid, presented himself to Ume.

"Who am I?" he asked, his neatly trimmed goatee framing a mischievous smile. "Can you guess?"

Baffled, and growing more embarrassed with each passing moment, Ume confessed that no, she could not.

"I am Ito," he said. "Don't you remember? You were only so high," holding his hand flat at waist height, "when I saw you last—and now you are back."

And so it was: Hirobumi Ito, who had once cheered up five homesick, seasick girls with pieces of pickle on the steamship carrying the Iwakura Mission to San Francisco, and entertained them with bedtime stories when they were snowbound in Salt Lake City. Then, he had been the youngest of the five senior ambassadors; now he was minister of the imperial household. (In another two years, he would become Japan's first prime minister.) "He is such a great man now," Ume wrote ruefully, "that I could not but feel embarrassed when he asked if I had forgotten him." Still, the encounter would prove fateful.

"WILL YOU REALLY believe it, when I tell you that I am at work already, begun since my last letter to you?" Ume scrawled to her foster parents. Barely a month had passed since she stood stammering before Ito at the foreign minister's ball, but her failure to recognize him had apparently done her no harm. "It seems he is very anxious to help women, education, and [in] every way, and he is very progressive," Ume wrote. She had found her patron.

Empress Haruko in court dress, 1872.
(Photo by Kyuichi Uchida. Courtesy
Getty Images, Hulton Archive.)

*From left to right: Shige, Tei, Ryo, Ume,
and Sutematsu, wearing the Western
dresses purchased for them in Chicago.*
(Courtesy Tsuda College Archives.)

*Tomomi Iwakura (center) with his senior ambassadors, including Takayoshi Kido
(far left), Hirobumi Ito (second from right), and Toshimichi Okubo (far right).*
(Courtesy Wikimedia Commons.)

Arinori Mori, Japanese chargé d'affaires in Washington, 1871. (© 2015 Museum of Fine Arts, Boston.)

Leonard Bacon, pastor of New Haven's First Church. (Courtesy Yale Divinity Library Special Collections.)

Adeline Lanman. (Courtesy Tsuda College Archives.)

Sotokichi Uriu as a naval cadet at Annapolis. (Courtesy Mrs. Setsuko Uriu.)

From left to right: Sutematsu, Shige, and their friend Martha Sharpe at Vassar. (Courtesy Vassar College Library Special Collections.)

Vassar's Class of 1882. Sutematsu sits fifth from the left, four rows back. (Courtesy Vassar College Library Special Collections.)

Ume in Tokyo, 1883. (Courtesy Tsuda College Archives.)

Sutematsu's graduation portrait, 1882. (Courtesy Vassar College Library Special Collections.)

Iwao Oyama, minister of war. (Courtesy National Diet Library, Tokyo.)

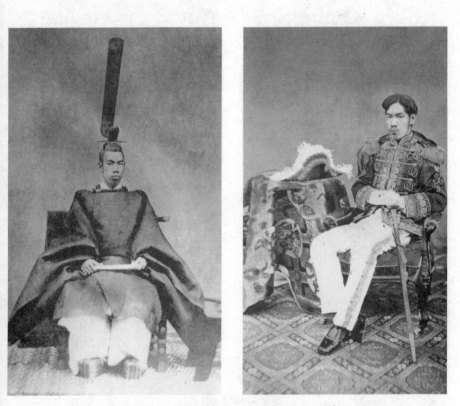

The Emperor Meiji in court dress, 1872, and in Western-style military uniform, 1873.
(Photos by Kyuichi Uchida. [Left] Courtesy Wikimedia Commons. [Right] Courtesy Getty
Images, Hulton Archive.)

Hirobumi Ito, Japan's first prime minister. (Courtesy Getty Images, Universal Images Group.)

Alice Bacon. (Courtesy Tsuda College Archives.)

The Rokumeikan. (Courtesy National Diet Library, Tokyo.)

Sutematsu, circa 1888. (Courtesy Vassar College Library Special Collections.)

The Empress Haruko, circa 1888–90. (Courtesy Getty Images, Hulton Archive, Apic.)

Ume upon matriculation at Bryn Mawr, 1889. (Courtesy Tsuda College Archives.)

The Women's Home School of English in its new home, 1901. (Courtesy Tsuda College Archives.)

COLLIER'S

SATURDAY, AUGUST 20, 1904

FIELD-MARSHAL MARQUIS OYAMA AND HIS FAMILY

The Oyama family, pictured in Colliers, 1904. From left to right: Sutematsu, Takashi, Marquis Iwao Oyama, Kashiwa, Hisako. (Courtesy Vassar College Library Special Collections.)

Ito introduced Ume to Utako Shimoda, a woman whose path to prominence had been as traditional as Ume's was radical. Ten years older than
Ume, and likewise from a samurai family fallen on hard times, Mrs. Shimoda had won a place at court following the restoration of the emperor.
Her fluency in the classics and her skill as a poet had made her a favorite of
the empress, who renamed her in honor of her talent: *uta* means "poem" or
"song." Utako had left the court to marry, but the marriage was a troubled
one, and powerful friends, including Ito, had helped her establish Toyo
Jojuku, a small private school for the wives and daughters of the elite. *Toyo*,
an allusion to Chinese poetry, translates as "young peaches"; it was feminine
polish that Mrs. Shimoda's school provided, not teacher training. Ito's own
wife (another former geisha) and daughter had been among the first pupils.

Ito hoped to add English instruction to Mrs. Shimoda's curriculum, and
who better to teach it than Ume? Meanwhile, the two women could tutor
each other—an hour of English in exchange for an hour of Japanese each
day—and since the Ito residence in Nagatacho was quite nearby, Ume
could afterward share lunch with Mrs. and Miss Ito, and give them a lesson
as well. Ume was beside herself. "Oh, I am so grateful and thankful—you
have no idea how I feel about it. It seems as if God had just raised up this
friend when most I needed it, and I do believe it is an answer to prayer,"
she wrote. "Just to think I am a teacher, and of these great people, and am
earning, and beginning my way for the future. Is it not good?" Ito's power
and charm dazzled her, and she tried not to dwell on his reputation as one
who was, in Sutematsu's words, "fond of the pleasures of Japanese life."
(Ito would later be suspected of carrying on an affair with Utako Shimoda,
but of this Ume remained happily unaware.)

Even Sutematsu blessed the arrangement: "If you have Mr. Ito as a
friend you need not fear." Privately, Sutematsu had never considered Ume
well suited to teaching—"she had so much petting in America," she confided to Alice—but Ume's new students, so few and so genteel, were a
good fit. "On the whole, I do like the work very much and really believe
I like to teach a great deal," Ume wrote, boasting to the Lanmans of the
"ingenuity and muscles" her conversation lessons required.

She savored the stiffly formal etiquette of lunch at the Itos'. It almost made up for Sutematsu's lavish new home next door, and the fact that the second Madame Oyama had recently been presented at court—an invitation Ume had no reason to expect anytime soon. Of the five girls who had bowed in awe before the empress a dozen years earlier and received her mandate to study abroad, the only one to have been invited back into her presence so far was the one who had married a government minister. Ume did not dwell on the implications. "[Sutematsu] said it was not formidable at all, but very easy and simple," she wrote breezily to the Lanmans. "The Empress talked to her through one of the ministers, and asked her a lot of questions, and then they had dinner and came away after that."

The string of fortuitous developments was not yet over. A week into Ume's new routine, Ito came to see her during her lessons. Would it not make more sense, he asked, if she took up residence in his household? There would be no jinrikisha commuting to eat up her earnings and her free time; her friend Sutematsu would be close by; and the Ito women could help Ume with Japanese, both language and manners. "He also wishes me to go out among the higher circles, get among people, and have an introduction into Japanese classes that I could not from my home," Ume wrote. "With any future idea of doing good, which must mostly be done among higher classes, I should have to learn now." However accomplished she might have been considered in Georgetown, what Ume needed now was a crash course in Japanese etiquette. In exchange, she could provide the Ito women with some essential training in Western dress and deportment, as befitted the family of a Meiji statesman.

It was hard to know how to respond. There could be no question of Ito's generosity, but would Ume feel like nothing more than the hired help? Then again, she mused, "we three girls must often consider that we are in part government property" and must do whatever possible to advance the condition of Japanese women. But beneath these sober considerations, Ume was having trouble restraining her excitement: "to think I might live in a minister's house!!" The next day, a letter from Ito arrived, addressed to her father. "I want to talk to you on business about Ume," it read. "Please come."

BUOYED BY THESE new developments, Ume was particularly pleased when an elegant invitation reached the farmhouse in Azabu. On the thirteenth of December, General and Madame Oyama would host a "grand evening entertainment." The ball would celebrate their recent marriage, and provide Ume with her first glimpse inside the building of the moment: the Rokumeikan.

Opened only weeks earlier, the Rokumeikan was the architectural embodiment of the Meiji government's ambitions. Conceived as a government guesthouse, it was an elaborate two-story Italianate pile in blinding white brick, with a ballroom, dining room, music room, billiard room, and elaborate suites for state visitors. Just as the general population was beginning to sour on Western fads, the Rokumeikan became the epicenter of foreign fashion for the most rarefied circles of society. Its name, translated as the "Deer Cry Pavilion," alluded to a classical Chinese poem, in which the bark of a stag is heard as guests from afar gather to enjoy the hospitality of a generous host.

In contrast to the traditional teahouses where statesmen met to drink sake and enjoy the talents of geisha, at the Rokumeikan wives in the latest Paris fashions would join their husbands, nibbling foreign delicacies and perhaps even attempting the steps of the waltz. To its admirers it was a glorious expression of the Meiji spirit, determined to put Japan on equal footing with the great powers of the West. To its conservative detractors it represented the worst excesses of Japan's slavish aping of undignified foreign ways. And to its foreign critics it brought to mind "a second-class casino in a French hot-springs resort."

On the night of the ball, the Oyamas stood together at the top of the wide staircase as nearly a thousand guests arrived. They received each foreigner with a handshake, and each Japanese invitee with a series of formal bows—"a gymnastic feat which would have killed any American woman," commented an American observer. Sutematsu, the epitome of cosmopolitan grace in her wedding gown, three star-shaped diamond pins in her hair, won the unqualified approval of all: "a perfect hostess and the most delightful ball ever given in Tokyo." Before long, she would be known as *Rokumeikan no kifujin*: the "Lady of the Rokumeikan."

Shige, nursing her newborn, had to stay home once again, but Ume was in her element. "I enjoyed myself so much talking and meeting people, and flourishing about in my train which I donned for the first time, and got along nicely in it," she wrote, allowing herself a moment of self-satisfaction. What could be better? A glittering evening in the best society, prestigious work and the prospect of more to come, and all without the ultimate compromise: a husband. Sutematsu, she reported with horror, "is almost like a regular Japanese wife," and even Shige deferred to Uriu in all things. "Such a life is killing to me," Ume wrote. "I get quite provoked with these horrid men, and yielding women, who surprise me so much. In America, how different!" Sutematsu's life might be full of parties and servants, but Ume claimed not to be tempted. "I am much more happy in my work, I am sure."

Already her work had wrought undreamed-of changes in her daily life. Ito's arguments for Ume's relocation had convinced her parents, who left the decision to their daughter. The very next week Ume moved in with the Itos, any nagging sense of guilt over deserting her cramped, impecunious home rapidly dispelled by the wonders of her new surroundings. "I have *two* rooms, upstairs, large and pleasant," she gloated. "You have no idea how it is—servants on every hand ready to wait and do." Her window looked out over exquisite gardens. Meals were served in foreign style and, as befitted an expert in foreign ways, Ume wore Western clothes exclusively. "I shall have all the comforts and luxuries that Sutematsu has," she wrote with satisfaction. "Of course, temporarily, without marrying for it as she did."

IN THE NEW year, 1884, Ume took to life at the Itos' with her usual mixture of enthusiasm and complaint. As her work at Mrs. Shimoda's school

would not begin until March, she found herself more of a ladies' companion than a teacher: helping young Miss Ito assemble a Western wardrobe at
the shops in Yokohama ("an awful bother"); introducing her to the piano;
standing awkwardly at Mrs. Ito's elbow during formal dinners, trying to
translate the platitudes of the foreign guests.

What she enjoyed most was the opportunity to converse with Ito himself, in English: "very serious talks on all sorts of subjects," the kinds of
discussions that she had joined regularly in Georgetown, and that she
missed acutely. Like the Lanmans, Ito seemed genuinely interested in
what Ume had to say. "Sometimes when I tell him about many things,
about books, or interesting things about women's work, he tells me I must
tell Japanese ladies all these sorts of things," Ume wrote. "He wants me to
learn and to bring me forward so that I can, and he is very kind."

But it was with the Ito women that Ume spent most of her time, including a three-week trip to the hot-spring resort of Atami, which, after briefly
admiring the scenery, Ume found painfully boring. She wanted to feel grateful, but struggling through English lessons with the stiffly polite Mrs. Ito and
her spoiled elder daughter was "very hard and rather slow," and outside of
lessons no one spoke any English at all. She knew she should be taking advantage of this immersion to advance her Japanese skills, but it was discourag-
ing to grope for simple words when she was so eager to discuss complicated
things. "I would give a great deal, a good many hours of my life," she wrote
to the Lanmans from Atami, "just to be your little girl and pet again."

It was a relief to return to Tokyo and a more convivial routine. Ume
taught English at Mrs. Shimoda's school three mornings a week, tutored
the Itos at home after lunch, and went home to Azabu on the weekends.
"You see how well-filled every moment is," she wrote proudly, though her
private thoughts about life as a working woman were ambivalent at best.
She remembered a composition she had written as a young schoolgirl: "Is
Labor a Blessing or a Curse?" "I suppose if I could have a life of pleasure
and nothing else, I should not want work," she wrote, knowing full well
that option was not available. If she had to work, she was happy to be a
teacher. But her confidence waxed and waned from one line to the next.

"You know I detest sewing, and am not fond of housework very much, so I think I am quite in my right corner and place, and am sure you too rejoice with me, though I am only a teacher; yet a teacher's work is a noble one."

AT LEAST UME could see Madame Oyama more now than she had in recent months. Sutematsu had organized a group to study *sumi-e* ink painting once a week and invited Ume to join, free of charge. Ume was delighted: "Is it not lovely," she asked Mrs. Lanman, "to take drawing lessons in such a pleasant way and company?" General Oyama had just left for Europe, sent by the Meiji government to study Prussian military systems, and though there had been some talk of Sutematsu accompanying him, she had been ill recently. He had embarked alone and would be away for nearly a year.

In his absence, relieved of the formal duties of a minister's wife, Sutematsu could turn her attention to the kinds of projects she had hoped her marriage might facilitate. Her visits to court—there had been a second one at New Year's, when she had been asked to translate for the empress—had been dismaying. "If I told you all I know about the life of our Empress, you would think Japan was absolutely a barbarous country," she wrote to Alice. "The court is a separate world and the people [who] live in it do not know any other or care to know any better one." A few years back, before the conservative reaction had set in, the imperial family had shaken off some of its archaic ways; the empress had even ridden out on horseback, with a sidesaddle. But since then, the gates had swung shut once more. How could Japanese women hope for enlightenment, Sutematsu wondered, when the empress herself was trapped by the traditions of centuries past?

Ito shared Sutematsu's concern, both for the backwardness of Japan's court and for the plight of its women. At the end of February he invited Sutematsu, Utako Shimoda, Foreign Minister Inoue, and several other "learned ladies" to his home. Ume, of course, was already there. To this illustrious and superlatively well-educated group he posed the question of how best to bring Japanese women out of the shadows. By the end of the meeting the group had sketched the outlines of a new idea: a school for wellborn girls under the patronage of the empress.

"Do you know that *the* dream of my life is to be now realized?" Sutematsu wrote excitedly to Alice. At last, a school where powerful men would be proud to send their daughters, and where those daughters could open their minds to Western ideas. At the same time, "as the school is to be partly supported by the court, the Empress and the ladies of the court will be obliged to visit the school, by which means education and western ideas are to [be] introduced to the very center of court." The new school would thus "kill two birds with one stone." Ito appointed a planning committee of two: Utako Shimoda and Sutematsu.

If they were successful, Ume would be appointed to teach English. "What a splendid thing if it could be established and arranged!" Ume wrote, though her attention at the meeting was distracted by her friend's newest piece of jewelry. "I must tell you that Sutematsu wore that night her wedding present from Mr. Oyama, a most tremendous diamond this size"—here she drew a circle half an inch in diameter—"or larger with five smaller ones around it making a most magnificent pin, one of the finest I ever saw. How it did glitter!"

For Sutematsu, the prospect of a Peeresses' School glittered more than any of Oyama's lavish gifts. "We are to set up a school just as we think best with no one to interfere, with much money to command, with the support of the most influential men of Japan," she told Alice. "Is not that just what I should like?" At first she had demurred; she had enough to do just then, learning to manage an elaborate household and three small stepdaughters. But Ito was adamant: she had a debt to repay her country; she was the only woman in Japan with a college degree; her marriage placed her in an ideal position of influence. At his request, Sutematsu sent him descriptions of her Vassar courses and the calendar of the college year.

ITO'S BRACING ENCOURAGEMENTS seemed to blow away the fog of uncertainty Sutematsu had come to feel about her ability to bring the lessons of her American past to bear on her Japanese future. In addition to long-range planning for the new school, she was soon immersed in another more immediate project—this one conceived to enlighten not just the daughters of Tokyo society, but their mothers as well.

Drawn to nursing ever since her brief stint at the Connecticut Training School, Sutematsu had recently toured Tokyo's Charity Hospital, founded only a couple of years previously. Whereas the University of Tokyo's hospital, influenced by German ideas, admitted indigent patients only insofar as they were useful in research, this new hospital followed a more humanitarian, English model—its explicit mission to serve the poor. Though the new venture enjoyed the patronage of an imperial prince, philanthropy was one Western habit that had not yet taken hold among Tokyo's elite, and the hospital was having trouble covering its expenses.

Raising funds for good causes had been part of the social fabric of New Haven, and Sutematsu had spent plenty of girlhood Saturdays sewing for charity with the members of Our Society or attending church sales. What better way to introduce the idea to her countrywomen than to raise money for the women's department of the new hospital? With Ito's encouragement, Sutematsu soon found herself spearheading the first charity bazaar Japan had ever seen.

"You don't know what an undertaking this is!!" Ume wrote to Mrs. Lanman. "These Japanese ladies, many of them, especially the high ones, never heard of charity, never worked to help, never probably gave a thought to it, and to work something with their own hands and give it and *sell* it! is something unheard of. To sell what they make is very lowering, and to them it is something very strange, for they are so proud and high and aristocratic."

Within a few weeks, a committee including Sutematsu, her French-speaking sister Misao, Ume, Mrs. Ito, and a few other well-placed matrons had persuaded more than two hundred ladies to participate. Their handicrafts poured into the Itos' home: paintings, embroidery, baskets, dresses, footstools, toys. Ume contributed two china dolls in foreign dress. Oyama's department donated the services of a military band, and the Rokumeikan itself was reserved for three days in June.

By the morning of the twelfth, all was in readiness. The Rokumei-kan was decked in Japanese flags and evergreen arches, and fifteen stalls showed off the dazzling array of items for sale, including fan-shaped hair-pins inscribed with "Ladies Benevolent Society" in English. "These were made for the occasion and are like souvenirs of the fair," wrote Ume, "and everyone, nearly, wished for one." Tobacco pouches bearing the same inscription "sold like anything." The lady organizers wore knots of purple silk cord. Ume helped Mrs. Ito at her table, and Shige joined Sutematsu at hers. A tearoom, likewise staffed by the ladies, offered lemonade and ice cream.

The opening morning was quiet; from ten o'clock until noon, only those of the highest rank were admitted. Behind their tables, the lady orga-nizers were demure, helping those who expressed interest in a purchase, and otherwise hanging back. But in the afternoon, when the doors opened to general ticket holders, they seemed to lose their inhibitions. Increas-ingly, to Ume's amusement, "they urged the people to buy and praised their own goods, and brought their own particular friends to their own particular table, and actually forced them to buy." Husbands found them-selves charmed out of their change; it was all, after all, for a good cause. "If you could have seen the way in which the gentlemen were really robbed of all their money by the persuasion of the ladies, you would not have believed that these were the shy, proper dames of Tokio," wrote Ume. The foreigners, among the most enthusiastic shoppers, "said they felt as if they were in America."

Sales of the pedigreed handicrafts were so good that the committee was forced to rush out and buy more merchandise to refill the stalls before reopening the next day. Jinrikishas clogged the road in front of the Roku-meikan, and lines of kimono-clad patrons waited patiently to take off their wooden clogs before entering. More than ten thousand people visited the bazaar, drawn by the novelty of buying a handmade trinket from a gov-ernment minister's wife. Sutematsu and the committee had hoped to raise a thousand yen. The net proceeds were six times that figure.

"It is a matter for universal admiration that ladies of such high rank should show themselves perfectly *au fait* in conducting the sale of the exhibits; and their kind and earnest manner left a most pleasing impression on all who visited the Bazaar," commented one Japanese newspaper. There were critical voices amid the general acclaim, however; another paper was less impressed, complaining that the event "was neither refined, elegant, nor admirable." The foreign press, though approving of the event itself, smirked that Japanese women might be taking things too far: "We have a very sincere admiration for the gentle grace and modest unobtrusiveness which distinguish the fair sex in this part of the world, and we cannot be pleased to see these charming qualities exchanged for the styles and methods which Western Ladies have thought fit to adopt at charity bazaars." The *Chugai Bukka Shimpo*, a financial paper founded by none other than Shige's brother Takashi Masuda, wryly proposed a bazaar at which merchants could unload stale goods, marked up several times, at stalls staffed by geisha.

It was impossible to deny the overall success of the endeavor, however. The bazaar at the Rokumeikan became an annual event, and a critical source of funding for the Charity Hospital. Sutematsu and her committee had shown Tokyo's highest-ranking women a way to participate in the welfare of their nation.

It was a moment to savor. Despite their various choices in regard to marriage, despite the relative indifference of most of the Meiji leaders, Sutematsu, Shige, and Ume were all engaged in work for the benefit of Japan. They were teaching, planning, and introducing Japanese girls and women to some of the ideas they had brought home from America. If Ito's new school could be realized, the future looked even brighter.

THE HIGH SPIRITS of June 1884 wilted somewhat in the heat of midsummer. The winter "illness" that had prevented Sutematsu from traveling to Europe with her husband, she now revealed to Ume, was morning sickness. She was halfway through her first pregnancy. "I must say she began early," Ume clucked. The baby, a girl named Hisako, would arrive in November, a week before Sutematsu's first wedding anniversary, and months before Oyama's return. Her birth would temporarily eclipse Sutematsu's involvement in planning the new Peeresses' School.

Shige, too, was beginning to suspect that another Uriu might be on the way, though it was too early to share the news with her friends. A second child, so close to the first, would put increased strain on Shige's teaching responsibilities at the music school. On top of these concerns, her husband's health was shaky; earlier in the spring he had suffered a hemorrhage in his throat, and Shige had suspended her teaching while he recovered.

And now a third pregnancy, from an unexpected quarter, hastened the end of Ume's sojourn within Tokyo's inner circle. Ume's mother was expecting yet another baby any day, and Ume could deny her responsibilities no longer. "At such a time, and by all laws of Japanese custom, and of ordinary human nature I must come home, and be home, and stay home," she wrote. She would return to Azabu to help her family. As wearying as the formalities of the Ito household had occasionally been for "free and easy-going Ume," as she described herself, it was difficult to leave the Itos. "I shall never regret the peep into the rank so different from mine, so different from America," she wrote. "I shall never go back again, I think. I do not know what will happen in the coming future."

THE BABIES ARRIVED in due course: Ume's newest sister, Tomi, that summer; Sutematsu's firstborn daughter, Hisako, in November; and Shige's second child, a boy named Takeo, in early spring. As she approached her twentieth birthday, Ume wrote a contemplative Christmas letter to Georgetown. "On the whole, I am glad this year '84 is most gone," she mused. "I had so much to worry about, trying to teach Miss Ito, and endeavoring to do my best in my ignorance of Japanese customs and language. Yes, it was hard and I am glad it is over. I hope the next year will somehow be better and smoother, and that my way will be clearer." Shige and Sutematsu were mothers now, their hands and minds full of responsibilities that Ume did not share. But before 1885 was over, Ume's life would be consumed with a comparably momentous event: the birth of a school.

In September, ending months of delay and doubt, a scroll arrived at the Tsuda home in Azabu, directing Ume to present herself at ten o'clock on a Monday morning at the Imperial Household Ministry, "accompanied by a relative," to receive her appointment as a founding member of the faculty at the new Peeresses' School.

"I must say that paragraph 'accompanied by a relative' was most thoughtfully put in, for it is not customary," Ume wrote, "and I had been on pins and needles wondering how in the world I was to get along at all alone to get my appointment, and my Japanese far from perfect." Dressed in her best blue silk, and with her father by her side, she threaded the hallways of the ministry and received the precious documents that made her an employee of the Meiji government, hired to teach English with a salary of 420 yen annually, and the bureaucratic rank of *jun sonin*. (Shige, she was quick to point out to Mrs. Lanman, held the lower rank of *hannin* in her position at the government music school.)

Accompanied by Utako Shimoda, who was appointed directress of the new school, Ume spent the rest of the day paying calls on Hirobumi Ito and all the officials who had had a part in her hiring. When, exhausted, she returned to Azabu at last, she found her home in an uproar: her father had spread the good news in her absence, and all the relatives had arrived. "We had quite a grand dinner in honor of the day, and I received congratulations from all around on my appointment, especially on the rank," she reported with pride. At least for the moment, all the doubt and frustration of the preceding years receded. "I have my papers, and am now a teacher in the school of the Empress."

Classes at the Peeresses' School, or Kazoku Jogakko, began on the fifth of October. Ume was pleased with her new surroundings, especially the faculty room. "I have such a nice desk here, a great big one in the farthest part of the room by the window, where it is light and pleasant. It is indeed the place of honor in this room, and it is the best place," she boasted to Mrs. Lanman. Without much to occupy her, and somewhat uncomfortable among her new colleagues, she wrote at unusual length to her foster mother that week; it gave her an excuse to sit at her new desk and look professional. She taught only three hours each day, and her scholars were somewhat distracted; everyone's attention was focused instead on the upcoming opening exercises of the school, which the empress herself would attend.

Ume found the rehearsals tiresome, and the prospect of the actual ceremony filled her with dread. "I know just how I ought to do, but I am afraid I will lose my head, and be put out, forget the many signals and not put the girls through the proper forms," she worried. "It is just like me to stare blankly when the signal is made and forget my part before so many." The little sprite who had blithely recited "The White-Footed Deer" before her elementary school classmates was no longer so sure of herself. In Georgetown, each accomplishment had made her a minor celebrity. Among the elite of etiquette-obsessed Tokyo, every public appearance was an opportunity for her to fail.

On the day of the ceremony Ume dressed carefully in a gold brocade gown made specially for the occasion. "My dress really did look nice, and it was praised as being very handsome, though it did not cost so much really as it seemed," Ume wrote, tempering her satisfaction with a show of pragmatism, as befitted a working woman. "It had a long train to it and I felt very dignified with it sweeping about." The empress arrived in a grand carriage, followed by a procession of smaller conveyances containing her ladies-in-waiting.

Before Ume had a chance to ask about protocol, she was summoned to make her bow. Though the setting was now a girls' school classroom rather than an imposing palace audience chamber, the twenty-year-old American-educated teacher who stood before her sovereign that morning felt very much like the bewildered kimono-clad six-year-old she had once been. "I did not know what to do, and I am sure I did not do it right, but I walked in without any instruction and bowed three times, as I believed must be done," she wrote. "But as I had to hold down my head, bow and come out, I could not see where the Empress was, nor how she looked at all."

After the empress had made the rounds of the various classes, the entire school gathered in the assembly hall, joined by an audience of illustrious guests. Ume took her place with the faculty in front of the long rows of girls; Sutematsu, now the Countess Oyama, stood to one side with the court ladies and others of noble rank. General Oyama had been raised to the rank of count by the Peerage Act of 1884, which conferred titles on non-nobles who had been of unusual service to Japan. "Countess" is "a very empty title, as [Sutematsu] herself said, and most absurd, but nevertheless hers in right, and that is what she is to be called in truth," Ume had written with poorly disguised envy. "It all sounds very fine, it seems to me, in name at least, and it may have some effect on the Europeans, at any rate."

A band played. "After the music ceased, the Empress arose and read something, of which I understood only a little," reported Ume, "but it spoke of the education of women, and the necessity of schools, urging both teachers and scholars to work upwards." Had Ume more perfectly comprehended the empress's words, she might have felt less approving. Though the empress had progressed to reading her own speeches rather than expressing them through an intermediary, she was hardly a progressive. "We consider women's duty is to possess the virtues of obsequiousness, to attend to their parents as well as to their fathers-in-law and mothers-in-law, assist their husbands, to conduct their family affairs properly, and, when they become mothers, to give their children home instruction," the empress had exhorted the assembled daughters of the nobility that afternoon. "To qualify themselves for these, they must acquire a proper knowledge of things."

Scholarship would assist these girls in the higher pursuit of chastity, benevolence, and filial piety. After all, went the prevailing wisdom, learning unanchored by sound moral teachings was at best useless and at worst dangerous. Though honored as their teacher, Ume—educated, unmarried, earning her own keep—was hardly a model for her highborn students to emulate.

Sutematsu, Shige, and Ume had accomplished a great deal since being uprooted and transplanted all over again. Largely forgotten by the government that had sent them abroad, they had preserved their sense of duty and made significant strides toward fulfilling it, despite Japan's growing ambivalence toward Western ways. But despite all this, they remained anomalies—Ume most of all. On the holiday celebrating the emperor's birthday that November, citizens of her rank were required to pay their respects at court—a privilege Ume had craved since her return to Japan, and to which she looked forward with nervous anticipation. But aside from Mrs. Shimoda, who as a former lady-in-waiting fell into a different category, Ume was the only woman of her bureaucratic rank. It would not do to have an unaccompanied woman among the men at the imperial audience. "So they asked me *privately*, you see, not to come, for they would not know what to do with me," Ume told Mrs. Lanman, covering her disappointment with a show of relief. On the appointed day, when her colleagues went to the palace, Ume had the day off—"far nicer than to have to bow one's head off at court," she insisted staunchly.

THE NEXT THREE YEARS passed swiftly for the trio, the regular rhythm of the academic year punctuated by the excitement of new babies. Shige doubled the size of her brood to four, on top of her teaching schedule. Sutematsu had a second child—which, with her three stepdaughters, brought her total to five—and found herself increasingly in the spotlight as her husband's star continued to rise.

Ume, secure at last in her prestigious teaching position and free of parental cares, had begun to enjoy herself, her letters preoccupied with gossip and social events. A cholera epidemic ravaged Tokyo in the summer of 1886, but Mrs. Lanman was not to worry, "as very few of the better classes catch it." The news that cholera had claimed the life of Ryo Yoshimasu, eldest of the original Iwakura girls, filled just half a paragraph. Ryo had married and borne a child, but beyond that Ume knew little, except that she lived in "reduced circumstances." The trio had not kept up with their old friend. "She seemed so different and changed, and we could not feel as we used to do, so we have lost sight of her," Ume wrote. "It is very sad to think that this is the end of poor Rio."

Ume's letters revealed a consciousness caught between cultures: she identified as a Japanese but thought more like an American. When Gilbert and Sullivan's *Mikado* opened in London and New York to great acclaim, she was full of righteous indignation. "Just suppose, if on the Japanese stage in one of the Tokyo theatres Queen Victoria and the British royal family were made the subject of a ridiculous play," she fumed to Mrs. Lanman, "why, the British representative would soon appeal for redress and make a great fuss." But her outrage was undermined by curiosity. "Can't you send me the libretto of it just for fun?"

That same fall, Japan was convulsed over the *Normanton* incident, in which a British cargo steamer, en route from Yokohama to Kobe, ran aground and sank. The two dozen Japanese passengers drowned, while the foreign captain and crew were saved. The British captain claimed that the victims, being Japanese, had not understood his exhortations in English to board the lifeboats. The Japanese press howled, and antiforeign sentiment exploded. "I send you a newspaper containing some accounts of the matter, which is indeed very curious," wrote Ume to Mrs. Lanman. But on to more important news: she had gotten a raise and a promotion in rank, and the emperor's mother had invited the whole school to see Giuseppe Chiarini's Royal Italian Circus, then visiting Tokyo.

Ume seemed somewhat oblivious to her compatriots' increasing wariness of foreign influence. When Prime Minister Ito hosted Japan's first costume ball at the Rokumeikan in April of 1887, Ume was pleased to receive an invitation, and dazzled by the scene: "old Emperors waltzing with peasant girls and Dutch maidens, old daimios polka-ing with the Goddess of Liberty and a jinricksha man and a Japanese carpenter in the same set with Queen Elizabeth." But those outside Ito's charmed circle were disgusted by the display, not to mention the rumors that in the wee hours Ito himself had seduced the pretty young wife of one of his councillors. The evening would come to be seen as a turning point in Japan's cultural history: the moment when the love affair with Western fashions soured for good. "The fancy ball made a great stir, and some of the newspapers made fun of the whole affair," Ume reported blithely. "Still it was a great success and everyone who went enjoyed it."

The following summer Ume left her parents' home and moved closer to the school with a widowed cousin who also taught there—a decision at once pragmatic and symbolic, confirming Ume's determination to remain independent. Her new household included the cousin's small niece and Ume's little sister Fuki, a Peeresses' student. The arrangement was congenial enough, though in quiet moments Ume betrayed the wistful longing that lurked always near the surface. "I love to think of you two, the same unchanged couple sitting by the fire in your own cozy room, just as I left you," she wrote to the Lanmans that winter. "Someday, when you are least expecting it, I will come in upon you, and find you in your old places, and I, I will take mine between you." With Shige and Sutematsu pouring their energies into motherhood, Ume had little opportunity to unburden herself to a kindred spirit.

THOUGH PROUD OF her job, Ume was less than enthralled by her daily responsibilities. "I have received notice to go to school," she wrote at the beginning of her second year, "and though the lessons do not begin until the first of the month, we teachers must go a week ahead of time. There we must decide our lessons, the hours, and make all the arrangements, which are too bothersome." She was unimpressed by the intellectual caliber of her highborn students, hampered as they were by the prescribed habits of their class and gender. "The girls of the nobility are stupid as a rule," she wrote, and on another occasion: "I wonder if these human dolls can learn much." Job security had not dispelled her underlying ambivalence about having a job in the first place: "It is far from easy work to go from class to class and room to room doing the same thing over and over again, and teaching the same things, although, you know, I am very fond of teaching and enjoy school very much indeed."

Her school bore little resemblance to the ones she had attended in Washington. Hirobumi Ito had become Japan's first prime minister in December 1885 and named Arinori Mori his minister of education, but their forward-thinking idealism and Sutematsu's Vassar-inspired input notwithstanding, the Peeresses' School was a strikingly conservative institution. Mrs. Shimoda, as directress, came to school each day in traditional court dress, and most of the students, ages six to eighteen, dressed in kimonos with purple *hakama*, the flowing skirt-like trousers worn on formal occasions. In addition to Japanese, Chinese literature, English or French, and history, the girls studied morals, calligraphy, drawing, sewing, tea ceremony, flower arrangement, household management, and formal etiquette. Instruction in arithmetic ceased once they reached their teens. Most of the students arrived by jinrikisha, the back of each conveyance emblazoned with a family crest, often followed by another carrying a maid. Maids and jinrikisha men waited at the school all day to escort their charges home again.

With enrollment growing, and English taught daily in the six higher grades, Ume was increasingly busy. By the end of the second year it was decided that the school would hire a foreigner to join the English department. But while Ume was eager to share her teaching load, the idea of a newcomer irked her; the school had recently hired a Frenchwoman who was paid more than Ume for fewer hours.

Then Ume had an idea. What if Alice Bacon was the new English teacher? Since 1883, Alice had been a teacher at the Hampton Normal and Agricultural Institute, the school where her late sister Rebecca had once been assistant principal. Alice had written to Ume not long before, expressing her concern for Sutematsu's shaky health, and Ume had the sense that a sojourn in Japan might be attractive to her. "You know, she has a very fine education, and has been used to teaching for ever so long, and she has had a good training with all those Indians and Negroes at Hampton," Ume wrote to Mrs. Lanman—once again revealing her American influences, and aligning herself with Alice as a bringer of enlightenment to the uncivilized. Hiring Alice, she felt certain, would please everyone: the Peeresses' School would gain a talented teacher, and Ume would enjoy the comfort of daily contact with a friend from her old life.

By the fall of 1887, the start of the school's third year, it was official. "Your letter with its unexpectedly good terms reached me a day or two ago," Alice wrote in October. "I have now decided to accept the offer for one year." She would arrange for a replacement at Hampton, and sail for Japan the following summer. A blizzard of questions followed: Could she bring her dog? Could she keep a horse? How many school days in the week? Would she need to learn some Japanese before she could start? "I mean to write to Stematz by this mail," she concluded, "so must close this catechetical letter."

Alice's salary at the Peeresses' School would be twice what Ume earned, but as it was Alice, Ume felt the sting far less than she might have otherwise. "It costs so much more for a foreigner to live than for a Japanese," she rationalized, "and then she has to come out on purpose, so I don't feel that my pay is too little."

NINE MONTHS LATER, Alice stepped ashore at Yokohama. Upon her arrival in June, she departed immediately to tour the country as far afield as Kyoto; she deputized Ume and Sutematsu, meanwhile, to arrange housing for her return to Tokyo. They found a perfect place: the vacant home of Japan's ambassador to Russia, ten minutes from the school and appointed half in Japanese and half in Western style, to facilitate the entertainment of foreign visitors. If Ume and Alice pooled their resources, the two households could share one roof and more spacious quarters than either could afford alone. Alice proclaimed herself delighted, and returned from her sightseeing in September to set up housekeeping. "Alice has been very busy getting things settled, getting her furniture, utensils, stove, carpets, and other things, and I have had to assist her as, of course, she could not talk to the tradesmen," Ume wrote in September.

The house was a perfect architectural expression of its bicultural occupants. Ume and her cousin, Mrs. Watanabe, lived with their gaggle of young girls (a few boarding students, in addition to Ume's little sister and Mrs. Watanabe's niece) in the larger Japanese side. Ume arranged her room with her Western bedstead and furniture, but otherwise the rooms were traditional. On Alice's side—accessible by a separate entrance through which it was permissible to walk in shoes—the windows were of glass instead of rice paper, the doors swung open instead of sliding, and there was carpet on the floors rather than tatami mats. The two halves of the house were connected by the *engawa*, a polished wood veranda roofed by the deep eaves of the house and overlooking the garden. Even the kitchen had two halves: Alice's cook prepared Western-style meals on an imported cast-iron stove, while a second cook steamed rice and grilled fish at an earthen Japanese stove. The servants lived in quarters behind the kitchen, and there was even a small stable for Alice's hoped-for horse.

Alice was an outsized presence in this hybrid household. This was partly literal: in height and breadth (not to mention opinionated self-confidence) she simply took up more space than tiny Ume and her equally diminutive dependents. And it was partly material: upon arrival, Alice promptly acquired new furniture, hung new wallpaper, and installed a state-of-the-art brass Rochester lamp, whose perforated burner provided a far more brilliant light than did the standard kerosene models. Mrs. Watanabe, "a dear little sweet-faced widow, the chaperon of our establishment," Alice wrote, "poetically remarked that my lamp was like the sun, and theirs was like a little star."

Then there was Bruce. Bruce was Alice's beloved border collie, and much to the chagrin of her housemates, she considered him part of the family. "He will insist on following Alice everywhere she goes, and so comes into our rooms sometimes," Ume complained to Mrs. Lanman. There was no teaching Bruce manners of any kind, let alone Japanese manners. "The dog is an attendant that I would willingly dispose of," Ume continued, "but I can't help that, and keep him out of our side as much as possible." The combination of ill-behaved Bruce and imposing Alice, her shrewd eyes taking in every detail from behind her glittering pince-nez, caused a sensation every time they left the house. An evening stroll along the nearest shopping street was never simple. "Apparently, a foreign lady with a dog shopping at that time of night is not a common sight in this part of the city, and we began to feel very much like a traveling show," Alice commented dryly.

Two weeks after moving in, Alice reported to work. As the Peeresses' School began its fourth academic year, the girls—among them Sutematsu's stepdaughters—lined up by size for the opening assembly, orderly as ever, though slightly more motley this year. The school now required foreign dress for its students, even though many of their parents had no experience wearing it. Uncomfortable as they were in scratchy wool stockings and ill-fitting leather shoes, the girls preserved the stillness of statues. Neither dazzled by their aristocratic pedigrees nor dismissive of their odd costumes, Alice saw only a group of children deserving of her sympathy, like the black students she had taught at Hampton. "Their lives are more or less stunted and cramped by the circumstances of their birth," she wrote of both groups, "the pickaninnies by poverty and the disabilities of their low social position, the peeresses by the rigid restraints and formalities that accompany their rank."

That evening, Alice looked over the English textbooks she had taken home from the school's library. One of them, a "Universal History," proclaimed, "The only historic race is the Caucasian, the others having done little worth recording." The line drew a sardonic smile. "It seems to me," she reflected, "that this will be a very interesting piece of news to a class of Japanese girls who are already quite familiar with the wonderfully stirring and heroic history of their own country." She asked Ume what the girls might think. "I should think they would say that the book was written by a Caucasian," Ume retorted smartly. Alice chuckled. "I have decided to skip the introduction which contains this statement," she wrote, "so as to avoid showing my pupils the self-conceit of my own race."

Though Alice's mind was very much her own, it remained always, and to a remarkable extent, open. She embraced her new surroundings with characteristic enthusiasm. Each morning she registered her attendance at school with her new signature seal. "I have just learned to seal my name right side up, and to recognize it when it is written in Japanese, and I regard this as a great advancement over my former state of ignorance," she reported with wry satisfaction. A bell signaled the start of each class, and after fifty minutes a man walking the corridors with a pair of clappers signaled its end. A great deal of ceremonial bowing took place between lessons. "The whole thing is very pretty, and I am charmed with this manner of calling to order and dismissing classes," Alice commented. "It might have a civilizing effect, if introduced into American schools."

At least as satisfying as the classroom work was the chance, after years of separation, to spend time with Sutematsu and her growing family. In the winter of 1886, Sutematsu had delighted her husband by giving him an heir, Takashi. (General Oyama protested merrily that he had hoped for yet another daughter to join his quartet of little girls, but that it was lucky this baby was a boy, because it was terribly ugly.) But since Takashi's birth, Sutematsu's health had wavered. She suffered a miscarriage in the wake of the 1886 cholera epidemic; pregnant yet again a year later, and tending to a daughter's sore throat, she was bending over a steam inhaler when it exploded, spraying her in the face with scalding water. The shock induced premature labor, and the baby, another girl, died two days later. Sutematsu recovered slowly.

Alice's bracing presence was a comfort—one that Sutematsu sorely needed. On top of all the pregnancies and illnesses, the Lady of the Roku-meikan had become something of a lightning rod for the conservative press. Her effortless Western ways and her public endorsement of women's education had made her a target of gossip; one paper even hinted that her marriage was doomed—a baseless rumor that was nevertheless picked up by American reporters. "Sutematsu feels very badly about the newspaper stories about her, and I don't wonder either," Ume wrote to Mrs. Lan-man. But even Ume's sympathy was tempered with criticism. "Sutematsu does not try to be popular, and her ill health and all makes society a kind of burden to her. Very often she refuses to see visitors, and I think that is wrong of a lady in her position." For once, Ume was content with her relatively low profile. "Japan has not quite made up its mind yet, whether women may have the same freedom as men," she wrote. "She is trying to find flaws in all who have gone ahead of time."

Sutematsu began to withdraw, turning away from the critical public eye toward her responsibilities at home. Her years at Vassar had begun to seem like a distant mirage. "Would that I could go about now in a green and blue plaid dress, with a turn-down collar under the left ear or other-wise!" she wrote to a Vassar classmate. "But alas! now my dresses have to come from Paris, and believe me, my dear Miss Howe, a plaid dress with a pig-tail hanging down one's back is a much more comfortable costume than all your French dresses." Concerned about Sutematsu's fragile health and low spirits, Alice called at her residence nearly every day.

Alice was especially fond of the Oyamas' son, who was not quite three. Little Takashi "regards me with great favor," she wrote, "partly because I ride horseback, and partly because I am so different from the rest of his small world." Whenever Alice came to visit, Takashi claimed her for his own. "When I have kissed him, he grows bolder, and stretches out his chubby hand to pat and smooth my cheeks," Alice wrote. "I think that the color of my face was what led him to begin this patting,—he wanted to see if it rubbed off." Alice's ruddy complexion wasn't the only difference Takashi noticed. After the patting, "he passes his little fingers all around my eye-sockets, with a view to ascertaining whether they really are as deep-set and hollow as they look." Though not usually fond of sitting still, Takashi loved to curl up in Alice's ample lap, to her private delight. "He calls me Bacon Chan, a kind of diminutive of Bacon San, or Miss Bacon."

Her own parents dead, her siblings married and scattered, Alice relished playing host to her Japanese "family." In November, she transported Ume, Sutematsu, and Shige to New England for the afternoon, racing home from school to prepare a Thanksgiving feast. The weather had turned cold at last, and Alice made chicken pie, turkey with oyster sauce, celery salad, and pumpkin pie. She even managed to get hold of some cranberry sauce, "most rare of all," exclaimed Ume, "which I had not eaten since I came back from America." The trio, cozy together in Ume's parlor (Alice's dining room was too small to hold them all), stuffed themselves silly and told Alice it tasted like home.

ALICE'S YEAR IN Tokyo was unusually full of pageantry. On the emperor's birthday in November of 1888, thanks to General Oyama, she had a front-row seat as the Heavenly Sovereign reviewed his well-equipped Western-style troops. "He did not look to me so very different from other people," Alice remarked matter-of-factly. "He is a skillful and daring horseman, it is said, but he rides in the old Japanese style, sitting all in a heap like a bag of meal, his legs dangling straight down on each side of the horse, and his elbows twitching and jerking with every motion of the animal."

Twenty years had wrought an extraordinary transformation: the Emperor Meiji, no longer invisibly "above the clouds," appeared before his subjects in much the same sort of gold-trimmed uniform as his fellow monarchs across the Western world. The ceremonial pomp that surrounded him was both awe inspiring and highly public; dazzled, few of his subjects reflected on the recent vintage of most of these "imperial traditions," many of them imported straight from Europe along with the guns and gold braid.

In December, the students of both the Peers' and Peeresses' schools were invited to tour the recently rebuilt Imperial Palace. Edo Castle, vacated by the shogun in 1868 as he capitulated to the young emperor, had subsequently burned; the audience chamber in which the girls had bowed before the empress no longer existed. Now at last the emperor was ready to move into a new home within the ancient ramparts. While the grand apartments remained vacant, the students would have the privilege of visiting them.

The girls would go at noon, followed by the boys two hours later. The short journey to the palace was an unexpected challenge. Two hundred and fifty girls needed to board two hundred and fifty jinrikishas, which then had to line up in order of their passengers' rank before the unwieldy procession could set out. "It was a funny sight when at last we were off, and our long, black line squirmed around the curves of the moats, looking like a procession of ants," Alice wrote. "I never before felt quite as much as if I were part of a circus."

There was another bottleneck at the palace gate, where everyone dusted off their shoes with their handkerchiefs, "lest a particle of dust from them should soil the sacred precincts," and then the unwieldy group proceeded along verandas and corridors affording views of grand public rooms and gardens. Alice was impressed in spite of herself ("The throne room is really magnificent"), but Ume, no longer an awestruck six-year-old, was more critical: "The one thing that strikes one is that there is too much [that is] brilliant and gay in one place—the richly ornamented ceilings take away from the gorgeous carpets; the one kills the other." Though the private quarters were furnished traditionally, the public rooms were not. The State Chamber featured a coffered ceiling lavishly painted with chrysanthemums, paulownias, and peonies, with ruby-colored drapes framing the carpeted dais, on which stood the emperor's throne, a gilded German armchair with scarlet cushions. The inlaid floors gleamed in the light of crystal chandeliers.

The girls, enthralled by their opulent surroundings, moved slowly; before they were halfway through, the boys had arrived at the palace gate. Alice looked on with some amusement. "As girls take more interest in upholstery than boys, the peers gained on the peeresses," she noted, but among the boys was the Crown Prince Haru;[*] if his group caught up, the girls would be forced to stop and bow until he passed. They hurried, but to no avail. "*Miya-sama!*" the cry went up. "His Majesty the Prince!" Everyone bent low, "all for the sake of a very minute boy in a little school uniform, with a little school knapsack on his back," Alice wrote. "I must say, that rather went against the grain with me. I don't mind bowing to officials and dignitaries, but when it comes to doubling myself up in an abject manner before a boy of seven, I don't like it."

The great event of the year—indeed of the Emperor Meiji's reign thus far—occurred just after the imperial family took up residence in the new quarters. Over the previous two decades it had become abundantly clear to Japan's leaders that the true mark of a civilized nation was representative government. On February 11, 1889, a state holiday commemorating the birth of Japan's mythical first ruler, the emperor bestowed upon his subjects Japan's first constitution, authorizing the creation of a bicameral Imperial Diet, on the Prussian model. No matter that sovereignty remained

---

[*] Crown Prince Haru—later Yoshihito, the Emperor Taisho—was the child of an imperial concubine. Unable to bear children herself, the empress had adopted him.

securely in the sacred person of the emperor, not the people; the promulgation of the constitution seemed to the Japanese a monumental step toward
recognition on the global stage, and they celebrated accordingly.

Sutematsu, Shige, and Ume must have found the occasion especially
satisfying. Of the ten officials whose signatures followed the emperor's
on the precious document, the first was Kiyotaka Kuroda, the man
whose idea it had been to send them to America so long ago. He was
now prime minister. Under Kuroda's name was that of his predecessor
and Ume's patron, Hirobumi Ito, regarded as the constitution's framer.
Ito and another signer, Justice Minister Akiyoshi Yamada, had both
traveled with the girls as part of the Iwakura Mission. Further down
the list were Iwao Oyama, Sutematsu's husband, and Arinori Mori, the
minister of education, who had greeted the shawl-wrapped girls on a
snowy Washington train platform once upon a time. The lives of those
bewildered children had become entwined with those of the most powerful men in Japan.

"The procession was the finest that I have seen yet," wrote Alice. For
the first time, the emperor and empress rode together in one carriage—an
unprecedented acknowledgment of the Western idea that marriage raised
the empress to the same exalted level as her husband. The coach was especially gorgeous, Alice thought, "drawn by six black horses, each led by a
magnificent black, white, and gold liveried groom." The coachman was
bedecked in so much gold trim that he didn't look real. The chrysanthemum crest glittered on the doors and panels, and crowning the roof was a
golden finial in the shape of a phoenix. But at this point Alice was forced
to bow with everyone else, "so that I saw nothing more but the top of the
Empress's bonnet as she turned to look at her little peeresses, who seem to
have a warm place in her heart."

Alice's interest in the event went deeper than its ceremonial trappings.
Several days later, she was visiting Sutematsu when General Oyama joined
them, bearing with him the official English translation of the new constitution. "With the greatest pride he pointed out to me the twenty-eighth
article, which guarantees religious liberty to all Japanese subjects," Alice

reported, equally proud. Leonard Bacon's exchanges with Arinori Mori seventeen years earlier had led directly to the article's inclusion.

The moment was bittersweet, however: on the very day of the constitution's promulgation, Mori was assassinated by an imperial loyalist who found his liberal attitudes toward Japanese tradition disrespectful. Five days after the emperor and empress rode by in triumphant splendor, Alice watched Mori's solemn funeral cortège pass near her house. "It seems so terrible that I can not realize it," Ume wrote of the man who had at first reacted to her seven-year-old self with such dismay. "I owed him a great deal when in America."

In April, Alice's eagerness to gaze directly upon the empress was at last satisfied. The chief patroness of the Peeresses' School was coming to visit and would be sitting in on Miss Bacon's English class. Empress Haruko had undergone a transformation quite as profound as her husband's in the years since the Iwakura Mission had sailed. Gone were the blackened teeth and shaved eyebrows, the cone-shaped ceremonial robes. The empress now ordered her gowns from Paris like any Western statesman's wife, and made regular appearances at charity bazaars and other public functions. For all her foreign finery, however, she was still an object of mysterious fascination.

When Alice arrived at school on the appointed day, the imperial accessories—lacquered tableware, silver smoking sets, upholstered chairs—had already arrived, and everyone was buzzing with adrenaline. After one last session of ceremonial bowing practice with Ume, Alice settled down by the window to wait. Gazing down into the yard, she watched as a mounted officer arrived bearing a purple silk flag embroidered with the gold chrysanthemum. After him came "quite a cavalcade" of soldiers with red and white pennants, and at last the red-and-gold coach containing the empress. Her ladies, having arrived earlier, formed a double line from the coach to the door, and Her Majesty entered the school.

When Alice reached her classroom, she found her girls in an uproar and an unfamiliar chair—exquisite black lacquer, with gold chrysanthemums and a purple brocade seat—standing near her desk. Claiming the class's attention with some difficulty, Alice had just begun the lesson when footsteps clattered along the hall and the door burst open. "The girls rose in their places, and I turned toward the door, expecting to see the Empress standing there, but no one appeared but a tousle-headed little secretary, who gazed distractedly into the room, muttered incoherently, and then shut the door with a bang," Alice wrote. "The girls dropped back into their seats, my heart began to beat again, and we went on with the lesson." A few minutes passed, and then the whole episode repeated itself: hurrying feet, wild-eyed secretary, incoherent exclamations, slammed door—followed by an explosion of nervous giggles from students and teacher alike.

"At last there was a rustle of silken skirts in the hall, and we knew that our hour was come," Alice continued. Everyone rose, bowed, and kept their heads down until the empress had taken her seat. Alice had low expectations for her girls after so much nervous excitement, "but there is where I did not fully understand my little peeresses," she wrote with admiration. "From the moment there was need for it they showed the most perfect self-possession, and I have never had better or less timid recitations in my life than those that they made in the Empress' presence."

The empress stayed for half an hour, during which time Alice managed to steal several good glimpses. She saw a small, slight woman, "rather loaded down by her heavy dove-colored silk dress and dove-colored Paris bonnet with a white plume," Alice reported. She was struck by the empress's air of patient melancholy. "They say that she is a very intellectual woman, and one of great strength and beauty of character."

When every girl had recited, the empress took her leave, and Alice dismissed her class, "feeling quite light hearted." But the day was not over. The foreign teachers, it seemed, would be received individually by the empress along with the senior Japanese faculty. No time for rehearsals now. Ume gave Alice a few hasty instructions and told her to stand with a view into the audience room so that she could watch Ume's example. But this eminently reasonable plan was quickly foiled. "As I was following this suggestion and moving toward a position in front of the door," Alice wrote, "I was seized and held by my old enemy, the little secretary, who had evidently taken the idea into his erratic little head that unless physical force were applied to restrain her, that outside barbarian would rush right into the imperial presence."

Luckily there was just time enough for a whispered conference when Ume reappeared moments later. Then it was Alice's turn. Enter, bow, walk straight ahead, turn right ninety degrees to face the seated empress, step forward, bow. An attendant appeared with a large, white paper-wrapped bundle on a tray, which Alice lifted to her breast and touched with her forehead. Bow again. Retreat backward, holding the bundle high in respect. At the door, bow once more. The bundles, when Ume and Alice unwrapped them, proved to contain yards and yards of the finest white silk, valuable enough even without their imperial provenance.

The empress spent the entire day at school, and then everyone went home, exhausted and relieved. "I was very glad," Alice remarked, "to order my horse and have a good ride to limber me up and make me feel myself once more a free American woman after all my unaccustomed bowing and cringing."

ALL TOO SOON it was summer again. Alice's year was drawing to an end. Her students brought farewell gifts: one class presented her with a doll dressed in the traditional costume of a girl of twelve, like themselves; another gave her emperor and empress dolls such as might appear on the topmost tier of a red-draped doll festival display, with doll-sized musical instruments, tea implements, and *bento* boxes to arrange around them.

There was a real baby to play with as well: Sutematsu had given birth to her second son, Kashiwa, at the beginning of June. Alice was fascinated by the novel details of the infant's first weeks: his loose cotton clothes, with cloth ties instead of buttons and pins; the serenity of his caregivers. "Here, nobody ever makes a noise at a baby, or jiggles or shakes it, to stop it crying," Alice marveled.

In the middle of July, just before Tokyo's heat made scholarship impossible, the Peeresses' School held its closing exercises—unusually grand in 1889, as the school was moving to brand-new quarters and the empress would be on hand to mark the occasion with a rare speech. Alice watched the elaborately choreographed proceedings with her usual mixture of avid interest and amusement, noting the graduates' diplomas—"not at all like the sheepskins of our native land, but dainty little Japanese scrolls on rollers, with brown and gold brocade mountings"—and the impeccable precision with which the girls executed so many bows ("my back fairly ached from sympathy"). There was music between the speeches, including a song written by the empress especially for the school, sung by the students with their heads reverently bowed:

> *Even a diamond, if not polished, will fail to shine;*
> *People, too, unless they study, will not demonstrate true virtue.*
> *If one is diligent every moment all day long,*
> *Like the hands of a clock that move without pause*
> *What is there that will not be achieved?*

Diamonds and clocks were daringly Western references, as was the empress's inspiration. Her lyric took its cue from the sixth of Benjamin Franklin's thirteen virtues: "Lose no time; be always employed in something useful; cut off all unnecessary actions." Franklin, as introduced by Samuel Smiles in *Self-help*, was the most famous American name in Meiji Japan. But the comparison of scholarship to the measured, mechanical ticking of a timepiece was, perhaps inadvertently, less than inspiring.

The empress, all in white this time, again struck Alice as a poignant figure, powerless to bridge the gulf between her elaborate black-and-gold lacquered chair on the dais and the rows of young faces in front of her. "Somehow I always feel sorry for her," Alice wrote, "and I think she would be sorry for herself, if she knew how much more fun it is to be a Yankee school-ma'am than an empress."

A little more than a week later, Alice left for Kyoto, ending her year with another month of travel before sailing for San Francisco in September. Pragmatic to the core, she wasted little ink on valediction, but she was no less aware of how her extraordinary year had changed her. Having lived more in the Japanese style than almost any other foreigner, she nevertheless felt conspicuously foreign among the Japanese; her purpose in Japan had been educational rather than spiritual, which set her apart from the missionaries, but her high-minded idealism distanced her as well from the foreign merchants and diplomats. Much like the three friends she had followed to Japan, she found herself in a category by herself—but where Sutematsu, Ume, and Shige wrestled with bouts of discouragement and loneliness, Alice's confident optimism, unobstructed by questions of identity, carried her forward, even when her path was less than clear. "The word 'civilization' is so difficult to define and to understand, that I do not know what it means now as well as I did when I left home," she wrote ruefully.

She remained undaunted by the ambiguity, however, and her engagement with Japan was far from over. She may have been leaving the trio behind, but she was carrying their legacy into the future. When she boarded the ship that would take her home, she was not alone. Under departures on the British steamer *Belgic*, for San Francisco, the *Japan Weekly Mail* listed "Miss A. Bacon, child, and native servant." Her young companion was Mitsu Watanabe, the five-year-old niece of Ume's cousin. Alice, unfettered by familial obligations but eager to remain connected to her Japanese "family," had adopted her. For the next decade, like Ume before her, Mitsu would grow up in America.

"My dear Mrs. Lanman," wrote Ume in August of 1889, barely a month after school had ended. "Where do you think I am?" Even as Alice Bacon was still traveling through the Japanese countryside, enjoying the last weeks of her year in Japan, Ume, to her profound delight, had just arrived in the suburbs of Philadelphia.

For some time, ever since joining the faculty of the Peeresses' School, Ume had been feeling the limitations of her education. The Women's Higher Normal School in Tokyo was beginning to graduate women trained as teachers, and though she could hardly criticize their achievements, these growing ranks of enlightened—and ambitious—women shook Ume's confidence in her own value. "I often wish I had had Sutematsu's training," she wrote, "which has been of no use to her," she added peevishly.

It was maddening: Sutematsu and Shige, simply by virtue of their few years' seniority, had made it to Vassar before their time in America was up, and yet it was their marriages, not their college years, that had ensured their social and financial security. Too young for college, Ume had also been too young to retain the language skills and cultural identity that might have made marriage to a Japanese man conceivable. Now, as she entered her twenties and contemplated the rest of her life as a single working woman, she regretted the lack of a college degree. "I feel that now my mind is more developed than at the time I came back," she wrote, "and that I would appreciate study more." Teaching might be her lot, but anonymity didn't have to be: "Though I may have enough education to carry me along through life in its ordinary paths, I want more than that."

Even before Alice's arrival in Tokyo, Ume had asked Mrs. Lanman to collect information for her: catalogs from Smith College, Wellesley, Mount Holyoke. Vassar was conspicuously absent from her list of requests, possibly because she was already familiar with the campus—but also perhaps because she preferred to choose her own path, rather than the one already trod by Sutematsu and Shige. Ume had reason to hope that the Peeresses' School would continue to pay her salary if she took a leave for further study abroad, but before she broached the question she needed a clear sense of what her expenses might be.

Help arrived suddenly, and from an unexpected quarter. Since her return to Tokyo, Ume had become close to Clara Whitney, an American missionary's daughter whose family had moved to Japan when she was fourteen, just a few years after Ume had left for America. Close in age, the two young women enjoyed each other's company: Clara spoke good Japanese and was one of the few foreigners Ume knew with a degree of real bicultural understanding. Ume wasn't particularly comfortable with the Whitneys' fervent strain of Christian piety, and both Clara's father and Ume's had been scandalized when Clara (already six months pregnant) married a Japanese man several years her junior. Still, Clara was a friend, and Ume told her in confidence of her ambition to study further in the States.

Clara wasted no time. She wrote to her friend Mary Harris Morris, a Philadelphia matron passionately engaged in a dizzying array of educational and missionary projects. Because her husband, Wistar Morris, was a director of the Pennsylvania Railroad, Mrs. Morris was in a position to dispense considerable philanthropic largesse, and she remembered Ume as a ward of the Lanmans. Without further ado, Ume became one of her causes: Mrs. Morris arranged for Ume to attend the newly founded Bryn Mawr College as a special student with reduced tuition, starting immediately. But having just gotten Alice settled in for her year of teaching in

Tokyo, Ume couldn't very well disappear; moreover, the administrators of the Peeresses' School would need diplomatic handling if Ume was to win their support for her plan. Gratified but cautious, she pocketed Mrs. Morris's offer for the time being.

The following spring Mrs. Morris renewed her encouragements. Ume dithered. "Mrs. Morris may be very kind, but don't you think it would be better to be sent from the school, not to depend on her entirely?" she asked Mrs. Lanman. In the end, and somewhat to Ume's surprise, the president of the Peeresses' School endorsed her plan, granting her leave to study at Bryn Mawr for two years at her present salary—provided, of course, that she came back. "Won't it be splendid!" she wrote, exultant. (Predictably, her delight was soon tempered with irritation: "You can not imagine the great mountain of work before me, and I dread to begin—it is such an undertaking.")

As soon as the closing ceremonies at school were over, Ume was off. The eager twenty-four-year-old woman who sailed bore little resemblance to the quaking child who had once made the same journey. This time she steered her own course. Her new phase would be at once a step forward and a respite: her studies would advance her career in Japan and also provide a much-needed break. Seven years of struggle to prove her worth to her country had left Ume weary. And while she would remain at least as anomalous in Philadelphia as she was in Tokyo, America still felt more like home.

UME ENROLLED AT Bryn Mawr in September of 1889, the beginning of the college's fifth year of existence. Immediately and joyfully in her element, she was surrounded by exactly the kind of unapologetically intellectual, independent women she had despaired of ever finding in Tokyo. Bryn Mawr's students were an ambitious bunch, determined to prove themselves. "Our failures only marry," the college's imposing dean, Martha Carey Thomas, was heard to say. Here, at least, no one was going to question the path Ume had chosen, or try to find her a husband.

It was at Bryn Mawr that Ume began the deepest friendship of her life—with Anna Cope Hartshorne, a fellow student who would later become the most important supporter of Ume's ambitions. From their first meeting, Anna was impressed with Ume's maturity. They met at an afternoon tea hosted by Rose Chamberlin, a square-jawed, six-foot Englishwoman who taught German. "Miss Tsuda was guest of honor, and looked very small and dainty as she stood beside our tall hostess, but as I remember my impression it was less of her smallness than of Miss Chamberlin's unusual height and breadth," Anna wrote. "It was easy to see that their relation was already that of friends rather than teacher and pupil." Ume, addressing the tea party guests on the subject of her life and work in Japan, was preternaturally poised: "Like a princess, and for the same reason, that she was used to being looked at and no longer gave a hoot, so to say."

Though Ume's nominal purpose in this second sojourn abroad was to learn more about American schools and teaching methods, at Bryn Mawr she chose biology, not English, as her focus. It is not hard to imagine her much-thwarted competitive streak driving her choice. Most of the male students sent abroad by the Meiji government had studied science or engineering, and returned to find prestigious positions waiting for them— a far cry from the lukewarm reception the trio had received. Here was a chance to prove that a woman could excel in a masculine field. And excel she did, eventually coauthoring an article with one of her professors entitled "The Orientation of the Frog's Egg" in the *Quarterly Journal of Microscopical Science.*

Ume's scientific achievements did not, however, eclipse her larger mission. She spent her first summer vacation at the Hampton Institute in Virginia, collaborating with Alice on a different sort of manuscript: a treatise on the daily life of Japanese women, from birth to old age, peeress to peasant, in the cities and in the fields. *Japanese Girls and Women*, the first comprehensive work on its subject, found a publisher immediately. "I have today handed over the manuscript to Mr. [Horace E.] Scudder, editor of the Atlantic & one of the big bugs of Houghton, Mifflin & Co.," Alice wrote to Ume after she returned to Bryn Mawr for the start of the fall term in 1890. "I don't want to be unduly hopeful, but I think he will take it and illustrate it."

By the summer of 1891, the book was in print. Despite Ume's extensive contributions to the project, Alice's name appeared alone on the title page. This was not selfishness on Alice's part: on the contrary, Alice took steps to ensure that the book's copyright would revert to Ume upon Alice's death; she also split the royalties scrupulously down the middle and sent Ume half of every payment. For all her ambition, Ume did not mind the omission; Alice's sole authorship was prudence, and it was not misplaced.

Though optimistic about the future of Japanese womanhood, *Japanese Girls and Women* was far from complimentary about the present. "Better laws, broader education for the women, a change in public opinion on the subject, caused by the study, by the men educated abroad, of the homes of Europe and America,—these are the forces which alone can bring the women of Japan up to that place in the home which their intellectual and moral qualities fit them to fill," the book declared. The Tokyo establishment was not amused. Even Ume's father, the iconoclastic Sen Tsuda, was not ready to see his daughter's name attached to such an explicit criticism of Japanese society. Her unusual position as a career woman was precarious enough.

The book was dedicated to Sutematsu, "in the name of our childhood's friendship, unchanged and unshaken by the changes and separations of our maturer years," and prefaced by sincere gratitude to Ume, "an old and intimate friend" who had made "many valuable additions." In several admiring reviews, the American press took note of Alice's unusual degree of familiarity with her subject. "She does not evade, but tells exactly what she sees," wrote the *New York Times*. "She has been industrious in finding the reasons for many things, and has been wise enough to have submitted her work to the criticism of Japanese ladies."

But the reaction in Japan, where the tide of conservatism continued to rise, was not as enthusiastic. Less than a year earlier the emperor had issued his Imperial Rescript on Education, celebrating the basic tenets of Confucian morality: hierarchy, consensus, obedience. "This is the glory of the fundamental character of Our Empire, and herein also lies the source of Our education," it read. Framed copies of the document hung in every school in Japan, and on national holidays schoolchildren chanted its text with heads bowed. The emperor, not Benjamin Franklin or Samuel Smiles, was the ideal they revered now. There wasn't nearly as much room for the advancement of women in the lines they recited.

"I do not think it is so compromising to Ume as [her father and others] seem to think," Sutematsu wrote to Ume and Alice during the summer of the book's publication, "but it is better to be on the safe side, especially as now there is so much conservative spirit cultivated even among the best and most educated classes." Alice offered to ask the publisher to remove Ume's name from the preface. "If it will do any good to shift the blame onto me," she suggested further to Ume, "you could write an open letter to one of the prominent Tokyo papers and say that your work on the book consisted largely in modifying my statements so that there should be nothing about them to hurt the Japanese national pride, and that at times I was so pigheaded that even your persuasions & arguments did not move me." (The unpleasant fallout in Tokyo taught Alice to protect her friends. When, a few years later, she published an epistolary memoir of her year in Tokyo entitled *A Japanese Interior*, she gave Ume and Sutematsu pseudonyms and dedicated the volume to her own siblings, to whom the original letters had been written.)

But Ume opted to ignore Alice's suggestions. The disgruntled conservatives in Tokyo were too far away to bother about, and meanwhile the book was proving an excellent springboard for her reputation in America. She began to promote the cause of Japanese women's education more widely and more forcefully—one lecture, to the Massachusetts Society for the University Education of Women, was titled "Education and Culture— What Japanese Women Want Now." By 1892, Ume had inspired her benefactress, Mary Harris Morris, and Bryn Mawr's Martha Carey Thomas to organize the American Women's Scholarship for Japanese Women, to be granted for study at Bryn Mawr. A fifteen-member committee of affluent Philadelphia matrons raised eight thousand dollars in short order.

Alice, too, used the attention garnered by her book to advance her own cause. In August 1891, vacationing with a sister in Norfolk, Connecticut—one town over from Colebrook—she held a "Japanese tea and chopstick supper" at the village hall, with girls in kimonos serving refreshments. "The tables were beautifully arranged and decorated and no end of amusement was caused by the ludicrous efforts of the hungry ones to satisfy their cravings with the chop-sticks, which by the way were the only instruments allowed under penalty of a fine," reported the local paper. The event raised two hundred dollars for the Hampton Institute.

DESPITE UME'S EFFORTS on behalf of female students, her idea of a woman's place was surprisingly old-fashioned. Where Martha Carey Thomas exhorted her students to leave domesticity behind for the higher calling of scholarship, Ume advocated education only insofar as it raised women to a level of intellectual equality with their own menfolk. Yes, a few exceptional (or perhaps unfortunate) souls would follow in her footsteps, advancing to the college level in order to become the teachers of the new generation. But that new generation would not necessarily aspire to the example of its teachers. "Wives must fit themselves to be companions of educated men, and mothers that they may wisely influence their sons," Ume told her audiences, "and there must be true sympathy of thought between them in the home." Good wife, wise mother: the Meiji ideal of *ryosai kenbo* persisted.

Sutematsu, whose retreat to domestic life had so disappointed Ume, was in fact a paragon of the new Japanese woman that Ume hoped to train: the intellectual equal of her husband, his helpmeet and companion rather than his obedient drudge, engaged with world affairs and charitable efforts, raising educated sons and daughters for the good of the nation. Sutematsu did not, however, share the rosy confidence in the future of Japanese womanhood that *Japanese Girls and Women* set forth. Alice and Ume had been "all together too sympathetic," Sutematsu insisted. "You left out, if I may be allowed to criticize, all that pettiness, envy and untruthfulness which seem to me to go side by side with some of the best qualities in a Japanese woman." Her frustrations made a striking counterpoint to Ume's speeches: raised for intellectual achievement, Sutematsu found the domestic sphere, even at her exalted level, claustrophobic, while Ume, having forsaken domesticity altogether, struggled with the loneliness of her professional path.

Ume disdained the concessions that her two married friends had made to Japanese convention—from the deference they showed their husbands to the slender *kiseru* pipes they now smoked. "Are you horrified?" Sutematsu wrote to her old Vassar friend Anne Southworth. "Almost all Japanese ladies smoke and we make no secret of it. Mrs. Uriu (Miss Nagai that used to be) began it and I followed. Miss Tsuda vainly tried to dissuade us from this pernicious practice, but now she has given it up as a bad job. You don't know what a soothing thing it is." Loneliness and financial insecurity may not have weighed as heavily on Sutematsu and Shige, but the tensions inherent in their hybrid identities were no less real. Ume could hold herself apart from other Japanese women, but Sutematsu and Shige, as the wives of prominent men, did not have that luxury.

Though her marriage to Iwao Oyama had proved unusually happy, Sutematsu found the scrutiny attached to her high social profile bruising. Her duties as the wife of the minister of war kept her busy enough, but on top of that she now held the official title of "Advisor on Westernization in the Court." Her post required frequent visits to the palace, either to guide the empress and her ladies in the details of wardrobe and etiquette, or to serve as an interpreter for the wives of foreign dignitaries. This she was glad to do, appalled as she was by the backward attitudes of the court conservatives, foremost among whom was Utako Shimoda herself, the former lady-in-waiting who directed the Peeresses' School. "I have no patience with her," Sutematsu fumed to Ume and Alice with uncharacteristic heat. "She ought to be kicked out of that school, I have no hesitation in saying that to every one, although it may not be for the good of my children if she hears it."

Mrs. Shimoda and Sutematsu might both have been deeply committed to educating girls, but there the affinity ended. The woman Sutematsu had once described as a "deep thinker" had proved unable to transcend her conservative roots. "What do you think the girls, especially her boarders, say?" Sutematsu raged. "That it is not patriotic to wear Japanese dresses made of *foreign stuffs*, and that to drink *milk* or eat *meat* are disloyal to Japan!!! What do you think of a teacher that puts such ideas into girls heads?" Unfortunately, too many parents of Peeresses' students shared Mrs. Shimoda's ideas.

Sutematsu's proximity to the empress did not endear her to the women of her own circle, and neither did her husband's place in the emperor's inner sanctum of advisers. The Oyamas had recently moved to a grand new house built on several acres of land two miles west of the palace, in the quiet suburb of Onden (near today's bustling pop-culture mecca of Harajuku). Designed by a German architect, the house satisfied General Oyama's florid European preferences: brick-built and massive, it was lavishly endowed with arches, dormer windows, French furniture, and a pointed turret rising from one corner. (Though the children grew up in Western clothing, they spent most of their time in the Japanese-style wing attached to the back of the house, "for their mother was too wise to bring them up as strangers to the customs of their own country," wrote a foreign friend.) In November 1890, just as the family finished settling in, the emperor himself paid a call.

Mutsuhito had embraced a new policy of visiting his most senior councillors in their homes, in order to know them more personally. He arrived at the Oyamas' at one o'clock in the afternoon and was still enjoying their hospitality—music, a performance of *noh* drama, staged readings of Chinese poetry—at ten o'clock that evening. His reluctance to leave was gratifying, but the elaborate event was exhausting and did nothing to alleviate the envy of Sutematsu's acquaintances. They clucked over her wealth, her Parisian gowns, her exalted rank—all this for a woman who couldn't even write decent Japanese and was known to address her husband by his first name!

HAVING WON THE esteem of her Philadelphia benefactors and the respect of her college, not to mention a year's extension on her original two-year plan, Ume returned to Tokyo in 1892. A certificate signed by Bryn Mawr's president called her "an intelligent, apt and diligent student" and declared, "Miss Tsuda has shown at this college all the virtues that grace and adorn the womanly character, and bears with her the honour, esteem and kindly regard of all the officers and students of the college." All, perhaps, save Martha Carey Thomas, who could not understand Ume's determination to resume her teaching career in Japan rather than pursue a scientific one in the United States. Bryn Mawr had offered Ume a position as a laboratory assistant, but she turned it down. "I don't believe Miss Thomas ever quite forgave her what probably seemed ingratitude and misprisal of true scholarship," wrote Anna Hartshorne.

Miss Thomas's view, with its emphasis on individual achievement, was a particularly American one; what she failed to grasp was that Ume, her American youth notwithstanding, had never relinquished her identity as a daughter of Japan. Tempting as it might have been to pursue an academic career in Pennsylvania, it was more important to fulfill the mission she had accepted as a child. Ume may have craved recognition, but always in the context of her larger obligation.

Ume resumed her work at the Peeresses' School and poured herself into her new project, promoting the newly created American Women's Scholarship that would encourage other young women to follow her example. While at Bryn Mawr, she had discovered a source of great energy in the audiences she addressed; back in Tokyo, she sought new ones. "Feeling as I do, that the one thing that Japan needs most at the present day is the elevation of the future wives and mothers, can you wonder that I most thoroughly desire a class of earnest, native women workers who can take up the work, showing in their own persons a happy combination of Japanese education, refinement, and culture, and the best results of Western civilization and religion?" she asked in the pages of the *Japan Weekly Mail*.

We want living examples to show the scoffing world that education does not spoil a woman. We want a woman to plead the wrongs of women. We want a clear head and a clever tongue to show the men how much is unjust in the lives of women. We want better teachers for our schools, and leaders in good movements pertaining to women.

Flush with a sense of renewed purpose in her vocation, Ume thought it especially galling, upon her return, to find that Sutematsu and Shige were still trying to play matchmaker. Ume was twenty-seven years old. When would her closest friends finally accept the path she had chosen? In her mail that fall, Alice found an exasperated screed from Ume, which she answered with the wisdom of personal experience. "I am afraid it is a fault of married women all the world over to patronize the unmarried and try to marry them off," she wrote to Ume. "Don't be worried by it. When you are as old as I am, I think that even Stematz & Shige will give you up."

Ume was equally irritated by her two dearest friends' relative lack of activist resolve. Here, too, the invaluable Alice provided perspective. "I am sorry that you find the gap widen between yourself & them, and sorry too that they are so inclined to be conservative & to drift with the tide," she wrote, "but a married woman is handicapped and has her husband's wishes and her children's future to think of while independent old maids like you and me can do as we choose and at least harm no one but ourselves by our enthusiasms or our mistakes and failures." Alice's soothing words must have had some effect. That fall, Ume convened a Japanese selection committee for the American scholarship, many of whose members had studied abroad. One of them was Shige.

Though she was now the mother of five with a sixth on the way, Shige had continued to teach, first at the Tokyo Music School and subsequently at the Women's Higher Normal School. Never as ambitious as Sutematsu or Ume, she had quietly managed to achieve a balance between teaching and family that was no less extraordinary. Her willingness to contribute her time to Ume's cause may have had something to do with a sudden shift in her household duties. Her responsibilities as a mother were growing, but she would soon have less work to do as a wife. In September of 1892, her husband left for Paris to take up a post as naval attaché to the Japanese embassy there. He would not return for four years.

· · ·

SOTOKICHI URIU WAS not the only military man who found his responsibilities increasing in 1892. After more than a decade of service, Iwao Oyama had recently submitted his resignation, but it was only a matter of months before he was recalled to his former office. Japan was mobilizing for war.

During the 1870s Japan had poured its energies into reform at every level, from education to industry to the structure of government. Domestic improvements took priority; the Western powers had made it quite clear they were not interested in negotiating with a nation they considered backward. But Japan's leaders remained acutely aware of their global context, and in the 1880s they watched with growing alarm as an increasingly industrialized Europe scrambled for new colonial territories. While the Meiji leaders were building a nation, other nations had been building empires, their reach drawing ever closer. The French were now in Indochina, the Americans in Hawaii, the Russians and the British fighting over central Asia. The "civilized" nations of the world were asserting sovereignty over the "unenlightened." If Japan had truly achieved its own enlightenment, it needed to protect itself from foreign encroachment, and perhaps do a little asserting of its own as well. Among all things Western that Japan had adopted in the previous decades, imperialism—an idea the West never meant to export—was rapidly becoming the most important.

Korea quickly became the focus of Japan's ambition. In 1876 the Japanese had taken a page from Commodore Perry's book and tried a little gunboat diplomacy of their own, "opening" Korea to trade as the Americans had once "opened" Japan: forcing the establishment of treaty ports and securing extraterritorial immunity for Japanese nationals. Ever since, China and Japan had eyed each other warily, each concerned about the other's domination of the Korean peninsula dangling between them.

By the early 1890s, Japan's leaders saw control of Korea as vital to Japanese national security. Only under enlightened Japanese influence—rather than the enfeebled patronage of China—could Korea withstand the predatory threat of the Western colonizers. The Meiji government, now firmly established, directed a steadily increasing flow of funds to the military: the army began to stage large-scale maneuvers, and the navy added larger warships and transports to its fleet. In the spring of 1894, a Korean peasant rebellion prompted both China and Japan to send in troops, setting the stage for direct confrontation. In July, Japanese forces seized the royal palace and forced the Korean king to endorse the expulsion of the Chinese.

For the first time since the sixteenth century, when the warlord Hideyoshi Toyotomi had launched his own brutal and ill-fated invasion of Korea, Japan faced war on foreign soil. On August 1, Japan declared war on China. At the head of Japan's Second Army was General Iwao Oyama.

"Of course I feel much anxiety," wrote Sutematsu to Alice that fall, "but at the same time I know that we shall be victorious in the end, and my husband though he may suffer many privations, still he will return after conquering China, all safe & well." The war effort was a tonic, chasing away the miasma of gossip and frustration that often sickened her. She rushed to gather whatever her warrior husband would need to face a frigid Chinese winter: fur linings for his coat and boots, woolen socks and flannel shirts, underwear padded with silk wadding, a hot-water bottle, and a supply of *kairo* hand warmers—cloth-covered tin boxes with holes in one end, inside which a stick of charcoal could burn for hours.

When she wasn't helping her husband, Sutematsu turned her attention to larger projects. "In July a committee of sixty ladies of which I was a member started to collect money among women & the result was a tremendous success," she wrote. "You have no idea—at least I cannot half express to you—of the enthusiasm of the people and the way they offer everything they possess to afford comfort to the soldiers." Primed by the example of the charity bazaars that Sutematsu had helped start a decade earlier, the female elite of Tokyo participated in full force. The empress herself led the Ladies' Volunteer Nursing Association, and Sutematsu joined in rolling bandages for the Red Cross. "We all wear nurses' costume and we carbolize our hands & clothes in a truly hospital style[,] for the Army is very strict about antiseptic treatment," she told Alice. "We have made millions of bandages but we are still making them."

Years later, Sutematsu was still struck by the efforts of her peers: "They who never dressed themselves without maids waiting on them, they who never held in their hands anything heavier than their handkerchiefs, they who never went outside of their houses without two or three attendants, all come alone to the hospital with their little lunch baskets and their bundles containing their nurse's uniforms." Behind the polished façade of the general's elegant wife, the spirit of the Aizu girl who had helped defend her castle survived. As she watched the bustle of preparation on the parade ground and at the train station, Sutematsu confided to Alice, "I felt as if I wanted to be a soldier too."

China's army was vastly larger than Japan's, and her navy boasted twice as many vessels. Western observers did not share Sutematsu's sublime confidence that her husband's forces could best their massive neighbor. But Japan had something to prove. Her navy crushed the Chinese fleet in one decisive battle, and her disciplined army pushed China's disorganized forces off the peninsula. Within a few months, Western newspapers had changed their tune regarding "the plucky little island empire." In America, doubt shifted quickly to self-congratulation. "Behind all this eagerness to learn of Japan's affairs there is a dot of pride in the fact that our American progression may have had something to do with her determination to force civilized 'ways and means' upon China," the *New York Times* reported.

The war was over in eight months. "I tell you," Alice wrote to Ume, "Japan is coming up in the eyes of Christendom now that she has proved her ability to carry on a successful war after civilized standards." The irony, of course, was not lost on her: "Unfortunately in spite of our avowed Christianity, physical force seems still to be the surest road to respect & consideration among nations."

Victory unleashed a storm of patriotic fervor in Japan. "Now we are no longer ashamed to stand before the world as Japanese," wrote Tokutomi Soho, founder of Japan's first news magazine, *Kokumin no tomo* ("The People's Friend"). "Before, we did not know ourselves, and the world did not yet know us. But now that we have tested our strength, we know ourselves and we are known by the world." (This national pride would suffer a blow just a month after the victory, when Russia along with France and Germany insisted that Japan return territory ceded by China. The so-called Triple Intervention turned Japan's joy to frustration and refocused its military energies against a new opponent, Russia.)

Just as the war had raised Japan's prominence on the international stage, it had also raised the profile of Japanese women, the mothers and wives of the soldiers who had won glory. General Oyama's name appeared regularly in the foreign papers, and it wasn't long before the American press found a way to take credit for his leadership: his wife. Raised by the sage Leonard Bacon and trained at the most venerable of American women's colleges, Madame Oyama was surely one secret to her husband's success. "Through Japan, China must soon give way to civilization, and when she does who can say that Uncle Sam has not materially aided in the result?" asked the *Times*. "As one of his disciples, grounded in his principles, and devoted to his methods and policies, Mme. Oyama has exerted a wide influence, and undoubtedly helped on the progressive spirit."

Elegant, educated, and at ease among the elite, Sutematsu was a deeply gratifying example of America's enlightening influence, proof of its successful transition from upstart to mentor nation. "Intensely loyal to her country, she yet left here thoroughly imbued with American principles, and determined to aid in the uplifting of her sex in Japan," another article declared. "There is little question that her early American education has been, through her consistent application of it, the keynote to the growing liberality of the Japanese toward women, and all American policy in general."

For the first time since her Vassar graduation speech, Sutematsu was visible to the world. "Whatever the war may have done," wrote Alice to Ume, "it has certainly been good for Stematz in giving her just the stirring up that she needed."

. . .

BUT THE PURPOSEFUL energies of the Sino-Japanese War ebbed quickly. Ume's routine at the Peeresses' School continued, as did her philosophical divergence from Utako Shimoda, a woman whose idea of "good wife, wise mother" was grounded in Confucian obedience, not Western liberal arts. For all the heady idealism of those planning meetings at Ito's house long ago, the scholarly ambitions of a Vassar or a Bryn Mawr had never taken root at the Peeresses' School. "Those students who study at this school must remember that in the future when they are married they are to become good wives; that when they become mothers, wise women; that to their parents and parents-in-law, they are to be gentle and kind homemakers," read the school's mission statement. Marriage and motherhood were not questions of if, but when. To this end, the girls should strive to "acquire such qualities and virtues as befit noble women," never allowing themselves to be distracted by "empty words, or swept by fancies." Etiquette, calligraphy, a smattering of the classics, perhaps a few words of English or French: these were virtues. Science, history, philosophy—for a woman, surely fanciful.

A Japanese educator of women, according to Mrs. Shimoda, should be like a gardener who works to make common plants as attractive as possible within their natural limits. "But if he attempts to raise something extraordinary and new—that is, if he tries to raise eggplants from cucumber vines, or to make cherry blossoms come out of willow trees, he will have spent his energy for no practical purpose," she wrote. "Not only that, but he may thereby kill the vines or break the branches of the willow trees."

Ume, a girl with Japanese roots who had flowered in America, must have found this particularly hard to hear. Her loneliness returned, redoubled. Alice was far away, absorbed in the foundation of a training hospital at the Hampton Institute. The stimulating companionship of Bryn Mawr classmates was out of reach. On top of that, just as all of Tokyo had become distracted by the outbreak of the war, Ume's younger sister Fuki had died of a kidney ailment. Nearly ten years younger than Ume, Fuki had been as much a daughter as a sister: Ume had brought Fuki to live with her when she first began to teach at the Peeresses' School and had paid her sister's tuition there.

"I can not realize she is dead," Ume wrote to Mrs. Lanman. "I have had so much to do with her and for her that she seems a part of my life." Within the year, yet another of Ume's dearest was gone: Charles Lanman died at the age of seventy-five. Her American father would never again beam with pride at his adopted daughter's achievements. The emotional bedrock that the Lanmans in Georgetown had always provided was no longer so solid.

Days of listening to the etiquette-obsessed daughters of the wealthy parroting beginner's English without comprehension or ambition left Ume depressed. "I feel quite at a loss, and do not seem as if I could pick up the threads of life again," she wrote to Bryn Mawr friends. "Nothing has changed in the aspects of affairs out here, educationally or otherwise. We still remain, as before, at a dead stand. Sometimes I think I shall get on board of a ship and steal away from it all, and not care or try anymore."

Ume's frustration was apparent to her students: the playful young teacher who had once delighted in showing the girls how to play prisoner's base at recess had become a terror in the classroom, pounding her desk with her fist when recitations went wrong. Alice, as always, tried to raise her spirits. "Don't be discouraged my dear," she wrote. "God is going to give you the chance to do plenty of good work before you are through. He doesn't put such women as you into the world for nothing."

SUTEMATSU, TOO, WAS wrestling with grief and hopelessness. Her eldest stepdaughter, Nobuko, had married at seventeen—too early in Sutematsu's private judgment, but as the girl was not actually her daughter, she deferred to the Oyama family's wishes. The groom, Yataro Mishima, was a promising (and strikingly handsome) young man, a viscount's son who had just returned from study in America to receive an appointment in the Ministry of Agriculture. Though traditional in its union of two powerful families, the match was also decidedly modern: the two young people adored each other. Their wedding, in 1893, had been a happy distraction from the threat of war. But the first winter of Nobuko's married life had been difficult: influenza struck Tokyo, and Nobuko became exhausted nursing her new husband's family. None too strong herself, she, too, fell ill and was slow to recover. Her in-laws sent her back to the Oyamas to convalesce. Tuberculosis had taken hold.

Mishima was an only son, honor bound to give his family an heir. Nobuko could not produce one, and her illness—stigmatized and poorly understood—posed a more direct threat as well: what if Mishima became infected too? His widowed mother charged her son to do his duty: divorce his wife and find a healthier bride to replace her. In the face of filial obligation, modern love was irrelevant.

Outraged for his daughter's sake, but recognizing the futility of argument, Oyama agreed to the Mishimas' request for a divorce. Nobuko, recuperating at the home of relatives in the country, was kept in the dark, her correspondence with Mishima intercepted by servants. It was only when a maid let one of Mishima's letters slip through by mistake that Nobuko learned what was afoot. By the fall of 1895 the marriage was over. "Because I am responsible for taking care of my family, my own opinions have no importance," Mishima wrote to Sutematsu in anguished apology. "I know it seems a cowardly excuse, but I believe this misfortune must be the result of something bad I did in a previous life." Alice, practical as ever, saw the affair in sociological terms rather than karmic ones. "I am so sorry to hear of that divorce," she wrote to Ume. "It simply confirms my opinion that nothing can go quite right in Japan until something is done about making the marriage tie more binding."

Nobuko's despair did nothing to improve her health. Her father brought her home to the big house in Onden, where her stepmother drew on everything she had once learned at the Connecticut Training School for Nurses to save her. The Oyamas built Nobuko a separate wing to protect the rest of the children from infection; they paid special attention to her diet and made sure she got outside when the weather was mild. But their efforts were in vain: by May of 1896, at the age of twenty, she was dead. Her tragedy was sickening proof that, American admiration notwithstanding, little had changed for Japanese women. Here was a daughter of privilege, blessed with an education and the most enlightened of parents, her heart broken and her life shortened by a social code that set the value of a wife far below the needs of her husband and his family. Sutematsu's desperate efforts to nurse her only set tongues wagging: what kind of evil stepmother exiled her ailing child to a distant part of the house and prevented her family from visiting her?

A novel based transparently on Nobuko and Mishima's doomed romance became a runaway best seller soon after Nobuko's death. It was titled *Hototogisu*, after a small cuckoo that symbolized tragic love in Japanese poetry; its mournful call was interpreted as a lament for a lost mate. Some legends held that the bird sang out its grief until blood poured from its throat—a particularly apt allusion for a tubercular heroine. Though the young couple and General Oyama were portrayed sympathetically, Sutematsu received less kindly treatment. The fictional stepmother, sent to England as a girl, had returned "knowing more about the English language, perhaps, than any one in Japan," but her bizarre skill served nothing but her own pride and brought unhappiness to her husband's family. "Her first concern, after entering the new household, was to change or abolish everything" that evoked the more traditional ménage presided over by the general's first wife. Though the novel came down firmly on the side of modern love, its author made it plain that a woman like Sutematsu took Western ideas several steps too far. "Dressed in the European fashion, exhaling a strange perfume," her fictional alter ego was "lacking all delicacy, egotistic, pedantic, and with manners hardly engaging."

Such criticisms were discomfiting enough when whispered behind the sleeves of high-ranking wives; in print for all of Japan to read, they were unbearable. All of Japan, that is, except Sutematsu. Written Japanese was still a challenge for her, and it is unlikely she read the book herself.

. . .

SHIGE SENT LOVE and support to her struggling friends when she could, but six children and a teaching schedule spread her cheerful energy thin. In August of 1896, while the Oyamas were still in mourning for Nobuko, the Urius enjoyed a moment of celebration: finished with his posting in Paris, Sotokichi Uriu came home at last. Shige greeted him with their youngest daughter, Sakae, in her arms; the four-year-old had never met her father.

The reunion was brief, however; early in the new year, Sotokichi Uriu began a new tour of duty at sea, taking the helm of a cruiser. His renewed absence was difficult enough, but then bad news arrived: in the course of practice maneuvers, Uriu's ship had collided with another and run aground. As befitted his position as captain, Uriu assumed full responsibility for the accident, and the naval authorities took him into custody.

Shige was distraught. Uriu was being held hundreds of miles away in Shikoku, the smallest of the four main Japanese islands, while she was in Tokyo with six children, one of whom—her eldest son, Takeo— happened to be quite ill. Shige's brother Takashi Masuda, who had always played the role of father figure, begged her to come stay with him or let him pay her way to visit husband. Shige wanted nothing more than to rush to Uriu's side, but like her stalwart husband, she remained at the helm of her household. A court-martial sentenced Uriu to three months in prison. Onlookers muttered that the Satsuma-dominated upper echelons of the naval command had made a fair hearing for a man with Uriu's Tokugawa-loyalist origins impossible, but the sentence held.

In the end, admiration for Uriu's forthrightness and humility prevailed, and upon his release he found his reputation surprisingly untarnished. He resumed his command, and with it, his extended absences from home. "No wonder Shige says she does not want her daughters to marry naval men!" Ume wrote to Mrs. Lanman.

. . .

AS THE NINETEENTH century drew to a close, it seemed as if there was a frustration for every triumph. Shige rejoiced in her large brood and her principled husband, and took pride in her teaching, though the strain of balancing it all was beginning to tell. Ume's second studious sojourn in America had raised her reputation as an educational crusader, which made the claustrophobic conservatism of the Peeresses' School all the more galling to her. Sutematsu had felt her energies return during the adrenaline-infused months of the Sino-Japanese War, and General Oyama's star continued to rise; after the victory the emperor had raised his title from count to marquis and had put him in charge of the crown prince's education. But though arguably in possession of a more powerful intellect than her two friends, Sutematsu had less to engage it with, constrained as she was by her rank and household duties. America might admire her, but many in Japan did not, and this ambivalence took a toll.

To Alice, the foster sister with whom she'd once dreamed of setting up house, eschewing husbands, and founding a school to educate girls for the benefit of Japan, Sutematsu now wrote with more resignation than enthusiasm: "My husband grows fatter every year and I thinner."

14

THE WOMEN'S HOME
SCHOOL OF ENGLISH

IT WAS A SNOWY afternoon in February 1897. The train from Tokyo to the seaside resort of Hayama was unheated, but Ume and Anna had a compartment to themselves. They took off their shoes, tucked their feet under them, and spread a traveling rug over their laps. Snug despite the storm, unable to see much beyond the windows, they talked of the future. Earlier that month, Anna's father had died in Tokyo, and Anna had reluctantly booked her passage back to Pennsylvania. To console her, and to cheer herself as well, Ume had invited her away for the weekend.

In the years since Ume had left Bryn Mawr, Anna and her widowed father had come to Japan twice. Henry Hartshorne, a Quaker doctor and the author of a respected medical textbook, had been invited to speak, and Anna, his only child, had taught English literature at a Quaker school that Ume's father helped to found. Later, the Hartshornes had returned as lay missionaries. Anna's presence delighted Ume; for her part, Anna described their acquaintance as having "ripened into one of the happiest friendships ever permitted to humanity." They liked to think their affinity had been foreshadowed: back in 1867, when Ume's father traveled to San Francisco for the shogun, one of the books he had carried home in his trunk was Henry Hartshorne's *Essentials of the Principles and Practice of Medicine*.

Ume and Anna had had countless discussions about the status of women in Japan, but as the train rattled through the outskirts of Tokyo, Ume began to describe an idea she had as yet shared with few others. Though the government now permitted women to sit the exam for an English Teachers' Certificate, there were almost no qualified candidates. A girl who attended missionary schools learned English but not much else; a graduate of the Women's Higher Normal School received teacher training but little advanced instruction in English. (The Peeresses' School, whose highborn students would never need to earn a living, did not figure in Ume's calculus.) "Here was a distinct practical demand," Anna remembered, "but further, said Miss Tsuda, through English rightly handled she could give her girls access to all that world of Western thought which educated men had part in, but which was a sealed book to most of their women-kind."

The rising tide of traditionalism had caused enthusiasm for Western ideas in government-run schools (especially for girls) to ebb; still, the need for English instruction remained. By opening a private school, Ume could both supply an undeniable demand and hold open a window on the West for her countrywomen. She believed, she confided to Anna, that her reputation would draw enough students and supporters to make her project a success. She was not ready to start quite yet, but when the time came, would Anna return to Tokyo and help? Anna was thirty-seven years old, free of family obligations and in possession of a prodigious intellect: like Alice Bacon, she had passed Harvard's Examinations for Women with high credit. Her bond with Ume was precious. "With grateful enthusiasm," she wrote later, "I promised that I would."

IN HER MIDTHIRTIES now, a confirmed career woman at last safe from the nagging of marriage-minded friends (as Alice had predicted), Ume had begun to widen her focus beyond the Peeresses' School and the American Women's Scholarship to larger questions of educational policy in Japan. She published her experiences and opinions in the English-language press: an account of her childhood journey to America for the *Chicago Record*; a lengthy article on the importance of women's education in the *Far East*, the English edition of Tokutomi Soho's popular news magazine. Another *Far East* essay called for stronger marriage and divorce laws and an end to concubinage. Enlightened women would surely not accept a status quo that expected them to share their husbands with other women. "One trembles to think of the future," Ume wrote, "if, through the broadening of their mental horizon, greater discontent and unrest come to women in their homes, and they forget that it is their noblest mission to guard the perfect peace of the home, even though in so doing, they are themselves sacrificed."

Ume's message was consistent: women needed education not to challenge men, but to better help them. "Without culture, education, and experience," she wrote, "women can only share the lowest side of a man's life and must indeed fall short of the ideal wife and mother." As a side note, she recommended that every woman seek proficiency in a skill that might win her an income, should misfortune require her to earn one. "This may be in anything suited to her tastes and capacities, in teaching, writing, nursing, cooking, or sewing," Ume explained, outlining a woman's sphere with a rather small diameter. (By the late 1890s, there were women in Japan who had pushed the boundaries further; Ginko Ogino, Japan's first female doctor, had become certified in 1885, and private medical colleges in Japan were beginning to allow female students to audit classes.)

Acquiring a useful skill need not indicate unwomanly inclinations; on the contrary, "such an acquisition not only takes the place of, but is better often than, the richest dowry." Ume must have thought of Shige, whose teaching salary had tided over her family during periods when her husband was ill. The thought that other women might actively choose a life like Ume's, full of work but empty of husband or children, never entered the argument. Her career in education was, paradoxically, dedicated to the perfection of the domestic.

Ume's rather modest credo, hewing always to the Meiji ideal of good wife and wise mother, protected her from the sharp tongues of the traditionalists. Now that her ideas were appearing under her own name, instead of Alice's, Ume paid more attention to the critics. "There have been one or two criticisms," she wrote to Mrs. Lanman about her *Far East* article, "but nothing especial and on every side I hear comment, because, you know, it is so unusual for a Japanese woman to do anything." But Ume's years of toil were beginning to yield dividends. In the spring of 1898, the government appointed her to teach at the Women's Higher Normal School in addition to the Peeresses' School—a welcome boost to both salary and ego, and proof that those in power approved of at least one Japanese woman doing something.

Further proof presented itself in May of that year. A Massachusetts matron by the name of Alice Ives Breed—"a remarkably handsome woman with magnificent physique and charming presence," according to one admiring reporter—was visiting Tokyo as vice president of the General Federation of Women's Clubs, an organization to whose presidency she hoped to be elected at that summer's convention in Denver. Having made a strong impression upon several Japanese statesmen in the course of her stay, she urged them to appoint a delegate to attend the convention. Whether influenced by Mrs. Breed's charm or her imposing physique, they were persuaded. There was one obvious candidate.

"What do you think has happened?" Ume wrote to Mrs. Lanman from the steamship *Olympia* two whirlwind weeks later. "Something very wonderful and very nice, too!!" The minister of education had broached the question of Mrs. Breed's invitation to Ume on a Friday evening; by the following Friday, she had sailed, along with a female colleague from the Peeresses' School. The government, moving with uncharacteristic efficiency, had granted them a five-month leave of absence.

By the end of June, Ume stood before an auditorium full of women in Denver, thanking them for their warm welcome and their inspiration. "Thus from one nation to another will be passed on the work of education and elevation for women," Ume told them; "thus, step by step, will woman arise, throughout all the world, from the slave and drudge of savage days, from the plaything and doll of later periods, to take her place as true helpmate and equal of man." American women had stretched their hands toward their Japanese sisters, who in turn would bring enlightenment to the women of other, as yet less civilized, Asian lands.

Denver was the beginning of a bold new phase. Ume hurried east after the convention, eager to reunite with Mrs. Lanman, now an elderly widow. She visited old friends not seen for six years, including Alice Bacon, of course, and Martha Carey Thomas of Bryn Mawr, and shared with them the dream she had outlined for Anna Hartshorne. She toured a number of schools as well, and in the course of her travels met an eighteen-year-old girl, deaf and blind since early childhood, who was studying for admission to Radcliffe College. "I have enjoyed meeting you, dear Miss Tsuda, more than I can tell you, and I wish you every success and happiness," wrote Helen Keller, commemorating their visit with an autographed sample of her extraordinary achievement. Ume saved the note as a keepsake. Was there any better example of the power of education to bring women out of the dark?

As the five months of her leave drew to a close, Ume was surprised to receive a second invitation, this time from several prominent English women via the Japanese ambassador in London. Would Miss Tsuda come and observe the progress of women's education on the far side of the Atlantic? Permission arrived swiftly from Tokyo: Ume's leave was extended until the following summer, and came with a stipend of a thousand yen. She sailed for Liverpool in November, hardly daring to believe her good fortune. "I have been thinking over what a lovely, lovely visit this has been to America," she wrote Mrs. Lanman from the ship. "I do not think it has a flaw. It has been so beautiful, too beautiful, it almost frightens me, and now to have so much lovely ahead of me . . . I can only rejoice and believe myself unworthy of it all."

For the first time Ume was traveling the world not as a student but as an independent adult, an educator, an authority on a nation in the ascendant, eagerly consulted by international peers. The trip was restorative— an extended break from the demands of professional life. In London she bought a raincoat, rode the underground railway, ate in restaurants, went to the theater. She made the rounds of the tourist attractions, and found it oddly sacrilegious to walk on the tombstones of the great in Westminster Abbey. "It seems very strange not to be in any hurry," she wrote. "I never in my life was so luxurious."

Her hosts in England were the wives of archbishops and the head-mistresses of colleges, women who displayed their considerable intellects with pride. At Cheltenham Ladies' College she met the formidable Dorothea Beale, "a most capable, powerful woman" who had grown a small school into an institution with over nine hundred students. "It is encouraging to see how education has progressed in England," Ume wrote in her journal, "for we are at a stage in Japan no worse than when Miss Beale began her life-long work." Ume spent several weeks at St. Hilda's Hall at Oxford, auditing lectures on Shakespeare and reading Addison and Pope, but also attending her share of tea parties and receptions. She met a niece of Tennyson and some relatives of Wordsworth; she took careful note of titles and much satisfaction in special treatment. "I have been about like a high-born lady with carriages and people to attend me wherever I went, and in fine style," she wrote. "I can hardly realize that it is I who am doing these things."

Back in London again, she was thrilled to be granted an interview with Florence Nightingale. "I would rather have seen her than royalty itself," she wrote. "I shall not soon forget my glimpse of that bright intelligent invalid face, whose clear mind & youthful activity seemed strange in that sick-room of a woman past her seventieth year." Even in her decline, propped up on white pillows under a red silk quilt, Miss Nightingale impressed Ume powerfully: a woman whose pioneering work had won her international acclaim, yet who had never actually strayed beyond the boundaries of feminine conduct. Nursing, like teaching, was a profession that supported the domestic ideal. The interview confirmed Ume's growing confidence in her own mission. She left Miss Nightingale's bedside at once starstruck and gratified. "I did so want to ask for her autograph or something from her, but I hardly dared today," she confided to her journal. As she left, a maid presented her with a nosegay of violets as a parting gift. Ume pressed them carefully.

Though Dorothea Beale and Florence Nightingale made stirring female models, Ume drew at least as much inspiration on her travels from discussions with a powerful man. This was true to form. Charles Lanman, indulgent and well connected, had delighted in engaging Ume's quick mind; the charismatic Hirobumi Ito had taken up the role in Ume's adulthood, enjoying her opinions on current topics during the months she lived in his home. In England, Ume found another distinguished father figure who took her ideas seriously: William Dalrymple Maclagan, the elderly archbishop of York. Invited to stay for several days at Bishopthorpe Palace, Ume was flattered to receive the prelate's personal attention on more than one occasion. "He is a lovely man, of a character simple and holy, and one that inspires reverence," Ume wrote. "He is *very* kind to me, and I do feel the honor very much."

To Maclagan, who seemed truly interested in Ume's work, she was moved to express her private doubts. "I told him that I really wished to do something, and to grow in grace and that I had had many advantages, but I must do something to pass them on to others, and how the weight of responsibility hung on me, although I was so unworthy of the blessings that God had given me in comparison with so many of my fellow countrywomen, that often I felt I would be glad of not having seen and known and heard so much," she wrote in a confessional rush. Were her ambitions self-aggrandizing, unwomanly, too aggressive? Could a woman "do something" and still remain humble? The archbishop confirmed the rightness of her vocation to act for the betterment of her society. "He gave me his blessing, and his prayers for my future work, and I felt indeed helped by his words and advice, so sympathetic, so wise and good."

Somewhat to her own surprise, Ume found she missed her professional routine. Swanning about like a great lady was "well enough for a year or six months, but in spite of hard times, and little money and hard grinding work, I like my busy life and enjoy feeling I am doing something," she wrote. She may have expressed a contentment born of necessity—the chance to live as a "lady of leisure" had evaporated with her refusal to consider marriage—but it was contentment nonetheless. At no point did she betray a longing to turn her back on Japan and remain in the West—not even in her letters to Mrs. Lanman.

In May of 1899, nearly a year after leaving Tokyo, Ume headed back across the Atlantic. There was time for one more glimpse of her friends in Philadelphia and Mrs. Lanman in Washington before the long westward trip across the continent. "How strange, how very strange it is that I am really going back after having been away so long to take up the broken threads of my life there," Ume wrote to her foster mother from Vancouver. "Wherever I am, you must remember how much I am thinking of you, how much I love and sympathize with you in your grief and loneliness, although perhaps you may not think I do, or feel that I care as much as I do." For once, Ume made no mention of her longing for the Georgetown fireside. Her year of travel and professional recognition had reoriented her. "Please do not in the least feel anxious for me," she closed her last letter before setting sail for Japan. "The *Empress of China* is a fine boat and runs well and I shall have every care and attention, I am sure, and in two weeks I shall be home again."

SUTEMATSU MISSED UME during her year away; with her youngest child now twelve, she felt the burden of too much time on her hands. Meanwhile, Shige was busier than ever: in addition to her brood of six, ages six to fifteen, she had taken over Ume's classes at the Women's Higher Normal School. During the New Year's holidays, on January 4, 1899—a day Ume filled with a visit to the British Museum, a ride on the upper deck of an omnibus, and preparations for a side trip to Paris—Sutematsu invited Shige to come for the day and spend the night. It was a rare and precious convergence for the two old friends.

Shige shared news and gossip from the Women's Higher Normal School, as well as the hopeful information that its principal, Hideo Takamine, was interested in raising the currency of Western ideas there. Takamine had been a classmate of Sutematsu's brothers long ago at the domain school in Aizu; during the years when Kenjiro had studied at Yale, Takamine had been a student at the Oswego Normal School in northern New York State. He was an old friend and an ideological ally, having learned in America that education was not simply a matter of texts memorized in a classroom.

Ever since Alice Bacon had left Tokyo a decade earlier, her Japanese friends had wished for her return. Now they saw their opportunity. Sutematsu asked Shige to sound out Takamine, and a few days later he paid a call on the Oyama residence. Sutematsu wrote to Alice that very evening. "It seems he wants just such a person as you for the school," she told her foster sister: "an American lady of the right kind" to serve as a cultural model both inside and outside the classroom. "I think the school needs a foreign teacher of a strong character, who will influence the girls in the right way," she went on. "Of course you may not be able to have your way always, still, Mr. Takamine is a man of very advanced ideas and he will be very sympathetic in your work."

In her next letter Sutematsu continued the hard sell. The Normal School couldn't pay much, but it would require Alice to teach only two hours a day, leaving her time for other pursuits—such as helping Ume, who had by now shared her pet plan with Alice. "You are very much admired by them and they are very anxious to secure your help," Sutematsu wrote of Takamine and his colleagues. She followed flattery with a dash of guilt, for good measure: "They want you to come as soon as you can and I hope to hear a favorable reply, for if you will not come, the responsibility rests on my shoulders and they will say that I did not write in sufficiently attractive light to induce you to accept the position."

Teaching at the Normal School would be even more attractive than Alice's earlier stint at the Peeresses' School. Shige would be a colleague, and Sutematsu suspected that Ume would shift her teaching duties to the Normal School upon her return, "for the other school is not at all to her liking and there are many teachers there who dislike her so much that it will not be pleasant for her when she comes back." With Alice and Shige and Ume all teaching together, and Sutematsu advising in the background, it would be as close as they had yet come to the girlhood dream of starting their own school in Japan.

Alice's responsibilities at Hampton prevented her from gratifying Sutematsu's request on the spot. She had recently finished the construction of Hampton's nurse-training hospital and was committed as well to a new project: in 1897, she had opened Deephaven, a summer retreat for academics and intellectuals on Squam Lake in New Hampshire. Life in America was full and rewarding for Alice, but still Japan beckoned; after all, at some point young Mitsu, Alice's adopted daughter, would be ready to bring her American education back to her native land. Alice wrote a long letter to Ume in England, which Ume relayed to Georgetown. "She really seems to be contemplating coming to Japan again, and I shall be so glad if she does come," Ume wrote to Mrs. Lanman. "She has such good, substantial, sterling qualities which one can always depend upon, and I think a great deal of her as a friend." As she contemplated her next chapter, reliable friends began to seem more important than ever.

UME RETURNED FROM her year of wonders in the heat of midsummer, 1899. Within days of her arrival, she was summoned to the palace (along with her co-delegate from the previous summer's Denver convention) to report her experiences to the empress herself. "It will be a fine ending to this year's travels," Ume told Mrs. Lanman. Here was the reception she had yearned for upon her first return to Tokyo in 1882, the recognition of her growing reputation as an authority on the education of women, and the satisfying conclusion of the empress's original mandate delivered in 1871: "When, in time, schools for girls are established, you shall be examples to your countrywomen, having finished your education." Ume had at last finished her education. She was ready to be an example.

The reality of the imperial audience was, as usual, less glorious than the prospect. Ume was pleased with her new dress—of foreign cut and Japanese fabric, appropriately—but August in Tokyo was a sticky time for bonnets and fitted bodices and lace collars. The encounter was mercifully brief. Ume and her colleague followed an official to the audience chamber and, after making their bows, stood before the empress—elegant in a pink morning gown trimmed in white—and answered her questions face-to-face. Ume had spoken nothing but English for the past year. "It was a great honor, of course," Ume wrote, "but a great trial to have to speak there before the Empress especially, as I feared I might make a mistake in speaking." A final round of corset-creaking bows, then on to an antechamber, where there were tea and cakes and the usual ceremonial gifts of white silk.

More recognition followed as the fall approached. A reporter paid a call, hoping to interview Ume for a series on notable women. "I told him it was too soon for any such things, and I did not want it at all," Ume told Mrs. Lanman. "I think he was much amused by my refusal." Ume was pleased that items mentioning her return had appeared in the papers, but the idea that the press might regard the year just ended as the apex of her career was deeply irritating.

Ume resumed her schedule at both the Peeresses' and the Women's Higher Normal School, her voice rasping with the unaccustomed strain of speaking for hours at a time. Her days were full, but her mind was elsewhere. In December she began to commit her intentions to paper. "My dear Mrs. Morris," she wrote to her benefactress in Philadelphia. "I have been wanting to write you especially of late to tell you that at the end of the present school year, I am going to ask to resign from my work in the Peeresses' School, and take up the school work about which I talked to you last summer." The letter went into the mail with another, to Martha Carey Thomas, restating Ume's plans and asking for help in raising the funds for a schoolhouse.

There was no turning back now, but there was still a school year to finish out. Ume closed her letters with pleas for discretion. "I should dislike to have exaggerated reports and rumors of my work get abroad and Tokyo is a very dreadful place for gossip," she wrote. "So please ask those who might speak of it to be careful, as I am not yet freed from my responsibilities to the government."

Most discreet of all was Ume herself. No one at the Peeresses' School or the Women's Higher Normal School (except Shige, of course) had any inkling of her distracted state of mind. In January the government showed its approval by raising her salary along with her court rank. Ume appreciated the extra money but barely paused to enjoy the news; she neglected to mention it in her letters for a month. A new century was dawning. "How strange it seems to be writing 1900!" she exclaimed. "I make mistakes all the time, and write eighteen and then have to correct it."

It was an auspicious moment for new beginnings. In 1899, still riding the wave of patriotism that followed the Sino-Japanese War, the Meiji government had passed the Girls' Higher School Law, mandating that every prefecture open at least one school for girls, equivalent to the middle schools that already existed for boys. Educated women were needed to raise educated sons to fight for Japan. A subsequent ordinance restricted mission schools by prohibiting religious education. Taken together, these moves expanded female education while placing it more firmly under government control.

Regardless of the political implications, though, two things were clear: the new schools would need new teachers to staff them, and at least some of their graduates would seek further study. By 1900, fifty-two schools had opened, serving twelve thousand middle-grade girls. Beyond that, the sole option for higher education was the Women's Higher Normal School in Tokyo.

There had never been a better moment for Ume's plan. Everything was coming together. "I had a letter from Alice Bacon, and she is expecting to come to Japan very soon now," Ume told Mrs. Lanman in February. In March, Alice traveled to Philadelphia to discuss with Ume's supporters— Anna Hartshorne, Martha Carey Thomas, Mrs. Morris, and others—the practical details of the English school Ume envisioned. Naming themselves the Committee to Help Miss Tsuda's School in Japan, they quickly raised two thousand dollars. A month later Alice was on her way. Mr. Takamine's offer of a position at the Women's Higher Normal School gave her security, but her true intent was to aid in the realization of Ume's dream.

She did not travel alone. Mitsu Watanabe, the five-year-old Alice had brought home with her in 1889, was now a young woman. Like Ume eighteen years earlier, Mitsu stepped off the boat in Yokohama with only the vaguest memories of her life before America. But she would avoid Ume's dispiriting struggle to claim a niche for herself in her homeland. Within a few months, a new school would urgently need her skills.

IN JULY OF 1900, when classes had ended for the summer, Ume resigned, giving up her rank, her salary, and her fifteen-year connection with the most prestigious school for girls in Japan. The news caused an uproar. "No one would believe me when I asked to resign and I had some fights to go thro' and some yet before me," Ume wrote in high spirits to Bryn Mawr friends. "But I am now *free* [she underlined the word twice] and have burned, so to speak, all my ships behind me." It felt purer, somehow, to work for the education of women unencumbered by imperial obligations. "I wanted to get away from all the Conservatism and Conventions of my old life, and now I am only a commoner, free to do what I like." Like her father before her, she had renounced her title to pursue a progressive ideal.

She wrote to Martha Carey Thomas in a more sober mood. "It has been a more difficult thing to leave the school than anyone in democratic America could realize, but I have been able to do so, I think, honorably. I do not feel, however, that I can, for two or three years yet, appeal to my Japanese acquaintances for help for my own plans." Even if the Tokyo elite could have fathomed her decision, they were unlikely to open their purses to support it; successful charity bazaars aside, the tradition of philanthropy had still not taken hold in Japan. If Ume's plan was to succeed, foreigners would have to fund it. She and Alice retreated to a hot-spring resort in the mountains for a brief summer respite before their work began in earnest. "Write me and keep me up in courage," Ume entreated her Bryn Mawr friends.

The first thing Ume needed was a house. The school she imagined was not simply a matter of desks and classrooms; it was to be a home for her students. Teachers and many of the girls would live under the same roof, with lessons springing as much from their informal interactions as from books and classroom instruction. The primary subject would be English, but the larger curriculum would emphasize character over scholarship.

The goal, as Ume saw it, was not just to produce English speakers, or even simply English teachers, but to graduate women who had absorbed Western ideas about the vital importance of women's education, whether or not they ever set foot in a classroom again.

On Friday, September 14, 1900, fourteen students squeezed into a small room in a small rented house for the opening ceremony of Joshi Eigaku Juku, the "Women's Home School of English."* Ten young women had signed on for Ume's three-year program; the other four were older students who were finishing their preparations for the English certification exam. Their teachers were Ume, Alice, and Utako Suzuki, who had lived with Ume while a student at the Peeresses' School. Alice's daughter Mitsu, though still a teenager, assisted them. Sutematsu—now the Marchioness Oyama—was present that day in her capacity as patron and official adviser, adding a note of distinction to the unprepossessing surroundings.

The ceremony began with a respectful recitation of the Imperial Rescript on Education. Though her resignation from the Peeresses' School may have been shocking, Ume had no intention of alienating those in power any further. The Confucian conservatism of the text made an odd counterpoint to Ume's own opening speech, which she delivered in Japanese, though she had written her notes in English.

Gesturing to their cramped surroundings, Ume reminded her new students that fine classrooms and large libraries were not the most essential components of a successful school. Far more important were "the qualifications of the teacher, the zeal, patience and industry of both teachers and pupils, and the spirit in which they pursue their work." The very smallness of their newborn institution was its greatest virtue, she continued: "It is possible to impart a certain amount of knowledge at one time to a large class, but in true education, each one ought to be dealt with as a separate individual, for we know that one's mental and

---

* Joshi Eigaku Juku is sometimes translated as "Women's English School" or "Women's Institute of English Studies," but *juku* carries a connotation of private, noninstitutional instruction, which Ume herself exploited when she described her school to English speakers.

moral characteristics vary as do the faces of each one of us." Ume's school would cultivate thoughtful individuals, not dolls reciting from memory: women who knew how to reason for themselves, independent of their teachers or their husbands.

Ume's philosophy strayed far from the Confucian idea of a woman's place, and she was acutely aware that the students of Joshi Eigaku Juku were pioneers, with a grave responsibility to disprove the disapproving. In Ume's mind, the very future of higher education for women in Japan was at stake. "Any criticism will mostly come, not so much on our courses of study or methods of work, but on points which simply require a little care and thoughtfulness on your part—the little things which constitute the making of a true lady," she told the girls: "the language you use, your manner in intercourse with others—your attention to the details of our etiquette." Though her pedagogy was progressive, her students must nonetheless be proper. "I ask you not in any way to make yourselves conspicuous or to seem forward, but to be always gentle, submissive and courteous as have always been our women in the past." Ume may have been inspired by Dorothea Beale and Martha Carey Thomas, but she could not entirely turn her back on Confucius.

THE HOUSE, RENTED for fifty yen—not much, but still more than Ume had earned in a month at the Peeresses' School—had seven rooms, including the kitchen and Alice's and Ume's bedrooms. Every room was a classroom during the school day. The furniture was no more than what a modest home would contain, and for many of their lessons the girls sat on the tatami. Ume's own books constituted their library, and her pictures were their only decoration. Her battered piano accompanied their hymns and, as they had no hymnbooks, Alice typed up new sheets for them to sing from each week.

In the first six months, enrollment more than doubled. Entrance standards were stiff; Ume knew that weak students would do nothing to help her school establish its reputation. Alice donated her teaching eight hours a week and gave a class on current affairs every Friday. English alone would not develop the integrity that Ume hoped to foster; "while endeavoring to perfect yourselves in this branch," she exhorted her students, "do not neglect other things, which go to make up the complete woman." In addition to English, course work included Japanese and Chinese literature, history, and ethics. Just as Bryn Mawr prided itself on matching Harvard's broad curriculum, Ume's school would demonstrate that girls could study at the same level as boys.

Ume's students were surprised to discover that school no longer consisted of scribbling down what the teacher said, memorizing it, and then regurgitating it for exams. Ume expected her girls to prepare their work before class, offer their own opinions during classroom discussions, and disagree with their teachers if those opinions diverged. In a culture that revered its teachers, no matter how mediocre, this was a revolutionary approach. Still, there was no excuse for sloppiness. The basics—grammar, pronunciation, spelling— were essential, Ume believed, and she drilled her girls relentlessly until they got the details right. "Try again! Once more! Repeat!"

Once her scholars were ready to move on to more advanced material, Ume created her own syllabi, choosing texts—*Little Lord Fauntleroy* and *Silas Marner* were favorites—that tended, self-consciously or not, to feature cheerful children buffeted by the winds of fate. Ume and Alice both contributed to a biweekly magazine, *The English Student*, and also published retellings of well-loved tales in English. One of these, *Popular Fairy Tales*, written by Mitsu and revised by Alice, presumably sprang from Mitsu's decade of childhood in America. "The English is excellent—simple, strong and pure," declared the *Japan Weekly Mail*.

By the following spring the little house was bursting. Still unable to purchase a suitable building, Ume moved her school to another cheap rented house, centrally located near the Imperial Palace. This one was spacious and came with a pedigree—it had once belonged to a nobleman— but that was the extent of its charms. The place leaked every time it rained, always in a different spot. There was no heat. The beams were warped, and seemed unlikely to hold the roof up much longer. The damp had opened such gaps in the walls and around the door frames that sound traveled freely between adjacent bedrooms and classrooms—"a great advantage, one of the pupils remarked, when one was ill and could not attend class, and yet could follow all the lesson in bed," Ume wrote. On top of all this, the place was said to be haunted: two rooms had apparently been the scene of a tragedy. Not one to indulge sentiment, Ume claimed these two as her bedroom and parlor, "and since I never saw the ghosts, our girls ceased to expect them."

Haunted or not, the extra space was welcome. Now that there was enough room for everyone, Ume and Alice began a series of monthly literary gatherings reminiscent of the club activities that Sutematsu and Shige had enjoyed at Vassar. The meetings moved English outside the classroom, and provided opportunities for friends of the school to observe the girls' progress. One of these occasions, in late May, was held in honor of the empress's birthday. "The girls had some recitations and dialogues, and then acted out *Little Red Riding Hood*," Ume reported to Mrs. Lanman. "Our musician in the house, who has a lovely voice, sang and one of our day scholars, who is a violinist, gave a performance, and so it was a very nice entertainment indeed." The evening finished with tea, cake, and strawberries.

Music, strawberries, Grandma and the Wolf—Ume was giving her students a taste of her own American childhood, with its lively social life. As the second year of classes began, Sutematsu invited everyone for a picnic. The entire school walked to the big house in Onden—no endless jinrikisha processions for this group—and spent the day. Sutematsu showed the girls her home—"we even went up to the cupola on the very tip top," wrote Ume—and fed them sandwiches and cake. There were games in the house and tennis on the lawn, and one of the Oyama boys showed the girls his Vistascope, a stereoscope with photo cards that seemed to move when you held the viewer to your face. The girls were enthralled. "Some of them had never seen a handsome foreign house and they thought it beautiful," wrote Ume. "We came home about six o'clock, very tired and happy." Whereas most Japanese students studied English as if it were Latin—to be conjugated and translated but never actually spoken—Ume's girls learned to live in it. "I am very proud of them," she wrote.

It would have been impolite to mention that she was proud of herself, but her satisfaction emerged in other ways. That fall, the second of her school's existence, the Ministry of Education appointed Ume to the Board of Examiners for the English Teaching Certificate. A few months later, Ume sat in a row with three other examiners (all male) as each of the sixty-four finalists for the certificate (only four of them women) stood before them to demonstrate their command of spoken English. The candidates "were not boys, either, but grown-up men, some of them teachers," Ume told Mrs. Lanman. "I tried to behave very properly and dignified." A woman—an unmarried woman at that—was sitting in judgment upon men. "It really was a great responsibility," she wrote, "and it is something to be proud of, something to add to my record that for once I did what never has been done by a woman before."

After the move to the new house, in Motozonocho, Kojimachi, Ume sent Mrs. Lanman her new address. "I am sorry it is so long, but letters are sure to reach me even if only Tokio is on them." It was true: a letter addressed to "Ume Tsuda, Educator, Tokyo" would reach its mark. Ume had chosen a far steeper path by remaining stubbornly single, but she had at last found her place.

IT HAD BEEN thirty years since three bewildered, shawl-wrapped girls emerged onto a snowy railway platform in Washington, thirty years since a group of newly minted Japanese statesmen traveled across an ocean and a continent to negotiate with the president of the United States. In March of 1902, the surviving members of the Iwakura Mission gathered for a reunion. It was held at the private Peers' Club, but the attendees remembered the ornate building by an earlier name: the Rokumeikan, symbol of the enthusiasm for all things Western that had propelled the mission on its journey in the first place. By the close of the 1880s, the Rokumeikan had come to represent the worst excesses of Meiji-era reform. The construction of the nearby Imperial Hotel had obviated the need for a government guesthouse for foreign visitors, and the building had been sold.

Sutematsu, Shige, and Ume, the only women invited to the gathering, attended together. "The gentlemen treated us beautifully," Ume reported. "Most of the men were old men, grey and baldheaded, and I was the baby of the party, as I was the baby on the ship in the old days, when the *America* went over from Japan to America." As in the old days, the men did the talking; dinner was followed by speeches, "to which we women only listened and enjoyed." The event made the papers, which published the reminiscences of the participants in installments for weeks after the fact.

What they remembered was not the blizzard of new information they had collected, now so thoroughly assimilated into Japan's armed forces, industries, and government. The stories they told instead recalled their mistakes and embarrassments: the craving for rice and pickles instead of yet another meal of rare roast beef; the relief at trading an ill-fitting suit for the comfort of a kimono in the privacy of a hotel room; the struggle with Western cutlery; the moment, during their audience with President Grant, when a vice-ambassador's headdress fell to the floor and he scooped it up and put it on backward in his haste. The hall rang with laughter as each man confessed his blunders or exposed his colleagues. The leaders of a modern twentieth-century nation looked back with fond amusement on the wobbly first steps of their nineteenth-century selves.

But for the girls, the embassy had been the beginning of their most formative years. The night of the reunion, both Marquis Oyama and Admiral Uriu happened to be away. The three women left the hall and climbed into Sutematsu's waiting carriage, their heads full of memories. They spent the night together, curled up on Sutematsu's foreign furniture, all considerations of rank and obligation laid aside. For that night they felt like girls again, "and it was a grand spree for all of us indeed," wrote Ume to Adeline Lanman.

Once more a country of three, they understood each other better than anyone in the world. The experiences that linked them transcended the great differences in the lives they had chosen: the grande dame; the working wife and mother; the unmarried educator. They had faced different challenges and found different sources of solace, but they had always held on to each other.

A YEAR INTO her second Japanese sojourn, Alice had been devastated to learn of her brother Alfred's sudden death; a bout of diphtheria shortly afterward compounded her low spirits. Though she was determined to see Ume through the second year of her fledgling venture, Alice knew her time in Japan was coming to an end. Before her departure, she and Ume, Sutematsu, and Shige all gathered at a photographer's studio. The group portrait taken that day—the only photo of all four together—captures a mixture of pride, optimism, and something like regret.

Alice—her broad shoulders squared in an unfussy black dress, a trace of gray at her temple, the strong line of her jaw beginning to soften in middle age—is the solid center of the group, her face directed with determination to one side. At her shoulder a kimono-clad Ume, not much taller standing than Alice is sitting, looks directly into the camera with a serene half smile. Shige stands on Alice's other side, bespectacled and more reserved in a kimono of a darker hue, meeting the lens with something less than her usual frank good cheer. Sutematsu, seated knee-to-knee with Alice, completes the composition, but where the other three are straight, she is curved, her gaze sliding out of the frame, her expression more tentative. Her hands are hidden in the pale silk of her kimono sleeves. It is tempting to read the photo as a record of the sitters' states of mind.

"The school is getting along so nicely now, and I have all the work I can possibly take, and with sixty scholars, I have quite enough to do," Ume had written in January. Whether propelled by fate or by her own will, she had traveled, arguably, farther than any Japanese woman ever had, and all the journeys now seemed to have been aimed directly toward this moment of fulfillment. "It was only a few days ago I was thinking how useful has been all that miscellaneous reading I did as a child in your library," she mused to Mrs. Lanman. Her childhood passions, so different from those of her peers in Japan, now seemed purposeful. "I feel quite sure now that my work will do some good, and perhaps my life and example will not be in vain—it was my wish for many years that it might be so, but now I feel it may be so," she wrote. The old ambivalence about her choices had faded; her school was now her home. "It has given me much happiness and friends, and I believe it is truly my life work." Alice's departure would be a blow, but there was reason to believe that Anna would shortly arrive to take her place, fulfilling the promise she had made on the train to the seaside years earlier.

That same year, Ume took legal steps to establish her own household, removing her name from her father's household register—an unheard-of step for a single woman. She added the suffix "-ko" to her first name: "Umeko" sounded more modern. She took care to record her status as *shizoku*, or samurai; she might have severed her ties to the imperial household and spent her life in the promotion of Western ideas and women's education, but she still claimed the proud past of her ancestors. In the photo Ume radiates a calm confidence. Her youthful face seems lit from within.

Shige had become a mainstay of the Women's Higher Normal School, beloved by everyone from the principal to the youngest student for her patience, her warmth, and her sympathy. For Uriu-*sensei*, everyone did their best work. She had chosen her path in 1881—as wife, mother, music teacher—and never strayed from it, or seemed to doubt it. But six children and an often-absent husband had tired her. Within the year, she would retire from teaching, suffering from nervous strain and the beginning, at age forty-one, of an unexpected seventh pregnancy.

As for Sutematsu, the girl who had left Vassar covered in glory had not fulfilled her promise in quite the way her classmates had predicted. Though she could look with satisfaction at the philanthropic projects she had inspired and the educational efforts she supported, her life was devoted mostly to the running of her prominent household. As the Vassar class of 1882 gathered for its twentieth reunion that year, Sutematsu sent in her news with a show of chagrin. Miss Tsuda's school was doing wonderfully well, she wrote. "As for myself, what can I say that will be of interest to you? Absolutely nothing," she wrote.

My life, compared with yours, is so uneventful . . . do you care to hear why I discharged one of my servants, or that I have engaged new ones, or that I have had some military officers to dinner who talked shop all the time, or that my youngest boy was very stupid at lessons and I lost my patience, or that my silk worms which I am rearing are not doing well on account of the cold weather, or that I am bothered out of my life with all sorts of societies, clubs and associations which send me letters by reams, etc., etc.? No, that kind of story is the same all over the world and in that respect I don't think my life is different from that of the average American woman.

Sutematsu had not founded a school, or joined the "noble army of spinsters." Japan's first college graduate had receded behind lacquered layers of prestige and position, her curled bangs the last outward trace that remained of the spirited Vassar girl. New Haven friends who visited her in Tokyo in 1900 found her "older, we felt, than she ought to be," graceful as ever, but somehow subdued.

"I haven't laughed so much for years," Sutematsu told them after an hour of delighted catching up. "In Japan we do not laugh much after we are old women." She was forty. Of the three Iwakura girls, she was the only one who never left Japan again. But the fact that this daughter of Aizu could write, with a self-deprecating chuckle, that she was no different from an average American woman was, in itself, extraordinary.

IN APRIL OF 1902, Alice started her packing, and she and the trio took every opportunity to spend a few last days together. There was a luncheon at Sutematsu's home, and Shige spent as much time as she could at Ume's school. On the day of departure, a crowd of well-wishers gathered at Shimbashi Station to see Alice off. Sutematsu, Shige, and Ume rode the train with her to Yokohama. There was time for a quiet lunch before the steamer sailed—four middle-aged women, at ease in their surroundings, chatting intimately in English. It was a very different meal from the Yokohama reunion twenty years earlier when Shige, welcoming her closest friends to their unfamiliar native land, wondered suddenly whether they could still handle chopsticks.

"I feel so strange," Ume had written to Mrs. Lanman after that long-ago lunch, "like a tree that is transplanted and takes a little while to get accustomed to new surroundings. And think to what different soil I have been transplanted." The three Iwakura girls, twice uprooted, had flourished by all outward measures, each in her own way fulfilling the mandate conferred upon them even as their government lost sight of it. Outside of themselves, only Alice, perhaps, truly understood the cost. They had grown into women with the odd ability to see their native land through foreign eyes. They were home, and yet at some deep level they would never cease to be homesick.

When lunch was finished, the women escorted Alice to the harbor. Her ship sailed at three o'clock. "None of us stayed until the steamer left the dock," Ume wrote. "It is so forlorn to see the steamer go off in the distance."

15

ENDINGS

UME'S SCHOOL GREW RAPIDLY. In 1903 it moved to a proper home at last, a well-equipped building next to the British embassy. The initial funding for this relocation had come from the Gaiyukai, a club made up of Japanese women, including Sutematsu and Shige, who had lived abroad; a surprise gift of six thousand dollars from a Boston benefactress arrived soon after, and the school settled into a space it would occupy for the next two decades. The following year it received government approval as a *senmon gakko*, or vocational college, the highest standard a women's private school could then attain, and by 1905 the Ministry of Education had ruled that Ume's graduates were not required to sit the certification exam for a teaching license.

Ume's sister Koto enrolled two daughters, where they joined Sutematsu's daughter, Hisako. Shige talked of sending her younger girls when they grew older. "So you see, the girls are gathering around this school as a center," Ume wrote to Mrs. Lanman with pride. She had nearly a hundred and fifty students that year, drawn from across Japan. Anna Hartshorne, who had indeed returned just as Alice departed, became vital to Ume's project as a teacher and administrator. Anna was also Ume's closest companion; the two women bought a cottage with an ocean view in Kamakura, to which they retreated whenever possible.

The school's role as a counterweight to government conservatism had never been more important. War was once more imminent, with its attendant surge of nationalism—especially since for the first time, Japan was facing off against a Western nation. Japan's defeat of China in 1895 had provided an opportunity for Russia in the region, and by the beginning of 1904, tensions between Russia and Japan had come to a head, once again over control of Korea. The Russo-Japanese War of 1904–5 was longer, bloodier, and more complicated than the conflict a decade earlier. Japan achieved a string of impressive victories over the Russian military machine, and the conflict ended in a stalemate broken only by the diplomatic intervention of Theodore Roosevelt, confirming Japan's arrival as a global power at last.

Once again Iwao Oyama played a central role, this time as commander-in-chief of Japan's forces in Manchuria, prompting the emperor to raise Oyama's rank from marquis to prince when the war was over. Vice Admiral Sotokichi Uriu was also in the thick of the action, leading a naval squadron that sank two Russian ships in the earliest engagement of the war; he was later made a baron. Their wives were equally prominent on the home front: raising money, assembling "comfort bags" for soldiers, and describing everything in letters to Alice Bacon, who used their reports to encourage donations from sympathetic Americans.

Sutematsu's and Shige's eldest sons, born a year apart, were too young to go to war against Russia, but they followed in their fathers' military footsteps as cadets. Sutematsu glowed with pride over reports from the naval academy: "Takashi, who used to give me so much anxiety, I am happy to say, has improved wonderfully," she wrote to Alice, "and he is a great comfort."

Sutematsu and Shige had always met their milestones in step: New Haven, Vassar, marriage, firstborn baby girls, and then sons born less than a year apart. In April 1908, they faced tragedy together. Takashi Oyama and Takeo Uriu were both assigned to training maneuvers aboard the cruiser *Matsushima*, a ship Takeo's father had once captained. They were at anchor in the Pescadores, shortly before dawn, when an accidental explosion tore through the gunpowder magazine. The ship sank rapidly, and nearly two-thirds of her crew died, Takashi and Takeo among them.

Alice wrote to both mothers as soon as she heard the devastating news. "It was a great comfort to receive such loving words," Sutematsu replied. "At times I am very rebellious and say to myself, why should such a bright young life be taken, when there are others who could be better spared? . . . I try not to grieve too much[,] for if I give away too much to my feelings, it distresses my husband and adds to his sorrow and hurts Chachan's* tender heart." Shige, warmhearted and generous as always, submerged her own loss in concern for Sutematsu. "Poor Stematz, she is taking the new grief bravely but she needs your beautiful thoughts and your deep love," she wrote to Alice. "You know how her life and soul depended upon Takashi, the bright, joyous boy who resembled her so much. I wished to see her and yet when I grasped her hands, I could not help weeping for her hair was turning grey and she tried to hide all her emotions."

Perhaps partly to distract herself with happier memories, Shige made a trip back to the United States in 1909, accompanying her husband on a tour that included a visit to the White House, the Naval Academy Ball at Annapolis, a stay with old friends in New Haven, and Vassar's commencement exercises. At the Vassar alumnae banquet, Shige rose to speak, "slowly and carefully as though she had grown somewhat rusty in her use of the English language," reported the *Poughkeepsie Eagle*. "There is no Vassar among us yet," Shige told the assembled guests, "but education for women and education methods are progressing." She presented the college with a gorgeous silver bowl, a gift from the empress in honor of Vassar's role in inspiring the development of women's education in Japan.

IN JULY OF 1912, a few months shy of his sixtieth birthday, the Emperor Meiji died and an era came to an end. His funeral procession, more than twenty thousand strong, stretched for miles. There were nobles in full-dress uniform, Diet members in tailcoats, rank upon rank of soldiers at

---

* "Chachan" was the family's pet name for Hisako, Sutematsu's daughter.

attention—and at the center, the emperor's hearse: a replica of an ancient wooden oxcart built in the old imperial capital of Kyoto, surrounded by attendants in traditional court dress. Born above the clouds, Mutsuhito had descended to become the symbol of Japan's rise. The forty-four years of his reign had been marked by vision and folly, blistering progress and deep frustration. His country was now a player on the world's stage, and his funeral was a chance to unite Japan's promising future and her glorious past in a single dazzling spectacle. The flood of public grief completed the project that the young leaders of the Iwakura Mission had first imagined: the Land of the Gods as a modern power, her citizens sharing a single proud national identity. The new emperor, Yoshihito, took the reign name of Taisho, "great righteousness."

The Empress Haruko—the era's most visible good wife, and a wise mother to her subjects, though not to any children of her own—lived less than two years longer. Just weeks before her death, Ume lost her own dearest mother figure: Adeline Lanman, nearly ninety. Ume had visited Mrs. Lanman one last time in 1913 during a trip to promote her school, and had found her lonely and infirm, the house in Georgetown crumbling around her. Putting her foster mother's finances in order, Ume called in carpenters and painters, leaving her old home much more comfortable than when she had arrived. But three months later, Mrs. Lanman was dead.

As she entered her fifties, Ume's momentum slowed. Her school—now a college—continued to thrive, but the cause on which she had based her life's work was shifting around her. One of her own early students, Raicho Hiratsuka, had founded a literary magazine, called *Seito* ("Bluestocking"), that gave voice to a new activist mood. Its first issue opened with a manifesto: "When Japan was born, woman was the sun, the true human being. Now she is the moon! She lives in the light of another star. She is the moon, with a pale face like that of a sickly person." Ume saw Hiratsuka as part of "a new generation of selfish women," bent on confirming the establishment's worst fears about educated women forgetting their place. It was unseemly, she insisted, for women to agitate and struggle; change would be granted from above to women who had proved the value of their scholarship. "The real work is now being done in quiet ways," she wrote, "which are after all our Oriental ways."

Sutematsu tended to agree with her. "I am sorry to say young girls nowadays are not like what they used to be," she wrote to Alice. "They have lost the best characteristics of Japanese women"—grace, forbearance, discipline, duty—"without gaining the best side of foreign education. It may be that I am rather old fashioned, but it seems to me that female education in Japan is not advancing in the right direction." In darker moments, Ume called the noisy radicals "agents of the devil." Her health began to fail; in 1917 she was hospitalized for the first time with complications of diabetes. The strain of her teaching schedule and the endless quest for financial security had begun to tell.

The one constant—impervious to time or political tide—was the sustaining friendship among the trio. On a gray afternoon in the fall of 1916, Shige and Sutematsu made their way to Ume's house for tea; hardly an unusual event, but that day they would be joined by one more. Before long a jinrikisha clattered to a halt at Ume's door, carrying a woman of about their age, dressed in a sober kimono, her hair pulled severely back from her long face. She climbed down, and the four women regarded each other speechlessly, abruptly transported to their first overwhelming weeks in America.

Tei Ueda, the fifth girl sent with the Iwakura Mission, had surfaced at last, married to a doctor and living in Ueno, not far from Shige. In the decades since her premature return to Japan with Ryo Yoshimasu, Tei had watched the successes of her erstwhile companions from the shadows of obscurity, ashamed of her own failure. The four women talked for hours, reaching back to the year when they had clung to one another, and trying to bridge the gap that had opened between them.

The occasion was noteworthy enough that the *Asahi Shimbun* sent a reporter to cover it. Whatever their struggles, their triumphs, or their legacies, the most astonishing thing about these women during their lifetimes remained their childhood journey to another world. "A Circle of Friends Missed Since Washington," read the headline two days later.

"Madame Ueda Invited to Miss Tsuda's Residence; All Rejuvenated by Innocent Reminiscences."

ALICE BACON MADE another visit to Japan just after the Russo-Japanese War, gathering material for her writing, but she never taught there again. Retired from the Hampton Institute, she settled in New Haven, where she was on hand to look after Sutematsu's nephew Makoto—Kenjiro's boy—when he arrived to study biochemistry at Yale. Alice's adopted daughter Mitsu married and started a family in Tokyo, where the trio kept an eye on her. Meanwhile, Alice adopted a second Japanese ward: Makiko Hitotsuyanagi, a former student of Ume's whose scholarship at Bryn Mawr had been interrupted by illness. Makiko became Alice's right hand at her camp in New Hampshire, the primary project of Alice's later life. Reflecting her two great passions, the camp was home to sixteen champion English sheepdogs and featured several buildings constructed and furnished in Japanese style. Alice was proud to tell visitors that Deephaven was the only place in America where one could enjoy a proper Japanese bath. It survives as a family camp to this day.

Alice died in 1918 at the age of sixty-one, her funeral held in New Haven's Center Church, where her father had preached his sermon every Sunday. She willed Deephaven to her two Japanese daughters. Her death was a blow to her friends in Tokyo, who had relied on her letters full of bracing Yankee wisdom.

It was especially hard on Sutematsu, who had recently found herself alone once again. At the end of 1916, two months after the birth of the first grandson to bear his name, Iwao Oyama had collapsed while accompanying the young Emperor Taisho to observe military maneuvers. The emperor sent his personal physician, a stream of gifts, and even a supply of soup to help save his trusted old counselor, to no avail. Oyama received a state funeral, and Sutematsu withdrew from public life, moving into her remaining son's household. "There is no use in telling you of all that the loss of my husband means to me," Sutematsu wrote to Alice. She had hoped her friend would make one last trip to Japan, to ease the loneliness of widowhood.

The First World War mobilized Japan once more, but this time Sutematsu left the Red Cross activities to her daughter-in-law. She remained active as a trustee of Ume's school, though; as Ume's health declined, the question of a successor became more acute. In January 1919, Ume resigned. Sutematsu had hoped that Alice's second daughter, Makiko, now back in Japan, might take Ume's place, but Makiko opted for marriage to an American architect instead.

The influenza pandemic had just reached Tokyo, and Sutematsu sent her family to their country retreat to escape it, but she couldn't bring herself to join them while the issue of Ume's replacement remained unresolved. On February 5, Sutematsu watched with relief as Matsu Tsuji, a member of Ume's faculty, was ceremonially named the college's acting president.

The next day Sutematsu woke with a sore throat. Within two weeks, the flu had claimed her. "Princess Oyama is characterized as having been naturally intellectual, sensitive and retiring, always in frail health but with energy and charm that made her socially brilliant," read one obituary. "She had an alert keen mind, a quick sense of humor, but with a spirit too kind for sarcasm. Her old samurai ideals of duty and selflessness had become a habit, and probably hastened her death." She was sixty years old.

First Adeline Lanman, then Alice, and now Sutematsu: three of Ume's staunchest supporters were gone. A week after Sutematsu's death, Ume suffered a small stroke, and six months later a larger one, which partly paralyzed her right arm; for the last ten years of her life she was largely housebound and increasingly isolated. When the Great Kanto Earthquake of 1923 flattened the college along with most of Tokyo, it was Anna Hartshorne, still full of energy in her midsixties, who left immediately for America to raise the money to rebuild. She was gone for more than two years, and though her campaign was triumphantly successful—eventually raising five hundred thousand dollars from donors including the Rockefeller Foundation and the Carnegie Foundation for International Peace—Ume missed her profoundly. Anna did return, however, and she would remain at her teaching post until 1940, when a trip home to Philadelphia was made permanent by the outbreak of another war.

ON NOVEMBER 3, 1928, two years after Yoshihito's death, with rising-sun flags flying from every house, his son Hirohito officially received the sacred imperial treasures—the sword, the mirror, and the jewel—that confirmed him as emperor. That same evening, after a brief battle with cancer, Shige died at home at the age of sixty-seven. The following evening, JOAK, Tokyo's first radio station, broadcast Carl Maria von Weber's *Invitation to the Dance* in her honor. A concert waltz, meant for a listening audience rather than a dancing one, it had been Shige's favorite piece, and the last she had performed in public—an apt choice for the woman who had helped teach her compatriots how to behave in a ballroom.

Sotokichi Uriu, always the sicklier member of the couple, would outlive his wife by nearly a decade. His grief was matched by that of his brother-in-law, Takashi Masuda, the young samurai who had sent his littlest sister to America. Masuda, like Uriu now a baron, had retired from the Mitsui Trading Company and turned his energies to the arts. On the occasion of his sister's death, he expressed his emotions in *tanka*, an ancient poetic form:

> *Her childish face lingers even now*
> *America-bound, long ago*

More than half a century had passed since seven-year-old Ume had watched her two dearest friends leave Washington for New Haven; now once again, she was the one left behind. She still had Anna, but as her health declined, what had always been a possessive relationship grew somewhat obsessive. The brief diary entries of Ume's last months make note of every moment spent in Anna's company.

Ume died less than a year after Shige, in August of 1929, at the age of sixty-four. After her death, the school she founded was renamed Tsuda Eigaku Juku—the "Tsuda Home School of English"—an unusually personal tribute. And when the post-earthquake rebuilding was at last complete, Ume's ashes were moved to a quiet corner of the new campus in the northwestern suburb of Kokubunji, marked by an imposing granite slab and surrounded by a grove of her namesake plum trees—a shrine in spirit, if not in fact.

Today, Japanese elementary school children learn Ume's name in social studies, though few recognize Sutematsu's or Shige's. Tsuda College, as it is known in English, still thrives, with an undergraduate enrollment of twenty-five hundred women studying English, mathematics, computer science, and international studies. They sometimes refer to themselves as "Umekos," and when a final examination or an important job interview looms, many find their way to that quiet, plum-shaded corner of campus to ask Ume for help.

ACKNOWLEDGMENTS

ON THE DAY, nearly a decade ago, when I first pulled Alice Bacon's *A Japanese Interior* from its basement shelf at the New York Society Library, I never imagined the voyage it would send me on, or the extraordinary people I would meet along the way.

Several descendants of the protagonists and their families shared stories and artifacts and provided a living link to the past: Jean Bacon Bryant, Akiko Kuno, Michio Tsuda, Setsuko Uriu, Yvonne Ying-yue Yung. Three generations of Tsuda College alumnae in the Fujita family shared their perspective on how the school has evolved across the decades.

Sachiko Tanaka and Takako Takamizawa were the fairy godmothers of my research in Tokyo, providing critically important encouragement and access. Librarians and archivists unlocked trove after trove of letters, documents, and photographs, especially Akira Sugiura and Yuki Nakada of Tsuda College, Dean M. Rogers of Vassar, James W. Campbell of the New Haven Museum, Rie Hayashi of the International House of Japan, Fernanda Perrone of Rutgers, and Brandi Tambasco of the New York Society Library.

Many experts, friends and strangers both, were startlingly generous with insights and advice: Margaret Bendroth, Lesley Downer, Elisabeth Gitter, Robert Grigg, Ann Havemeyer, James Huffman, James Lewis, James Mulkin, Anne Walthall, Barbara Wheeler. Special thanks to Daniel Botsman, chair of the Council on East Asian Studies at Yale, whose extensive and thoughtful comments were a gift.

For close reading (and close friendship) I am grateful to Jessica Francis Kane, Gail Marcus, Zanthe Taylor, Carlton Vann, and Isaac Wheeler.

This project would never have become a book without Rob McQuilkin, who makes the most extravagant promises and keeps them; and Alane Salierno Mason, whose editorial wisdom never falters. The indefatigable Stephanie Hiebert devoted countless hours to the details. Nancy Howell drew the beautiful map.

My profoundest thanks go to Yuzo Nimura, tireless researcher, translator, and father-in-law. My work would have been impossible without him.

But the true inspiration for this book is my husband, Yoji Nimura, who took me to the other side of the world, and our children, Clare and David, who brought us back again. Home is wherever you are.

NOTES

PROLOGUE

15 motley uniforms: William Elliot Griffis, *The Mikado's Empire* (New York: Harper & Brothers, 1896), 366.

16 Oiled hair: Julia Meech-Pekarik, *The World of the Meiji Print: Impressions of a New Civilization* (New York: Weatherhill, 1986), 112.

17 Her teeth were blackened: Basil Hall Chamberlain, *Things Japanese: Being Notes on Various Subjects Connected With Japan, For the Use of Travellers and Others*, new ed. (London: Kegan Paul, Trench, Trubner, 1892), 57; Gina Collia-Suzuki, "Beautiful Blackened Smiles," *Andon* 92 (2012): 46–48.

17 They did not touch the refreshments: Shige Uriu, "The Days of My Youth," *Japan Advertiser*, September 11, 1927.

17 "Considering that you are girls": Yoshiko Furuki, *The White Plum, a Biography of Ume Tsuda: Pioneer in the Higher Education of Japanese Women* (New York: Weatherhill, 1991), 11–12.

1: SAMURAI DAUGHTER

19 The Yamakawa compound: Sutematsu Yamakawa, "Recollections of Japanese Family Life," *Vassar Miscellany*, November 1, 1880, 49–54.

23 "Serve the shogun": Teruko Craig, introduction to *Remembering Aizu: The Testament of Shiba Goro*, by Goro Shiba (Honolulu: University of Hawai'i Press, 1999), 4.

24 "1. We must not disobey our elders": Ibid., 6.

25 And then they were free: Goro Shiba, *Remembering Aizu: The Testament of Shiba Goro* (Honolulu: University of Hawai'i Press, 1999), 34; R. P. Dore, *Education in Tokugawa Japan* (London: Routledge & Kegan Paul, 1965), 105–6.

25 "Instructions for the Very Young":

Craig, introduction to *Remembering Aizu*, 7.

26 "The five worst maladies": Basil Hall Chamberlain, *Things Japanese: Being Notes on Various Subjects Connected with Japan, for the Use of Travellers and Others*, new ed. (London: Kegan Paul, Trench, Trubner, 1892), 459–61.

28 taking Dutch sobriquets: Donald Keene, *The Japanese Discovery of Europe, 1720–1830* (Stanford, CA: Stanford University Press, 1969), 124.

29 One of his officers bragged: Noel Perrin, *Giving Up the Gun: Japan's Reversion to the Sword, 1543–1879* (Boston: David R. Godine, 1979), 72.

29 Perry's men, naturally: Matthew C. Perry, *The Japan Expedition, 1852–1854: The Personal Journal of Commodore Matthew C. Perry* (Washington, DC: Smithsonian Institution Press, 1968), 91.

30 "Our historians bid us to obey": Henry Heusken, *Japan Journal, 1855–1861* (New Brunswick, NJ: Rutgers University Press, 1964), 183.

2: THE WAR OF THE YEAR OF THE DRAGON

33 "brocade banner": Peter Duus, *Modern Japan* (Boston: Houghton Mifflin, 1998), 80.

34 "potato samurai": Goro Shiba, *Remembering Aizu: The Testament of Shiba Goro* (Honolulu: University of Hawai'i Press, 1999), 42.

34 Girls of the samurai class: Shiba, *Remembering Aizu*, 44.

36 "Hand in hand": Teruko Craig, introduction to Shiba, *Remembering Aizu*, 17.

36 The rhythmic pop of rifle fire: Shiba, *Remembering Aizu*, 51.

36 Not quite strong enough: Sakumi Hanami, *Danshaku Yamakawa Sensei Den* [The biography of Baron Yamakawa] (Tokyo: Iwanami Shoten, 1939), chap. 2.

36 The tale is retold to this day: The story of the Byakkotai traveled far beyond Aizu, morphing from a heroic tale of Old Japan into a rallying symbol for militarists both in Japan and beyond. In 1928, impressed by the depth of the young fighters' loyalty to their lord, Benito Mussolini sent a Pompeian column to be erected at the gravesite on Iimori Hill overlooking the castle. The monument still stands, inscribed in Italian and dated "year VI of the Fascist Era."

37 Her sister was among: John Dwight, "The Marchioness Oyama," *Twentieth Century Home*, 1904.

38 The night of his surrender: Harold Bolitho, "Aizu, 1853–1868," *Proceedings of the British Association for Japanese Studies* 2 (1977): 16.

38 the paddle wheel steamer *Yancy*: Akiko Kuno, *Unexpected Destinations: The Poignant Story of Japan's First Vassar Graduate*, trans. Kirsten McIvor (New York: Kodansha International, 1993), 46.

39 Desperate to feed his mother: Shiba, *Remembering Aizu*, 91.

39 "To those who ask": Hiraku Shimoda, *Lost and Found: Recovering Regional Identity in Imperial Japan* (Cambridge, MA: Harvard University Asia Center, 2014), 59.

39 "If those scoundrels": Shiba, *Remembering Aizu*, 89.

39 The boys now read: Shiba, *Remembering Aizu*, 91–92.

39 "Although Europe is now": Akiko Uchiyama, "Translation as Representation: Fukuzawa Yukichi's Representation of the 'Others,'" in *Agents of Translation* (Philadelphia: John Benjamins, 2009), 67–68.

41 "The curio-shops displayed": Basil Hall Chamberlain, *Things Japanese: Being Notes on Various Subjects Connected with Japan, for the Use of Travellers and Others*, new ed. (London: Kegan Paul, Trench, Trubner, 1892), 397.

3: "A LITTLE LEAVEN"

43 "Western-style" suit: Sakumi Hanami, *Danshaku Yamakawa Sensei Den* [The biography of Baron Yamakawa] (Tokyo: Iwanami Shoten, 1939), chap. 2.

44 "as a little leaven leavens": Charles Lanman, ed., *The Japanese in America* (New York: University Publishing, 1872), 46.

46 "Over sea, hither from Niphon": Walt Whitman, "The Errand-Bearers," *New-York Times*, June 27, 1860.

46 Even a smoke: Yukichi Fukuzawa, *The Autobiography of Yukichi Fukuzawa*, trans. Eiichi Kiyooka (1899; New York: Columbia University Press, 1980), 113.

46 "One burly fellow": Masao Miyoshi, *As We Saw Them: The First Japanese Embassy to the United States* (New York: Kodansha America, 1994), 65.

50 Bowling along on wheels: Edward Seidensticker, *Low City, High City: Tokyo from Edo to the Earthquake: How the Shogun's Ancient Capital Became a Great Modern City, 1867–1923* (New York: Alfred A. Knopf, 1983), 47; Julia Meech-Pekarik, *The World of the Meiji Print: Impressions of a New Civilization* (New York: Weatherhill, 1986), 86.

51 The Empress Haruko: Donald Keene, *Emperor of Japan: Meiji and His World, 1852–1912* (New York: Columbia University Press, 2002), 105.

51 "delicate and effeminate": Ibid., 201.

52 Superstitions: Japan Photographers Association, *A Century of Japanese Photography* (New York: Pantheon, 1980), 7.

52 "tools of civilization and enlightenment": Japan Photographers Association, *Century of Japanese Photography*, 9.

54 "urge them on toward civilization": Albert A. Altman, "*Shinbunshi*: The Early Meiji Adaptation of the Western-Style Newspaper," in *Modern Japan: Aspects of History, Literature, and Society* (Berkeley: University of California Press, 1975), 63.

54 "Five Young Girls": "Five Young Girls Leave for Study in America," *Shinbun Zasshi*, November 1871.

4: "AN EXPEDITION OF PRACTICAL OBSERVERS"

55 "If we would profit": Charles Lanman, ed., *The Japanese in America*, (New York: University Publishing, 1872), 6–7.

56 "What heartless people": Yoshiko Furuki, *The White Plum, a Biography of Ume Tsuda: Pioneer in the Higher Education of Japanese Women* (New York: Weatherhill, 1991), 6.

57 its settlers dead or dispersed in poverty: The grave of one of the women, a nursemaid named Okei, still stands. It is believed to be the first grave of a Japanese woman in America.

57 "What wonder": Ume Tsuda, "Japanese Women Emancipated," *Chicago Record*, February 27, 1897. Reprinted in Ume Tsuda, *The Writings of Umeko Tsuda* [*Tsuda Umeko monjo*] (Kodaira, Japan: Tsuda College, 1984), 77.

59 "Sailors on the decks": Kunitake Kume, *The Iwakura Embassy, 1871–73: A True Account of the Ambassador Extraordinary & Plenipotentiary's Journey of Observation through the United States of America and Europe*, ed. Graham Healey and Chushichi Tsuzuki (Chiba, Japan: Japan Documents, 2002), 30.

59 In his account of their departure: Ibid.

59 "It was a very beautiful day": Ume Tsuda, *The Writings of Umeko Tsuda* (Kodaira, Japan: Tsuda College, 1984), 475; Barbara Rose, *Tsuda Umeko and Women's Education in Japan* (New Haven, CT: Yale University Press, 1992), 18.

60 "The bride was left alone": Shige Uriu, "The Days of My Youth," *Japan Advertiser*, September 11, 1927.

62 Japanese for "what do you want?": Tsuda, *Writings of Umeko Tsuda*, 475.

62 "All our entreaties": Uriu, "Days of My Youth."

62 "Passengers are forbidden": Kume, *Iwakura Embassy, 1871–73*, 31.

62 Those who had acquired pocket watches: Kunitake Kume, *Japan Rising: The Iwakura Embassy to the USA and Europe 1871–1873*, ed. Chushichi Tsuzuki and R. Jules Young (Cambridge: Cambridge University Press, 2009), 8.

62 "We did not see so much as": Ibid., 8–9.

63 "He told us to come": Uriu, "Days of My Youth."

63 held tutorials on Western table manners: Akiko Kuno, *Unexpected Destinations: The Poignant Story of Japan's First Vassar Graduate*, trans. Kirsten McIvor (New York: Kodansha International, 1993), 60.

64 Though there were two secretaries called Nagano: The other Nagano with the Iwakura mission, Fumiakira Nagano, was

secretary to the chief judicial minister, Sasaki. Some scholars think the man who molested Ryo was Fumiakira: he was a southern samurai and therefore predisposed to abuse the girls, whose families were on the losing side; and he was close to Sasaki, which would explain why Sasaki argued vehemently against holding a trial at all. Sasaki, unfortunately, referred to both Naganos indiscriminately by surname in his journal, so we may never know which it was.

64 He wrote love notes: Masao Miyoshi, *As We Saw Them: The First Japanese Embassy to the United States* (New York: Kodansha America, 1994), 43.

64 "Wives and maids": "Tommy Polka" (Philadelphia: Lee & Walker, 1860), Lester S. Levy Collection of Sheet Music, Sheridan Libraries, Johns Hopkins University.

65 "Little irregularities": Furuki, *White Plum*, 7.

65 "To divert our boredom": Ibid.

65 "Apparently, when crossing the ocean": Kume, *Iwakura Embassy, 1871–73,* 35.

5: "INTERESTING STRANGERS"

69 "Interesting Strangers": "The Japanese Embassy," *San Francisco Chronicle,* January 10, 1872. In anticipation of the embassy's arrival, the *Chronicle* exhorted its readers to extend a warm welcome to the Japanese visitors: "The Japanese people occupy toward this nation a very important position; they send their youth here for education, who, unlike the Chinese, adopt our costume and our customs, and will in time carry to their Oriental homes many of the habits and feelings acquired among us . . . It is necessary that some steps should be immediately taken by our civic authorities and leading men to give these interesting strangers, and to Minister DeLong, a proper reception when they land upon our shores."

69 "America is a democratic country": Donald Keene, *Modern Japanese Diaries: The Japanese at Home and Abroad as Revealed through Their Diaries* (New York: Henry Holt, 1995), 93.

70 "in the most outlandish": "The Japanese," *New-York Times,* January 17, 1872.

71 "as densely packed as": Kunitake Kume, *The Iwakura Embassy, 1871–73: A True Account of the Ambassador Extraordinary & Plenipotentiary's Journey of Observation through the United States of America and Europe,* ed. Graham Healey and Chushichi Tsuzuki (Chiba, Japan: Japan Documents, 2002), 64.

71 The Grand Hotel: Kume, *Iwakura Embassy, 1871–73,* 65.

71 "I was shocked": Keene, *Modern Japanese Diaries,* 93–94.

72 *"Annata, anaata ohio"*: "The Orientals," *San Francisco Chronicle,* January 17, 1872.

73 Iwakura was gracious: Ibid.

74 "Western people are ever eager": Kunitake Kume, *Japan Rising: The Iwakura Embassy to the USA and Europe 1871–1873*, ed. Chushichi Tsuzuki and R. Jules Young (Cambridge: Cambridge University Press, 2009), 16.

74 "Let the Chinese be not confounded": "Orientals," *San Francisco Chronicle*, January 17, 1872.

74 "American idea": Cullen Murphy, "A History of the *Atlantic Monthly*" (from a presentation given in 1994), Atlantic Monthly Group, 2001, http://www.theatlantic.com/past/docs/about/atlhistf.htm.

74 "for, in spite of all Celestial": "Japan," *Atlantic Monthly*, June 1860, 722.

75 Iwakura ordered samples: "Iwakura's Head," *San Francisco Chronicle*, January 19, 1872.

75 "And that is what we want with Japan": "The Japanese," *San Francisco Chronicle*, January 18, 1872.

77 "Several milliners": "The Orientals," *San Francisco Chronicle*, January 25, 1872.

77 "*furore*": Ibid.

77 "We hardly dared to go out": Ume Tsuda, *The Writings of Umeko Tsuda* [*Tsuda Umeko monjo*] (Kodaira, Japan: Tsuda College, 1984), 81–82.

78 "could not be creatures of this world": Ibid., 82.

78 "The simplicity of these daughters": "Various Notes," *San Francisco Chronicle*, January 19, 1872. The girls were not the only ones to be perplexed by foreign women's fashion. In the early 1870s, a young man studying English in Japan expressed his frank concern for the practice of wearing corsets in an essay entitled "My First Impression of Foreigners": "One thing which attracted my attention was the narrowness of the bellies [of] women, and I asked one of my friends who knew a little of foreign customs and manner[s] if their bellies were so narrow from their birth; and I was quite astonished when I was told that they [were] made so by their own will, and the narrower the bellies the more beautiful they were said to be. I can not understand even at the present day why those civilized countries of Europe and America retain such a foolish custom, because it may possibly do some harm, but I dare say it does not make any good even to the slightest possible degree. Moreover, I guess it is worse than the shaving of eyebrows and the blackening of the teeth of the Japanese women. It may be compared with the lessening of the feet of Chinese, so that they can not walk without the aid of some other person." Takasu, "My First Impression on [*sic*] Foreigners," William Elliot Griffis Collection, Box 108, Folder 135, Special Collections and University Archives, Rutgers University Libraries.

78 "to impart a classic inspiration": "Japanese Wonders," *San Francisco Chronicle*, January 21, 1872.

78 "a splendidly executed group": "Photographs of the Embassy," *San Francisco Chronicle*, February 9, 1872.

78 "our Japanese visitors": "Our Japanese Visitors," *Harper's Weekly*, March 16, 1872, 209.

79 "The streets were so densely packed": Kume, *Japan Rising*, 17.

79 "Japan extends the hand": "The Japanese Embassy," *Daily Alta California*, January 20, 1872.

79 "The Embassy from Japan": "The Orientals," *San Francisco Chronicle*, January 24, 1872.

80 The climax of the embassy's stay: "Banquet to the Japanese Embassy and United States Minister C. E. DeLong at the Grand Hotel," *Daily Alta California*, January 24, 1872.

80 "the Great Britain of the Pacific": Newton Booth, quoted in "Orientals," *San Francisco Chronicle*, January 24, 1872.

80 "Our Daimios": Hirobumi Ito, quoted in "Orientals," *San Francisco Chronicle*, January 24, 1872.

81 "seems a repetition of the old story": Horatio Stebbins, quoted in "Orientals," *San Francisco Chronicle*, January 24, 1872.

81 "Your visit to this country": "The Orientals," *San Francisco Chronicle*, January 26, 1872.

82 "It is all quite opulent": Kume, *Japan Rising*, 30.

82 Wags insisted: "The Orientals," *San Francisco Chronicle*, January 31, 1872.

82 They ate what was placed before them: Tsuda, *Writings of Umeko Tsuda*, 82.

83 miniature statues of President Grant: "Legislative Banquet," *San Francisco Chronicle*, February 2, 1872.

83 The festivities ended: "The Orientals," *San Francisco Chronicle*, February 3, 1872.

83 "Far below, at the foot": Kume, *Japan Rising*, 32.

83 "Having journeyed through a realm": Ibid., 36.

84 Salt Lake City's leading hotel: Dean W. Collinwood, Ryoichi Yamamoto, and Kazue Matsui-Haag, eds, *Samurais in Salt Lake: Diary of the First Diplomatic Japanese Delegation to Visit Utah, 1872* (Ogden, UT: US-Japan Center, 1996), 42.

84 "lascivious cohabitation": Leonard Arrington, *Brigham Young: American Moses* (New York: Knopf, 1985), 372.

84 "We came to the United States": "Why Iwakura Declined to See Brigham Young," *San Francisco Chronicle*, February 13, 1872.

84 "His power is equivalent": Collinwood, Yamamoto, and Matsui-Haag, *Samurais in Salt Lake*, 47.

85 "Mrs. DeLong, with the bearing": "The Orientals," *San Francisco Chronicle*, February 14, 1872.

85 "The social customs": Kume, *Japan Rising*, 40.

85 "We had seen everything": Ibid., 37.

85 Warm Springs Bath House: Collinwood, Yamamoto, and Matsui-Haag, *Samurais in Salt Lake*, 43.

85 From the windows: Shige Uriu, "The Days of My Youth," *Japan Advertiser*, September 11, 1927.

86 "Although one may tire": Kume, *Japan Rising*, 42–43.

86 At Omaha, memorably: Tsuda, *Writings of Umeko Tsuda*, 83.

86 "Show yourselves": "Our Oriental Visitors," *Chicago Tribune*, February 27, 1872.

86 "Their features are less intellectual": Ibid.

87 "intelligent, bright, and vivacious": "Our Japanese Visitors," *Chicago Tribune*, February 26, 1872.

87 "Most of the stations": Kume, *Japan Rising*, 48.

87 "His city was not at its best": Tremont House, like Chicago, was struggling, but the fact that it existed at all was something of a miracle. The hotel had, in fact, burned to the ground in the Great Fire. At the height of the blaze, its proprietor, John B. Drake, had had the presence of mind to buy the nearby Michigan Avenue Hotel, placing a brash bet that it would escape the inferno. Its current owner, sure it was doomed, was only too happy to sell. It was the only hotel on the South Side to survive. Drake renamed it New Tremont House until the old Tremont House was rebuilt on the original site two years later. Reference report by Chicago Historical Society library staff, July 2, 1974,

Clipping Files, Chicago History Museum.

87 "the wonderful recuperative powers": "Our Oriental Visitors," *Chicago Tribune*, February 27, 1872.

87 "the first money contribution": [No title], *Chicago Tribune*, February 29, 1872.

87 "little almond-eyed gentlemen": "The Views of Young Japan," *San Francisco Chronicle*, February 28, 1872.

88 with drivers on each car blowing horns: Kume, *Japan Rising*, 54.

89 "a Westerner born of Japan": Ivan Parker Hall, *Mori Arinori* (Cambridge, MA: Harvard University Press, 1973), 1.

89 "The princesses": "Our Japanese Visitors," *Evening Star*, February 29, 1872.

89 "What am I to do?": Katharine McCook Knox, *Surprise Personalities in Georgetown, D.C.* (Washington, DC: author, 1958), 17–18.

90 "It is said they parted": "Georgetown Affairs," *Daily National Republican*, March 2, 1872.

91 Mrs. Hepburn: Coincidentally, Mrs. Hepburn's brother-in-law, the medical missionary James Curtis Hepburn, was living at the time in Yokohama, where he ran a clinic and an English school. The Hepburn system for transliterating Japanese into the Roman alphabet is named for him.

91 The scribe Kume: Kume, *Japan Rising*, 56.

91 "the veritable 'Japanese Tommy'":

"Our Oriental Visitors," *Evening Star*, March 1, 1872.

92 "The separation between white and black": Kume, *Japan Rising*, 63.

92 "Did you see those Japs": Mark Twain and Charles Dudley Warner, *The Gilded Age: A Tale of Today* (1873: New York: Library of America, 2002), 274.

92 "the helmets worn by Roman warriors": "The Japanese Embassy," *Evening Star*, March 4, 1872.

92 "upon which the Japanese were to walk": "The Japanese Embassy," *Daily National Republican*, March 5, 1872.

92 "A confused idea": "De Temporibus et Moribus," *Vassar Miscellany*, April 1872, 47.

93 "the members of the Embassy": "The Japanese Embassy," *Evening Star*, March 6, 1872.

93 "It will be a pleasure": "Japanese Embassy," *Daily National Republican*, March 5, 1872.

93 "Their mission is to be educated": "Our Japanese Visitors," *Evening Star*, February 29, 1872.

94 "Ume, in particular, is quick": Adeline Lanman to Hatsuko Tsuda, March 4, 1872, in Yoshiko Furuki, *The White Plum, a Biography of Ume Tsuda: Pioneer in the Higher Education of Japanese Women* (New York: Weatherhill, 1991), 20.

94 "I wish you to understand": Hatsuko Tsuda to Adeline Lanman, April 17, 1872, in Furuki, *White Plum*, 20.

95 "They don't understand": Joseph Niijima to Mr. and Mrs. Hardy, March 5, 1872, in Arthur Sherburne Hardy, *Life and Letters of Joseph Hardy Neesima* (Boston: Houghton, Mifflin, 1891), 122.

95 A gossip columnist: "The Japanese Ladies," *New-York Times*, May 20, 1872.

95 Miss Annie Loring: [No title], *Daily National Republican*, May 21, 1872.

96 "First I am happy": Ume Tsuda to Hatsuko Tsuda, May or June 1872, TCA, LT0002.

6: FINDING FAMILIES

97 "everything passed off pleasantly": "Farewell Entertainment to the Japanese Embassy," *Evening Star*, July 27, 1872.

98 "The ordinary dinner parties": Charles Lanman, unpublished manuscript for a biography of Ume Tsuda, TCA, IV-6-1.

99 "If these girls are not taught": Kenjiro Yamakawa to Charles Lanman, June 8, 1872, TCA, IX-C-1.

100 The response was overwhelming: Edward J. M. Rhoads, *Stepping Forth into the World: The Chinese Educational Mission to the United States, 1872–81* (Hong Kong: Hong Kong University Press, 2011), 49–50.

101 Doctor after doctor: "The Japanese Girls," *San Francisco Chronicle*, October 20, 1872.

101 "I went to see Mrs. Van Name": Rebecca Bacon to Leonard Bacon, July 1872, BFP, Box 9, Folders 162 and 164, YMA.

101 "sunbeam from the land of the rising sun": Charles Lanman, unpublished manuscript for a biography of Ume Tsuda, TCA, IV-6-1.

103 "They don't stand this climate": Rebecca Bacon to Leonard Bacon, July 1872, BFP, Box 9, Folder 162, YMA.

103 "Mrs. Hotchkiss suggests": Ibid.

103 Northrop's original call: Rhoads, *Stepping Forth*, 64.

103 "What we propose": Leonard Bacon to Addison Van Name, August 12, 1872, BFP, Box 9, Folder 162, YMA.

103 "However I beseech him": Kenjiro Yamakawa to Addison Van Name, August 17, 1872, BFP, Box 9, Folder 162, YMA.

104 "During their stay in the East": "The Returning Japanese Young Women," *New-York Times*, November 9, 1872.

104 "My Dear American mother": Ume Tsuda to Adeline Lanman, 1872, TCA, I-B-2.

105 "The two Japanese girls": Leonard Bacon, date book, October 31, 1872, BFP, Box 2, Folder 6, YMA.

106 "Mrs. Bacon and my daughters": Leonard Bacon to Arinori Mori, October 31, 1872, BFP, Box 9, Folder 163, YMA.

106 "I have all along regarded": Theodore Bacon, ed., *Delia Bacon: A Biographical Sketch* (Boston: Houghton, Mifflin, 1888), 310.

106 "We expect them to acquire": Leonard Bacon to Arinori Mori, October 31, 1872, BFP, Box 9, Folder 163, YMA.

107 "We were sorry to part": Leonard Bacon to Leonard W. Bacon, December 9, 1872, BFP, Box 9, Folder 163, YMA.

7: GROWING UP AMERICAN

108 "and if they are aware": Leonard Bacon to Leonard W. Bacon, December 9, 1872, BFP, Box 9, Folder 163, YMA.

108 "Barnum's great menagerie": Leonard Bacon to Catherine Bacon, April 26, 1873, BFP, Box 9, Folder 165, YMA.

109 "the Little Professor": Carolyn Quick Tillary, *A Taste of Freedom: A Cookbook with Recipes and Remembrances from the Hampton Institute* (New York: Citadel Press, 2002), 59.

110 "Cease your chatter": in classmate Carrie's autograph book, 1870–75, New Haven Museum, MSS 17, Box VI, Folder F.

111 "I remember how": Marian P. Whitney, "Stematz Yamakowa, Princess Oyama," *Vassar Quarterly*, July 1919, 265.

111 "Do you remember saying": Yew Fun Tan to Catherine Bacon, September 18, 1874, BFP, Box 9, Folder 172, YMA.

112 "Analyze the following sentence": *Annual Report of the Board of Education of the New Haven City School District, for the Year Ending August 31, 1874* (New Haven, CT: Tuttle, Morehouse & Taylor, 1874), 54–55.

113 "As the mother is the guardian": John S. C. Abbott, *The Mother at Home; or The Principles of Mater-*

nal *Duty* (New York: American Tract Society, 1833), 2.

113 "A single day's absence": "Private Day School for Young Ladies and Children," pamphlet, 1876–77, New Haven Museum.

114 In the summer: Sumie Ikuta, *Uryu Shigeko: Mo hitori no joshi ryugakusei* [Uriu Shigeko: One more female foreign student] (Tokyo: Bungei Shunju, 2009), 51–61.

114 One memorable evening: Ibid., 56.

115 "The fear of the Lord": Ibid., 66.

115 "unruly spirits": Katsunobu Masuda, *Recollections of Admiral Baron Sotokichi Uriu, I. J. N.* (Tokyo: privately published, 1938), 3–6.

115 What a lovely boy: Ikuta, *Uryu Shigeko*, 68.

116 "Ume is as talkative as ever": Sutematsu Yamakawa to Catherine Bacon, December 20, 1874, BFP, Box 9, Folder 174, YMA.

116 "Dear Mrs. Lanman": Ume Tsuda to Adeline Lanman, 1872, TCA, I-B-3.

116 "I dreamt that I went home": Ume Tsuda to Hatsuko Tsuda, 1872, TCA, I-A-4.

117 "I am always thinking": Hatsuko Tsuda to Adeline Lanman, March 22, 1873, Dorothea Lynde Dix Additional Papers, 1866–87 (MS Am 2157), Houghton Library, Harvard University.

117 The Lanmans enrolled Ume: Richard P. Jackson, *The Chronicles of Georgetown, D.C.: From 1751 to 1878* (Washington, DC: R. O. Polkinhorn, printer, 1878), 230.

117 A neighbor child: Katharine McCook Knox, *Surprise Personalities in Georgetown, D.C.* (Washington, DC: author, 1958), 19.

117 "She always decidedly objected": Charles Lanman, unpublished manuscript for a biography of Ume Tsuda, TCA, IV-6-1.

117 "A large number of premiums": "The Collegiate Institute of Georgetown," *Daily National Republican*, June 27, 1874.

118 "If there is any merit": Knox, *Surprise Personalities*, 34.

118 Ume's accomplishments: Ibid., 21.

118 Kiyo Kawamura: Charles Lanman to Sen Tsuda, June 11, 1873, TCA, I'-1; Hatsuko Tsuda to Adeline Lanman, March 22, 1873, Dorothea Lynde Dix Additional Papers, 1866–87 (MS Am 2157), Houghton Library, Harvard University.

118 "Mr. Yoshida said": Ume Tsuda to Hatsuko Tsuda, January 20, 1875, TCA, I-A-7.

118 "Ume herself was wont to say": Charles Lanman, unpublished manuscript for a biography of Ume Tsuda, TCA, IV-6-1.

119 "You asked me to write": Ume Tsuda to Charles Lanman, May 21, 1875, TCA, I-B-4.

120 "I think I have baptised": Octavius Perinchief to Charles Lanman, July 12, 1873, in Charles Lanman, *Octavius Perinchief; His Life of Trial and Supreme Faith* (Washington, DC: James Anglim, 1879), 148.

120 "Ume will be glad to know": Sen Tsuda to Charles Lanman, July 10, 1875, TCA, I'-2.

120 "You went away from us": Koto Tsuda to Ume Tsuda, January 11, 1875, TCA, II-2-1.

121 "O sir, she was a good child": Charles Lanman, unpublished manuscript for a biography of Ume Tsuda, TCA, IV-6-1.

121 "A kiss to your little Japanese ward": Ume Tsuda, *The Writings of Umeko Tsuda [Tsuda Umeko monjo]* (Kodaira, Japan: Tsuda College, 1984), 510.

121 "International Exhibition of Arts": "Exhibition Facts," Centennial Exhibition Digital Collection, Free Library of Philadelphia, 2001, http://libwww. freelibrary.org/CenCol/exhibitionfax.htm.

121 "Have you been at the Centennial?": William Dean Howells, "A Sennight of the Centennial," *Atlantic Monthly*, July 1876, 92.

122 "sooner or later lift the nation": "The Centennial: The Government Exposition," *New-York Times*, March 29, 1876.

122 *The Dreaming Iolanthe*: Pamela H. Simpson, "Butter Cows and Butter Buildings," *Winterthur Portfolio*, Spring 2007, 4.

122 "Wherever else the national bird": Howells, "Sennight," 96.

122 "Let the new cycle": John Greenleaf Whittier, "Hymn Written for the Opening of the International Exhibition, Philadelphia, May 10, 1876," *Atlantic Monthly*, June 1876, 744–45.

122 "dragons, and mats": "The Great Exposition," *Hartford Courant*, May 18, 1876.

123 "a plesaunce for a palace": "Characteristics of the International Fair V," *Atlantic Monthly*, December 1876, 733.

123 "The quaint little people": Robert W. Rydell, *All the World's a Fair: Visions of Empire at American International Expositions, 1876–1916* (Chicago: University of Chicago Press, 1984), 30.

123 In contrast, when 113 young members: Edward J. M. Rhoads, *Stepping Forth into the World: The Chinese Educational Mission to the United States, 1872–81* (Hong Kong: Hong Kong University Press, 2011), 109–13.

124 "The first day crowds come": Fukui Makoto, *Harper's Weekly*, July 15, 1876, quoted in "Exhibition Facts—Period Testimony: Quotations & Random Thoughts," Centennial Exhibition Digital Collection, Free Library of Philadelphia, 2001, http://libwww.library.phila.gov/CenCol/exh-testimony.htm.

124 "The Main Building is one third of a mile": Ume Tsuda to Miss Marion, July 18, 1876, TCA, I-C-1.

124 The commencement exercises: Hillhouse High School graduation program, April 1877, Dana Collection 109, New Haven Museum.

125 "I went to see Miss Abbott": Rebecca Bacon to Catherine

Bacon, July 8, 1877, BFP, Box 9, Folder 195, YMA.

126 fifty dollars to cover expenses: Saburo Takaki to Leonard Bacon, August 2, 1877, BFP, Box 9, Folder 195, YMA.

8: AT VASSAR

127 "Most of us in Japan": Stranger, "Japanese Children," *Gleaner*, February 21, 1878.

128 "I have never seen such a wonderful place": Catherine Bacon to Leonard Bacon, June 5, 1872, BFP, Box 9, Folder 161, YMA.

128 "I considered that the mothers": Moses Tyler, "Vassar Female College," *New Englander*, October 1862, 8.

129 "heated by steam": Ibid., 5.

129 "I think of Alice constantly": Catherine Bacon to Leonard Bacon, June 5, 1872, BFP, Box 9, Folder 161, YMA.

129 They were the first nonwhite: Nearly twenty years later, in 1897, a scandal erupted on campus when it was discovered that one Anita Florence Hemmings, an outstanding student who had been voted class beauty, was the daughter of black parents and had been passing as white for four years. Her identity was revealed just weeks before graduation, but she was permitted to receive her diploma. Though a trickle of Japanese women studied at Vassar beginning in 1912, the college would not formally enroll another black student until 1940.

129 There were indoor bathrooms: Dorothy Plum and George B. Dowell, *The Magnificent Enterprise: A Chronicle of Vassar College* (Poughkeepsie, NY: Vassar College, 1961), year 1865 on time line.

129 provided her own napkin: *Fourteenth Annual Catalogue of the Officers and Students of Vassar College, Poughkeepsie, N.Y., 1878–79* (Poughkeepsie, NY: E. B. Osborne, printer, 1879), 47.

130 Twenty minutes of quiet privacy: Ibid., 46.

130 "He waked us up": Cornelia M. Raymond, *Memories of a Child of Vassar* (Poughkeepsie, NY: Vassar College, 1940), 36–37.

130 "You should see his Cassius-like proportions": *Letters from Old-Time Vassar: Written by a Student in 1869–1870* (Poughkeepsie, NY: Vassar College, 1915), 58.

130 "What's the matter?": Ibid., 116–17.

130 "I expect to talk about him": Ibid., 17–18.

130 "He is our oasis": Ibid., 116.

130 At Vassar, male professors were addressed: Ibid., 56.

131 "How are you getting on?": Frances A. Wood, *Earliest Years at Vassar* (Poughkeepsie, NY: Vassar College Press, 1909), 86.

131 "Learn as if you will live forever": Ibid., 85.

131 "dome parties": Maryann Bruno and Elizabeth A. Daniels, *Vassar College* (Charleston, SC: Arcadia, 2001), 20.

131 "Who lifting their hearts": Wood, *Earliest Years*, 97.

132 "I have no memory": "Japanese Vassar Girls," *Sunday Advertiser*, October 1, 1893.

132 "Japanese arias": Sheet music, Ritter Papers, Box 13, Folder 19, VSC.

132 "like a beautiful Jewess": "Japanese Vassar Girls," *Sunday Advertiser*.

132 "When the class-room was depressed": Helen Hiscock Backus, "A Japanese Lady of High Degree," *Vassar Miscellany*, February 1901, 201.

133 one of her older sisters, Misao: Akiko Kuno, *Unexpected Destinations: The Poignant Story of Japan's First Vassar Graduate*, trans. Kirsten McIvor (New York: Kodansha International, 1993), 117.

133 When a letter from this distant sister: "History of the Class of 1882, Vassar College, Prepared for Their Fiftieth Anniversary, June, 1932," SYOP, Box 2, Folder 4, p. 114, VSC.

133 "I believe it was on account of": Ume Tsuda to Hatsuko Tsuda, June 15, 1879, TCA, I-A-8.

133 Sophomore Party: Marian P. Whitney, "Stematz Yamakowa, Princess Oyama," *Vassar Quarterly*, July 1919, 265.

134 "Miss Yamakawa's essay": "Home Matters," *Vassar Miscellany*, November 1, 1880, 73.

134 "the sacred lotus spread": Sutematsu Yamakawa, "Recollections of Japanese Family Life,"

Vassar Miscellany, November 1, 1880, 49–54.

134 Ocean View Hotel: "Block Island," *Hartford (CT) Courant*, August 5, 1881.

135 "who is a fine swimmer": Ume Tsuda to Hatsuko Tsuda, September 7, 1880, TCA, I-A-11.

135 "The girls say I was very convenient": Ume Tsuda to Adeline Lanman, June 23, 1881, TCA, I-B-5.

136 "as to whether the negro is doomed": "Commencement at Vassar," *New-York Times*, June 23, 1881.

136 "It is evident from their actions": Ume Tsuda to Adeline Lanman, June 23, 1881, TCA, I-B-5.

136 "Through her connection": "Off for Japan," *New-York Times*, October 24, 1881.

137 "of Spanish descent": "Detaining a Japanese Girl," *New-York Tribune*, August 10, 1881.

138 "When it came time for Louisa": "The Japanese Girl Disposed Of," *New-York Tribune*, August 24, 1881.

138 "But for her queer little": "Wakayama's Daughter," *New-York Times*, August 19, 1881.

138 "creamy skin, jet-black hair": "Off for Japan," *New-York Times*.

138 "I think of Shige": Sutematsu Yamakawa to Ume Tsuda, October 9, 1881, TCA, II-6-1.

138 Mrs. Rutherford B. Hayes: Ume Tsuda to Hatsuko Tsuda, June 15, 1879, TCA, I-A-8.

138 "an ambitious persevering & truly polite pupil": Ume Tsuda, *The Writings of Umeko Tsuda*

[Tsuda Umeko monjo] (Kodaira, Japan: Tsuda College, 1984), 511.

138 "If I could see you": Sutematsu Yamakawa to Ume Tsuda, October 9, 1881, TCA, II-6-1.

139 "I cannot, I must not": Shige Nagai to Adeline Lanman, 1881–82, TCA, IX-C-6.

139 "Bring lots of buttons": "History of the Class of 1882, Vassar College, Prepared for Their Fiftieth Anniversary, June, 1932," SYOP, Box 2, Folder 4, p. 114, VSC.

140 "In spite of modern sources": Sutematsu Yamakawa, "De Temporibus et Moribus," Vassar Miscellany, December 1, 1881, 128.

140 "Could he have foreseen": H. C. Kingsley, Leonard Sanford, and Thomas R. Trowbridge, eds., Leonard Bacon: Pastor of the First Church in New Haven (New Haven, CT: Tuttle, Morehouse & Taylor, printers, 1882), 224.

140 "I have never expressed": Yew Fun Tan to Catherine Bacon, January 3, 1882, BFP, Box 9, Folder 210, YMA.

141 "It is such a perfect likeness": Sutematsu Yamakawa to Catherine Bacon, January 28, 1882, BFP, Box 9, Folder 210, YMA.

141 "I was nearly wild": Ibid.

141 "However[,] she does not have much rest": Class Day prophecies, 1882, SYOP, Box 2, Folder 4, VSC.

142 "Ironic and Otherwise": Scrapbook 1, Jessie F. Wheeler Papers, Box 1, VSC.

142 "The Conscience of Science": Commencement program, 1882, SYOP, Box 2, Folder 3, VSC.

143 "Never before had a foreigner's speech": Kuno, Unexpected Destinations, 104–6.

143 "To Students Leaving College": Scrapbook 1, Jessie F. Wheeler Papers, Box 1, VSC.

9: THE JOURNEY "HOME"

144 "I cannot realize": Sutematsu Yamakawa to Alice Bacon, August 2, 1882, SYOP, Box 1, Folder 5, VSC.

145 Alice received certificates: Edward T. James, ed., Notable American Women: A Biographical Dictionary (Cambridge, MA: Radcliffe College, 1971), 78.

145 "I am now in the diet kitchen": Sutematsu Yamakawa to Alice Bacon, August 2, 1882, SYOP, Box 1, Folder 5, VSC.

146 "You see we would live in American style": Ibid.

146 "Perhaps I am counting the chickens": Ibid.

146 "I hope I shall see you": Sutematsu Yamakawa to Jessie Wheeler, September 17, 1882, SYOP, Box 1, Folder 7, VSC.

146 "Do you mean to say": Sutematsu Yamakawa to Jessie Wheeler, September 22, 1882, SYOP, Box 1, Folder 7, VSC.

147 "Every thing is already upside down": Sutematsu Yamakawa to Jessie Wheeler, September 26, 1882, SYOP, Box 1, Folder 7, VSC.

147 "Miss Tsuda's progress": Yoshiko

Furuki, *The White Plum, a Biography of Ume Tsuda: Pioneer in the Higher Education of Japanese Women* (New York: Weatherhill, 1991), 33.

147 "The regret for her departure": "Society," *Evening Critic*, October 6, 1882.

148 "I was thunderstruck": Sutematsu Yamakawa to Alice Bacon, October 1882, SYOP, Box 1, Folder 5, VSC.

148 "I did not know what to say": Ibid.

148 "Indeed we have been lionized": Ibid.

149 "Their mother remarked": Furuki, *White Plum*, 39–40.

149 "We have since we've been here": Sutematsu Yamakawa to Jessie Wheeler, October 25, 1882, SYOP, Box 1, Folder 7, VSC.

149 "We all climbed a tree": Ume Tsuda to Adeline Lanman, October 22, 1882, TCA, I-B-7 (1).

149 "It is so strange": Ume Tsuda to Adeline Lanman, October 25, 1882, TCA, I-B-7 (2).

150 "I hardly wonder": Ibid.

150 "You know he talked very bad English": Ume Tsuda to Adeline Lanman, November 9, 1882, TCA, I-B-8 (3).

151 "I think I realize": Ume Tsuda to Adeline Lanman, October 30, 1882, TCA, I-B-8 (4).

151 "Ume Tsuda and Stematz Yamakawa": J. H. C. Bonté to Charles and Adeline Lanman, November 1, 1882, TCA, IX-C-2.

151 "I expect after the first days": Ume Tsuda to Adeline Lanman, October 30, 1882, TCA, I-B-7 (4).

151 "The purser who has crossed": Sutematsu Yamakawa to Alice Bacon, November 18, 1882, SYOP, Box 1, Folder 5, VSC.

152 "Although it is very pleasant": Ume Tsuda to Adeline Lanman, November 6, 1882, TCA, I-B-8 (2).

152 "He says that the storms": Sutematsu Yamakawa to Alice Bacon, November 18, 1882, SYOP, Box 1, Folder 5, VSC.

152 "plenty of waiters & China boys": Ume Tsuda to Adeline Lanman, November 6, 1882, TCA, I-B-8 (2).

152 "the object of some curiosity": Ume Tsuda to Adeline Lanman, November 9, 1882, TCA, I-B-8 (3).

153 "We must not make enemies": Ume Tsuda to Adeline Lanman, October 25, 1882, TCA, I-B-7 (2).

153 "Come and see me": Ume Tsuda to Adeline Lanman, November 12, 1882, TCA, I-B-8 (3).

154 "Japan is no longer a land of mysteries": Sutematsu Yamakawa, "Recollections of Japanese Family Life," *Vassar Miscellany*, November 1, 1880, 49–50.

155 "Consequently, you must constantly": Ibid., 51.

155 "What will be the end": Sutematsu Yamakawa, "De Temporibus et Moribus," *Vassar Miscellany*, December 1, 1881, 131.

156 "splendid except for a nasty cold": Sutematsu Yamakawa to

Alice Bacon, November 18, 1882, SYOP, Box 1, Folder 5, VSC.

156 "They swam all around us": Ume Tsuda to Adeline Lanman, November 19, 1882, TCA, I-B-8 (4).

156 "Tomorrow turns a new page": Ibid.

157 "How do you feel now": Sutematsu Yamakawa, draft manuscript, December 24, 1882, SYOP, Box 1, Folder 5, VSC.

10: TWO WEDDINGS

161 Yet as they thanked: Ume Tsuda to Adeline Lanman, November 21, 1882, in Yoshiko Furuki, ed., *The Attic Letters: Ume Tsuda's Correspondence to Her American Mother* (New York: Weatherhill, 1991), 13–14.

161 "who though very polite": Sutematsu Yamakawa, draft manuscript, December 24, 1882, SYOP, Box 1, Folder 5, VSC.

161 "so nice and comfortable": Ume Tsuda to Adeline Lanman, November 21, 1882, in Furuki, *Attic Letters*, 13–14.

162 "I ate the lunch": Sutematsu Yamakawa, draft manuscript, December 24, 1882, SYOP, Box 1, Folder 5, VSC.

162 "I get along as well": Ume Tsuda to Adeline Lanman, November 21, 1882, in Furuki, *Attic Letters*, 13–14.

162 eleven more members of Ume's family: Ume Tsuda to Adeline Lanman, November 23, 1882, in Furuki, *Attic Letters*, 14–19.

163 who promptly burst into tears:

Akiko Kuno, *Unexpected Destinations: The Poignant Story of Japan's First Vassar Graduate*, trans. Kirsten McIvor (New York: Kodansha International, 1993), 115.

163 "They are so afraid": Sutematsu Yamakawa to Alice Bacon, December 11, 1882, SYOP, Box 1, Folder 5, VSC.

163 "After the first week": Sutematsu Yamakawa, draft manuscript, December 24, 1882, SYOP, Box 1, Folder 5, VSC.

163 "American Aunt": Ibid.

163 "As soon as I touched": Ibid.

163 "My knees at this moment": Sutematsu Yamakawa to Alice Bacon, December 11, 1882, SYOP, Box 1, Folder 5, VSC.

164 "She does not show": Ume Tsuda to Adeline Lanman, November 23, 1882, in Furuki, *Attic Letters*, 14–19.

164 "The day the steamer sails": Ibid.

164 "every kind of mess imaginable": Ibid.

164 "Shige is a great help": Ibid.

165 "So you see my return": Ibid.

165 "so much lighter and warmer": Ibid.

165 "The hardest thing": Ibid.

165 "I can't yet sit down": Ibid.

165 "My dresses have been shown": Ibid.

166 "If I could only speak": Ume Tsuda to Adeline Lanman, November 19, 1882, TCA, I-B-8 (4).

166 "I am bound hand and foot": Ume Tsuda to Adeline Lanman, December 1882, in Furuki, *Attic Letters*, 22–23.

166 "Oh, I don't want to lose": Ume Tsuda to Adeline Lanman, November 23, 1882, in Furuki, *Attic Letters*, 14–19.

166 "But now in Japan": Ibid.

166 "Much to my alarm": Ume Tsuda to Mattie, Maggie, and Mamie, February 20, 1883, TCA, I-C-6.

167 "I long to jump around": Ume Tsuda to Adeline Lanman, November 23, 1882, in Furuki, *Attic Letters*, 14–19.

167 "My father was talking": Ibid.

167 "Sutematsu and I hate": Ume Tsuda to Adeline Lanman, November 29, 1882, in Furuki, *Attic Letters*, 21.

167 "for twelve yen": Ibid.

167 "a sort of tea concern": Sutematsu Yamakawa to Alice Bacon, December 29, 1882, SYOP, Box I, Folder 5, VSC.

168 "Such a curious mixture": Ume Tsuda to Adeline Lanman, December 1882, in Furuki, *Attic Letters*, 22–23.

168 Shige in maroon silk: Ume Tsuda to Adeline Lanman, November 23, 1882, in Furuki, *Attic Letters*, 14–19; Sutematsu Yamakawa to Jessie Wheeler, December 28, 1882, SYOP, Box I, Folder 7, VSC.

168 "which Mr. Uriu had presented": Ume Tsuda to Adeline Lanman, December 1882 in Furuki, *Attic Letters*, 22–23.

169 "A fine distinguished soldier-like man": Ume Tsuda to Adeline Lanman, November 27, 1882 in Furuki, *Attic Letters*, 19–20.

170 "As we could not refuse": Ibid.

170 "All these great men": Ibid.

170 "I am not willing": Sutematsu Yamakawa to Alice Bacon, December 11, 1882, SYOP, Box I, Folder 5, VSC.

170 "My Father": Ume Tsuda to Adeline Lanman, November 29, 1882, in Furuki, *Attic Letters*, 21.

171 "Sutematsu and I inwardly lament": Ume Tsuda to Adeline Lanman, December 23, 1882, in Furuki, *Attic Letters*, 26–28.

171 "They seem to think": Ume Tsuda to Adeline Lanman, January 16, 1883, in Furuki, *Attic Letters*, 33–34.

171 "young men who have been abroad": Sutematsu Yamakawa to Alice Bacon, January 8, 1883, SYOP, Box I, Folder 5, VSC.

172 "perfectly at home": Ibid.

172 "[She] has presented me": Sutematsu Yamakawa to Jessie Wheeler, December 28, 1882, SYOP, Box I, Folder 7, VSC.

172 "Oh, Alice, I don't know": Sutematsu Yamakawa to Alice Bacon, January 16, 1883, SYOP, Box I, Folder 5, VSC.

173 a "private theatrical": Sutematsu Yamakawa to Alice Bacon, January 18, 1883, SYOP, Box I, Folder 5, VSC.

173 "The party will be a large affair": Sutematsu Yamakawa to Alice Bacon, January 24, 1883, SYOP, Box I, Folder 5, VSC.

173 "Can you imagine me as Portia?": Ibid.

173 "the best amateur performer": Ibid.

173 "were relieved from the formalities": Ume Tsuda to Adeline

Lanman, January 29, 1883, in Furuki, *Attic Letters*, 36–37.

174 "So we met very often": Sutematsu Yamakawa to Alice Bacon, February 20, 1883, SYOP, Box 1, Folder 5, VSC.

174 "What a trouble it is to live!": Sutematsu Yamakawa to Alice Bacon, January 28, 1883, SYOP, Box 1, Folder 5, VSC.

175 "I did have serious thoughts": Sutematsu Yamakawa to Alice Bacon, February 20, 1883, SYOP, Box 1, Folder 5, VSC.

175 "crazy boy": Ibid.

175 "It is just the place for me": Sutematsu Yamakawa to Alice Bacon, February 3, 1883, SYOP, Box 1, Folder 5, VSC.

176 "Oh Alice, my views": Sutematsu Yamakawa to Alice Bacon, February 20, 1883, SYOP, Box 1, Folder 5, VSC.

176 "I wonder if you think": Sutematsu Yamakawa to Alice Bacon, March 18, 1883, SYOP, Box 1, Folder 5, VSC.

176 "I have so much to write": Ume Tsuda to Adeline Lanman, March 27, 1883, in Furuki, *Attic Letters*, 52–57.

178 Oyama's dapper cousin: Kuno, *Unexpected Destinations*, 143.

179 "What must be done": Sutematsu Yamakawa to Alice Bacon, April 5, 1883, SYOP, Box 1, Folder 5, VSC.

179 "By the way do you remember": Ibid.

180 "I wonder what he thought": Ume Tsuda to Adeline Lanman, March 27, 1883, in Furuki, *Attic Letters*, 52–57.

179 "Mr. Oyama is rich": Ibid.

180 "Although they all love me": Sutematsu Yamakawa to Alice Bacon, July 2, 1883, SYOP, Box 1, Folder 5, VSC.

182 a diamond ring: Ume Tsuda to Adeline Lanman, April 11, 1883, in Furuki, *Attic Letters*, 58–60.

182 "all together too magnificent": Sutematsu Yamakawa to Alice Bacon, July 2, 1883, SYOP, Box 1, Folder 5, VSC.

182 "so matter-of-fact": Ume Tsuda to Adeline Lanman, November 11, 1883, in Furuki, *Attic Letters*, 103–6.

182 *Le Ministre de la Guerre*: Wedding announcement, SYOP, Box 2, Folder 7, VSC.

182 "acting hostess to all the ladies": Ume Tsuda to Adeline Lanman, November 11, 1883, in Furuki, *Attic Letters*, 103–6.

182 "I must get used to the idea": Ibid.

11: GETTING ALONG ALONE

183 "Please don't write marriage": Ume Tsuda to Adeline Lanman, June 6, 1883, in Yoshiko Furuki, ed., *The Attic Letters: Ume Tsuda's Correspondence to Her American Mother* (New York: Weatherhill, 1991), 74–75.

183 "A few years ago": Ume Tsuda to Adeline Lanman, March 18, 1883, in Furuki, *Attic Letters*, 50–51.

185 "It is said that Grant": Clara Whitney, *Clara's Diary: An American Girl in Meiji Japan*

(New York: Kodansha International, 1979), 256-57.

185 Geisha danced for him: Ibid., 260.

185 The emperor himself stood: Julia Meech-Pekarik, *The World of the Meiji Print: Impressions of a New Civilization* (New York: Weatherhill, 1986), 107.

185 "The spirit of self-help": Samuel Smiles, *Self-help: With Illustrations of Character and Conduct* (Boston: Ticknor and Fields, 1866), 15.

186 "building up their characters": "Preamble to the Fundamental Code of Education" (1872), in William Theodore de Bary, Carol Gluck, and Arthur E. Tiedemann, eds., *Sources of the Japanese Tradition, 1600 to 2000: Part Two, 1868–2000*, abridged (New York: Columbia University Press, 2006), 95.

186 "Help from without": Smiles, *Self-help*, 15.

186 "In recent days, people": Nagazane Motoda, "Great Principles of Education" (1879), in De Bary, Gluck, and Tiedemann, *Sources of the Japanese Tradition*, 97.

187 "There must be a certain kind": Ume Tsuda to Adeline Lanman, September 21, 1883, in Furuki, *Attic Letters*, 95–96.

187 "In the normal school": Ume Tsuda to Adeline Lanman, October 13, 1883, in Furuki, *Attic Letters*, 97–100.

188 "If I thought that by my dying": Ume Tsuda to Adeline Lanman,

May 23, 1883, in Furuki, *Attic Letters*, 69–70.

188 "devoured with fleas": Ume Tsuda to Adeline Lanman, April 27, 1883, in Furuki, *Attic Letters*, 62–67.

188 Sen Tsuda, Ume's father: Charles Lanman, *Japan; Its Leading Men* (Boston: D. Lothrop, 1886), 34–39.

188 Tsuda had fathered a child: Yoshiko Furuki, *The White Plum, a Biography of Ume Tsuda: Pioneer in the Higher Education of Japanese Women* (New York: Weatherhill, 1991), 107.

189 "Mrs. Lanman she misses you": Shige Uriu to Adeline Lanman, 1883, TCA, IX-C-7.

189 "I think music would not do much": Ume Tsuda to Adeline Lanman, February 1, 1883, in Furuki, *Attic Letters*, 38.

189 "I think it very unwise": Ume Tsuda to Adeline Lanman, May 26, 1883, in Furuki, *Attic Letters*, 71–73.

189 Sutematsu was trying: Sutematsu Yamakawa to Alice Bacon, April 12, 1883, SYOP, Box 1, Folder 5, VSC.

189 "Please don't write anything": Ume Tsuda to Adeline Lanman, May 26, 1883, in Furuki, *Attic Letters*, 71–73.

189 "They are entirely too stuck up": Ume Tsuda to Adeline Lanman, April 27, 1883, in Furuki, *Attic Letters*, 62–67.

190 "which only poorer classes attend": Ume Tsuda to Adeline Lanman, December 17, 1882, in Furuki, *Attic Letters*, 24–26.

190 Kaigan Jogakko: Barbara Rose, *Tsuda Umeko and Women's Education in Japan* (New Haven, CT: Yale University Press, 1992), 61.

190 "Now are you not surprised": Ume Tsuda to Adeline Lanman, May 25, 1883, in Furuki, *Attic Letters*, 70–71.

190 "I am so busy": Ume Tsuda to Adeline Lanman, June 6, 1883, in Furuki, *Attic Letters*, 74–75.

190 "Do not suppose, Mrs. Lanman": Ume Tsuda to Adeline Lanman, June 18, 1883, in Furuki, *Attic Letters*, 77–79.

191 "I think I am young yet": Ume Tsuda to Adeline Lanman, July 15, 1883, in Furuki, *Attic Letters*, 83.

191 "I want to have my school": Ume Tsuda to Adeline Lanman, June 6, 1883, in Furuki, *Attic Letters*, 74–75.

191 "But what a position": Ume Tsuda to Adeline Lanman, November 2, 1883, in Furuki, *Attic Letters*, 101–2.

191 "I don't hide it": Ume Tsuda to Adeline Lanman, October 31, 1883, in Rose, *Tsuda Umeko*, 62.

191 "very curious and very beautiful": Ume Tsuda to Adeline Lanman, November 5, 1883, in Furuki, *Attic Letters*, 102–3.

192 "lovely in blue crepe": Ibid.

192 "Who am I?": Ume Tsuda, "Personal Recollections of Prince Ito," in *The Writings of Umeko Tsuda* [*Tsuda Umeko monjo*] (Kodaira, Japan: Tsuda College, 1984), 489–90.

192 "He is such a great man now": Ume Tsuda to Adeline Lanman, November 5, 1883, in Furuki, *Attic Letters*, 102–3.

192 "Will you really believe it": Ume Tsuda to Adeline Lanman, December 4, 1883, in Furuki, *Attic Letters*, 108–10.

192 "It seems he is very anxious": Ume Tsuda to Adeline Lanman, November 20, 1883, in Furuki, *Attic Letters*, 106–8.

193 "young peaches": Furuki, *White Plum*, 61.

193 "Oh, I am so grateful": Ume Tsuda to Adeline Lanman, December 4, 1883, in Furuki, *Attic Letters*, 108–10.

193 "fond of the pleasures": Ume Tsuda to Adeline Lanman, December 18, 1883, in Furuki, *Attic Letters*, 113–16.

193 "If you have Mr. Ito": Ume Tsuda to Adeline Lanman, December 4, 1883, in Furuki, *Attic Letters*, 108–10.

193 "she had so much petting": Sutematsu Yamakawa to Alice Bacon, January 18, 1883, SYOP, Box 1, Folder 5, VSC.

193 "On the whole, I do like": Ume Tsuda to Adeline Lanman, December 4, 1883, in Furuki, *Attic Letters*, 108–10.

194 "[Sutematsu] said it was not formidable": Ibid.

194 "He also wishes me to go out": Ume Tsuda to Adeline Lanman, December 18, 1883, in Furuki, *Attic Letters*, 113–16.

194 "we three girls": Ibid.

194 "to think I might live": Ume Tsuda to Adeline Lanman,

December 9, 1883, in Furuki, *Attic Letters*, 110–13.

195 "I want to talk to you": Ibid.

195 "grand evening entertainment": Ibid.

195 "a second-class casino": Meech-Pekarik, *World of the Meiji Print*, 148.

195 "a gymnastic feat": John Dwight, "The Marchioness Oyama," *Twentieth Century Home*, 1904.

196 three star-shaped diamond pins: Akiko Kuno, *Unexpected Destinations: The Poignant Story of Japan's First Vassar Graduate*, trans. Kirsten McIvor (New York: Kodansha International, 1993), 154–55.

196 "a perfect hostess": Dwight, "Marchioness Oyama."

196 "I enjoyed myself so much": Ume Tsuda to Adeline Lanman, December 18, 1883, in Furuki, *Attic Letters*, 113–16.

196 "I have *two* rooms": Ume Tsuda to Adeline Lanman, February 29, 1884, in Furuki, *Attic Letters*, 139–40.

196 "Of course, temporarily": Ume Tsuda to Adeline Lanman, December 21, 1883, in Furuki, *Attic Letters*, 116–17.

197 "an awful bother": Ume Tsuda to Adeline Lanman, January 4, 1884, in Furuki, *Attic Letters*, 121–24.

197 "very serious talks": Ibid.

197 "very hard and rather slow": Ume Tsuda to Adeline Lanman, January 13, 1884, in Furuki, *Attic Letters*, 125–28.

197 "I would give a great deal": Ume Tsuda to Adeline Lanman, January 27, 1884, in Furuki, *Attic Letters*, 131–32.

197 "You see how well-filled": Ume Tsuda to Adeline Lanman, March 27, 1884, in Furuki, *Attic Letters*, 146–47.

197 "Is Labor a Blessing": Ume Tsuda to Adeline Lanman, February 29, 1884, in Furuki, *Attic Letters*, 139–40.

198 "Is it not lovely": Ume Tsuda to Adeline Lanman, February 26, 1884, in Furuki, *Attic Letters*, 135–37.

198 Her visits to court: Ume Tsuda to Adeline Lanman, January 4, 1884, in Furuki, *Attic Letters*, 121–24.

198 "If I told you all I know": Sutematsu Yamakawa to Alice Bacon, March 1884, SYOP, Box 1, Folder 5, VSC.

198 "learned ladies": Ume Tsuda to Adeline Lanman, February 26, 1884, in Furuki, *Attic Letters*, 135–37.

199 "Do you know that *the* dream": Sutematsu Yamakawa to Alice Bacon, March 1884, SYOP, Box 1, Folder 5, VSC.

199 "What a splendid thing": Ume Tsuda to Adeline Lanman, February 26, 1884, in Furuki, *Attic Letters*, 135–37.

199 "We are to set up a school": Sutematsu Yamakawa to Alice Bacon, March 1884, SYOP, Box 1, Folder 5, VSC.

200 Tokyo's Charity Hospital: "Our Roots—To Serve the Suffering Poor," The Jikei University

School of Medicine, 2004, http://
www.jikei.ac.jp/eng/our.html.

200 "You don't know what an undertaking": Ume Tsuda to Adeline Lanman, April 5, 1884, in
Furuki, *Attic Letters*, 147–50.

200 Their handicrafts: Ume Tsuda to
Adeline Lanman, June 15, 1884,
in Furuki, *Attic Letters*, 160–63.

201 "These were made for the occasion": Ibid.

201 Ume helped Mrs. Ito: "Notes,"
Japan Weekly Mail, June 14,
1884.

201 "they urged the people to buy":
Ume Tsuda to Adeline Lanman,
June 15, 1884, in Furuki, *Attic
Letters*, 160–63.

201 "It is a matter for universal admi-
ration": "The Opening of the
Charity Bazaar," *Japan Weekly
Mail*, June 14, 1884. (Trans-
lated from *Mainichi & Choya
Shimbun*.)

202 "was neither refined, elegant":
"Notes," *Japan Weekly Mail*,
June 28, 1884.

202 "We have a very sincere admiration": Ibid.

202 The *Chugai Bukka Shimpo*: Ibid.

202 "I must say she began early":
Ume Tsuda to Adeline Lanman,
July 17, 1884, in Furuki, *Attic
Letters*, 166.

203 "At such a time": Ume Tsuda to
Adeline Lanman, June 23, 1884,
in Furuki, *Attic Letters*, 163–65.

203 "On the whole, I am glad":
Ume Tsuda to Adeline Lanman,
December 21, 1884, in Furuki,
Attic Letters, 171–72.

204 "'accompanied by a relative'":

Ume Tsuda to Adeline Lanman,
September 25, 1885, in Furuki,
Attic Letters, 219–22.

204 "We had quite a grand dinner":
Ibid.

204 "I have such a nice desk here":
Ibid.

205 "I know just how I ought to do":
Ume Tsuda to Adeline Lanman,
November 10, 1885, in Furuki,
Attic Letters, 229–30.

205 gold brocade gown: Ume Tsuda
to Adeline Lanman, September
15, 1885, in Furuki, *Attic Letters*,
218–19.

205 "My dress really did look nice":
Ume Tsuda to Adeline Lanman,
November 20, 1885, in Furuki,
Attic Letters, 230–32.

205 "I did not know what to do":
Ibid.

206 "a very empty title": Ume Tsuda
to Adeline Lanman, July 14,
1884, in Furuki, *Attic Letters*,
165–66.

206 "After the music ceased": Ume
Tsuda to Adeline Lanman,
November 20, 1885, in Furuki,
Attic Letters, 230–32.

206 "We consider women's duty":
Miki Yamaguchi, "The Educa-
tion of Peeresses in Japan," *Far
East*, January 20, 1898, 406.

207 "So they asked me *privately*":
Ume Tsuda to Adeline Lanman,
November 9, 1885, in Furuki,
Attic Letters, 227–28.

12: ALICE IN TOKYO

208 "as very few of the better classes
catch it": Ume Tsuda to Adeline Lanman, August 9, 1886, in

Yoshiko Furuki, ed., *The Attic Letters: Ume Tsuda's Correspondence to Her American Mother* (New York: Weatherhill, 1991), 257.

208 Ryo Yoshimasu: Ume Tsuda to Adeline Lanman, September 10, 1886, in Furuki, *Attic Letters*, 260–61.

209 "Just suppose, if on the Japanese stage": Ume Tsuda to Adeline Lanman, September 23, 1886, in Furuki, *Attic Letters*, 263.

209 "I send you a newspaper": Ume Tsuda to Adeline Lanman, November 23, 1886, in Furuki, *Attic Letters*, 268–69.

209 "old Emperors waltzing": Ume Tsuda to Adeline Lanman, April 22, 1887, in Furuki, *Attic Letters*, 283–85.

209 "The fancy ball made a great stir": Ume Tsuda to Adeline Lanman, May 1, 1887, in Furuki, *Attic Letters*, 285.

210 "I love to think of you two": Ume Tsuda to Adeline Lanman, January 29, 1887, in Furuki, *Attic Letters*, 276–77.

210 "I have received notice": Ume Tsuda to Adeline Lanman, September 22, 1886, in Furuki, *Attic Letters*, 261–62.

210 "The girls of the nobility": Ume Tsuda to Adeline Lanman, September 25, 1885, in Furuki, *Attic Letters*, 219–22.

210 "I wonder if these human dolls": Ume Tsuda to Adeline Lanman, October 20, 1885, in Furuki, *Attic Letters*, 224–26.

210 "It is far from easy work": Ume Tsuda to Adeline Lanman, October 20, 1886, in Furuki, *Attic Letters*, 266.

211 In addition to Japanese: Miki Yamaguchi, "The Education of Peeresses in Japan," *Far East*, January 20, 1898, 408.

211 Most of the students arrived: Barbara Rose, *Tsuda Umeko and Women's Education in Japan* (New Haven, CT: Yale University Press, 1992), 71.

211 "You know, she has": Ume Tsuda to Adeline Lanman, July 20, 1887, in Furuki, *Attic Letters*, 292–94.

211 "Your letter with its unexpectedly": Alice Bacon to Ume Tsuda, October 12, 1887, TCA, II-3-4 (1).

212 "It costs so much more": Ume Tsuda to Adeline Lanman, September 5, 1887, in Furuki, *Attic Letters*, 297–98.

212 "Alice has been very busy": Ume Tsuda to Adeline Lanman, September 9, 1888, in Furuki, *Attic Letters*, 316–17.

213 "a dear little sweet-faced widow": Alice Mabel Bacon, *A Japanese Interior* (Boston: Houghton, Mifflin, 1894), 5.

213 "He will insist on following": Ume Tsuda to Adeline Lanman, September 9, 1888, in Furuki, *Attic Letters*, 316–17.

213 "The dog is an attendant": Ume Tsuda to Adeline Lanman, September 18, 1888, in Furuki, *Attic Letters*, 317–18.

213 "Apparently, a foreign lady": Bacon, *Japanese Interior*, 3–4.

214 "Their lives are more or less": Ibid., 10.

214 "Universal History": Ibid., 13.

214 "I have just learned": Ibid., 15.

215 General Oyama protested merrily: Ume Tsuda to Adeline Lanman, February 19, 1886, in Furuki, *Attic Letters*, 240–42.

215 she was bending over a steam inhaler: Akiko Kuno, *Unexpected Destinations: The Poignant Story of Japan's First Vassar Graduate*, trans. Kirsten McIvor (New York: Kodansha International, 1993), 168.

215 one paper even hinted: Ume Tsuda to Adeline Lanman, August 27, 1887, in Furuki, *Attic Letters*, 296–97; Kuno, *Unexpected Destinations*, 166.

215 "Sutematsu feels very badly": Ume Tsuda to Adeline Lanman, May 2, 1887, in Furuki, *Attic Letters*, 285–86.

215 "Japan has not quite": Ume Tsuda to Adeline Lanman, December 7, 1887, in Furuki, *Attic Letters*, 304–5.

215 "Would that I could go about": Sutematsu Oyama to Elizabeth Howe, 1886 SYOP, Box 1, Folder 8, VSC.

216 Little Takashi "regards me with great favor": Bacon, *Japanese Interior*, 81–82.

216 "most rare of all": Ume Tsuda to Adeline Lanman, December 6, 1888, in Furuki, *Attic Letters*, 321.

216 it tasted like home: Bacon, *Japanese Interior*, 82–83.

216 "He did not look to me": Ibid., 50–51.

217 "It was a funny sight": Ibid., 88.

217 "lest a particle of dust": Ibid.

218 "The one thing that strikes one": Ume Tsuda to Adeline Lanman, January 5, 1889, in Furuki, *Attic Letters*, 325–26.

218 "As girls take more interest": Bacon, *Japanese Interior*, 89–90.

219 "The procession was the finest": Ibid., 134.

219 "With the greatest pride": Ibid., 145.

220 "It seems so terrible": Ume Tsuda to Adeline Lanman, February 15, 1889, in Furuki, *Attic Letters*, 326–28.

220 the imperial accessories: Bacon, *Japanese Interior*, 189–92.

221 "The girls rose in their places": Ibid., 193–94.

221 "At last there was a rustle": Ibid., 194–95.

221 "rather loaded down": Ibid., 195.

221 "feeling quite light hearted": Ibid.

221 "As I was following": Ibid., 197.

222 Then it was Alice's turn: Ibid., 197–98.

222 "I was very glad": Ibid., 199.

222 Her students brought farewell gifts: Ibid., 232.

222 "Here, nobody ever makes a noise": Ibid., 224–25.

223 "not at all like the sheepskins": Ibid., 234.

223 "my back fairly ached": Ibid., 236.

223 "Even a diamond": Julia Meech-Pekarik, *The World of the Meiji Print: Impressions of a New Civilization* (New York: Weatherhill, 1986), 119.

223 "Lose no time": Meech-Pekarik, *World of the Meiji Print*, 119–20.

223 "Somehow I always feel sorry": Bacon, *Japanese Interior*, 237.

224 "The word 'civilization'": Ibid., 228.

224 "Miss A. Bacon": "Passengers: Departed," *Japan Weekly Mail*, September 28, 1889.

13: ADVANCES AND RETREATS

225 "My dear Mrs. Lanman": Ume Tsuda to Adeline Lanman, August 1889, in Yoshiko Furuki, ed., *The Attic Letters: Ume Tsuda's Correspondence to Her American Mother* (New York: Weatherhill, 1991), 332–33.

225 "I often wish I had had": Ume Tsuda to Adeline Lanman, May 6, 1886, in Furuki, *Attic Letters*, 248–50.

226 catalogs from Smith College: Ume Tsuda to Adeline Lanman, July 10, 1888 and August 5, 1888, in Furuki, *Attic Letters*, 314, 315–16.

227 "Mrs. Morris may be very kind": Ume Tsuda to Adeline Lanman, March 9, 1889, in Furuki, *Attic Letters*, 328–29.

227 "Won't it be splendid!": Ume Tsuda to Adeline Lanman, May 26, 1889, in Furuki, *Attic Letters*, 331.

227 "You can not imagine": Ume Tsuda to Adeline Lanman, June 13, 1889, in Furuki, *Attic Letters*, 331–32.

227 "Our failures only marry": Barbara Rose, *Tsuda Umeko and Women's Education in Japan* (New Haven, CT: Yale University Press, 1992), 82.

228 "Miss Tsuda was guest of honor": Anna C. Hartshorne, "The Years of Preparation: A Memory of Miss Tsuda," in Ume Tsuda, *The Writings of Umeko Tsuda* [*Tsuda Umeko monjo*] (Kodaira, Japan: Tsuda College, 1984), 513.

228 "Like a princess": Rose, *Tsuda Umeko*, 84.

228 Here was a chance to prove: Ibid., 94.

228 "I have today handed over": Alice Bacon to Ume Tsuda, September 26, 1890, TCA, II-3-4 (2).

229 "Better laws, broader education": Alice Mabel Bacon, *Japanese Girls and Women*, rev. ed. (Boston: Houghton, Mifflin, 1902), 115.

229 "in the name of our childhood's friendship": Ibid., viii.

229 "She does not evade": "New Publications," *New-York Times*, August 17, 1891.

229 "This is the glory": "The Imperial Rescript on Education," Children and Youth in History, Item 136, 1996–2014, http://chnm.gmu.edu/cyh/primary-sources/136.

230 "I do not think it is so compromising": Sutematsu Oyama to Alice Bacon and Ume Tsuda, August 6, 1891, TCA, II-6-1 (3).

230 "If it will do any good": Alice Bacon to Ume Tsuda, August 9, 1891, TCA, II-3-4 (4).

230 "Education and Culture": Rose, *Tsuda Umeko*, 89.

231 "Japanese tea and chopstick sup-

per": *Norfolk (CT) Tower*, August 13, 1891.

231 "Wives must fit themselves": Ume Tsuda, "The Education of Japanese Women," in *Writings of Umeko Tsuda*, 31.

231 "all together too sympathetic": Sutematsu Oyama to Alice Bacon and Ume Tsuda, August 6, 1891, TCA, II-6-1 (3).

232 "Are you horrified?": Sutematsu Oyama to Anne Southworth Wyman, May 30, 1893, SYOP, Box 1, Folder 8, VSC.

232 "Advisor on Westernization": Akiko Kuno, *Unexpected Destinations: The Poignant Story of Japan's First Vassar Graduate*, trans. Kirsten McIvor (New York: Kodansha International, 1993), 178.

232 "I have no patience with her": Sutematsu Oyama to Alice Bacon and Ume Tsuda, August 6, 1891, TCA, II-6-1 (3).

233 "deep thinker": Sutematsu Yamakawa to Alice Bacon, March 8, 1884, SYOP, Box 1, Folder 5, VSC.

233 "What do you think the girls": Sutematsu Oyama to Alice Bacon and Ume Tsuda, August 6, 1891, TCA, II-6-1 (3).

233 "for their mother was too wise": Marian P. Whitney, "Stematz Yamakawa, Princess Oyama," *Vassar Quarterly*, July 1919, 270.

233 He arrived at the Oyamas': Kuno, *Unexpected Destinations*, 180.

234 "an intelligent, apt and diligent student": Yoshiko Furuki, *The White Plum, a Biography of Ume*

Tsuda: Pioneer in the Higher Education of Japanese Women (New York: Weatherhill, 1991), 86.

234 "I don't believe Miss Thomas": Furuki, *White Plum*, 85.

234 "Feeling as I do": "Questions to Specialists," *Japan Weekly Mail*, July 22, 1893.

235 "I am afraid it is a fault": Alice Bacon to Ume Tsuda, October 19, 1892, TCA, II-3-4 (6).

235 "I am sorry that you find the gap widen": Ibid.

237 "Of course I feel much anxiety": Sutematsu Oyama to Alice Bacon, October 28, 1894, SYOP, Box 1, Folder 5, VSC.

237 "In July a committee": Ibid.

238 "They who never dressed themselves": Sutematsu Oyama, "War Work of Japanese Ladies," *Collier's*, April 1, 1905.

238 "I felt as if I wanted": Sutematsu Oyama to Alice Bacon, October 28, 1894, SYOP, Box 1, Folder 5, VSC.

238 "the plucky little island empire": "Noted Vassar Graduate," *New-York Times*, December 2, 1894.

238 "I tell you," Alice wrote: Alice Bacon to Ume Tsuda, October 6, 1894, TCA, II-3-4 (10).

238 "Now we are no longer ashamed": Kenneth B. Pyle, *The Making of Modern Japan* (New York: D. C. Heath, 1996), 138.

239 "Through Japan, China must soon": "Noted Vassar Graduate," *New-York Times*.

239 "Intensely loyal to her country": "A Remarkable Japanese

Woman," *New-York Times*, April 19, 1896.

239 "Whatever the war may have done": Alice Bacon to Ume Tsuda, July 22, 1895, TCA, II-3-4 (12).

240 "Those students who study": Furuki, *White Plum*, 101.

240 "But if he attempts to raise": Utako Shimoda, "The Virtues of Japanese Womanhood," in Naoichi Masaoka, ed., *Japan to America: A Symposium of Papers by Political Leaders and Representative Citizens of Japan on Conditions in Japan and on the Relations between Japan and the United States* (New York: G. P. Putnam's Sons, 1914), 187–88.

241 "I can not realize she is dead": Ume Tsuda to Adeline Lanman, August 9, 1894, in Furuki, *Attic Letters*, 335.

241 "I feel quite at a loss": Ume Tsuda to Abby Kirk and Emily Bull, August 31, 1894, in Tsuda, *Writings of Umeko Tsuda*, 371–74.

241 the playful young teacher: Ume Tsuda to Adeline Lanman, October 20, 1885, in Furuki, *Attic Letters*, 224–26.

241 a terror in the classroom: Rose, *Tsuda Umeko*, 117.

241 "Don't be discouraged": Alice Bacon to Ume Tsuda, October 6, 1894, TCA, II-3-4 (10).

242 "Because I am responsible": Kuno, *Unexpected Destinations*, 182.

242 "I am so sorry to hear": Alice Bacon to Ume Tsuda, May 10, 1894, TCA, II-3-4 (8).

243 "knowing more about the Eng-

lish language": Roka Tokutomi, *Hototogisu (The Heart of Nami-San)*, trans. Isaac Goldberg (Boston: Stratford, 1918), 62.

243 "Her first concern": Ibid., 13.

243 "Dressed in the European fashion": Ibid., 15.

244 Shige was distraught: Sumie Ikuta, *Uryu Shigeko: Mo hitori no joshi ryugakusei* [Uriu Shigeko: One more female foreign student] (Tokyo: Bungei Shunju, 2009), 196.

244 "No wonder Shige says": Ume Tsuda to Adeline Lanman, November 25, 1899, in Furuki, *Attic Letters*, 354–55.

245 "My husband grows fatter": Sutematsu Oyama to Alice Bacon, August 5, 1899, SYOP, Box 1, Folder 5, VSC.

14: THE WOMEN'S HOME SCHOOL OF ENGLISH

246 "ripened into one of the happiest": Anna C. Hartshorne, "The Years of Preparation: A Memory of Miss Tsuda," in Ume Tsuda, *The Writings of Umeko Tsuda* [*Tsuda Umeko monjo*] (Kodaira, Japan: Tsuda College, 1984), 514.

247 "With grateful enthusiasm": Ibid., 515.

248 "One trembles to think": Ume Tsuda, "A Woman's Plea," *Far East*, January 20, 1898, 124.

248 "Without culture, education": Ume Tsuda, "The Future of Japanese Women," *Far East*, January 20, 1897, 16.

248 "such an acquisition": Ibid., 17.

249 "There have been one or two":

Ume Tsuda to Adeline Lanman, April 24, 1898, in Yoshiko Furuki, ed., *The Attic Letters: Ume Tsuda's Correspondence to Her American Mother* (New York: Weatherhill, 1991), 339.

249 "a remarkably handsome woman": "Among Maine Women's Clubs," *Lewiston (ME) Saturday Journal*, January 1, 1898.

249 "What do you think has happened?": Ume Tsuda to Adeline Lanman, June 10, 1898, in Furuki, *Attic Letters*, 339–40.

249 "Thus from one nation to another": Ume Tsuda, "Speech Given at the Denver Convention of the General Federation of Women's Clubs," June 24, 1898, in *Writings of Umeko Tsuda*, 484.

250 "I have enjoyed meeting you": Yoshiko Furuki, *The White Plum, a Biography of Ume Tsuda: Pioneer in the Higher Education of Japanese Women* (New York: Weatherhill, 1991), 92.

250 "I have been thinking over": Ume Tsuda to Adeline Lanman, November 4, 1898, in Furuki, *Attic Letters*, 341.

251 "It seems very strange": Ume Tsuda, "Journal in London," in *Writings of Umeko Tsuda*, 276.

251 "a most capable, powerful woman": Ibid., 287.

251 "I have been about like": Ibid., 300–301.

251 "I did so want to ask": Ibid., 337.

252 "He is a lovely man": Ibid., 292–93.

252 "I told him that I really wished": Ibid., 295–96.

252 "well enough for a year": Ibid., 277.

252 "lady of leisure": Ibid., 276.

253 "How strange, how very strange": Ume Tsuda to Adeline Lanman, July 9, 1899, in Furuki, *Attic Letters*, 347–48.

253 Takamine had been a classmate: Akiko Kuno, *Unexpected Destinations: The Poignant Story of Japan's First Vassar Graduate*, trans. Kirsten McIvor (New York: Kodansha International, 1993), 190.

254 "It seems he wants just": Sutematsu Oyama to Alice Bacon, January 7, 1899, SYOP, Box 1, Folder 5, VSC.

254 "for the other school is not": Sutematsu Oyama to Alice Bacon, March 4, 1899, SYOP, Box 1, Folder 5, VSC.

255 "She really seems to be contemplating": Ume Tsuda to Adeline Lanman, February 16, 1899, in Furuki, *Attic Letters*, 346.

255 "It will be a fine ending": Ume Tsuda to Adeline Lanman, August 3, 1899, in Furuki, *Attic Letters*, 349–50.

256 "It was a great honor": Ume Tsuda to Adeline Lanman, August 11, 1899, in Furuki, *Attic Letters*, 350.

256 "I told him it was too soon": Ume Tsuda to Adeline Lanman, August 28, 1899, in Furuki, *Attic Letters*, 351.

256 her voice rasping: Ume Tsuda to Adeline Lanman, October 19, 1899, in Furuki, *Attic Letters*, 353.

256 "I should dislike to have exaggerated": Ume Tsuda to Mary Harris Morris, December 28, 1899, in *Writings of Umeko Tsuda*, 382–85.

257 "How strange it seems": Ume Tsuda to Adeline Lanman, February 5, 1900, in Furuki, *Attic Letters*, 359–60.

257 Women's Higher Normal School in Tokyo: The Women's Higher Normal School would later become Ochanomizu Women's University, today one of two national women's universities in Japan.

257 "I had a letter from Alice Bacon": Ume Tsuda to Adeline Lanman, February 16, 1900, in Furuki, *Attic Letters*, 360.

258 "No one would believe me": Ume Tsuda to Abby Kirk and Emily Bull, August 6, 2000, in *Writings of Umeko Tsuda*, 374–78.

258 "It has been a more difficult thing": Ume Tsuda to Martha Carey Thomas, August 9, 2000, in *Writings of Umeko Tsuda*, 389–91.

258 "Write me and keep me up": Ume Tsuda to Abby Kirk and Emily Bull, August 6, 2000, in *Writings of Umeko Tsuda*, 374–78.

259 "Women's Home School of English": Ibid.; Barbara Rose, *Tsuda Umeko and Women's Education in Japan* (New Haven, CT: Yale University Press, 1992), 137.

259 and Utako Suzuki: Furuki, *White Plum*, 103.

259 "the qualifications of the teacher": Furuki, *White Plum*, 104.

260 "Any criticism will mostly come": Rose, *Tsuda Umeko*, 129.

260 Alice typed up new sheets: Ume Tsuda, "Introductory," *Alumnae Report of the Joshi-Eigaku-Juku*, June 1905, in *Writings of Umeko Tsuda*, 104.

261 "while endeavoring": Furuki, *White Plum*, 105.

261 at the same level as boys: Rose, *Tsuda Umeko*, 130.

261 "Try again!": Furuki, *White Plum*, 123.

261 *Little Lord Fauntleroy*: Rose, *Tsuda Umeko*, 131.

261 "The English is excellent": "The Bookshelf," *Japan Weekly Mail*, May 3, 1902.

262 "a great advantage": Ume Tsuda, "Teaching in Japan," *Bryn Mawr Alumnae Quarterly*, August 1907, in *Writings of Umeko Tsuda*, 94.

262 "The girls had some recitations": Ume Tsuda to Adeline Lanman, June 1, 1901, in Furuki, *Attic Letters*, 367–68.

262 "we even went up to the cupola": Ume Tsuda to Adeline Lanman, October 28, 1901, in Furuki, *Attic Letters*, 376–77.

263 "I am very proud of them": Ume Tsuda to Adeline Lanman, June 1, 1901, in Furuki, *Attic Letters*, 367–68.

263 The candidates "were not boys": Ume Tsuda to Adeline Lanman, January 22, 1902, in Furuki, *Attic Letters*, 378–79.

263 "It really was a great responsibility": Ume Tsuda to Adeline Lanman, February 3, 1902, in Furuki, *Attic Letters*, 379–80.

263 "I am sorry it is so long": Ume Tsuda to Adeline Lanman, April 6, 1901, in Furuki, *Attic Letters*, 365.

263 a letter addressed to "Ume Tsuda": William Elliot Griffis to Ume Tsuda, December 18, 1920, envelope, William Elliot Griffis Collection, Box 160, Folder 2, Special Collections and University Archives, Rutgers University Libraries.

264 "The gentlemen treated us": Ume Tsuda to Adeline Lanman, March 22, 1902, in Furuki, *Attic Letters*, 380–81.

264 The stories they told: "Yoko no yume" [A dream of travel to the West], *Yomiuri Shimbun*, March 22 to April 11, 1902.

264 "and it was a grand spree": Ume Tsuda to Adeline Lanman, March 22, 1902, in Furuki, *Attic Letters*, 380–81.

265 "The school is getting along": Ume Tsuda to Adeline Lanman, January 22, 1902, in Furuki, *Attic Letters*, 378–79.

266 she would retire from teaching: Sumie Ikuta, *Uryu Shigeko: Mo hitori no joshi ryugakusei* [Uriu Shigeko: One more female foreign student] (Tokyo: Bungei Shunju, 2009), 203–4.

266 "As for myself": Sutematsu Oyama, "Stematz Yamakawa Oyama," *Records of the Class of '82: 1882–1902*, SYOP, Box 2, Folder 4, VSC.

267 "I haven't laughed so much": Marian P. Whitney, "Stematz Yamakawa, Princess Oyama," *Vassar Quarterly*, July 1919, 269.

268 "I feel so strange": Ume Tsuda to Adeline Lanman, November 23, 1882, in Furuki, *Attic Letters*, 14–19.

268 "None of us stayed": Ume Tsuda to Adeline Lanman, April 21, 1902, in Furuki, *Attic Letters*, 382.

15: ENDINGS

269 "So you see, the girls": Ume Tsuda to Adeline Lanman, September 27, 1904, in Yoshiko Furuki, ed., *The Attic Letters: Ume Tsuda's Correspondence to Her American Mother* (New York: Weatherhill, 1991), 417–18.

270 "Takashi, who used to give me": Sutematsu Oyama to Alice Bacon, January 10, 1907, SYOP, Box 1, Folder 5, VSC.

271 "It was a great comfort": Sutematsu Oyama to Alice Bacon, June 8, 1908, SYOP, Box 1, Folder 5, VSC.

271 "Poor Stematz": Shige Uriu to Alice Bacon, July 7, 1908, SYOP, Box 1, Folder 12, VSC.

271 "slowly and carefully": "Brilliant Features Mark the Vassar Class Day Exercises," *Poughkeepsie (NY) Eagle*, June 9, 1909.

272 "When Japan was born": Barbara Rose, *Tsuda Umeko and Women's Education in Japan* (New Haven, CT: Yale University Press, 1992), 142.

272 "a new generation of selfish women": Ume Tsuda, "To the Members of the Doso-Kwai,"

Alumnae Report of the Joshi-Eigaku-Juku, July 1908, in *The Writings of Umeko Tsuda* [*Tsuda Umeko monjo*] (Kodaira, Japan: Tsuda College, 1984), 119.

273 "The real work": Rose, *Tsuda Umeko*, 150.

273 "I am sorry to say": Sutematsu Oyama to Alice Bacon, March 12, 1912, SYOP, Box 1, Folder 5, VSC.

273 "agents of the devil": Rose, *Tsuda Umeko*, 146.

273 "A Circle of Friends": "Washinton irai no natsukashiki danran" [A circle of friends missed since Washington], *Asahi Shimbun*, October 22, 1916.

274 "There is no use in telling you": Sutematsu Oyama to Alice Bacon, March 10, 1917, SYOP, Box 1, Folder 5, VSC.

275 "Princess Oyama is characterized": "Influenza Fatal to Noted Princess," *Japan Advertiser*, February 20, 1919.

276 "Her childish face": Sumie Ikuta, *Uryu Shigeko: Mo hitori no joshi ryugakusei* [Uriu Shigeko: One more female foreign student] (Tokyo: Bungei Shunju, 2009), 269.

BIBLIOGRAPHY

In addition to the primary and secondary sources listed individually in this Bibliography, I drew upon letters, diaries, photographs, and printed material from the following archives: Bacon Family Papers, Yale University Manuscripts and Archives; Houghton Library, Harvard University; Terry and Bacon Family Papers, Connecticut Historical Society; Sutematsu Yamakawa Oyama Papers, Vassar College Library Special Collections; Tsuda College Archives, Tokyo; Whitney Library, New Haven Museum; William Elliot Griffis Collection, Rutgers University. Frequently cited archival sources are abbreviated in the notes as follows:

BFP   Bacon Family Papers
SYOP   Sutematsu Yamakawa Oyama Papers
TCA   Tsuda College Archives
VSC   Vassar College Library Special Collections
YMA   Yale University Manuscripts and Archives

Newspapers and magazines of the period—especially the *Atlantic Monthly*, *Frank Leslie's Illustrated Newspaper*, *Harper's Weekly*, the *New York Times*, the *San Francisco Chronicle*, the Washington *Evening Star*, and *Daily National Republican*—provided important context for the world the girls encountered in America, including lavish coverage of the Iwakura Mission's movements in 1872. Meiji periodicals—including the *Japan Weekly*

Mail, the *Japan Advertiser*, the *Far East*, and *Shinbun Zasshi*—also proved invaluable in their coverage of the three women after their return to Japan.

PRIMARY SOURCES

Abbott, John S. C. *The Mother at Home; or The Principles of Maternal Duty*. New York: American Tract Society, 1833.

Alcock, Rutherford. *The Capital of the Tycoon: A Narrative of a Three Years' Residence in Japan*. London: Longman, Green, Longman, Roberts & Green, 1863.

Annual Report of the Board of Education of the New Haven City School District, for the Year Ending August 31, 1874. New Haven, CT: Tuttle, Morehouse & Taylor, 1874.

Bacon, Alice Mabel. *In the Land of the Gods: Some Stories of Japan*. Boston: Houghton Mifflin, 1905.

Bacon, Alice Mabel. *Japanese Girls and Women*, rev. ed. Boston: Houghton, Mifflin, 1902. First published 1891.

Bacon, Alice Mabel. *A Japanese Interior*. Boston: Houghton, Mifflin, 1894.

Black, John Reddie. *Young Japan. Yokohama and Yedo: A Narrative of the Settlement and the City from the Signing of the Treaties in 1858, to the Close of the Year 1879, with a Glance at the Progress of Japan during a Period of Twenty-One Years*. Yokohama, Japan: Kelly, 1880.

Chamberlain, Basil Hall. *Things Japanese: Being Notes on Various Subjects Connected with Japan, for the Use of Travellers and Others*, new ed. London: Kegan Paul, Trench, Trubner, 1892.

Dwight, John. "The Marchioness Oyama." *Twentieth Century Home*, 1904. (Sutematsu Yamakawa Oyama Papers, Vassar College Archives and Special Collections, Box 2, Folder 3.)

Fourteenth Annual Catalogue of the Officers and Students of Vassar College, Poughkeepsie, N.Y., 1878–79. Poughkeepsie, NY: E. B. Osborne, printer, 1879.

Fukuzawa, Yukichi. *The Autobiography of Yukichi Fukuzawa*. Revised translation by Eiichi Kiyooka. (New York: Columbia University Press, 1980). First published by Jiji Shinposha, 1899.

Furuki, Yoshiko, ed. *The Attic Letters: Ume Tsuda's Correspondence to Her American Mother*. New York: Weatherhill, 1991.

Griffis, William Elliot. *The Mikado's Empire*. New York: Harper & Brothers, 1896. First published 1876.

Griffis, William Elliot. *The Rutgers Graduates in Japan: An Address Delivered in Kirkpatrick Chapel, Rutgers College, June 16, 1885*, rev. and enl. ed. New Brunswick, NJ: Rutgers College, 1916.

Griffis, William Elliot. *Townsend Harris, First American Envoy in Japan*. Boston: Houghton, Mifflin, 1895.

Hardy, Arthur Sherburne. *Life and Letters of Joseph Hardy Neesima*. Boston: Houghton, Mifflin, 1891.

Harris, Townsend. *The Complete Journal of Townsend Harris: First American Consul General and Minister to Japan*. New York: Doubleday, Doran, 1930.

Heusken, Henry. *Japan Journal, 1855–1861*. Translated and edited by Jeannette C. van der Corput and Robert A. Wilson. New Brunswick, NJ: Rutgers University Press, 1964.

Jackson, Richard P. *The Chronicles of Georgetown, D.C.: From 1751 to 1878*. Washington, DC: R. O. Polkinhorn, printer, 1878.

"Japan." *Atlantic Monthly*, June 1860, 721–33.

Katsu, Kokichi. *Musui's Story: The Autobiography of a Tokugawa Samurai*. Translated by Teruko Craig. Tucson: University of Arizona Press, 1988.

Kingsley, H. C., Leonard Sanford, and Thomas R. Trowbridge, eds. *Leonard Bacon: Pastor of the First Church in New Haven*. New Haven, CT: Tuttle, Morehouse & Taylor, printers, 1882.

Kume, Kunitake. *The Iwakura Embassy, 1871–7 : A True Account of the Ambassador Extraordinary & Plenipotentiary's Journey of Observation through the United States of America and Europe [Tokumei zenken taishi Bei-O kairan jikki]*. Edited by Graham Healey and Chushichi Tsuzuki. Chiba, Japan: Japan Documents, 2002.

Kume, Kunitake. *Japan Rising: The Iwakura Embassy to the USA and Europe 1871–1873 [Tokumei zenken taishi Bei-O kairan jikki, abridged translation]*. Edited by Chushichi Tsuzuki and R. Jules Young. Cambridge: Cambridge University Press, 2009.

Lanman, Charles. *Haphazard Personalities; Chiefly of Noted Americans*. Boston: Lee and Shepard, 1886.

Lanman, Charles. *Japan; Its Leading Men*. Boston: D. Lothrop, 1886.

Lanman, Charles, ed. *The Japanese in America*. New York: University Publishing, 1872.

Lanman, Charles. *Octavius Perinchief; His Life of Trial and Supreme Faith*. Washington, DC: James Anglim, 1879.

Letters from Old-Time Vassar: Written by a Student in 1869–1870. Poughkeepsie, NY: Vassar College, 1915.

Masaoka, Naoichi, ed. *Japan to America: A Symposium of Papers by Political Leaders and Representative Citizens of Japan on Conditions in Japan and on the Relations between Japan and the United States*. New York: G. P. Putnam's Sons, 1914.

Masuda, Katsunobu. *Recollections of Admiral Baron Sotokichi Uriu, I. J. N.* Tokyo: privately published, 1938.

Masuda, Takashi. *Jijo Masuda Takashi ou den* [Biography of Takashi Masuda in his old age, told by himself]. Tokyo: Chuokoronsha, 1989.

Mori, Arinori. *Education in Japan: A Series of Letters Addressed by Prominent Americans to Arinori Mori.* New York: Appleton, 1873.

Perry, Matthew C. *The Japan Expedition, 1852–1854: The Personal Journal of Commodore Matthew C. Perry.* Edited by Roger Pineau. Washington, DC: Smithsonian Institution Press, 1968.

Raymond, Cornelia M. *Memories of a Child of Vassar.* Poughkeepsie, NY: Vassar College, 1940.

Shiba, Goro. *Remembering Aizu: The Testament of Shiba Goro.* Edited by Ishimitsu Mahito. Translated by Teruko Craig. Honolulu: University of Hawai'i Press, 1999.

Shimoda, Utako. "The Virtues of Japanese Womanhood." In *Japan to America: A Symposium of Papers by Political Leaders and Representative Citizens of Japan on Conditions in Japan and on the Relations between Japan and the United States,* edited by Naoichi Masaoka, 187–92. New York: G. P. Putnam's Sons, 1914.

Smiles, Samuel. *Self-help: With Illustrations of Character and Conduct.* Boston: Ticknor and Fields, 1866.

Sugimoto, Etsu Inagaki. *A Daughter of the Samurai: How a Daughter of Feudal Japan, Living Hundreds of Years in One Generation, Became a Modern American.* Rutland, VT: Charles E. Tuttle, 1990. First published by Doubleday, 1926.

Tokutomi, Roka. *Hototogisu (The Heart of Nami-San).* Translated by Isaac Goldberg. Boston: Stratford, 1918. First published in serial form in *Kokumin Shimbun,* 1898.

Tsuda, Ume. "The Future of Japanese Women." *Far East* 2, no. 1 (January 20, 1897): 14–18.

Tsuda, Ume. "A Woman's Plea." *Far East* 3, no. 24 (January 20, 1898): 120–24.

Tsuda, Ume. *The Writings of Umeko Tsuda* [*Tsuda Umeko monjo*]. Kodaira, Japan: Tsuda College, 1984.

Twain, Mark, and Charles Dudley Warner. *The Gilded Age: A Tale of Today.* New York: Library of America, 2002. First published by American Publishing Company, 1873.

Tyler, Moses. "Vassar Female College." *New Englander,* October 1862, 1–23.

Uriu, Shige. "The Days of My Youth." *Japan Advertiser,* September 11, 1927.

Whitney, Clara. *Clara's Diary: An American Girl in Meiji Japan.* New York: Kodansha International, 1979.

Yamakawa, Sutematsu. "Recollections of Japanese Family Life." *Vassar Miscellany*, November 1880, 49–54.

SECONDARY SOURCES

Altman, Albert A. "*Shinbunshi*: The Early Meiji Adaptation of the Western-Style Newspaper." In *Modern Japan: Aspects of History, Literature, and Society*, edited by William G. Beasley, 52–66. Berkeley: University of California Press, 1975.

Arrington, Leonard. *Brigham Young: American Moses*. New York: Knopf, 1985.

Auslin, Michael R. *Pacific Cosmopolitans: A Cultural History of U.S.-Japan Relations*. Cambridge, MA: Harvard University Press, 2011.

Bacon, Theodore, ed. *Delia Bacon: A Biographical Sketch*. Boston: Houghton, Mifflin, 1888.

Barr, Pat. *The Deer Cry Pavilion: A Story of Westerners in Japan 1868–1905*. London: Macmillan, 1968.

Beasley, William G. *Japan Encounters the Barbarian: Japanese Travellers in America and Europe*. New Haven, CT: Yale University Press, 1995.

Beebe, Lucius. *Mr. Pullman's Elegant Palace Car*. New York: Doubleday, 1961.

Benfey, Christopher. *The Great Wave: Gilded Age Misfits, Japanese Eccentrics, and the Opening of Old Japan*. New York: Random House, 2003.

Bolitho, Harold. "Aizu, 1853–1868." *Proceedings of the British Association for Japanese Studies* 2 (1977): 1–17.

Bruno, Maryann, and Elizabeth A. Daniels. *Vassar College*. Charleston, SC: Arcadia, 2001.

Collinwood, Dean W., Ryoichi Yamamoto, and Kazue Matsui-Haag, eds. *Samurais in Salt Lake: Diary of the First Diplomatic Japanese Delegation to Visit Utah, 1872*. Ogden, UT: US-Japan Center, 1996.

Davis, Hugh. *Leonard Bacon: New England Reformer and Antislavery Moderate*. Baton Rouge: Louisiana State University Press, 1998.

Dore, R. P. *Education in Tokugawa Japan*. London: Routledge & Kegan Paul, 1965.

Duus, Peter. *The Japanese Discovery of America: A Brief History with Documents*. New York: Bedford/St. Martin's, 1997.

Duus, Peter. *Modern Japan*, 2nd ed. Boston: Houghton Mifflin, 1998.

Furuki, Yoshiko. *The White Plum, a Biography of Ume Tsuda: Pioneer in the Higher Education of Japanese Women*. New York: Weatherhill, 1991.

Hall, Ivan Parker. *Mori Arinori*. Cambridge, MA: Harvard University Press, 1973.

Hammersmith, Jack L. *Spoilsmen in a "Flowery Fairyland": The Development of the U.S. Legation in Japan, 1859–1906*. Kent, OH: Kent State University Press, 1998.

Hanami, Sakumi. *Danshaku Yamakawa sensei den* [The biography of Baron Yamakawa]. Tokyo: Iwanami Shoten, 1939.

Hopkins, Vivian C. *Prodigal Puritan: A Life of Delia Bacon*. Cambridge, MA: Belknap Press, 1959.

Hoshi, Ryoichi. *Yamakawa Kenjiro den: Byakkotaishi kara Teidai socho e* [The biography of Kenjiro Yamakawa: From Byakkotai soldier to dean of Tokyo University]. Tokyo: Heibonsha, 2003.

Huffman, James L. *Japan in World History*. New York: Oxford University Press, 2010.

Husband, Joseph. *The Story of the Pullman Car*. Chicago: A. C. McClurg, 1917.

Ikuta, Sumie. *Uryu Shigeko: Mo hitori no joshi ryugakusei* [Uriu Shigeko: One more female foreign student]. Tokyo: Bungei Shunju, 2009.

Iriye, Akira. *Across the Pacific: An Inner History of American-East Asian Relations*. New York: Harcourt, Brace & World, 1967.

Izumi, Saburo. *Meiji yonen no anbassadoru: Iwakura Shisetsudan bunmei kaika no tabi* [The ambassadors of the fourth year of Meiji: The Iwakura Mission's journey of civilization and enlightenment]. Tokyo: Nihon Keizai Shimbunsha, 1984.

James, Edward T., ed. *Notable American Women: A Biographical Dictionary*. Cambridge, MA: Radcliffe College, 1971.

Japan Photographers Association. *A Century of Japanese Photography*. New York: Pantheon, 1980.

Johnson, Joan Marie, ed. *Southern Women at Vassar: The Poppenheim Family Letters, 1882–1916*. Columbia: University of South Carolina Press, 2002.

Keene, Donald. *Emperor of Japan: Meiji and His World, 1852–1912*. New York: Columbia University Press, 2002.

Keene, Donald. *The Japanese Discovery of Europe, 1720–1830*. Stanford, CA: Stanford University Press, 1969.

Keene, Donald. *Modern Japanese Diaries: The Japanese at Home and Abroad as Revealed through Their Diaries*. New York: Henry Holt, 1995.

Knox, Katharine McCook. *Surprise Personalities in Georgetown, D.C.* Washington, DC: author, 1958.

Kuno, Akiko. *Unexpected Destinations: The Poignant Story of Japan's First Vassar Graduate*. Translated by Kirsten McIvor. New York: Kodansha International, 1993. First published as *Rokumeikan no kifujin Oyama Sutematsu: Nihon hatsu no joshi ryugakusei* (Tokyo: Chuo Koronsha, 1988).

Lambourne, Lionel. *Japonisme: Cultural Crossings between Japan and the West*. London: Phaidon, 2005.

Matsuoka, Naomi. "Tsuda Umeko as University Founder and Cultural Intermediary." In *Crosscurrents in the Literatures of Asia and the West*, edited by Masayuki Akiyama and Yiu-nam Leung, 209–23. Newark: University of Delaware Press, 1997.

Meech-Pekarik, Julia. *The World of the Meiji Print: Impressions of a New Civilization*. New York: Weatherhill, 1986.

Mencken, August. *The Railroad Passenger Car: An Illustrated History of the First Hundred Years with Accounts by Contemporary Passengers*. Baltimore: Johns Hopkins University Press, 2000. First published 1957.

Miyoshi, Masao. *As We Saw Them: The First Japanese Embassy to the United States*. New York: Kodansha America, 1994. First published by University of California Press, 1979.

Nish, Ian Hill, ed. *The Iwakura Mission in America and Europe: A New Assessment*. Surrey, UK: Curzon Press (Japan Library), 1998.

Oba, Minako. *Tsuda Umeko*. Tokyo: Asahi Shimbunsha, 1990.

Perrin, Noel. *Giving Up the Gun: Japan's Reversion to the Sword, 1543–1879*. Boston: David R. Godine, 1979.

Plum, Dorothy, and George B. Dowell. *The Magnificent Enterprise: A Chronicle of Vassar College*. Poughkeepsie, NY: Vassar College, 1961.

Pyle, Kenneth B. *The Making of Modern Japan*. New York: D. C. Heath, 1996.

Rhoads, Edward J. M. *Stepping Forth into the World: The Chinese Educational Mission to the United States, 1872–81*. Hong Kong: Hong Kong University Press, 2011.

Rose, Barbara. *Tsuda Umeko and Women's Education in Japan*. New Haven, CT: Yale University Press, 1992.

Rydell, Robert W. *All the World's a Fair: Visions of Empire at American International Expositions, 1876–1916*. Chicago: University of Chicago Press, 1984.

Schlereth, Thomas J. *Victorian America: Transformations in Everyday Life 1876–1915*. New York: HarperCollins, 1991.

Seidensticker, Edward. *Low City, High City: Tokyo from Edo to the Earthquake: How the Shogun's Ancient Capital Became a Great Modern City, 1867–1923*. New York: Alfred A. Knopf, 1983.

Shiba, Ryotaro. *The Last Shogun: The Life of Tokugawa Yoshinobu*. Translated by Juliet Winters Carpenter. New York: Kodansha International, 2004. First published as *Saigo no shogun* (Tokyo: Bungei Shunju, 1967).

Shimoda, Hiraku. *Lost and Found: Recovering Regional Identity in Imperial Japan*. Harvard East Asian Monographs 364. Cambridge, MA: Harvard University Asia Center, 2014.

Stevenson, Louise L. *The Victorian Homefront: American Thought & Culture, 1860–1880*. Ithaca, NY: Cornell University Press, 2001. First published by Twayne, 1991.

Tillary, Carolyn Quick. *A Taste of Freedom: A Cookbook with Recipes and Remembrances from the Hampton Institute*. New York: Citadel Press, 2002.

Uchiyama, Akiko. "Translation as Representation: Fukuzawa Yukichi's Representation of the 'Others.'" In *Agents of Translation*, edited by John Milton and Paul Bandia, 63–83. Philadelphia: John Benjamins, 2009.

Vassar College. *Life at Vassar: Seventy-Five Years in Pictures*. Poughkeepsie, NY: Vassar Cooperative Bookshop, 1940.

Wood, Frances A. *Earliest Years at Vassar*. Poughkeepsie, NY: Vassar College Press, 1909.

Yamakawa, Kikue. *Women of the Mito Domain: Recollections of Samurai Family Life*. Translated by Kate Wildman Nakai. Stanford, CA: Stanford University Press, 2001. First published as *Buke no josei* (Tokyo: Mikuni Shobo, 1943).

CREDITS

INDEX

Page numbers in *italics* refer to photographs.

Abbott, Ellen "Aunt Nelly," 113–14, 125–26, 176
Abbott, John S. C., 107, 112–13
Abbott family, 114, 136
abolitionists, 102
Addison, Joseph, 251
African Americans, 77, 91–92, 102, 109, 120–21,
    150, 214
Ainu people, 43, 146
Aizu code, 23, 24, 34, 39
    junior version of, 24–25
Aizu domain, 19, 23–24, 28, 32, 43, 49, 56, 89, 177,
    178, 238, 267, 282n
    Boshin War and, 33–38
    education in, 24–25, 39–40
    exile to Tonami of, 38–39, 40, 46, 47
    hierarchy in, 36
    malnutrition of refugees within, 39, 40, 47,
      49
    remoteness of Wakamatsu and, 23, 27, 31,
      50
    retainers of, 23–24
    samurai of, 25, 26–27, 38, 39, 99, 170
    Tonami school of, 39–40
    Wakamatsu school of, 24–25, 35, 253
    weaponry in, 34
    see also Tonami; Wakamatsu
Aizu prison camp, 38, 40, 48
alternate attendance, 22
Alvord, William, 72
Amaterasu, 21
America, 58–59, 65, 69, 264
American Oriental Society, 111
American Women's Scholarship for Japanese
    Women, 230, 234, 235, 247
Amherst College, 94, 171
Andover Theological Seminary, 94

Annapolis, U.S. Naval Academy at, 114–15, 135,
    168, 189, 271
Anthony, Susan B., 127
Antisell, Thomas, 104
antislavery movement, 102
Arabic, 151–53, 156–57, 161
Archer, Mrs., 138
Archer Institute, 138
Arlington Hotel, 90
Asahi Shimbun, 143, 273
Atami, 197
Atlantic Monthly, 74, 122
Aurora, Ill., 86
Azabu, 162, 188, 195, 203, 204

Backus, Truman, 130
Bacon, Alfred, 265
Bacon, Alice Mabel, 12, 102, 108, 110, 111, 129,
    140, 144–45, 146–48, 176, 247
    death of, 274, 275
    Hampton Institute and, 109, 211, 214, 228,
      231, 240, 255, 274
    Imperial Palace tour and, 217–18
    in Japan, 211–24, 225, 226–27, 257–60, 262,
      265, 274
    Japanese constitution and, 219–20
    Japanese customs/etiquette and, 222, 223
    on Japanese empress, 223
    Japanese Girls and Women of, 228–29, 230,
      231–32
    Japanese house of, 212–13
    Mitsu adopted by, 224, 255, 257, 274
    open mind of, 214
    at Peeresses' School, 212, 213–14, 220–22,
      223, 226–27, 254
    photograph of, *159*, 265

Bacon, Alice Mabel (*continued*)
  plans to go to Japan, 146, 147
  retirement of, 274
  return to U.S., 223–24, 265, 266, 267–68
  Russo-Japanese War and, 270, 274
  salary of, 212
  Shige and, 216, 271
  Sutematsu and, 109, 114, 144, 151–52, 156,
    163–64, 168, 170, 171, 173, 174–75, 176,
    179, 180–81, 182, 193, 198, 199, 211, 212,
    215, 216, 237–38, 242, 245, 254–55, 271,
    273, 274–75
  as teacher, 109, 211, 212, 213–14, 220–21,
    226–27, 254, 259, 260, 262
  Tsuda College and, 257, 258, 259, 260, 262
  Ume and, 211–13, 214, 216, 220, 221, 228–
    29, 235, 238, 239, 241, 242, 248–49, 250,
    254, 267–68
  at Women's Higher Normal School, 254, 257
Bacon, Catherine, 103, 106, 108, 109, 111–12,
  116, 125, 129, 140, 141, 144, 145
Bacon, Delia, 106
Bacon, Francis, 145
Bacon, Georgeanna, 145
Bacon, Leonard, 101–2, 103, 105, 108, 110, 112,
  220, 239, 274
  death of, 140–41
  on women's duties, 106, 113
Bacon, Nelly, 108, 109, 140
Bacon, Rebecca, 101, 102, 103, 109, 125–26, 145,
  176, 211
Bacon, Sir Francis, 106
Bacon family, 107, 108, 110–11, 117, 126, 129,
  146, 170
Barnum, P. T., 108
Beale, Dorothea, 251, 252, 260
Belgic, 224
Bishopthorpe Palace, 252
Block Island, R.I., 134
Bonté, Fannie, 149
Bonté, John H. C., 149, 151
Bonté family, 150
Booth, Newton, 80
Boshin War, 33–38, 60, 155, 177
Bowdoin College, 112
Bradley & Rulofson, 78
Breed, Alice Ives, 249
British Museum, 253
Bruce (Alice's dog), 213
Bryant, William Cullen, 117–18
Bryn Mawr College, 226, 227, 228–29, 230,
  234, 240, 241, 246, 250, 258, 261, 274
Byakkotai, 36, 282n

California, 56–57, 69, 80, 149
  Chinese laborers in, 74, 75, 149–50
  gold rush in, 76
California, University of, 149
Cape Horn, 83
Carnegie Foundation for International Peace,
  275
Carrie (Sutematsu's classmate), 110
Carrington, Kate, 111
Carrington, Sarah, 111
Centennial Exhibition, 121–24
Chamberlin, Rose, 228
charity, 110, 200–202, 258
Charter Oath, 44–45, 47, 53
Cheltenham Ladies' College, 251
Cheyenne, Wyo., 148–49
Cheyenne Opera House, 148
Chiarini, Giuseppe, 209
Chicago, Ill., 80, 85, 86–88, 147, 288n
Chicago Record, 247–48
Chicago Tribune, 87, 88, 142
China, Chinese, 28
  American labor of, 74, 75, 102, 150
  appearance of, 75
  Christian influence feared by, 140
  Japanese trade with, 27
  Japanese vs., 74–75
  laborers' return to, 152–53
  military of, 238
  in Opium Wars, 27
  in San Francisco, 149–50
  Sino-Japanese War and, 236–38, 239, 269
  study abroad of, 100, 103, 111, 123
  as uncivilized, 238
Chinese Educational Mission, 100, 111, 123
Chinese Exclusion Act, 150
Chinese immigration, 150
Choshu domain, 33, 39, 40, 41
Christianity, 115, 153, 170, 226, 238
  Chinese feared influence of, 140
  as illegal in Japan, 27, 104, 105
  Iwakura girls and, 102, 103–4, 114, 120–21,
    153
  in Japan, 165, 168
  Tsuda family and, 165, 188
  Western strength and, 120
Chugai Bukka Shimpo, 202
Civil War, U.S., 91, 109, 113, 145, 150, 184
Classic of Filial Piety, 25
Colebrook, Conn., 111, 116, 117, 140, 145
Committee to Help Miss Tsuda's School in Japan,
  257
concubinage, 248

Confucianism, 23, 25, 33, 39, 99, 110, 186, 259
    education and, 25, 186, 187, 229
    hierarchy and, 23, 27, 99, 229
    obedience and, 25, 99, 229, 240; *see also* obedience
    women and, 23, 25, 240, 260
Congregationalism, 102
Connecticut, 100, 101, 103–15, 145–47
Connecticut Board of Education, 100
Connecticut Training School for Nurses, 145–46, 200, 242
Cornell University, 171
corsets, 286*n*

Daily National Republican, 117
daimyo, 21
    alternate attendance required of, 22
    domain abolishment and, 41
    expenses of, 22
    trading treaties and, 31
Daughter of the Samurai, A (Sugimoto), 7, 13, 67, 159
Davis, J. D., 147, 148, 152
Davis, Mrs., 147, 148, 152, 153
Deephaven, 255, 274
Dejima, 27
DeLong, Charles, 47, 69–70, 72, 74, 84, 90, 285*n*
DeLong, Elida Vineyard, 47, 56, 62, 70, 71, 73, 78, 81, 87, 90
Denver, Colo., General Federation of Women's Clubs convention in, 249–50
Dickens, Charles, 110, 147
divorce laws, 248
dolls, 26, 34, 222
domains, 23
    abolishment of, 41
    as reorganized into prefectures, 155
    rivalries among, 23, 33, 39, 41
    schools of, 24; *see also* Nisshinkan
    see also specific domains
Drake, John B., 288*n*
Dreaming Iolanthe, The, 122
Dutch learning, 28, 31

Edo, *see* Tokyo
Edo Castle, 33, 60, 217
education, 26, 57, 185–86
    in Aizu domain, 24–25, 39–40
    Confucianism and, 25, 186, 187, 229
    in Great Britain, 251
    during Meiji era, 163, 178, 185–86, 188, 190,

193, 199, 210–11, 229–30, 234–35, 247–48, 257, 269–70
    morality as primary focus of, 186
    for women/girls, 17, 44, 55–56, 57, 81, 113, 128, 145, 163, 170, 178, 187, 188, 190, 193, 199, 210–11, 231, 234–35, 247–50, 257, 259, 260, 269–70, 271, 272–73
    see also Iwakura Mission, girls of; study abroad; *specific schools*
education, American, 254
    of Iwakura Mission, 109–10, 112, 117, 124–25, 127, 128, 129, 131, 135, 138, 139–40, 141–43, 147
    for women and girls, 44, 128; *see also specific schools*
"Education and Culture—What Japanese Women Want Now" (U. Tsuda), 230
emancipation, 92
Emerson's Minstrels, 77
Empress of China, 253
English Student, The, 261
English Teachers' Certificate, 247, 263
"Errand-Bearers, The" (Whitman), 46
Essentials of the Principles and Practice of Medicine (Hartshorne), 246
Europe, 31, 39–40
    colonization and, 27, 236
Evening Critic, 147
Evening Star, 89, 93, 97
Ezo, *see* Hokkaido

Fairmount Park, Pa., 122
Far East, 248, 249
Fillmore, Millard, 29
Finance Ministry, Japanese, 61, 62
First Unitarian Church, 81
Fish, Hamilton, 79, 97
France, 30, 236, 239
Franco-Prussian War, 110
Franklin, Benjamin, 223, 230
freed slaves, 102, 109
Fukuchi, Gen'ichiro, 62–63
Fukui, Makoto, 124
Fukuzawa, Yukichi, 39–40, 46, 112
Fundamental Code of Education, 185

Gaiyukai, 269
geisha, 180*n*, 185, 193, 202
General Federation of Women's Clubs, 249–50
Geneva, 177
Georgetown, Wash. D.C., 90, 104, 115, 118, 120–21, 124, 147, 148, 166, 188, 189, 194, 197, 203, 205, 241, 255, 272

Georgetown Collegiate Institute, 117
Germany, 239
Gilbert, W. S., 208
Gilded Age, 91
Gilded Age, The (Twain & Warner), 92
Girls' Higher School Law, 257
Gleaner, 127
gold rush, 76
Grand Hotel, 71–72, 76, 78, 80, 83, 104, 166
Grant, Ulysses S., 83, 84, 91, 93, 123, 184–85, 186, 188, 264
Great Britain, 27, 42, 50, 209, 236
    education in, 251
    Japanese trade with, 30
    Japanese visits to, 80
    Ume's trip to, 250–52
Great Chicago Fire, 87, 288n
"Greater Learning for Women," 187
Great Kanto Earthquake (1923), 275
"Great Principles of Education" (Nagazane Motoda), 186
Grove Hall Seminary, 109–10

"Hail Columbia," 73, 122
Hakodate, 47, 48, 49, 60
Hampton Normal and Agricultural Institute, 109, 176, 211, 214, 228, 231, 240, 255, 274
Handbook of Nursing for Family and General Use, A (G. Bacon), 145
Handel, George Frideric, 125
Harper's Weekly, 78
Hartshorne, Anna Cope, 228, 234, 246–47, 250, 257, 266, 269, 275–76
Hartshorne, Henry, 246
Haru, Crown Prince, 218
    see also Yoshihito, Taisho Emperor of Japan
Haruko, Meiji Empress of Japan, 16–17, 51, 52, 99, 107, 128, 191, 194, 198–99, 219, 232, 255–56, 271
    adopted son of, 218n
    birthday of, 262
    charity work of, 237
    death of, 272
    Peeresses' School and, 199, 205–6, 220–22, 223
    as trapped by traditions, 198
    Western-style clothing for, 220
Harvard's Examinations for Women, 247
Harvard University, 129, 144–45, 261
Hawaii, 236
Hawthorne, Nathaniel, 112
Hayama, 246

Haydn, Joseph, 125
Hayes, Mrs. Rutherford B., 138
Haynes & Lawton, 78
Hemmings, Anita Florence, 293n
Hepburn, James Curtis, 288n
Hepburn, Mrs., 91, 288n
Hepburn family, 95
Heusken, Henry, 30
Hillhouse High School, 112, 124–25, 127
Hillhouse Society, 110
hinamatsuri (Doll Festival), 26, 34
Hiratsuka, Raicho, 272
Hiscock, Helen, 132
Hitotsuyanagi, Makiko, 274, 275
Hokkaido (Ezo), 27, 43, 47
Hokkaido Colonization Board, 43, 47, 49, 61, 104, 169
Honshu, 33, 38
Hoterukan, 119–20
Hototogisu (Roka Tokutomi), 243
Howe, Julia Ward, 131
Howells, William Dean, 122–23
hyaku monogatari (hundred tales), 20–21

Imperial Army, 170
Imperial Diet, 218–20, 271
Imperial Household Ministry, 204
imperialism, 236
Imperial Naval Academy, 115
Imperial Palace, 15, 51, 162, 217–18, 261
Imperial Rescript on Education, 229–30, 259
Indochina, 236
influenza, 242, 275
Inoue, Kaoru, 191, 198
"Instructions for the Very Young," 25
Invitation to the Dance (Weber), 276
Irwin, Robert, 168
"Is Labor a Blessing or a Curse?" (U. Tsuda), 197
Ito, Hirobumi, 47, 62–63, 64, 80, 85, 89, 93, 97, 192–93, 194, 197, 198–99, 200, 204, 209, 210, 219, 240, 252
Ito, Miss, 193, 194, 197, 203
Ito, Mrs., 193, 194, 197, 200, 201
Ito residence, 192, 194, 196, 203
Iwakura, Tomomi, 45, 46, 58, 70, 72, 73, 74, 75, 79–80, 84–85, 89, 92, 93, 97, 143
    Chicago donation given by, 87
    sons of, 79–80, 87–88
Iwakura Mission, 17, 46–47, 55, 100, 137, 177, 219, 220, 272, 284n
    American music and, 73–74
    Americans' interest in, 78–79, 86

in Chicago, 86–88
crossing of U.S. by, 82–88
departure of, 58–59, 184
and first impressions of U.S., 71–72
ocean voyage of, 59–60, 61–63, 192
purpose of, 59, 73, 93, 97
racially polarized U.S. and, 92
reunion of, 263–64
in Sacramento, 82–83
in Salt Lake City, 84–85, 192
in San Francisco, 69–82
scribe for, *see* Kume, Kunitake
sitting and, 72, 73
theater attended by, 76–77
U.S. arrival of, 69
in Washington, D.C., 88–91, 185
Iwakura Mission, ambassadors of, 70, 86, 143
as ambitious, 63
Grant's reception for, 91, 92–93, 184
international travels of, 97–98
tours and entertainments for, 76–77, 78–79
Western-style suits of, 57, 75
wives not brought along by, 56
Iwakura Mission, girls of, 47, 48, 49–50, 59, 89,
95, 208, 268, 273
African Americans and, 77
American education of, 99, 109–10, 112, 117,
124–25, 127, 128, 129, 131, 135, 138, 139–40,
141–43, 147
American food and, 82
American women and, 78
appearance of, 15–16, 70, 86–87, 121
chaperone for travels of, *see* DeLong, Elida
Vineyard
Christianity and, 102, 103–4, 114, 120–21,
153
Connecticut Avenue house of, 95–96, 98,
104
departure of, 56
education as purpose of, 17, 48, 51, 89, 93
English learned by, 95, 107, 112, 185
English not spoken by, 77, 95, 112
as indebted to Japan, 167, 176, 187–88, 194,
199, 207, 268
isolation of, 77, 82, 86, 87
Japanese spoken by, 98
Japanese-style dress of, 15–16, 50–51, 70, 77,
85, 86
in journey back to western U.S., 147–48
in journey to eastern U.S., 82, 85, 88
lack of preparation for, 57
as left behind in America, 98

as looked after by Lanmans, 90, 94, 98, 99,
123, 126, 134–35, 147
loss of Japanese identity by, 110, 116, 117, 153
Mori as guardian of, 98, 99–101, 105
neighborhood children and, 94
in ocean voyage from U.S., 151–53, 156–57
in ocean voyage to U.S., 59, 61–64, 192
photographs of, *13*, 52–53, *67*, 78, 121
piano lessons of, 95
recruitment of, 47–50, 53, 61
Ryo and Tei's return home and, 101, 104
as samurai daughters, 50
separation of, 100, 104, 107
stipends for host families of, 103
as subject of newspapers, 53–54
theater attended by, 77–78
Western-style clothing for, 77, 87, 89, 93–94,
97, 104
see also Oyama, Sutematsu Yamakawa;
Tsuda, Ume; Ueda, Tei; Uriu, Shige Nagai;
Yoshimasu, Ryo

Japan, Edo-era (1603–1868):
Christianity declared illegal in, 27
coastal batteries of, 29
commoners in, 28
economy in, 21
guns and gunsmithing as viewed in, 29
martial hierarchy in, 21–22, 23
trade within, 22
understanding of West lacked by, 31, 45
unequal trade agreements in, 30–31, 45
weapons in, 29
Westerners as viewed in, 30–31
xenophobia of, 27, 42
see also Tokugawa shogunate
Japan, Japanese, 11
American occupation of, 81
American trade with, 28, 30, 73
British and, 30, 50
charity and, 110, 200–202, 237–38, 258
China/Chinese and, 27, 28, 74–75
Christianity in, 165, 168
customs/etiquette of, 72, 73, 154, 163–64,
165, 167, 168, 187, 195–96, 205, 214, 222,
223
Dutch and, 24, 27, 28, 30, 52
extreme topography of, 23
foreign commerce as viewed in, 27–30, 48
as global power, 270, 272
Great Kanto Earthquake in (1923), 275
marriage and, 167, 171, 172, 179, 248

Japan, Japanese (*continued*)
obedience as important in, 25, 37, 43, 48, 128, 171, 186, 240
in racially polarized U.S., 92
Russia and, 27, 30
samurai population in, 21
schools for girls in, 12, 17, 163, 188, 190, 193, 199, 210–11, 257, 269–70; *see also specific schools*
suffrage in, 81
superstitions about photography in, 52
women and girls in, *see* women and girls
World War I and, 275
Japan, Meiji-era (1868–1912), 11–12, 42
American missionaries in, 189–90
appearance/dress of girls in, 15–16, 50–51
Boshin War in, 34–38
cholera epidemic in, 208, 215
Christianity banned in, 104, 105
as civilized nation, 40, 44
conversion to Christianity in, 153, 165, 188
education in, 163, 178, 185–86, 188, 190, 193, 199, 210–11, 229–30, 234–35, 247–48, 257, 260, 269–70
end of, 271
enlightenment as goal for, 55–56, 102, 153, 186, 198, 236, 239
exile of Aizu domain in, 38–39
Hoterukan and, 119–20
Imperial Diet of, 218–20
Iwakura Mission of, *see* Iwakura Mission
journalism in, 53–54, 62, 202, 209
Korea and, 236–37, 270
marriage and divorce laws in, 248
men's Western-style clothing in, 17, 42, 57, 75
military in, 237–38
modernization and reform efforts of, 48, 52, 53–54, 80–81, 100, 106, 183–85, 236
National Exhibition in, 184
national security and, 236
Normanton incident and, 209
patriotism in, 238–39, 257, 270
railway built in, 50, 162
reaction to *Japanese Girls and Women* in, 229
revival of conservative traditions in, 186–87, 229, 247, 248
Russia and, 239, 270
Russo-Japanese War (1904–5) and, 270
samurai class abolished in, 155
Sino-Japanese War (1894–95) and, 236–40, 257, 269
and travels to America and, 43–44, 46–47

Western agriculture and, 120
Westernization and, 43, 44–45, 48, 75, 183–84, 185, 186–87, 247
women's personal grooming during, 17
Japanese Girls and Women (A. M. Bacon and U. Tsuda), 228–29, 230, 231–32
Japanese Interior, A (A. M. Bacon), 12, 230
Japanese mythology, 21
"Japanning," 154*n*
Japan Weekly Mail, 224, 234–35, 261
Japonisme, 78
jinrikishas, 50, 161, 162, 182, 190, 194, 201, 211
JOAK (radio station), 276
Joshi Eigaku Juku, *see* Tsuda College

Kaga domain, 115
Kagoshima, 42, 184
Kaigan Jogakko, 190
Kamakura, 269
Kanda, Naibu, 173, 174–75, 189
Kawamura, Kiyo, 118
Keller, Helen, 250
Kido, Takayoshi, 47, 53–54
kimonos, 50–51, 77, 85, 164, 165, 168
Koishikawa, 60
Kokubunji, 277
Kokumin no tomo, 239
Korea, 27, 236–37, 270
Kume, Kunitake, 47, 59, 62, 65, 69, 71–72, 74, 79, 82, 83, 84, 86, 87, 89
Kuroda, Kiyotaka, 42–44, 45, 47, 48, 99, 169–70, 219
Kyoto, 21, 23, 31, 51, 212, 223, 272
Kyushu, 33

Ladies' Volunteer Nursing Association, 237
Lagler, Miss, 95
Lanman, Adeline, 97
death of, 272, 275
home of, 90–91, 117, 138
Iwakura girls looked after by, 90, 94, 96, 123, 126, 134–35, 147
as lavish, 116
Shige and, 126, 134, 139, 189, 204
Sutematsu and, 126, 134–35, 138
Ume's correspondence with, 153, 156, 161, 164–65, 167, 170–71, 173–74, 180–82, 187–88, 190–93, 198, 200, 204–5, 207, 208–10, 213, 225–27, 241, 244, 249, 253, 255–57, 262–65, 268, 269
as Ume's foster mother, 94, 101, 104–5, 116, 117, 189, 197

Ume's notes written to, in U.S., 104, 116, 119, 135–36, 149, 151
Ume's reunions with, 250, 272
Ume's stay with, 91, 94, 101, 104–5, 116–19, 123, 124, 126, 134–35, 153, 166, 226
vacations of, 126, 134–35
Lanman, Charles, 149
death of, 241
home of, 90–91, 117, 138
Iwakura girls looked after by, 90, 94, 98, 99, 123, 126, 134–35, 147
as lavish, 116
Mori and, 89–90, 97
Ume and, 91, 94, 101, 104–5, 116–21, 123–25, 126, 153, 166, 192, 193, 197, 210, 226, 252
vacations of, 126, 134–35
Litchfield Hills, Conn., 111, 145
Little Lord Fauntleroy (Burnett), 261
Little Red Riding Hood, 262
London, 97, 250–51
Longfellow, Henry Wadsworth, 112, 114, 121
Long Island, N.Y., 125
Loring, Annie, 95, 96

Machinery Hall, 122
Maclagan, William Dalrymple, 252
Manchuria, 270
Manifest Destiny, 73
Masonic Temple, 91
Massachusetts, 100
Massachusetts Society for the University Education of Women, 230
Masuda, Eisaku, 173
Masuda, Shige, *see* Uriu, Shige Nagai
Masuda, Takanosuke, 60–61
Masuda, Takashi, 60–61, 139, 168, 172–73, 189, 202, 276
Masuda family, 173–74
Matsudaira, Katamori (Aizu daimyo), 34, 37, 38
Matsudaira clan, 23, 49
Matsushima, 270
Medill, Joseph, 87
Meiji Emperor, *see* Mutsuhito
Meiji restoration, 33–34
Meirokusha, 188
Mendelssohn, Felix, 125, 132
Merchant of Venice, The (Shakespeare), 173–75
Methodist Mission, 190
Mikado, The (Gilbert and Sullivan), 208–9
millennium, 257
Miller, Martha "Mattie," 117, 166
Ministry of Agriculture, Japanese, 241

Ministry of Education, Japanese, 49, 169, 172, 263, 269
Mishima, Yataro, 241–42, 243
Mishima (village), 61
Miss Abbott's School, 113–14, 124, 176
Mitchell, Maria, 130–31
Mitsui Trading Company, 139, 276
Monfort, Maria, 109
Mori, Arinori, 44, 88–89, 91, 95, 106, 120, 210
assassination of, 220
as guardian of Iwakura girls, 98, 99–101, 105
Imperial Diet and, 219
Lanman and, 89–90, 97
Mormons, Mormonism, 84–85
Morris, Mary Harris, 226–27, 230, 256, 257
Morris, Wistar, 226
Morse, Samuel, 79
Mother at Home, The, or The Principles of Maternal Duty (Abbott), 113
Motoda, Nagazane, 186
Motozonocho, Kojimachi, 263
Mount Holyoke College, 226
Mozart, Wolfgang Amadeus, 132
music, western, 73–74, 169
Music Investigation Committee, 169
Mussolini, Benito, 282*n*
Mutsuhito, Meiji Emperor of Japan, 17, 21, 33, 40, 51–52, 55, 60, 70, 119, 209, 216–17
birthday celebrations for, 191–92, 207, 216
Charter Oath of, 44–45
death of, 271–72
domains abolished by, 41
Imperial Diet of, 218–20
Imperial Rescript on Education of, 229–30
Japan declared unenlightened by, 55
Oyamas visited by, 233
as symbol of Japan's rise, 272
Western-style military uniforms of, 185, 217

Nagai, Gen'ei, 61
Nagai, Shige, *see* Uriu, Shige Nagai
Nagano, Fumiakira, 284*n*-85*n*
Nagano, Keijiro "Tommy," 63–64, 91, 285*n*
Nagasaki, trading post at, 24, 27, 52
Nagatacho, 193
National Guard, U.S., 79
Native Americans, 149
Naval Academy, U.S., 114–15, 135, 168, 189, 271
Negishi, 171
Netherlands, 28
Japanese trade with, 24, 27, 30, 52
New Hampshire, 274

New Haven, Conn., 12, 100–103, 105, 111, 112,
    115, 116, 134, 140, 144, 146–47, 148, 162,
    163, 200, 267, 271, 274
New Jersey, 80, 87
newspapers, 53–54
New York, N.Y., 45–46, 137
New York State, 254
New York Times, 95, 138, 229, 238, 239
New York Tribune, 138
Nightingale, Florence, 251, 252
Niijima, Joseph, 94–95
Nisshinkan, 24–25, 35
Norfolk, Conn., 231
Normanton incident, 209
Northern Alliance, 60
Northrop, Birdsey Grant, 100, 101, 115–16
Norwich, Conn., 99

obedience, 25, 37, 43, 48, 128, 171, 186, 240
Oceanic, 136
Ogden, Utah Territory, 83
Ogino, Ginko, 248
Okubo, Toshimichi, 47, 53, 64, 76, 93, 96
Omaha, Nebr., 86
Onden, 233, 242, 262
Onna daigaku ("Greater Learning for Women"),
    25
opium, 150
Opium Wars, 27, 75
"Orientation of the Frog's Egg, The," 228
Orleans Hotel, 82
Oswego Normal School, 254
Our Society, 110, 200
Oxford University, 251
Oyama, Hisako "Chachan," 202–3, 269, 271
Oyama, Iwao, 177, 200, 216, 243
    ball hosted by, 195–96
    death of, 274
    foreign travels of, 198, 203, 264
    Imperial Diet and, 219
    proposal and marriage of, to Sutematsu,
        178–82, 184n, 187, 196, 199, 225, 232
    rank of, 206
    Russo-Japanese War and, 270
    Sino-Japanese War and, 236, 237, 239, 245
    Takeo's death and, 271
Oyama, Kashiwa, 222
Oyama, Nobuko, 241–43, 244
Oyama, Sutematsu Yamakawa, 12, 19, 20, 21,
    23, 24, 25–26, 27, 31, 32, 33, 34–35, 38, 43,
    57, 59, 60, 64, 67, 71, 89, 99, 111, 219, 224,
    266–67, 277

admirers of, 172, 174–75, 177–79
Alice and, 109, 114, 144, 151–52, 156, 163–64,
    168, 170, 171, 173, 174–75, 176, 179, 180–81,
    182, 193, 198, 199, 211, 212, 215, 216, 237–38,
    242, 245, 254–55, 273, 274–75
American education of, 109–10, 112, 124–25,
    127, 128, 129, 131, 135–36, 138, 139–40,
    141–43, 225
appearance of, 121, 166
Bacon family and, 107, 108–9, 110, 125–26,
    140
ball hosted by, 195–96
at Centennial Exhibition, 123, 179
character of, 132–33, 139, 275
charity work of, 110, 200–202, 237–38, 270
children of, 202–3, 208, 215, 216, 222, 241–43,
    253, 270–71
Christianity and, 103–4
in Connecticut, 101, 103–4, 105–12, 115,
    145–47, 175–76, 200
court visits of, 194, 198
death of, 275
education outside classroom of, 110
essays on Japan written by, 134, 140, 154–56
French lessons of, 181
Gaiyukai club and, 269
in Grove Hall Seminary, 109–10
in Hillhouse High School, 112, 124–25
Hototogisu alter ego of, 243
as indebted to Japan, 176, 199, 207
Iwakura Mission recruitment of, 47–50, 53
at Iwakura Mission reunion, 264
Japanese Girls and Women and, 229, 230,
    231–32
Japanese identity of, 110, 154
Japanese practiced by, 110, 116, 131–32, 163
Japan understood by, 153–54
in journey back to western U.S., 147–49
Marian Whitney and, 111, 114
marriage and, 171, 172, 174–75, 179–81, 191
at Masudas' party, 173–74, 176–77
as natural leader, 133
negative newspaper stories about, 215
noble rank of, 206
nursing charity sale organized by, 200–202
nursing school attended by, 145–46, 200, 242
in ocean voyage home, 151–53, 156–57
Oyama's proposal and marriage to, 178–82,
    184n, 187, 196, 199, 225, 232
Peeresses' School and, 199–200
photographs of, *13*, 52–53, *67*, 78, 121, 143,
    159, 265

poor health of, 211, 215, 216
pregnancies of, 202–3, 215
reeducation in being Japanese of, 162,
 163–64
in return to Japan, 144, 146, 156, 157, 161–63,
 168, 169–70
Russo-Japanese War and, 270
sent to prison camp, 38, 48
Shige and, 107, 108, 109, 112, 131–32, 133, 138,
 139, 141, 161, 164, 179, 183, 253, 267–68,
 271, 273
Shige's wedding and, 167–68
Shimoda and, 232–33
siege of Wakamatsu and, 36, 48, 96, 238
Sino-Japanese War victory and, 239
smoking and, 232
Takeo's death and, 271
Tonami exile of, 38–39, 40, 48
on training children, 127–28
Tsuda College and, 259, 262, 269
Ume and, 108, 109, 115–16, 117, 133, 134–35,
 138, 179, 182, 183, 189, 193, 198, 203–4, 210,
 215, 235, 253, 273
as unable to read or write Japanese, 155, 175
Vassar attended by, 129, 131–34, 135–36, 138,
 139–40, 163, 225, 226, 262, 266–67
Vassar commencement of, 141–43, 144, 147,
 148, 179, 239
in Washington, D.C., 91, 95, 105
wedding of, 181–82, 192
Western-style clothing and, 215–16
withdrawal of, 215–16, 274–75
on women's rights, 127
see also Iwakura Mission, girls of
Oyama, Takashi, 215, 216, 270–71
Oyama family, 233, 241, 242, 244

Paris, 78
Peerage Act of 1884, 206
Peeresses' School, 199, 200, 204–5, 209–12, 213,
 225, 226, 232–33, 247, 249, 254, 256, 259
as conservative, 233, 245
Empress Haruko and, 199, 205–6, 220–22,
 223
foreign dress required by, 213–14
Imperial Palace tour for, 217–18
mission statement of, 240
Peers' Club, see Rokumeikan
Peers' School, 217, 218
Pennsylvania, 234, 246
Pennsylvania Railroad, 226
Perinchief, Octavius, 120, 123–24

Perry, Matthew, 28–29, 30, 45, 48, 52, 54, 75, 115,
 119, 236
Pescadores, 270
Philadelphia, Pa., 97, 225, 233, 253, 257
 Centennial Exhibition in, 121–24, 179, 184
Philalethean Society, 134, 139–40, 154, 173
Philippines, 27
photography, Japanese superstitions about, 52
Pitman, Helen, 114, 168
Pitman, Leila, 114, 168
Pitman, Lizzie, 114, 168
Pitman family, 114, 115
Pocket Edition of Japanese Equivalents for the Most
 Common English Words, A, 57
Pope, Alexander, 251
Popular Fairy Tales, 261
Porter, Noah, 140
Portugal, 27, 29
"potato samurai," 34, 41, 177
Poughkeepsie, N.Y., 128–34, 135–36, 138, 139–
 40, 141–43, 144, 148
Poughkeepsie Eagle, 142, 271
Promontory Summit, 82
Protestants, Protestantism, 118
Pullman, George M., 82, 85

Quakers, 246
Quarterly Journal of Microscopical Science, 228

Radcliffe College, 144, 250
Raleigh, Walter, 106
"Recollections of Japanese Family Life"
 (Yamakawa Oyama), 154–55
Red Cross, 237, 275
Richardson Incident (1862), 42
Ritter, Frederick, 132, 136
ritual suicide, 25, 36, 37
Rockefeller Foundation, 275
Rokumeikan, 195–96, 200–202, 209, 263–64
Roosevelt, Theodore, 270
Rouge et Noir, 76
Royal Italian Circus, 209
Russia, 27, 30, 43, 236, 270
Russian Orthodoxy, 48
Russo-Japanese War (1904–5), 270, 274
Rutgers Grammar School, 80

Sacramento, Calif., 82–83
Saigo, Takamori, 184
Saigo, Tsugumichi, 178, 184n
St. Hilda's Hall, 251
St. Petersburg, 133, 141

Salt Lake City, Utah, 84–85, 192
samurai, samurai families, 19, 89
    abolished class of, 155
    coastlines patrolled by, 27–28, 119
    code of loyalty and honor of, 21
    discipline of, 21, 26, 94
    dolls collected by, 26
    domain abolishment and, 41
    as emperor's intimate advisors, 51
    farming and, 38
    girls in, 34
    as hereditary warrior class, 21
    humiliation of, 39
    intimacy and, 116
    in Iwakura Mission, 63
    money and, 28
    morals of, 99
    population of, 21
    pride and, 110
    as shishi, 31, 33
    sleep and, 94
    status of, 188
    stipends provided to, 21, 28, 41
    sword as signature weapon of, 29
    training for, 39, 89
    wives, 43
samurai culture, 21
samurai mansions (bukeyashiki), 19, 50
Sanders, Mr., 148
San Francisco, Calif., 65, 69–82, 104, 149–51,
    164, 165–66, 192, 223
San Francisco Assaying and Refining Works, 76
San Francisco Bulletin, 104
San Francisco Chronicle, 72, 75, 77, 78, 136, 285n
Sasaki, Takayuki, 64, 65, 285n
Satsuma domain, 33, 34, 39, 41, 42, 53, 89, 169,
    177, 178, 184, 244
Satsuma Rebellion, 184
Savell, Jeffrey and Margaret, 120–21
Sawabe, Takuma, 48
Schnell, John Henry, 56
Schubert, Franz, 132
Scott, Walter, 147
Scudder, Horace E., 228
Second Artillery Band, 73
Seito, 272
Self-help (Smiles), 185, 223
Serata, Tasuku, 168, 189
Seven Sisters, 129
Shakespeare, William, 106, 147, 173, 176, 251
Shakespeare Society, 133
Shanahan, Julia, 137–38

Sheffield Scientific School, 99
Shimbun Zasshi, 54
Shimoda, Utako, 193, 196, 197, 198, 204, 207,
    210–11, 232–33, 240
Shinagawa, 164
shishi, xenophobia of, 31, 33
shogun, 21
    alternate attendance required by, 22
    bureaucracy of, 33
    daimyo and, 22
    shishi and, 31
    see also Tokugawa shogunate
Sierra Nevada, 83
Silas Marner (Eliot), 261
Sino-Japanese War (1894–95), 236–40, 245, 257
Smiles, Samuel, 185, 186, 223, 230
Smith College, 128, 226
Society for the Collegiate Instruction of Women
    (Harvard Annex), 145
Soho, Tokutomi, 238–39, 248
Soper, Junius, 120
Southworth, Anne, 232
Spain, 27
Spenser, Edmund, 106
Squam Lake, N.H., 255
Stanton, Elizabeth Cady, 127, 131
"Star-Spangled Banner, The," 122
State Central Woman Suffrage Committee of
    California, 81
State Department, U.S., 91, 92
Stebbins, Horatio, 81
Stephenson, Lucy, 117
study abroad:
    in America, 43, 80, 87–88, 94, 99, 102, 114–15,
        118, 227, 228–34
    of Chinese, 100, 103, 111, 123
    for men, 43, 44, 46, 80, 87–88, 89, 94, 99,
        114–15, 118, 228
    for women and girls, 17, 44, 48, 51, 99, 227,
        228–34
    see also Iwakura Mission, girls of
suffrage, 81
Sugimoto, Etsu Inagaki, 7, 13, 67, 159
Sullivan, Arthur, 208
Sumner, Charles, 121
Suzuki, Utako, 259

Takaki, Mrs., 162
Takaki, Saburo, 142, 161–62
Takamine, Hideo, 253–54, 257
Tan Yaoxun (Yew Fun Tan), 111–12, 140
telegraph, 79

ten-men groups, 24–25

Tennyson, Alfred, Lord, 251

Thomas, Martha Carey, 227, 230, 231, 234, 250, 256, 257, 258, 260

Tokugawa, Iesada (shogun), 30

Tokugawa, Ieyasu (shogun), 21, 27

Tokugawa, Ieyoshi (shogun), 30

Tokugawa, Yoshinobu (shogun), 32, 33

Tokugawa family, 23

Tokugawa shogunate, 21–22, 24, 26–30, 61, 217
    American travels and, 45
    antiforeign stance of, 27
    Christianity declared illegal by, 27
    end of, 33, 41
    foreigners and, 28
    guns and, 29
    isolationist policies of, 30
    opposition to, 31, 32, 33
    peace in rule of, 23, 27, 28
    see also Japan, Edo-era

Tokyo (Edo), 12, 22, 23, 30, 52, 60, 95, 115, 119, 146, 184, 225, 226, 274
    American missionaries in, 189–90
    cannons in, 29
    cholera epidemic in, 208, 215
    city name changed to, 40
    Emperor and Empress relocation to, 51
    Great Kanto Earthquake in (1923), 275
    influenza in, 242, 275
    Iwakura girls' recruitment in, 48, 49–50
    jinrikishas in, 50, 162
    Tokugawa shogunate headquarters in, 21

Tokyo Charity Hospital, 200, 202

Tokyo Imperial University, 162

Tokyo Music School, 169, 189, 235

Tonami, 38–39, 40, 47, 48, 49

Townsend House, 84, 85

Toyo Jojuku, 193

Toyotomi, Hideyoshi, 237

Tremont House, 87, 288*n*

Triple Intervention, 239

True Account of the Ambassador Extraordinary & Plenipotentiary's Journey of Observation through the United States of America and Europe (Kume), 47

Tsuda, Fuki, 210, 240–41

Tsuda, Hatsuko, 94, 116–17, 203

Tsuda, Koto, 58, 116–17, 120, 165, 166, 190, 269

Tsuda, Sen, 57–58, 95, 116, 118, 119–20, 166, 169, 170–71, 188–89, 190, 195, 204, 229, 246, 258, 266

Tsuda, Tomi, 203

Tsuda, Ume, 12, *13*, 49, 50, 53, 57–58, 59–60, 62, *67*, 71, 78, 89, 95, 98, 172, 202, 206–7, 219, 224
    Adeline Lanman as foster mother to, 94, 101, 104–5, 116, 117, 189, 197
    Adeline Lanman's reunions with, 250, 272
    Alice and, 211–13, 214, 216, 220, 221, 226–27, 228–29, 235, 238, 239, 241, 242, 248–49, 250, 254, 267–68, 275
    American education of, 117–18, 135, 138, 147, 227, 228–29, 234
    American identity of, 153, 154, 208
    on American missionaries in Tokyo, 189–90
    American scholarship program and, 230, 234, 235, 247
    Anna Hartshorne and, 228, 234, 246–47, 250, 269, 275–76
    appeal of West to, 119–20
    appearance of, 121, 147, 166–67
    appointed to Board of Examiners for English Teaching Certificates, 263
    Archer Institute attended by, 138, 147
    articles on women's education written by, 234–35, 247–49
    biology studied by, 228
    Bryn Mawr attended by, 227, 228–29, 234, 246, 250, 258
    at Centennial Exhibition, 123, 124, 179
    Charles Lanman and, 91, 117, 118–19, 120–21, 166, 192, 193, 197, 210, 252
    on Chinese people, 149–50, 152
    Christianity of, 120–21, 153
    death of, 276
    diabetes of, 273
    at emperor's birthday celebration, 191–92
    during empress's visit to school, 221, 222
    in England, 250–52
    in first return to Japan, 147, 151, 153, 156, 157, 161, 162, 167, 168, 169–71
    at General Federation of Women's Clubs convention, 249–50, 255
    in Georgetown, 104–5, 115–19, 120–21, 147, 148, 166, 188, 189, 191, 194, 197, 205
    at Georgetown Collegiate Institute, 117–18
    as historical figure, 277
    household established by, 266
    on Imperial Palace, 218
    as indebted to Japan, 167, 187–88, 194, 207, 234
    isolation and loneliness of, 189, 240
    Ito family and, 192–94, 197

Tsuda, Ume (*continued*)
in Ito residence, 196–97, 198, 203
at Iwakura Mission reunion, 264
Iwakura travel preparations of, 57
Japan as viewed by, 153
Japanese communication skills lacked by, 153,
166, 191
Japanese customs/etiquette and, 165, 167, 187,
194, 205
Japanese Girls and Women of, 228–29, 230,
231–32
Japanese identity of, 116, 118, 153, 208, 225,
234
Japanese lessons for, 118, 193, 194
in journey back to western U.S., 147–48, 149
letters written to Lanmans by, 153, 156, 161,
164–65, 167, 170–71, 173–74, 180–82,
187–88, 190–93, 198, 200, 204–5, 207,
208–10, 213, 225–27, 241, 244, 249, 253,
255–57, 262–65, 268, 269
marriage and, 171, 183, 189, 191, 225, 227, 235
Martha Miller and, 117
on Mori assassination, 220
in move closer to Peeresses' School, 209–10
new millennium and, 257
notes written to Adeline Lanman by, in U.S.,
104, 116, 119, 135–36, 149, 151
at nursing charity sale, 200, 201
in ocean voyage home, 151, 152–53, 156–57
as official representative of Japan, 150–51
at Oyamas' ball, 195–96
at Peeresses' School, 204–5, 206, 209–12,
220, 221, 222, 225, 226, 227, 234, 240, 241,
247, 249, 256, 260
photographs of, *13*, 52–53, *67*, 78, 121, *159*,
265, 266
poor health of, 273, 275
rank of, 204, 207, 209, 256, 258
recognition for, 191, 255, 256
reeducation of, in being Japanese, 162, 164
resignation of, 258, 259
salary of, 204, 211, 212, 256, 258, 260
samurai status of, 266
school founded by, *see* Tsuda College
in shared house with Alice, 212–13
Shige and, 115–16, 134, 164, 182, 183, 203–4,
210, 235, 256, 267–68, 273
Shige's wedding and, 167–68
Shimoda and, 240
smoking and, 232
in stay with Lanmans, 91, 94, 101, 104–5,
116–19, 123, 124, 126, 134–35, 153, 166, 226

strokes of, 275
subsequent American sojourns of, 225, 226,
227–34, 245, 249–50, 253, 272
Sutematsu and, 108, 115–16, 117, 133, 134–35,
138, 179, 182, 183, 189, 193, 198, 203–4, 210,
215, 235, 253, 273, 275
Sutematsu's wedding and, 182–83
as teacher, 190–91, 193, 194, 196–98, 204,
208, 210, 211–12, 234, 249, 254, 259, 273
Vassar visited by, 135–36
Western-style clothing of, 165, 196
at Women's Higher Normal School, 249, 256
women's place as viewed by, 231, 260,
272–73
see also Iwakura Mission, girls of
Tsuda College, 259–61, 265–66, 269, 272, 275,
276–77
enrollment at, 260, 269, 277
first house of, 258–59, 260
funds raised for, 256, 257, 258, 269
goal of, 259
monthly literary gatherings at, 262
progressive pedagogy of, 260
role as counterweight to conservatism of,
269–70
second house of, 261–62, 263
teaching methods at, 261, 262–63
third house of, 269
Ume's planning of, 247, 257, 258
Tsuda family, 56–57, 117, 119, 120, 165,
170–71
Tsuda rope, 188
Tsugaru Straits, 47
Tsuji, Matsu, 275
Tsukiji, 190
Tsuruga Castle, 19, 35–37
siege of, 36–38, 49, 177, 238
Twain, Mark, 92

Ueda, Tei, *13*, 49–50, 52–53, 63, 89, 91, 164,
273–74
return to Japan of, 101, 104, 273
Ueno, 60, 273
Ueno Park, 184
Union Pacific Railroad, 83
United States, 27, 31
centennial of, 121–24
Chinese labor in, 74, 75, 102, 150
Chinese study abroad in, 100, 103, 111,
123
Edo-era visits to, 45–46
Hawaii and, 236

higher education for women in, 128
Japanese females' travels to, 56–57
Japanese study abroad in, 43, 80, 87–88, 94, 99, 102, 114–15, 118
Japanese trade with, 28, 30, 73
Meiji-era visits to, 43–44, 46–47, 80
music in, 73–74
racial issues in, 92, 102, 150
Sino-Japanese War and, 238, 239
success of men in, 44
women from, 43–44
see also Iwakura Mission
Uriu, Chiyo, 182, 192
Uriu, Sakae, 244
Uriu, Shige, 12, 49, 50, 59–61, 62, 63, 71, 89, 125–26, 157, 181, 202, 206–7, 219, 224, 277
Abbott family and, 114
Alice and, 216
American scholarship program and, 235
appearance of, 121, 136
at Centennial Exhibition, 123, 179
character of, 132
children of, 182, 192, 196, 208, 235, 244, 245, 253, 266, 270–71
Christianity and, 114
in Connecticut, 101, 105, 107, 112–15, 176
death of, 276
English fluency lost by, 166, 271
Gaiyukai club and, 269
gatherings hosted by, 171–72
at Iwakura Mission reunion, 264
Japanese practiced by, 131–32, 163
Lanmans and, 126, 134, 139, 204
marriage of, 164, 168, 196, 225, 244, 266
maternal qualities of, 189
as mother, 182, 192, 196, 203, 266
music studied by, 95, 132
at nursing charity sale, 201
photographs of, 13, 52–53, 67, 78, 121, 159, 265
Pitman girls and, 114
rank of, 204
in return to Japan, 135, 136–37, 138, 139, 168–69
in return to U.S., 271
Russo-Japanese War and, 270
salary of, 169, 175, 248
smoking and, 232
Sotokichi and, 115, 116, 135, 137, 139, 164, 168, 173, 174, 196, 244, 271
Sutematsu and, 107, 108, 112, 116, 131–32, 133,

138, 139, 141, 161, 164, 179, 183, 253, 267–68, 271, 273
Takeo and Takashi's deaths and, 271
as teacher, 168–69, 203, 204, 208, 235, 244, 245, 253, 266
Tsuda College and, 267, 269
Ume and, 115, 164, 182, 183, 203–4, 210, 235, 256, 267–68, 273
Vassar attended by, 129, 131–32, 133, 134, 135–36, 225, 226, 262
in Washington, D.C., 91, 96, 105
wedding of, 167–68
at Women's Higher Normal School, 253, 254, 266
Uriu, Sotokichi, 171–72, 173, 174, 189, 192, 271
death of, 276
in Japanese navy, 235, 236, 244, 264, 270
poor health of, 203, 276
in return to Japan, 135, 137
Shige's marriage to, 164, 168, 196
in United States, 114–15, 116, 135
Uriu, Takeo, 203, 244, 270–71
Ushigome, 162
Utah Territory, 82

Van Ingen, Henry, 130
Van Name, Addison, 101, 103
Vassar, Matthew, 128, 133–34
Vassar College, 128–34, 135–36, 139–40, 141–42, 146, 163, 173, 175, 225, 226, 239, 262, 271, 293n
Vassar Miscellany, 132, 134, 140, 155
Victoria, Queen of England, 209
Vienna Exposition (1873), 188

Wakamatsu, 19, 23, 49
remote Aizu domain in, 23, 27, 31, 50
siege at, 36–38, 48, 49, 105, 238
Tsuruga Castle of, 19, 35–37, 49
Wakamatsu Tea and Silk Colony, 57
Wakayama, Norikazu, 137
Wakayama, Shiori Louisa, 137–38
Warner, Charles Dudley, 92
warrior honor, 36
Washington, D.C., 46, 82, 88–91, 97, 100, 104, 105, 115–16, 118, 151, 185, 189, 210, 253, 263
blacks in, 92–93, 150
Washington, George, 73
Watanabe, Mitsu, 224, 255, 257–58, 259, 261, 274
Watanabe, Mrs., 212, 213
Weber, Carl Maria von, 276
Wellesley College, 128, 226

Western clothing, 17, 42, 57, 75, 77, 87, 89, 93–94, 97, 104, 123, 165, 168, 185, 196, 197, 213–14, 215–16, 220, 286n
Western military technology, 28, 29, 33, 34, 185
Western Union, 79
whaling, 27
Wheeler, Jessie, 146, 149, 172
Whitman, Walt, 46
Whitney, Clara, 185, 226
Whitney, Marian, 111, 114
Whitney, William Dwight, 111
Whittier, John Greenleaf, 122
women and girls:
    attitudes toward, 12, 24, 127, 187, 206, 240, 260, 272–73
    college degrees for, 128
    Confucianism and, 23, 25, 240, 260
    education for, 17, 25, 44, 55–56, 57, 81, 113, 128, 145, 163, 170, 178, 187, 188, 190, 193, 199, 210–11, 231, 234–35, 247–50, 257, 259, 260, 269–70, 271, 272–73
    enlightenment of Japan and, 56, 102, 198
    marriage and, 167, 171, 172, 179, 248
    Meiji-era dress and appearance of, 15–16, 50–51, 70
    obedience and, 25, 37, 43, 48
    personal grooming for, 17
    qualities required of, 25–26
    salaries of, 169
    as samurai wives, 43
    Sino-Japanese War and, 239
    smoking by, 232
    on stage, 174
    studies abroad for, 17, 44, 48, 51, 99, 227, 228–34
    as subordinate, 23, 187
    suffrage for, 81
    weapons used by, 25, 34–35
    work and, 248
    see also Iwakura Mission, girls of
women and girls, American, 43–44, 78, 145, 175–76, 249–50
    corsets worn by, 286n
    higher education for, 128
    suffrage for, 81
Women's Higher Normal School, 163, 175, 178, 225, 235, 247, 249, 253, 254, 256, 257, 310n

Woodward, R. B., 76
Wordsworth, William, 147, 251
World War I, 275
Wyoming Territory, 86

Yale University, 99, 100, 101–2, 105, 111, 112, 129, 145, 171, 253, 274
Yamada, Akiyoshi, 219
Yamakawa, Futaba, 163, 175
Yamakawa, Hiroshi, 36–37, 41, 47, 48–49, 163, 170, 177
    as Aizu domain leader in Tonami, 38–39, 48
Yamakawa, Kenjiro, 36, 40, 41, 43, 120, 133, 140, 154, 162, 170, 253, 274
    American study abroad of, 43, 44, 48, 99–100
    Sutematsu looked after in U.S. by, 99–100, 101, 103–4, 105, 107, 110, 112, 116, 163
Yamakawa, Makoto, 274
Yamakawa, Misao, 133, 163, 200
Yamakawa, Shigekata, 19
Yamakawa, Toi, 35, 37, 48–49, 146, 162, 163
Yamakawa, Tose, 37
Yamakawa compound, 19–20, 35, 155
    servants of, 20, 155
Yamakawa family, 48, 155, 162–63, 170, 177, 178
    dolls collected by, 26, 34
    ferried on American ships, 38
    malnutrition of, 39, 40
    security and prestige of, 41
Yamakawa, Sutematsu, see Oyama, Sutematsu Yamakawa
Yancy, 38
Yokohama, 50, 56, 59, 70, 156, 161–62, 197, 212, 257, 267, 288n
Yoshida, Kiyonari, 118, 123–24, 179–80
Yoshida, Mrs., 180
Yoshihito, Taisho Emperor of Japan, 218n, 272, 274, 276
Yoshimasu, Ryo, 23, 49–50, 52–53, 59, 63–64, 65, 89, 95, 164, 285n
    death of, 208
    eye troubles of, 85, 96, 100–101, 164
    return to Japan of, 101, 104, 117, 273
Young, Brigham, 84
Yung Wing, 100, 101